Esports Business Management

David P. Hedlund, PhD
St. John's University

Gil Fried, JD
University of New Haven

R.C. Smith III, MAA, MSJ
Marietta College

Editors

HUMAN KINETICS

Library of Congress Cataloging-in-Publication Data

Names: Hedlund, David P., editor. | Fried, Gil, 1965- editor. | Smith, R. C., III, 1983- editor.
Title: Esports business management / David P. Hedlund, Gil Fried, R.C. Smith III, editors.
Description: Champaign, IL : Human Kinetics, Inc., 2021. | Includes bibliographical references and index.
Identifiers: LCCN 2020034235 (print) | LCCN 2020034236 (ebook) | ISBN 9781718200227 (paperback) | ISBN 9781492597230 (epub) | ISBN 9781492597223 (pdf)
Subjects: LCSH: eSports (Contests)--Management. | eSports (Contests)--Economic aspects.
Classification: LCC GV1469.34.E86 E77 2021 (print) | LCC GV1469.34.E86 (ebook) | DDC 794.8068--dc23
LC record available at https://lccn.loc.gov/2020034235
LC ebook record available at https://lccn.loc.gov/2020034236

ISBN: 978-1-7182-0022-7 (print)

Acquisitions Editor: Andrew L. Tyler; **Developmental Editor:** Jacqueline Eaton Blakley; **Managing Editor:** Hannah Werner; **Copyeditor:** Joanna Hatzopoulos Portman; **Indexer:** Nan N. Badgett; **Permissions Manager:** Dalene Reeder; **Senior Graphic Designer:** Joe Buck; **Cover Designer:** Keri Evans; **Cover Design Specialist:** Susan Rothermel Allen; **Photograph (cover):** Suzi Pratt / Getty Images; **Photographs (interior):** © Human Kinetics, unless otherwise noted; **Photo Asset Manager:** Laura Fitch; **Photo Production Manager:** Jason Allen; **Senior Art Manager:** Kelly Hendren; **Illustrations:** © Human Kinetics, unless otherwise noted; **Printer:** Walsworth

Printed in the United States of America

10 9 8 7 6 5 4 3 2 1

The paper in this book was manufactured using responsible forestry methods.

Human Kinetics
1607 N. Market Street
Champaign, IL 61820
USA

United States and International
Website: **US.HumanKinetics.com**
Email: info@hkusa.com
Phone: 1-800-747-4457

Canada
Website: **Canada.HumanKinetics.com**
Email: info@hkcanada.com

E8167

IESF

The International Esports Federation (IESF) is a global group of more than 70 member nations (and growing) that works to promote esports as a true sport that transcends language, race, and cultural barriers. Since its founding, the IESF has produced meaningful and tangible results through the creation of (1) an organized esports world with services provided to members and national esports associations, (2) regulations and disciplinary systems for stakeholders in which fair and clean competition is offered, (3) training and education for referees, managers, and other professionals through our International Esports Academy, and (4) the hosting of the Esports World Championship, where esports athletes compete and represent their nation. The IESF strives to become the world's first internationally recognized governing body for esports.

"As the esports industry has rapidly evolved, professional education, academia, and literature have come into high demand. Only by influencing positive and educated professionals around the industry are we able to solidify a sustainable ecosystem and promote further growth. We congratulate David P. Hedlund, Gil Fried, and R.C. Smith III for their hard work. Creating this book will add to the value of esports in academia."

USEF

The United States Esports Federation (USEF) is the national governing body for esports in the United States and a full member of the International Esports Federation (IESF). USEF runs live and online annual events across the United States promoting amateur and youth development of esports and promoting education and development of esports. USEF is a not-for-profit organization with the responsibility to promote, grow, and develop the quality, diversity, and beauty of esports as part of the fabric of our communities and our day-to-day lives, as well as to nurture, inspire, and protect athletes and the esports culture. The organization's ambition is to unite all esports stakeholders, including athletes, event organizers, technology producers, innovators and inventors, IP holders, parents, sponsors, and fans.

"*Esports Business Management* provides incredible vision and in-depth insight into the global esports ecosystem. The publication of *Esports Business Management* is integral to the development of education within esports as an industry."

ESPORTS RESEARCH NETWORK

The Esports Research Network (ERN) is a collaboration of various researchers fostering interdisciplinary research on the emerging phenomenon of esports. Esports is truly global and digital, and, therefore, esports can be used to research existing social issues and forecast the future increasingly digitalized world. In other words, research on esports can be seen as a future lab. Furthermore, in order to understand esports, it is necessary to research in depth the social impact and evolution of esports as well as the current and future role of esports in society. The goals of the Esports Research Network are to gain rigorous insights into esports, foster the sustainable growth of esports, shape the role of esports in society, and translate this knowledge to obtain knowledge for the digitalized world.

"Esports has grown substantially in recent years, and there is a substantial need for young talent and professionals who can navigate through the esports ecosystem dynamically and proactively. Therefore, it is essential to educate the next generation today. *Esports Business Management* lays the vital foundation for teaching esports management. It is a must-read for anybody to level up in their esports skills."

Contents

Foreword

James O'Connor, President and Founder of the Pittsburgh Knights

As people become more connected, the world seems to grow smaller. The technologies of the 21st century enable people to call, text, video chat, and communicate with others in every country and on every continent. People connect with each other like never before. Many industries are keeping up with the rapid changes. With the mere click of a button, businesses can advertise to millions of people through social networking sites. Content is created, shared, and available for everyone in the world to enjoy. Organizations have transformed from local to multinational, products are quickly shipped around the world, and long-distance travel and communication have become common.

It only makes sense that the rich human traditions of game play, competition, and fandom (allegiance) would also transform and share in this phenomenon of a large yet shrinking world. However, as the world becomes more connected, the technological means of these connections allow (and somewhat encourage) people to actually become more isolated. As people's digital social reach flourishes, their need for a physical social reach diminishes. While many people deride this evolution of human interaction, the esports industry does not criticize or pass judgment; rather, esports embraces the paradox of worldwide connections born from remote endeavors. They encapsulate this new dichotomy.

Gaming is, by nature, an isolated undertaking. The industry that has formed around gaming mirrors that independence, and through that shared independence it is able to bring people together. You do not have to live in a certain place to be a fan of your team; you do not have to travel to a specific location to socialize with fellow fans; and you do not need a particular social status or level of affluence to watch a game, participate in a match, or even train with a team. Just like the current world, the esports community is open. It is accessible. It inspires closeness for people who are thousands of miles apart and have worlds of cultural differences between them.

Esports offers a global camaraderie that is unmatched by any other industry. For this reason, esports is poised to dominate this dynamic digital 21st-century world. Esports will not only be its own self-contained entertainment powerhouse, it will be a model for other industries looking to welcome more fans into their fold. The time to study and understand the inner workings of esports and the business that surrounds it is now.

CONTRIBUTING EDITORS

Roger M. Caramanica, PhD, SHRM-SCP

Adjunct Professor at Post University, Mercy College, and Central Connecticut State University

Director of Learning and Development at Lightbox

Owner of FirstPerson LLC

Anthony Palomba, PhD

Assistant Professor at the University of Virginia

CONTRIBUTORS

Stanley Nana Anyang-Kaakyire

Founder and Executive Director of Spero Sports Consultancy

Jason Batzofin

Chairperson of the International Esports Federation (IESF) Players' Commission

Aaron Castellan

Senior Copywriter at PlayVS

Alexander Champlin, PhD

Senior Analyst of Esports at Niko Partners

Katelyn Chapin, AIA

Architect and Associate at Svigals + Partners

Jason Chung

Executive Director of Esports and Assistant Professor of Sport Management in the Pompea College of Business at the University of New Haven

Aaron "TheParadoxMuse" Colaiacomo

Professional League of Legends Coach and Analyst

Program Lead for Johnson and Wales University

Former Coach for Providence College Esports

Joanne Donoghue, PhD, ACSM-CEP

Associate Professor and Director of Clinical Research for the College of Osteopathic Medicine at the New York Institute of Technology

Robert Dranoff, EdD

Commissioner of the East Coast Conference

Adjunct Associate Professor at St. John's University

Graciano Gaillard

Intellectual Property and Sports Lawyer at Gaillard Consulting LLC

(continued)

CONTRIBUTORS *(CONTINUED)*

Matt Grimm
Assistant Athletic Director and Director of Campus Recreation at Stevenson University

Ryan Hagen
Director of Campus Recreation for CENTERS LLC at the University of New Haven

Lisa Cosmas Hanson
President of Niko Partners

Rob Holub, JD
Associate Director of Enrollment Operations at the University of New Haven

Courtney James
Director of Student Involvement and Esports at DePaul University

Taylor Johnson
Chief Performance Engineer at Statespace

Eric Kammeyer
Director of Esports and Gaming Technology at Butler University

Clint Kennedy, PhD
Director of Education at PlayVS

Ronald "Rambo" Kim
World Champion Gamer and Coach at FPS Coach

Raffaele Lauretta
Founder and CEO of Athletic Genetix

Sang-ho Lee, PhD
Research Professor in the Center for Cognition and Behavior of Esports at KyungSung University

Daniel Liang
Marketing Analyst at Ader

Moira McArdle
Principal Consultant for McArdle Education Marketing

John McDermott
Head Coach of Esports at Long Island University

Matt McGivern
Cofounder and CEO of Spark Virtual Reality

Lance Mudd
Founding Member and Sport Director for the United States Esports Federation (USEF)

Michael L. Naraine, PhD
Assistant Professor at Brock University

Michael Newhouse-Bailey, PhD
Associate Dean at Southern New Hampshire University

James O'Connor
President and Founder of the Pittsburgh Knights

Jide Osipitan
Founder of Gaming Insomniacs

Sheng Qiang

Volunteer Department and Resource Development Department in the Esports Association of Jiangsu Province, China

Nick Rider

Founder and President of Esports Ohio

Director of Technology for the Carey Exempted Village School District

Ryan Rogers, PhD

Associate Professor and Academic Coordinator of Esports Programs at Butler University

Tobias M. Scholz

Cofounder of the Esports Research Network (ERN)

Assistant Professor at the University of Siegen

Justin Smith

Head of the Computer Academy and Esport Coordinator for Hudson Park Primary School

Henry Wear, PhD

Assistant Professor of Sports Communication at the University of Oregon

Colin Webster

Past President and IESF Board Member for the International Esports Federation (IESF)

Melissa Welby, MD

Psychiatrist

Writer

Former President of the Connecticut Psychiatric Society

Janelle E. Wells, PhD

Associate Professor at the University of South Florida

Matthew Williamson, PhD

Associate Professor of Computer Science at Marietta College

Ashley Witt

Accreditation Coordinator for the University of Massachusetts at Amherst

Hallie Zwibel, DO, MPH, FAAFP

Associate Professor of Family Medicine, Medical Director for the Academic Healthcare Centers, and Director of Sports Medicine at the New York Institute of Technology

Preface

The thought of writing a book on the subject of esports was not on our radar 10 or even 5 years ago. At those times, the industry was slowly growing, yet it was still small compared to many traditional sports. In addition, because many considered esports to be a niche market in which gaming activities were just for a few gamers, they thought no money was to be made in it. Today, these people have been proven wrong.

Even before the global COVID-19 pandemic in 2020, the esports and video gaming industry was a fertile area for business opportunities, as evidenced by the millions of dollars invested since 2017. During the COVID-19 pandemic, while traditional sports were essentially shut down around the world, esports rose and filled the gap for millions of people. Moving forward, esports and new types of related and innovative activities (e.g., virtual, augmented, and mixed reality) will continue to receive attention and investments. By 2030, when people watch sports programming and news, headlines about both traditional sports and esports will undoubtedly be side by side and often combined, because professional sport franchises will continue to invest in and support both types of organized activities and teams. Interestingly, in 2030, there may be esports franchises that also own professional sport teams. While some of these activities are already apparent, in the near future, soccer (football) fans will be able to watch their favorite team play the physical game; and before, during halftime, and after the game they can watch the team's esports team compete against the same opponent in the FIFA video game *Pro Evolution Soccer* (*PES*) and other games such as *League of Legends*, *Dota 2*, *Fortnite*, and *Clash of Clans*.

Today, people have many questions about the current issues and challenges facing existing stakeholders in esports and how the industry will evolve in the coming years. These and many more questions underpin much of the work that has brought together contributors from around the world to write this textbook.

In addition, because of continuing calls (which are growing louder by the day) from the industry as a whole for employees and a workforce with specialized knowledge and skills, today more than ever, it is important to bring attention to the multifaceted and diverse nature of the business and management of esports. Similar to the challenges that traditional sport faced throughout the 1960s, 1970s, and 1980s to be taken seriously as a specialized type of business and industry, the esports industry, which traces its lineage to both video games and sports, faces the same type of challenge today.

In esports, each game has a story line, and players face a multitude of evolving opportunities and challenges when they play. In one of the most popular recent games, *Fortnite*, the battle royale setting of the game facilitates 100 separate players (who are logged in from around the globe) being dropped on an island on a quest to eliminate other competitors, survive in the ever-shrinking world, and be the last one standing at the end. These details are the basics of one current game setting within *Fortnite*, but a growing number of ways exist in which *Fortnite* might host other activities or evolve into a virtual universe. Not unlike the OASIS depicted in Ernest Cline's bestselling book *Ready Player One*, which was later adapted by Steven Spielberg for a movie of the same name in 2018, *Fortnite* and other games have the opportunity to create a platform—a virtual universe—where people can log in and do or be whatever they want. Already *Fortnite* has hosted music concerts; it will likely not be long before sporting events, digital festivals, dating activities, and both personal and business meetings are hosted on the platform. All of this lays the foundation for the ever-increasing movement and transfer of human lives from the real to the digital world. For those wishing to better understand this new world, not to mention those that also strive to work in the industry, this book is for you. Let's begin with how many people in 2020 may still perceive esports.

For many years, the stereotypes of those having an interest in and playing esports and video games include terms such as *nerds*, *geeks*, and *loners*. Purportedly, these people, predominantly males, stay at home in their bedroom or basement. They are antisocial or prefer not to socialize with others face-to-face, favoring online interactions. They eat microwaveable high-calorie foods and drink highly caffeinated beverages; as a result, they are often obese. They understand computers and technology, but they do not understand other human beings.

Despite parallel media depictions in television, movies, and other popular culture media, the stereotypes no longer match reality. Esports and video games are played by men and women, mothers and fathers, athletes and musicians, and more than 2.7 billion people worldwide. Global venues ranging from PC bangs in Asia to gaming cafés in Europe to Madison Square Garden in New York and back to Beijing National Stadium (also known as the Bird's Nest) in China have all hosted esports events. The sponsors of esports have evolved from a select few endemic computer equipment manufacturers to non-endemic companies and brands spanning the business world, including but not limited to credit card companies, automobile manufacturers, and sponsors of traditional sports. In essence, esports has become the next big sport. It has the attention of the coveted young generation of consumers to whom companies want to sell their goods and services. Esports influencers leverage social media in a manner very few others can achieve. Over the course of a few days, relatively unknown players can become world famous through winning competitions and tournaments. All this growth leads to opportunities for players, for spectators, for teams and their owners, for businesses and sponsors, for entrepreneurs, and for investors. The existence of these opportunities means that jobs need to be filled. Today, esports needs an educated workforce that is knowledgeable about the esports industry.

Those that play esports and video games have often felt underappreciated and stereotyped. Even when homage has been paid, such as episode 8 of the 10th season of *South Park* when the central characters played *World of Warcraft* in an attempt to save the game from another player who had become too strong (IMDB 2020), stereotypes were still abound. For example, after playing the game near constantly for months and eating and drinking highly processed foods and drinks, the main characters were depicted as sedentary, obese, and with poor hygiene and pimples. More recently, a major happening occurred when singer, songwriter, and entrepreneur Drake played *Fortnite* with well-known player Tyler "Ninja" Blevins on March 15, 2018, and more than 600,000 people tuned in to watch the livestream on Twitch (CNN 2018). In a matter of hours, many people started asking questions about and exploring opportunities to play, watch, invest, and allocate resources toward esports. The interest in esports further advanced and reached a potential tipping point when a 16-year-old from Pennsylvania won the first-ever *Fortnite* World Cup solo championship in July 2019 and pocketed a $3 million prize (Lapin 2019). Following the championship event, the American late-night comedy show *Saturday Night Live* satirized esports in a skit where a news reporter, played by Chance the Rapper, was tasked with interviewing players at an esports event. Needless to say, the character in the skit did not understand and could not explain what was going on at the esports event. The skit ended with the esports champion leaving the facility arm-in-arm with attractive fans, and the reporter appeared dumbfounded about what he just witnessed.

Many have been dumbfounded by the meteoric growth of esports. Globally, more than 2.7 billion people play video games, and an estimated 150 million play in the United States (Jabr 2019). The average American spends around 12 hours per week playing video games, and 32 million Americans play over 22 hours a week. Some of the incredible global esports numbers include the following (Newzoo 2020):

- In 2020, the global gaming market is valued at $159.3 billion, with mobile gaming comprising $77.2 billion, console gaming equaling $45.2 billion, and PC gaming totaling $36.9 billion.
- In 2020, total esports revenues are projected to be USD $1.1 billion, a 10.6 percent increase year-over-year (YOY).
- The esports audience is estimated at 459 million people in 2020, an 11.7 percent YOY growth. Projections for 2023 suggest a total esports audience of approximately 646 million people around the world.

These are just a few of the current statistics showing how the industry is rapidly growing. Another example can be seen in how advertisers have shifted resources from other sports to esports. Around 2017 and 2018, the U.S. Navy spent $20.2 million on television advertising, which represented almost half of their total advertising budget. A significant portion of that total was a campaign featured during the 2017 Army–Navy football game. In 2020, the U.S. Navy's total advertising budget is projected to be approximately $33 million; however, they anticipate spending nothing on television ads. Instead, approximately 97 percent of the budget will be reportedly spent on online advertising (Werner 2019). Broken down, approximately $1 million of that amount will be spent on traditional advertising such as billboards and local radio stations, while the remaining funds will be spent on online advertising. The digital strategy they will use focuses on esports advertising (advertising in and around esports digital content), and the U.S. Navy will field an esports team made up of active-duty recruits.

At the same time, the industry still faces a number of growing challenges. It is a cut-throat industry with stakeholders fighting for market share and consumers. Similar to the competition between linear broadcasters for traditional sport content, significant battles are being fought for streamers and content between Twitch, YouTube Gaming, Facebook Gaming, and more. Government oversight is another concern. For example, in China, the government limits the amount of time people are allowed to spend playing online games. Health is an important consideration in esports; people question how healthy it is to play video games and esports in near-constant seated positions, not to mention the potential for becoming addicted to it. Health-related esports questions first came to prominence around 2018 when the World Health Organization (WHO) identified gaming disorder as an official disease (Price and Snider 2018). Gaming disorder is defined as excessive and irresponsible preoccupation with video games resulting in significant personal, social, academic, or occupational impairment for at least 12 months (Jabr 2019). One group, Game Quitters, which was formed to counter this issue, has around 75,000 members in 95 countries (Jabr 2019). Thus, similar to chronic gambling or alcoholism, the joy of gaming can sometimes lead to significant trouble through gaming too much.

Another area where many questions are raised is whether or not the esports bubble will sooner or later burst. For example, recent years have seen a dramatic rise of estimated values of esports franchises (Upton 2019). With many investors investigating and pursuing opportunities in esports, casualties are bound to occur. One example is that of Echo Fox, a now defunct organization. Originally founded by former NBA player and entrepreneur Rick Fox, a well-publicized battle played out in the media between investors, and eventually the team was disbanded and all staff and players let go (McHugh 2019). In order to navigate the opportunities and challenges of financially investing in esports, individuals and groups wishing to know more need to have a solid understanding of numerous aspects of the esports industry.

This book started with the goal of bringing together a large and diverse group of authors and contributors who all operate in the esports space. No one or two people know everything there is to know about the esports industry—at least not yet. As a result, the three editors gathered 44 experts from around the world to share their perspectives, insights, and experiences. It has been a rewarding effort to compile the content and materials for this book. Because the global perspective is often not considered in many industries, we intentionally sought out multiple international perspectives on esports from around the world. Those that have contributed to this book represent esports-focused industry professionals and experts, CEOs and entrepreneurs, presidents and managers, athletes and coaches, academics and researchers, leaders and governing body representatives, and many more. Each contributor was tasked with exploring and sharing how their knowledge and expertise can be used by those in the field or those wishing to enter the industry.

Toward that end, the contents and organization of this textbook consider all the most important aspects of the business and management of esports. We start our journey with a foreword from James O'Connor, the President and Founder of the Pittsburgh Knights, a leading global esports team (2020 Pittsburgh Knights teams compete in *Rocket League*, *Smite*, *PlayerUnknown's Battlegrounds* (*PUBG*), *Gears of War*, *Madden '20*, and *Trackmania*), about the importance of learning more about esports and business. From there, chapter 1 dives right in with an introduction to esports and the industry, including some history and an examination of what esports is, its ecosystem, different platforms and types of games, and industry statistics. Chapter 2 provides a discussion of four levels of esports (youth, high school, college, and professional). Chapter 3 includes information about and comparisons of esports culture and issues from different perspectives, both positive and negative. Chapter 4 provides a framework of tiered stakeholders, and thoroughly describes and discusses each group. Chapter 5 offers various perspectives and information about the governance and organization of esports in various contexts.

The next seven chapters share in-depth information about key areas of the esports industry. Chapter 6 explores esports marketing, including both how it is done and to whom it is targeted. Because of its modern-day importance to the bottom line of many organizations in the industry, esports sponsorship and related opportunities, issues, and evaluation are examined in chapter 7. Chapter 8 describes and discusses the creation, execution, and evaluation of esports events. Because face-to-face (in-person) events are held in one of any number of possible locations, esports venues and facilities are discussed in chapter 9. In addition, because events can also be virtual, chapter 10 focuses on explaining esports communications as both a platform and a business function. Underpinning all of these business functions and activities is money; as a result, chapter 11 discusses the essentials of esports finance and economics. Due to the importance of numerous legal issues facing the industry, its organization, and its growth, chapter 12 provides information about esports and the law.

The final two chapters explore opportunities in the esports industry. Chapter 13 examines and discusses the management of esports teams and players from multiple perspectives. Chapter 14 surveys the esports industry landscape and focuses particularly on jobs and careers in the industry, all while being mindful that the industry is changing at a rapid pace and new knowledge and skills may be required in the near future. Finally, the book concludes with an international expert's perspective on the future of esports. Tobias M. Scholz, a highly respected esports author and researcher, discusses the potential future of digitalized society in which esports achieves both growth and sustainability.

While some in the esports industry may now be taking a victory lap, many topics and issues still require discussion and examination. In other words, it is too early to celebrate.

This book is the first step (and first edition). In the coming years, esports will evolve, likely in ways and at a speed that we now can barely imagine. So we begin this journey here, mindful that this textbook will also need to evolve and include more expert voices from around the world. The accompanying case studies and industry highlights available online through HK*Propel* provide an opportunity to learn from more experts and receive new information about the ever- and rapidly changing world of esports. We hope you enjoy reading and learning from the expert contributors, and we also hope some of what you read raises questions and ideas. This book has been written to provide as much up-to-date information as possible about the evolving esports industry. We hope our collective passion for esports energizes and excites all of you as you read and learn. Thank you for joining all of us on this journey into the esports industry.

Acknowledgments

I would like to start by thanking my wife, Yi-Hsin, and my son, Jayden, for their love, patience, and willingness to support me during this process. I could not have successfully completed this process without your love and support. I would also like to thank my parents, Dr. Ronald D. Hedlund and Dr. Ellen L. Hedlund for their constant and unwavering support, guidance, and mentoring. I would also like to acknowledge my sister for her lifelong love and sibling rivalry. Without the challenge of attempting to overcome all the sibling issues we faced over the years, I am certain I would not be as motivated as I am to persevere through challenges. I would also like to express my deep gratitude to both of my coeditors, Gil Fried and R.C. "Rick" Smith III, for their counsel, diligence, and perseverance through this process. I also have the same feelings of gratitude for the two additional editors, Roger Caramanica and Anthony Palomba, who both stepped up when we needed more editorial assistance. I would also like to recognize the 42 additional contributors from around the world whose expertise and experiences fill many pages of this book and the accompanying online resources. In addition, this book could not have happened without the multitude of professionals at Human Kinetics, many of whom I never directly communicated with, but whose work is on display in the production of this book and all its materials. Drew Tyler, Jacqueline Blakley, Hannah Werner, and Aimee Minyard led their respective teams at Human Kinetics, and we are all grateful for their professionalism, insights, counsel, and willingness to deal with the complexities and realities of putting together one of the first textbooks on esports. Finally, I would be remiss if I did not acknowledge and thank the students and faculty with whom I have collaborated on esports at St. John's University and institutions around the world. Because many of us wear multiple hats, often with one foot in academia and the other in both the for-profit and nonprofit sides of the industry, I would also like to thank all these professionals and experts who have shared their stories, knowledge, and experiences, all while lighting the esports path we will now recount in this textbook.

—David P. Hedlund

I would like to acknowledge my entire family for their patience with my crazy schedule during creation of yet another book. They are very patient. Besides my family, I would like to thank David Hedlund and Rick Smith for all their hard work in helping this book evolve from just an idea to a real book. I would also like to thank all the industry executives who have given us such valuable insight to help provide the most in-depth text to date focused on their experiences and knowledge. Lastly, I would like to thank all the folks at Human Kinetics for all their hard work. Numerous individuals have helped make this text what it is; from the bottom of my heart, I thank you all.

—Gil Fried

I would like to express my gratitude to our contributors, my coeditors, and Human Kinetics for making this book a reality. Coeditors Gil and David were instrumental in keeping me grounded and focused to finish my portions of this book—my first textbook publication ever, which was intimidating but rewarding. It was a daunting task but one I enjoyed doing with them. I also want to acknowledge Marietta College for being a true pioneer by starting an esports program and for having me involved in the administration of it, including believing in Matt and me to recruit athletes, manage a scholarship budget, and continue building the brand of the college. A special thank-you goes to Dr. Matt Williamson, Marietta College's esports coach, for helping me learn the ins and outs of esports at a local level. On a personal note, I thank my family for their continued support of my endeavors, which have been diverse and varied over the years (Mom, Dad, Elie, Janelle and Dustin, Caitlyn, Jenisse, Julie, Deanna, Emery, Amelia, and Cole; and my aunts, uncles, and cousins). When I told them I was assisting with this project, they were not surprised that I had gotten my hands "into something else." The best part about them listening to me talk about the book was that I had to explain esports to them, which helped me with writing some of the content for the book. Perhaps those who will be most impacted by this book are my nieces and nephew (Deanna, Cole, Emery, and Amelia), who will grow up with esports in their schools as we grew up with football, volleyball, and marching band in our schools. "Big ups" and thanks to the students in my classes; without you, I wouldn't be a teacher. You keep me motivated to be a better person, role model, and teacher. Finally, specifically at Marietta College, thank you to President, Dr. Bill Ruud; Provost, Dr. Janet Bland; my department chair, Dr. Greg Delemeester; and a mentor of mine on campus, Mrs. Linda Roesch, whose combined leadership, guidance, and patience has continued to motivate me to be better than I was yesterday.

—R.C. Smith III

1

Introduction to Esports

David P. Hedlund | R.C. Smith III | Gil Fried
Stanley Nana Anyang-Kaakyire | Sang-ho Lee
Michael Newhouse-Bailey | Janelle E. Wells

OBJECTIVES

- Explain the definition, history, and development of esports.
- Explain similarities and differences between traditional sports and esports.
- Identify various stakeholders within the esports ecosystem.
- Identify various esports platforms on which users play.
- Identify unique types and categories of esports games.
- Draw conclusions from research on the past, present, and future of the business of esports.

INTRODUCTION

Electronic sports, also known as **esports**, is an overarching term used in reference to numerous types of video games played on personal computers (PCs), mobile devices (e.g., mobile phones, tablets), video game consoles (e.g., Microsoft Xbox, Sony PlayStation), and hybrid portable console devices (e.g., Nintendo Switch). In the near future, games played with virtual reality (VR), augmented reality (AR), and mixed reality (MR) devices could also fall under the category of esports. When computers and arcade machines were first used to play video games in the 1970s and 1980s, most games were played one player at a time. As technology evolved, some video games allowed two players to compete with or against each other in the same game at the same machine. For example, the Mortal Kombat arcade game included two joysticks and two sets of buttons, and this facilitated two players to simultaneously play against each other. Later, the Nintendo Entertainment System (NES) had two controllers, and many games were designed for simultaneous collaborative or competitive play. With the advent of the Internet, players no longer needed to be located at the same machine in order to compete with or against each other. Current technology allows individuals and teams from every corner of the globe to connect in real time and play esports at their leisure. Because the word *esports* is often used to describe many types of gaming, the first task in this introductory chapter is to define and explain it.

WHAT IS ESPORTS?

As noted previously, the word *esports* is used to describe a number of activities, including both recreational and competitive electronic video game play, electronic games played by individuals and teams, games played on a single device or multiple connected devices, and multiple genres of games (e.g., sport, fighting, and shooting games). Alongside spirited debate about whether it is accurate to call esports an actual sport, confusion still exists about how esports are best defined due to the evolving nature of video games and technology.

Multiple definitions of esports have been put forward over the years. Wagner (2006) did much of the initial work of bringing together the conceptual pieces that defined esports. Drawing from sport-focused literature, Wagner noted the importance of playing video games in a professional setting, developing game-playing abilities, and comparing one's own game-playing skills against the skills of others, all within a system consisting of generally accepted rules. In the end, Wagner defined esports simply as "an area of sport activities in which people develop and train mental or physical abilities in the use of information and communication technologies" (p. 439). Based on the limited scope of this definition, Taylor (2012) and Witkowski (2012) examined the electronic nature of esports and argued this is the key difference from traditional sports (i.e., competitive games played in the "real world" versus those played within electronic systems).

Jenny, Manning, Keiper, and Olrich (2017) later compared traditional sports with esports based on similarities and differences: involving voluntary or intrinsically motivated play; being organized and having rules, including competition (i.e., a winner or loser); being based on skill and not chance, including physical skills and body movement; having a broad following of players and fans; and having an overarching institution that regulates and oversees the game (read more about this in chapters 2 , 4, and 5). In all of these areas, except the inclusion of physical skills and body movement, evidence suggested esports met the criteria to be defined as a sport. Within a discussion of the mixed evidence that esports includes physical skills and body movements, Jenny and colleagues noted the importance of distinguishing between gross motor skills (e.g., throwing, hitting or kicking a ball, running from place to place) and fine motor skills (e.g., organizing coordinated movement of one's fingers or hands in a proper sequence, such as playing a video game with a controller based on what one sees on a screen). As discussed later in this chapter in more detail, the argument about the importance of, and perhaps requirement of, using gross motor skills as a prerequisite for consideration as a sport continues, and it is the primary argument against labeling esports a true sport.

In one of the most recent attempts at creating a concise definition, Hamari and Sjöblom (2017) defined esports as "a form of sports where the primary aspects of the sport are facilitated by electronic systems; the input of players and teams as well as the output of the esports system are mediated by human-computer interfaces" (p. 213). Within this definition are two components. First, while teams of esports players may be located in the same physical space and be able to communicate face-to-face, the game itself is occurring online (i.e., within an electronic system). Therefore, the electronic system connecting players to the game is an important component of the definition of esports. Second, in contrast to traditional sports, where players either use physical objects to play (e.g., a ball is necessary to play soccer, football, baseball, rugby, tennis, or golf) or players physically move (e.g., running, jumping), esports players need to connect with a computer, device, or controller that is then electronically converted into video, audio, and haptic outputs. In other words, esports cannot occur without electronic devices. As a result, esports includes interfaces that connect players and devices together. Technology such as game-streaming services and cloud gaming (e.g., Google Stadia, Microsoft xCloud) will further enhance the interfaces needed to play esports.

The major issue remaining with existing definitions, however, is about whether playing certain types of video games in specific game play modes may still be considered esports. As discussed by Funk, Pizzo, and Baker (2018), "while all esports are video games, not all video gaming should be classified as sport" (p. 9). Therefore, before a more encompassing definition of esports is put forward, an examination and comparison of video games and esports is undertaken.

The confusion over defining and explaining esports is likely based on its precursor, video games. In the beginning, video games were electronic games played using a device that housed or facilitated the game to be played (e.g., a video game console, a stand-alone arcade video game machine); a monitor, television, screen, or other

Zoning

THE EVOLUTION OF ESPORTS THROUGH ENTERTAINMENT AND CULTURE

Janelle E. Wells

Culture and entertainment are constantly evolving. From one second to the next, interests, perspectives, and values can align to influence individuals and society. Video content has evolved from scripted television shows to original reality shows with vloggers and streamers (McVerry and Wells 2019). In today's hyperconnected world, technology has fueled gaming's growth to the mainstream, penetrating everything from music to fashion to sports.

Artists from all music genres, particularly hip-hop, are engaging and investing in esports—for example, Canadian rapper Drake became a co-owner of 100 Thieves, and American rapper Offset invested in FaZe Clan (Webster 2019). Offset suggested the main unifying force between hip-hop and esports is that both are "about entertainment" (Webster 2019, p. 1). In fashion, according to Rouse (2019), an online street wear destination, more partnerships are being created between fashion brands and esports teams, such as the special-edition jersey that Undefeated created for *Overwatch* team New York Excelsior. In sports, the National Basketball Association (NBA) created its own gaming league, the NBA 2K League, and some of its players found themselves at major esports events. For example, NBA guard Josh Hart attended the Fortnite Celebrity Pro-Am charity event and then went to the Call of Duty World League (CWL) Anaheim Open (Parker 2018). These examples highlight how the rise of gaming has transcended the online experience by affecting merchandise, culture, and ultimately entertainment.

Slowly ascending to the mainstream, gaming has been at the center of a digital ecosystem full of platforms (e.g., YouTube, Twitch) and digital networks (e.g., Discord, Reddit) that support immersive interactive entertainment. According to Entrepreneur Outlet (Austin 2018), Vine became a factor of mass culture and helped pave the way for social media influencers such as Amanda Cerny, Logan Paul, King Bach, and Curtis Lepore. Launched in 2012, Vine was one of the first short-form video applications where creators could film, edit, and post from their cell phones. Alexander (2019) identified Logan Paul as one of the most popular Vine influencers, which parlayed him into acting roles and earned him an estimated $200,000 for branded Vine content. Four years later, one reason Vine shut down was because the initial creators fled to other social media platforms, particularly YouTube. With the popularity of YouTube and YouTubers, the outlet for creative expression has provided lucrative earning potential for content creators. According to Forbes (Robehmed and Berg 2018), in 2018, of the top 10 highest-paid YouTube stars, 5 were gamers (DanTDM, Markiplier, PewDiePie, VanossGaming, and JackSepticEye). In total, the top 10 YouTube stars earned a combined income of $180.5 million, which was a 42 percent increase from the previous year.

Around the world, esports has become a cultural force in attracting audiences and creating connective experiences. The rise in popularity of gaming has allowed gamers and streamers a newfound level of respect and influence, as was evident by YouTube's top 10 gaming influencers in 2018.

device on which the playing of the electronic game could be displayed; or a device that allowed a user to control the actions shown on the monitor. While video games were originally an activity purely for entertainment, it did not take long for these recreational activities to escalate into competitions. With "high score" boards listing the best scores achieved by users, and later with opportunities for users to play the same game side by side and compete in real time, the games soon became increasingly competitive. Herein lies the first additional important aspect of defining esports: the opportunity for competition. It was not long before video game developers began to build in options for both one- and two-player versions of the game, where players could play with or against each other in real time. It is important to note that video games can be played asynchronously, where only one player would play at a given moment in time and later another player would play. An example is the popular game *Words With Friends*, which is downloaded onto mobile devices and where one player creates a word with letters they have, then places that word on a board; their opponent then takes a turn doing the same thing. Minutes or hours could pass between activities undertaken by each player. As a result, real-time competition—where two or more players or teams compete at the same time in the same game—is a central component of esports. This is the second important aspect of defining esports: real-time competition with or against other players or teams.

In the early years of video games in the 1970s and 1980s, in order to compete with or against other people, players needed to be located in the same location with machines that were physically connected. The earliest local area network (LAN) events capitalized on this phenomenon, where computers could be physically attached and a main computer (e.g., server) would facilitate the competition. With the advent of the Internet and the ability to remotely connect devices, it was no longer necessary for individuals to be located in the same place in order to compete with or against each other. As a result, the next important aspect of the esports definition includes non–geographically bound real-time competitions with or against other players or teams.

Finally, player-organized competitions lacked standardized rules and organization, so game developers and publishers began to include opportunities for competitions based on standardized rules that included number of players, game length, acceptable practices, and standards for winning and losing. As a result, having some type of organization and standardization is essential because otherwise each competition could be played under different rules and game parameters, some of which might not epitomize competitive gaming.

Based on its current yet evolving and unique characteristics, here is an encompassing definition of esports:

> Esports are any video game that allows for organized multiplayer non–geographically bound real-time competitions with or against other players or teams, where the primary aspects of the game are facilitated by electronic systems, and the input of players and teams as well as the output of the electronic systems are mediated by human–computer interfaces.

In order to organize and increasingly monetize esports, game developers and publishers have begun to create competitions and leagues, based in some cases on the franchise model popular in traditional sports. Creating different tiers of players, teams, and leagues (recreational, amateur, professional) is also a valuable component of a video game but not necessarily a prerequisite to be considered an esport. As will be discussed in subsequent chapters, in addition to the game developers and publishers, a growing number of organizations are attempting to bring structure and governance to multiple levels of esports.

A BRIEF HISTORY OF VIDEO GAMES AND ESPORTS

The Stanford University Artificial Intelligence Lab hosted the first organized competitive video game contest when it brought students together to compete in the computer game *Spacewar* in 1972 (Baker 2016). The prize for the winner was a magazine subscription to *Rolling Stone*, which ran a feature on the event. The year 1972 also saw the birth of the Atari video game system and the development of the game *Pong*, which was one of the first commercially successful video games ever developed (Casey 2017).

Golden Age of Arcade Video Games

According to Steven Kent (2001), the golden age of arcade video games began with the release of *Space Invaders* in 1978 and continued until 1983. Atari hosted what is considered the first large-scale video game competition when it attracted over 10,000 competitors for the *Space Invaders* high score in 1980. Within a few years, Walter Day opened an arcade called Twin Galaxies and immediately became interested in the "high-score culture" of video games (Wright 2018). He was known to visit and record high scores at various sites and eventually published his findings as a "national scoreboard" for video games. Day's activities became the basis for officially reporting high scores, and Twin Galaxies eventually became the official video game scorekeeper for Guinness World Records (Wright 2018). Video games continued to grow in popularity during the close of the golden age, punctuated by *Starcade*, a television show featuring video game programming from 1982 to 1984. *Starcade* aired over 120 episodes, featured over 200 games, and over 120 contestants participated in timed competitions (Starcade n.d.).

Video Games at Home

The first video game console that allowed people to play games at home was the Odyssey from Magnavox (Martin 2014). Other companies attempted to jump on the home video game bandwagon, with Atari 2600 being the most successful early on in 1977 (Martin 2014). Early games, such as *Space Invaders*, *Asteroids*, and *Centipede*, had rudimentary graphics. A few years later, Nintendo helped energize the video game market with its 1983 release of the Famicom in Japan, known in the United States as the Nintendo Entertainment System (NES) (Mlot 2014). Sega also joined the home console business when it released the Master System in the United States in 1986 (Horowitz 2018). This prompted the console wars as Nintendo and Sega battled for market dominance. Video games such as *The Oregon Trail*, *Castle Wolfenstein*, *Ultima I*, *Frogger*, *Zaxxon*, *King's Quest*, and *The Black Cauldron* also entered the home on personal computers starting in the late 1970s and early 1980s with the success of Apple, Commodore, and Tandy computer systems (Purcaru 2014). Many of these games were **player versus environment (PvE)** in which competitors competed against the computer instead of another player.

Growth of Organized Events

Nintendo took advantage of the interest in organized events and launched the Nintendo World Championships in 1990 (Cifaldi 2015). Nintendo created a special tournament cartridge and embarked on a 30-city tour that started in Dallas, Texas. Three age categories competed in the Championship Arena in each city. The winner from each was flown to Universal Studios to compete for the world championship title.

While organized events around video games continued into the 1990s, the **player versus player (PvP)** concept took off thanks to the rise in fighting games. The Evolution Championship Series (Evo) is the world's largest fighting game tournament. It began as the Battle by the Bay in 1996 (Rinaldi 2018). By the end of the 1990s, other organizations were forming that started to resemble modern esports gaming organizations. For example, the Cyberathlete Professional League (CPL) was founded as a small LAN group in Dallas, Texas, in 1997 (Chalk 2008). The CPL was acquired in 2008 after hosting many successful video game championships and doling out more than $3 million in cash prizes during its existence (Liquipedia 2019c).

Modern Esports

With the development of broadband technology and increased Internet speeds, competitive video games were positioned to become a global affair. South Korea was an early adopter in terms of esports and formed the Korea e-Sports Association (KeSPA) in 2000 (Larch 2019). KeSPA is part of the South Korean government's Ministry of Culture, Sports, and Tourism, which provides financial backing to support the growth of esports (Larch 2019).

Blizzard, publisher of popular esports titles *World of Warcraft* and *StarCraft II*, held its first Battle.net World Championship Series in 2012 (Hillier 2012). More than 30 events were held over the course of the season, leading to a grand finale featuring the national champions from 28 countries. The champion, Won "PartinG" Lee-sak from South Korea, was awarded $100,000 (Liquipedia 2019a).

Esports gained mainstream attention when the *League of Legends* World Championship was hosted in Los Angeles at the Staples Center in 2013. Tickets for the event sold out in about an hour (Tassi 2013). The following year, the *League of Legends* World Championship was held in Seoul, South Korea, in front of over 40,000 fans (Chalk 2014). The opening and closing ceremonies resembled the type of fanfare that the Olympic Games command, and the event was streamed online to over 27 million viewers (Tassi 2013).

The first dedicated esports facility in the United States, aptly named Esports Arena, opened in 2015 in Santa Ana, California (Esports Arena n.d.). More recently, facilities have opened hosting professional franchises and teams, college and university teams, and publishers' studios. The following year, Turner Broadcasting System (TBS) launched its first foray into esports programming with *ELEAGUE* in 2016 (Heitner 2015). The show originally broadcast *Counter-Strike: Global Offensive* competitions surrounding a 24-team league, and has since expanded to include *Street Fighter*, *Overwatch*, and *Rocket League*. Since 2016, *ELEAGUE* has hosted and broadcast nine seasons of competitions (Liquipedia 2019b).

Even brick-and-mortar stores such as Walmart and the Simon Property Group, the "global leader in the ownership of premier shopping, dining, entertainment and mixed-use destinations" (Simon n.d., para. 1), are investing in bringing esports to their respective locations (Fitch 2019; Fogel 2018). In the United States, there has been an increasing interest in esports based on the overlap of traditional sports and competitive video games. For example, in 2018, Major League Soccer (MLS) launched the eMLS, and the National Basketball Association (NBA) launched its NBA 2K League. eMLS started with 19 teams in 2018 and expanded to over 22 teams in 2019 (MLS Soccer Staff 2018). The NBA 2K League also launched in 2018, and over time, members of the esports teams have garnered the same benefits as the players on the traditional basketball team, including access to personal trainers and team facilities (NBA 2K League 2018). In addition, Blizzard created the *Overwatch* League in 2018 with a goal of developing geographically centered fans around local teams, much like traditional sports. In its first year, all the teams competed at Blizzard Arena in California, but by the 2020 season, all teams were required to have a local facility in which they could host home competitions. In the 2020 season, the *Overwatch* League had 20 teams based in six countries: the United States, Canada, China, South Korea, England, and France (Blizzard Entertainment n.d.).

In July of 2019, the *Fortnite* World Cup was held in New York City over three days in front of a sold-out Arthur Ashe Stadium (Spangler 2019). In the 10 weeks leading up to the event, over 40 million players from more than 200 countries competed in qualifying events (Fortnite Team 2019). During the finals, in which 16-year-old Kyle "Bugha" Giersdorf reigned supreme and won $3 million, concurrent viewership "peaked at over 2.3 million across YouTube and Twitch, making the *Fortnite* World Cup the most-watched competitive gaming event (excluding China) of all time" (para. 2). In the next section, a description of the esports ecosystem is provided.

THE ESPORTS ECOSYSTEM

A depiction of the esports ecosystem, consisting of eight key stakeholders is shown in figure 1.1. Later in chapter 4, a more complete list of stakeholders is provided and discussed, with a focus on categorizing stakeholders into different tiers based on their importance.

Players

The central component of the esports ecosystem is the players. Players bring excitement, interest, and intrigue. It is feasible that video games and esports could be played only by automated computers; however, the "human element"—and how it results in achieving success and dealing with failures—provides opportunities for others to spectate and motivation to play. As soon as people begin watching others play esports, the opportunity to monetize and leverage gaming becomes important. When recreational gaming for personal entertainment transforms into a competitive profession, then multiple stakeholders may leverage players and their game play in order to monetize the competitive activities. This is when esports business begins to take shape.

Teams and Franchises

The next stakeholder is teams and franchises. As briefly discussed earlier in this chapter and in more detail later in this book, some games are played by teams of players (e.g., 3v3, 5v5, 6v6). In order to create successful teams of like-minded and skilled players, first, players come together and form teams. Over time, some players may leave and join another team, while new players may be recruited. Because there are numerous types of esports and games available for players with different interests and skill sets, and because players' interests and skills may also change, it should not be surprising that over time, esports franchises housing players and teams competing in numerous different games would develop.

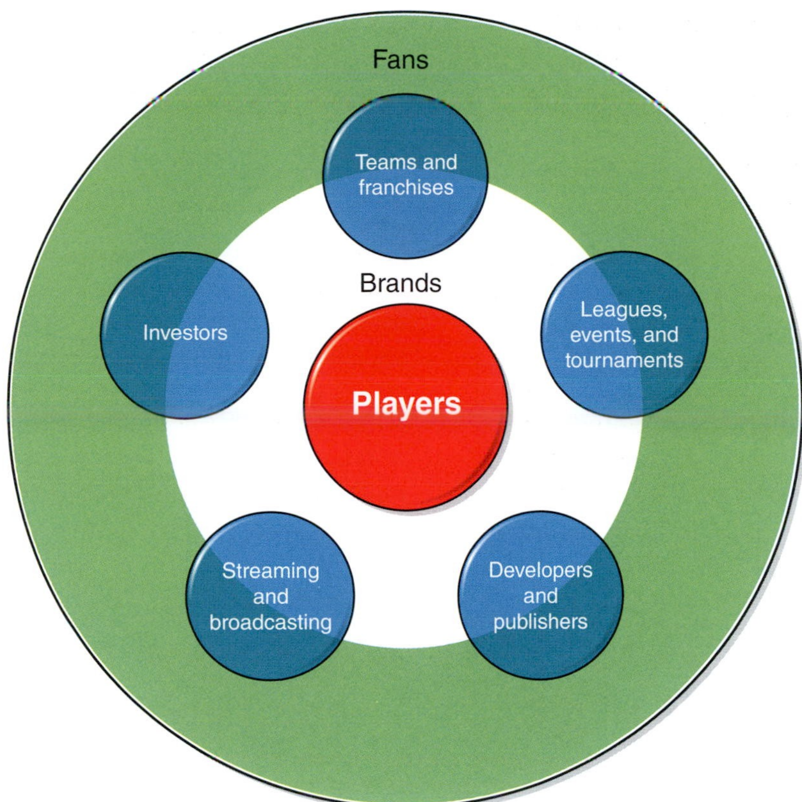

Figure 1.1 The esports ecosystem.

Leagues, Events, and Tournaments

Due to the increasing popularity of certain games in various national and international markets, leagues, events, and tournaments are organized by various stakeholders, including publishers, developers, and event management and production groups. In some places, such as the United States, China, and South Korea, game-specific leagues are being operated (NBA 2K League, *PlayerUnknown's Battlegrounds* [*PUBG*] Champions League, Korea StarCraft League). Around the world, teams competing in leagues around specific games are also growing in popularity (e.g., *Overwatch* League, *League of Legends* Championship Series [LCS]). Throughout the year, companies like ESL (Electronic Sports League) host game-specific competitions in cities around the world. In contrast, after being on a multiyear hiatus, the World Cyber Games (WCG) returned in 2019 with Olympic-style competitions (e.g., 506 players from 34 countries) in six different games (WCG 2019).

Game Developers and Publishers

The leagues, events, and tournaments could not be hosted without the work and support of the game developers and publishers. In fact, some might argue that without games being developed and published for users to play, the esports industry would not be possible. As will be discussed later in this chapter, because some games are played on specific platforms (e.g., PC, console, mobile devices, AR/VR/MR technology), game developers and publishers may focus on only one platform to publish their games. However, with enhanced technology such as game-streaming services and cloud gaming (e.g., Google Stadia, Microsoft xCloud), in the near future it may be possible for games to be played on any device or platform. Already, some games like *Fortnite* have been developed for all major platforms.

Streaming and Broadcasting Services

In order to provide opportunities for spectating esports competitions and activities, during the last five years streaming services (e.g., Twitch, YouTube Gaming) have become more popular and allow fans around the world to watch others play esports. According to Bogorad (2020), Twitch remains the most popular streaming website for esports content. In early 2020, usage statistics for Twitch were viewed on Twitch Tracker. The data showed that during 2019, Twitch had more than 660 billion minutes of content watched, with an average of 3.6 million monthly streamers, more than 1.25 million concurrent viewers on average, and nearly 50,000 concurrent live channels on average streaming content (Twitch Tracker 2020). While several well-known esports influencers (e.g., Tyler "Ninja" Blevins, Michael "Shroud" Grzesiek, Cory "King Gothalion" Michael) began exclusively streaming on the Mixer platform rather than Twitch in 2019 (Stephen 2019), in mid-2020, Mixer closed down its service as Facebook Gaming and YouTube Gaming were both rising. There are also very popular streaming platforms (e.g., DouYu TV, Huya) catering to large numbers of Chinese players and spectators.

Investors

The next group of stakeholders is the investors. Without a doubt, one of the most pervasive messages about esports in the media today is about how its popularity is growing with plentiful opportunities for investment. With publications such as Deloitte's (2019) "The Rise of Esports Investments" laying out information about the state of the industry, numerous professional athletes, musicians, and entertainers (e.g., Michael Jordan, Drake, Steve Young, Sean "Diddy" Combs) have all invested in esports organizations. As will be described in chapter 13, numerous investors have bought stakes in esports franchises and now are owners or managing partners. Some professional athletes, such as former NFL player Jay Ajayi, have segued from competing in traditional sports to playing professional esports (Webster 2020).

Fans and Brands

The last two groups of stakeholders are fans and brands. Later in this book, both groups will receive more attention, in addition to other stakeholders not listed here. However, in brief, without fans and spectators, esports would undoubtedly revert to a recreational activity played solely for fun and entertainment. At the same time, today's esports fans are on average substantially younger than fans of other traditional sports. According to data compiled by Skillshot (see figure 1.2), the average age of esports fans is 26 years old, while fans of traditional sports range from 40 (Major League Soccer) to 64 (Professional Golf Association) (Harris 2020).

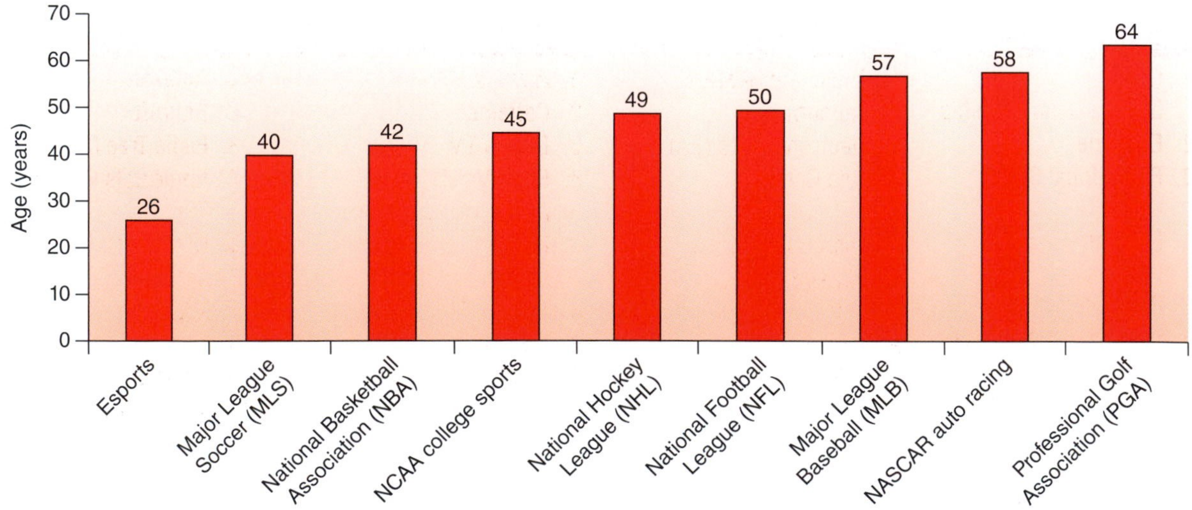

Figure 1.2 Average age of fans of esports and traditional sports leagues.
Data from Harris (2020).

In part due to the young average age of esports fans, both **endemic** and **non-endemic** brands have explored opportunities for marketing, advertising, and branding activities in the esports ecosystem. Due to factors such as the ability to record and skip over broadcasted advertisements on television and cable, coupled with the strong connection and identification fans often feel with their favorite sport team and a desire to watch sports and esports events live, an increasing number of brands, especially those focusing on 18- to 35-year-old consumers, are embracing the esports ecosystem. With endemic brands initially populating the esports ecosystem (e.g., computer companies, chair companies), followed by those with some connection such as food and drink companies, there are now non-endemic brands (e.g., car companies, credit card companies) using esports to connect with fans and consumers. Table 1.1 provides examples of stakeholders in each of the seven major categories.

ESPORTS PLATFORMS

As mentioned at the outset of this chapter, there are five major platforms on which esports and video games are currently developed: PCs; consoles; hybrid portable console devices; mobile devices; and AR, VR, and MR technologies.

Table 1.1 Stakeholders in the Esports Ecosystem

Former and current players	Franchises and teams	Leagues
1. Jian "Uzi" Zihao	1. Astralis	1. *Call of Duty* League
2. Katherine "Mystik" Gunn	2. Cloud9	2. *CS:GO* Pro League
3. Kuro "KuroKy" Salehi Takhasomi	3. Evil Geniuses	3. eMLS League
4. Lee "Faker" Sang-hyeok	4. FaZe Clan	4. ePremier League
5. Marcelo "coldzera" David	5. Fnatic	5. ESL Pro League
6. Matthew "Nadeshot" Haag	6. G2 Esports	6. Korean *Starcraft* League
7. Michael "Shroud" Grzesiek	7. Immortals	7. *League of Legends* Championship Series (LCS)
8. Park "SaeByeolBe" Jong-yeol	8. Invictus Gaming	8. NBA 2K League
9. Sasha "Scarlett" Hostyn	9. Ninjas in Pyjamas	9. *Overwatch* League
10. Soleil "Ewok" Wheeler	10. NRG Esports	10. *PUBG* Champions League
11. Spencer "Gorilla" Ealing	11. OG	
12. Stephanie "missharvey" Harvey	12. Team Dignitas	
13. Turner "Tfue" Tenney	13. Team Liquid	
14. Tyler "Ninja" Blevins	14. Team Vitality	
15. Xiaomeng "VKLiooon" Li	15. Virtus.pro	

Events and tournaments	Developers and publishers	Streaming and broadcasting	Investors
1. Call of Duty World League Championship	1. Activision Blizzard	1. Afreeca TV	1. Amazon
2. ESL One	2. Capcom	2. Caffeine	2. Bitkraft
3. FIFA Global Series and eWorld Cup	3. Electronic Arts (EA)	3. DouYu TV	3. Eagle Tree Capital
4. Fortnite World Cup	4. Epic Games	4. ESL TV	4. Immortals Gaming Club
5. Hearthstone World Championship	5. Hi-Rez Studios	5. Facebook Gaming	5. Modern Times Group
6. Intel Extreme Masters	6. Microsoft Studios	6. Huya	6. Softbank
7. League of Legends World Championship	7. Nintendo	7. Smashcast.tv	7. Techstars
8. Rocket League Championship Series	8. Riot Games	8. Steam TV	8. Tencent
9. The International	9. Ubisoft	9. Twitch	9. Valor Equity Partners
10. World Cyber Games	10. Valve	10. YouTube Gaming	10. Y Combinator

Personal Computers

PCs have been around since at least the 1970s, but at the time they were extremely expensive, in some cases costing upwards of the 2016 equivalent of half a million dollars (Comen 2018). In the beginning, PC games were very basic and contained low-quality graphics. However, over the years as hardware within PCs improved (e.g., central processing unit [CPU], graphics processing unit [GPU], random-access memory [RAM]), in addition to the production of high-quality monitors (e.g., 4K, curved displays) and enhanced peripherals (e.g., mouse, keyboard), PCs have become one of the most popular means of playing esports in the United States (Waddell 2019). Today, services such as Steam allow users to log in to their personal account and download (if necessary) and play more than 30,000 games on their PC or mobile device (Steam n.d.).

Consoles

Consoles, such as the Microsoft Xbox, Sony PlayStation, and the hybrid portable console device Nintendo Switch, have traditionally been lower-cost alternatives to PCs. In the case of the Xbox and PlayStation, the console plugs directly into a television, while the Switch has a small display built in to the device. Due to several factors, such as the lower cost, ergonomic controllers, the ability to play games more comfortably from a couch (compared to the table and chair needed for a PC), and the simplicity of console use (i.e., turn it on and play), playing esports and video games on consoles remains very popular within the United States (Waddell 2019). Also, manufacturers have gone to great lengths to make the most popular games available on their respective console platforms (Agarwal 2018).

Mobile Devices

Mobile gaming, currently the most popular platform for playing esports within the United States (Waddell 2019) and around the world (Wijman 2018), includes playing games on mobile phones, tablets, and other portable and mobile devices. Wijman notes, "In the span of a decade, mobile gaming will have grown from the smallest segment in 2012 to a 100-billion-dollar industry in 2021" (2018, para. 5). Based on the tremendous growth in mobile gaming, in addition to expanding opportunities in pairing mobile devices with VR, AR, and MR technology, there are increasing opportunities for publishers and developers to create games played on all mobile platforms.

Virtual, Augmented, and Mixed Reality

The final types of gaming platforms are VR, AR, and MR. Perhaps popularized most recently by the game *Pokémon Go* in 2016 (which primarily leverages AR technology), VR, AR, and MR platforms are the next step in the future of gaming development. As described by Bryksin (2018), VR technology (e.g., Oculus products, PlayStation VR, Samsung Gear VR, HTC Vive) offers a fully artificial digital environment in which there is complete immersion in a virtual world. In practice, players of VR games put on a head-mounted display or VR headset, and they would feel like they are in a virtual and digital world (Marr 2019). AR technology allows virtual and digital objects to be overlaid on the real world and viewed via a digital device (Bryksin 2018). Based on the example of *Pokémon Go*, players use their mobile device to view the real world, and the game overlays digital and virtual objects (e.g., Pokémon creatures) onto their screen. In the near future, AR technology (e.g., Apple's ARKit, Google's ARCore) will allow consumers to see how aspects of the real world could be changed with digital and virtual overlays (Marr 2019). Finally, MR is the combination of real and virtual worlds to produce a new environment. MR technology (e.g., Acer Windows Mixed Reality, Lenovo Explorer, Microsoft HoloLens, Samsung Odyssey) allows users to see one's own surroundings and at the same time be immersed in a virtual experience with digital objects overlaid on the real world (Bryksin 2018). Currently, there are relatively few VR, AR, and MR games (notable exceptions include *Pokémon Go, EVE: Valkyrie, EVE: Project Galaxy, Raw Data,* and *Smash Tanks!*), because "current headsets are bulky, inconvenient, uncomfortable, underpowered, and expensive" (Leong 2019, para. 14). Despite current barriers to adoption in Internet speeds (4G vs. 5G), cost, and the limited availability of games, in the next few years as these hurdles are overcome, VR, AR, and MR technology and platforms are likely to see a rise in use similar to that of gaming on mobile devices during the 2010s. In chapter 9, more information about VR and facilities hosting related technology is provided.

TYPES OF ESPORTS GAMES

Esports can be classified into eight major categories or genres of games: (1) multiplayer online battle arena (MOBA); (2) first-person shooter (FPS); (3) fighting games; (4) sports games; (5) racing games; (6) real-time strategy (RTS); (7) hybrid games, card games, and other games; and (8) mobile-only games (see table 1.2).

Multiplayer Online Battle Arena Games

MOBA games are played with two teams competing against one another in an effort to destroy or eliminate the opposing team or its base. At the beginning of each game, players can choose from a number of different characters (also known as avatars), each with unique skills and abilities to use during the game. In 2016, the MOBA game *League of Legends* reported over 100 million monthly active players worldwide (Volk 2016).

First-Person Shooter Games

The next type of game, FPS, can be played by individuals or teams in both PvE and PvP competitive scenarios. As the name suggests, FPS games allow players to feel like they are actually holding and operating the weapons in their hands (which they can see on-screen). Throughout the game, players feel like they are looking through the eyes of their in-game character. In the early 2000s, two of the most popular FPS games for PCs were *Call of Duty* and *Counter-Strike* (Evans-Thirlwell 2017). More recently, the game *Apex Legends* set numerous records during its initial launch in early 2019, including signing up 10 million players during its first 72 hours of operations (Zampella n.d.) and garnering 8.28 million hours of Twitch viewership eight days after its unveiling (McAloon 2019). Surpassing those records, *Fortnite*, which can now be played on all three major gaming platforms, had a total of 250 million players at its peak and 100 million downloads on Apple's iOS platform in its first five months (Iqbal 2019). In 2020, *Valorant* joined the growing list of FPS games.

Table 1.2 Esports Games and Categories

Multiplayer online battle arena (MOBA)	First-person shooter (FPS)	Fighting games	Sports games
• *Defense of the Ancients 2 (Dota 2)* • *Heroes of the Storm* • *League of Legends (LoL)* • *Smite* • *Vainglory*	• *Apex Legends* • *Call of Duty (COD)* • *Counter-Strike: Global Offensive (CS:GO)* • *Fortnite* • *Overwatch* • *PlayerUnknown's Battlegrounds (PUBG)* • *Rainbow Six (R6)*	• *BlazBlue* • *Dragon Ball FighterZ* • *Marvel vs. Capcom* • *Street Fighter* • *Super Smash Bros.* • *Tekken*	• *FIFA* • *Madden* • *MLB: The Show* • *NBA 2K* • *NHL* • *Pro Evolution Soccer (PES)*
Racing games	**Real-time strategy (RTS)**	**Hybrid games, card games, and other games**	**Mobile-only games**
• *F1* • *Forza Motorsport* • *Gran Turismo* • *iRacing* • *NASCAR Heat* • *Project CARS* • *Trackmania*	• *Age of Empires* • *Starcraft* • *Warcraft*	• *Gears of War* • *Hearthstone* • *Magic: The Gathering Online* • *Pokémon Trading Card Game Online* • *Rocket League* • *World of Tanks*	• *Arena of Valor* • *Brawl Stars* • *Clash of Clans* • *Clash Royale* • *Free Fire* • *Honor of Kings* • *Lords Mobile* • *Mobile Legends* • *Pokémon Go* • *Summoners War*

Zoning

THE RISE OF ARTIFICIAL INTELLIGENCE IN ESPORTS AND GAMING

Gil Fried

Artificial intelligence (AI) is more than just an abstract concept. There are numerous applications that are being analyzed. Applications for medicine, voting, law, and human resources are starting to utilize AI. For example, AI can help analyze numerous photographs of people's eyes, and then identify what might be precursors to identifying adult-onset diabetes. In fact, Google has a division focused on analyzing millions of pieces of data and numerous eye photographs to help identify possible future diabetics in India. Being able to identify the most likely candidates using a computer analysis of photographs may significantly reduce adult-onset diabetes. This is the benefit of AI and how numerous points of data can be analyzed by a computer. The same concept can be applied to esports.

Computers have been used to help battle humans in various games such as chess. However, AI has helped make machines almost unbeatable. In 2015, the DeepMind Technologies AI project was able to master 49 Atari games (ranging from *Pong* to *Space Invaders*) in only a few hours of training. In 2017, DeepMind's AlphaGo became the best Go "player" in the world. Also in 2017, Libratus, an AI poker-playing system, defeated four professional poker players in no-limit Texas Hold'em. Then in 2019, DeepMind's AlphaStar ranked in the top 99.8 percent of the world's players in *StarCraft II* (Kahn 2020). This might indicate that in the future, the top players could be computers battling against each other to determine who the best programmers are.

Fighting Games

The fighting game category, as the name suggests, include titles in which players can choose a character based on a multitude of skills and abilities and then engage in PvP or PvE combat. Oftentimes, in-game combat is undertaken via martial arts or fighting activities, and competitions occur over multiple rounds. Fighting game tournaments are frequently held as open-bracket tournaments over multiple days, where anyone willing to pay the entry fee has the opportunity to compete (Murray 2018).

Sports Games

Sports games are generally modeled after traditional sports competitions, and teams and players frequently license their likeness to the game developer. In recent years, sports games representing traditional sports such as soccer, gridiron football, basketball, baseball, and ice hockey have all become more popular. As evidenced by the creation of the eMLS and NBA 2K League, in which professional traditional sport franchises have formed esports teams consisting of top players of the game title, organized competitions in sports games are starting to make their breakthrough. In the near future, it is likely that soccer fans will be able to watch their favorite team play a traditional soccer match, followed by the opportunity to watch esports players from those same two teams compete in *FIFA* or *PES*.

Racing Games

Racing games, similar to sports games, are played in ways meant to mirror the action of driving a car in a competitive race. Moreover, many of today's most popular racing games are designed to feel like a driving simulator (Janas 2019). In fact, driving simulations have a specialized category called "sim racing." Interestingly, in early 2019 while competing in a traditional racing competition, the Race of Champions, a novice driver trained in sim racing defeated a former Formula 1 driver (Tangermann 2019). Moving forward, as evidenced during the COVID-19 pandemic, it is increasingly likely that professional race car drivers will spend more time training using sim racing games, and competitions such as the eNASCAR iRacing Pro Invitational Series are likely to become more commonplace. Furthermore, there will be opportunities for those wishing to become professional race car drivers to first show their skills in sim racing games before having the opportunity to apply those skills in traditional race car driving (Janas 2019).

Real-Time Strategy Games

The goal of RTS games is for players to build armies consisting of different types of characters and destroy an opponent's base. Compared to MOBA games, RTS games are generally played in PvP or PvE modes instead of as two teams of five players each. Additionally, to succeed in RTS games, players must build and accumulate increasing amounts of structures and resources, while in MOBAs, players generally earn rewards for accomplishing different tasks such as destroying important buildings or in-game characters. To be successful as an RTS player, one needs to learn how to manage all of the resources (e.g., armies, buildings) under one's control, while at the same time strategically positioning oneself to limit the opponent who is attempting to complete similar tasks.

Hybrid Games

The next category of games are hybrid games, digital collectible card games (not including games such as poker and blackjack), and other unclassified types of games. The best example of a hybrid game is *Rocket League*, which combines driving a car (e.g., racing games) with the game of soccer (e.g., sports game). It is set in a three-dimensional arena where cars can drive up the walls, onto the ceiling, and around the arena, all in the pursuit of hitting or deflecting an oversize ball at the proper angle into a soccer goal. To be successful, players need to effectively combine racing game and sports game skills. In terms of online digital collectible card games, *Hearthstone* is the most popular game today. However, many people are introduced to this genre through other games such as the *Pokémon Trading Card Game Online* and *Magic: The Gathering Online* (Switzer 2020). Based on traditional trading and collectible card games, online card games consist of electronic decks of cards, and different cards display different characters with unique skills and abilities. Players draw cards and have a chance to use them to attack or defend against their opponent. All of this is done electronically on-screen, with players being able to see only their cards or the cards in play. Finally, there are other types of games such as *Gears of War*, which may be best classified as a "third-person shooter" game (Boyd 2019), and *World of Tanks*, which is similar to a MOBA, except it uses teams of tanks instead of characters.

Mobile Games

Finally, due to the size of the industry, it is important to note there are a number of very popular games currently available only on mobile devices. According to PocketGamer.biz (n.d.), in January of 2020, there were over 931,000 active games available in Apple's U.S.-based app store. While esports games such as *Fortnite* and *PUBG* can now be played on all types of platforms, some developers have decided to support the game only on mobile device platforms such as phones and tablets. At the same time, developers like Supercell (publisher of *Clash Royale*, *Clash of Clans*, and *Brawl Stars*) have also created large-scale competitions and tournaments for the best players from around the world. Mobile game developers monetize by charging users when they buy items in-game or download the game up-front. Based on data collected by Sensor Tower, from 2014 to 2019 *Clash of Clans* players' in-game spending totaled on average $1.09 billion a year (Williams 2020). After surveying the esports ecosystem, Jeff Chau describes how mobile games are creating more access and opportunities for more players to play the games they want, when they want, with whom they want, how they want, and in what physical location they want (2019a, 2019b). He further notes, "Mobile esports is an awakening, growing phenomenon that will displace and forever change the landscape of the global esports industry over the next decade" (Chau 2019b, para. 40).

ESPORTS INDUSTRY STATISTICS

When you read any current story on esports, somewhere within its content will likely be important statistics describing or displaying some aspects or trends within the industry. In recent years, Dutch company Newzoo has been one of the most oft-cited market research companies on the global esports industry. Using a self-described "panel of over 14 million game enthusiasts across 28 markets" (Newzoo n.d., para. 6), Newzoo produces both proprietary and free-to-view articles, reports, infographics, and other information about the esports industry such as the global games market, esports revenues, and esports audience size. In Asia, Niko Partners has emerged as a leader in gaming market intelligence. Providing data, reports, market analysis, and other insights, in addition to focused reports on the Chinese market, Niko Partners offers "qualitative and quantitative data collection and analysis, market models, forecasts, and strategic advisory services to give you the intelligence and answers you need to truly understand the region" (Niko Partners n.d., para. 2). Another market research firm, SuperData Research, was acquired by Nielsen in 2018. SuperData Research offers data and reports about video games, esports, virtual reality, markets, and consumers (SuperData Research n.d.). In summary, these three companies represent the tip of the iceberg in terms of the regional and global leaders in market research and intelligence on the esports industry.

Because the esports industry is a fast-moving, often-changing industry, with major changes sometimes happening in just minutes or hours, there is competition to be the first to report on a topic. Moreover, because stakeholders may want only the newest and most up-to-date research and insights, another valuable resource is the German company Statista. Statista "consolidates statistical data on over 80,000 topics from more than 22,500 sources and makes it available on four platforms: German, English, French and Spanish" (Statista n.d., para. 5).

As esports have evolved from recreational to competitive video gaming, people from around the world have become increasingly aware of the phenomenon (Li 2016). Focusing on 2015 through 2016 and based on projections from 2017 through 2019, data from Newzoo indicates the number of people aware of esports worldwide has increased from 809 million people in 2015 to a projected 1.572 billion people in 2019.

While consumer awareness is important to the success of any business, another useful aspect is the actual behavior of different types of customers. For example, after separating esports viewers into (1) occasional and (2) frequent viewers, Newzoo (2019) projected steady growth from 2012 to 2018 and continuing increases in 2019 and 2022 projections based on measured and projected data. In 2012, for example, there were 58 million frequent viewers and 76 million occasional viewers (Statista 2019d). Those numbers grew to 120 million frequent and 115 occasional viewers in 2015, 201 million frequent and 253 occasional viewers projected in 2019, and 297 million frequent and 347 occasional viewers projected in 2022 (Statista 2019d). The increases in consumer awareness and behaviors have also coincided with increases in revenues. According to data collected by Newzoo and reported by Statista (2019a), revenues increased from $130 million in 2012 to $865 million in 2018, and were projected to hit $1.1 billion in 2019 and $1.79 billion in 2022.

Based on popularity, interest, and revenue opportunities, six esports games were played at the 2019 Southeast Asian (SEA) Games (Celera 2019). In the lead-up to the Tokyo 2020 Olympic Games (moved to 2021 due to the COVID-19 pandemic), *Tekken* and *Rocket League* will both be played at the Intel World Open esports tournament (Intel 2019). In addition, esports games, with an emphasis on sport-focused titles, are expected to be officially included in the 2022 Asian Games hosted in Hangzhou, China (Potkin 2018). Not to be left out, the International Olympic Committee (IOC) has indicated it is open to "exploring the possibility of including esports in future games" (BBC 2018, para. 6). The movement toward including esports in and around mega sporting events may lie in the opportunity for the event and its sponsors to generate revenues from viewership, attendance, and other consumption behaviors. Newzoo's 2019 estimates of the esports revenues broken down by segment indicate sponsorships totaled $456.7 million, media rights were $251.3 million, advertising contributed $189.2 million, merchandising and ticketing equaled $103.7 million, and game publisher fees were $95.2 million. These estimates do not include money generated from betting, fantasy leagues, and in-game revenues (Statista 2019b).

Because esports are a global phenomenon, it is important to understand and compare the market size of different geographical regions. Figure 1.3 shows Newzoo's (2019) projections for estimated percentages of global esports market revenues for four regions of the world. The importance of China and South Korea in the esports marketplace is evident.

Many countries have begun to recognize professional esports gamers as sports athletes. In the United States, for instance, professional gamers can now obtain P-1 visas, which are designated for internationally recognized athletes partaking in athletic competitions in the United States (U.S. Citizenship and Immigration Services n.d.). In 2013, professional gamer Danny "Shiphtur" Le

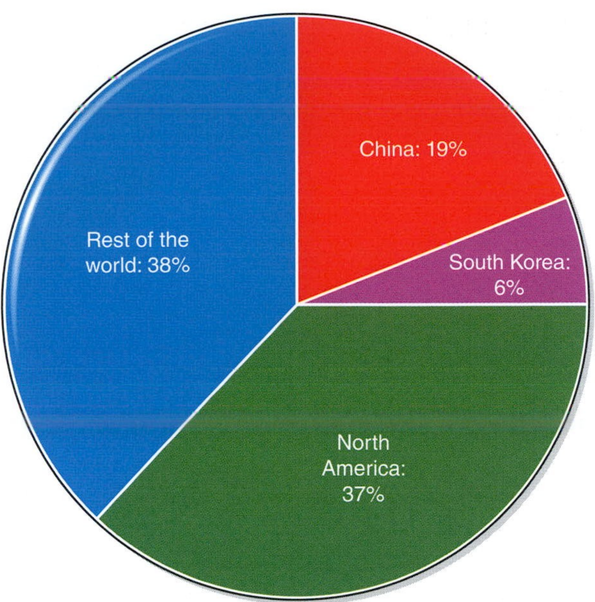

Figure 1.3 Global shares of esports market revenues as projected in 2019.

Data from *Statista* (2019c).

became the first esports athlete to receive a P-1 visa (Dave 2013). Because of the opportunities for esports tourism through hosting mega esports events, many game developers and event promoters are organizing competitions and tournaments around the world. With large prize pools, such as *Dota 2*'s $34.3 million prize pool for The International 2019 (Prizetrac.kr 2019), player interest in competing in prize-winning events is likely to continue to grow. The top five games in terms of the number of tournament players, prize money, and the number of tournaments are shown in table 1.3.

CONCLUSION

This chapter covered information about esports and its ecosystem, stakeholders, platforms, and industry statistics. It also provided a new and expanded definition of esports, details on its shared history with video games, and an introduction to the debate about whether esports is indeed a sport. Subsequent chapters will explain various aspects of the esports industry in more detail, including job functions of various areas (e.g., esports management, marketing, communications, finance, law, events, and coaching). In addition, the culture and issues facing esports will be examined. Chapter 2 will discuss the different levels of esports (youth, high school, college, and professional).

Table 1.3 Top Five Games for Tournaments, Players, and Prize Money in 2019

Game	Number of tournament players	Prize money	Number of tournaments
1. *Dota 2*	3,532	$219,095,635.31	1,284
2. *Counter-Strike: Global Offensive*	12,293	$87,119,453.26	4,411
3. *Fortnite*	3,243	$84,420,164.25	523
4. *League of Legends*	6,775	$73,091,646.37	2,400
5. *StarCraft II*	1,982	$32,084,645.74	5,602

Data from Esports Earnings (n.d.).

DISCUSSION QUESTIONS

1. What is the definition of esports?
2. How have esports developed over the years?
3. What are the similarities and differences between traditional sports and esports?
4. Who are the various stakeholders within the esports ecosystem?
5. What are the various esports platforms on which users play?
6. What are the unique types and categories of esports games?
7. What might the future of the business of esports look like?

2

Levels of Esports

R.C. Smith III | *Roger M. Caramanica*
Robert Dranoff | *Eric Kammeyer* | *Daniel Liang*
Nick Rider | *Justin Smith*

INTRODUCTION

The esports industry is growing quickly. To keep pace, governing bodies are being created to set rules and minimum expectations, such as eligibility for high school and college students (e.g., minimum grade point average, full-time student). In addition, there is now a path to playing professional esports that runs through the educational system. A player can begin playing esports as a young child, progress through various levels as a high school and college student, then move up to the professional level. High school students applying to college now have opportunities to earn a scholarship to play while completing their degree. If they have performed well in college, after graduation they may have opportunities to compete at the professional level. This path is not an exclusive one; many top players join the professional ranks when (or even before) they finish high school.

At the youth and secondary levels, local communities and organizations are predominantly forming esports organizations through grassroots efforts. Other governing bodies such as state- and national-level groups help create competitions and events, set guidelines for participation, and mirror the traditional sport experience for esports athletes.

At the time of writing this book, multiple groups are vying to organize youth and high school esports activities, and the National Collegiate Athletic Association (NCAA) does not yet sanction it as an official varsity sport. As a result, the National Association of Collegiate Esports (NACE) was founded to help manage issues such as eligibility rules and competitions. Moreover, NACE also acts as a conduit between game publishers and schools while also giving teams, coaches, and other stakeholders a forum to share ideas, collaborate and cooperate with each other, and assist in advocating for collegiate esports. NACE is just one organization currently vying for a stake in the collegiate marketplace. More organizations are covered in chapter 5.

Professional esports is also becoming mainstream, with some competitive events being televised on large cable networks such as ESPN. Some professional players are guaranteed a minimum salary, have practices throughout the week, and

OBJECTIVES

- Understand the governing structures of esports in high schools and colleges, including state-level organizations and college conferences.
- Identify potential pathways to playing competitive esports at multiple levels.
- Learn about professional esports organizations.

thus are treated much like a traditional professional sport athlete would be treated, including inking endorsement deals.

This chapter explores the multiple levels of esports and gives context to some of the key issues facing those working at each level.

YOUTH ESPORTS

Thinking of young children playing esports should immediately conjure up images of fun and laughter. At the grade school and youth levels, kids should be gaming for pure pleasure. Through esports they learn to enjoy themselves, connect with others, be respectful, and have fun. At these levels, playing solely to win should be minimized.

Youth and recreational esports activities are also increasing in popularity. Today's generation of young people have grown up playing fun and recreational gaming activities on their electronic devices such as mobile phones, tablets, personal computers, and gaming consoles. As a result, many young people frequently are gaming, connecting, and bonding over and through electronic activities. Moreover, friendly competitions and recreational opportunities occurring around gaming result in socialization and contribute to friendship among participants (Lenhart 2015). These trends toward online recreational gaming and identifying and making friends are likely to continue increasing in the years to come.

Because some game titles require minimum ages (e.g., *League of Legends* requires players to be at least 13 years old), gaming titles for players of grade school ages can vary. One of the most popular games among young people is *Minecraft*. The game "increasingly is used by school districts to promote STEM—science, technology, engineering and mathematics" (Baker 2017, para. 11). Much like other traditional after-school programs, esports activities can also be scheduled after school with opportunities for practice and competition.

Matches at the youth level can be stressful, especially considering the amount of time spent practicing and the pressure to find convenient times when all can play. Individual school programs and players' playing time can vary. Some coaches and programs may allow youth players to challenge others for roster spots, while other schools may adopt an "everyone plays" mentality. In youth esports, a focal point should be to unite children who game. Esports promotes inclusiveness. It is a great social platform for both children who are introverted and those who are extroverted to interact; this environment had not existed until recently.

In addition to modeling good behaviors and respect for coaches and other players, the importance of teamwork should be stressed at the youth level. Because many games are created for teams, young players have the opportunity to realize that they can accomplish success only when they work together. All these activities require adult supervision, which is what esports teachers and coaches can offer; they provide a guided, educational approach to gaming.

At around ages 11 to 13 (about the sixth grade), many youth players begin to experiment with different genres of games, such as multiplayer online battle arena (MOBA), first-person shooter (FPS), collectible card games (CCG), and sports games. The maturity of each child should be taken into account during this process. It is possible for gamers to continue this experimental phase throughout life, but many players have found their favorite game genre or title by age 15. The kind of dedication required to play and successfully compete at a high level in many esports titles can be overwhelming for some young children. As a result, the teacher or coach needs to ensure that balance is maintained between gaming and other activities. Moreover, because each child is different, those overseeing esports activities (parents, coaches, teachers) should help players find a proper balance between having fun and competing to win.

Ideally, all young gamers are taught how to cope with frustrations and deal with potentially **toxic gamers**. Promoting fairness and good sporting behavior, such as having teams congratulate each other after each match, is a good way to instill positive values. Young gamers learn that emotions will run high, but mistakes are opportunities for learning how to improve their own abilities. Involving parents may also be a useful tool for ensuring that the values related to good sporting behavior taught at school can be reinforced at home.

Enjoyment is an important outcome of esports at the youth level. The values learned in the esports setting are similar to those learned in the traditional youth sports setting: good sporting behavior, teamwork, fair play, and doing one's best. Some children play multiple sports (in the case of esports, multiple gaming titles) to explore what they are good at and enjoy, while others zero in on one specific game title in an attempt at mastery. Whether through structured matches and ranking systems, or through in-house tournaments, it is important that those overseeing youth esports create an environment that promotes fun and excitement, determination to improve, a sense of acceptance of oneself and others, and the ability to forge friendships that last. This environment will help not only to instill a love of esports but also to foster gamers with strong characters who will go out and inspire more young people to participate in esports.

HIGH SCHOOLS AND PATHWAYS TO COLLEGE

"Video games don't belong in school" used to be a common phrase. Over the last few years, it is heard less and less as high school esports programs continue to grow into valid competitive, scholastic, and career opportunities. With over 300 universities offering competitive esports programs (Buzby 2020), many with scholarship opportunities and some with academic esports degree programs or classes, the reasons to start a high school program have never been more relevant. Student interest in video games has continued to grow, with over 80 percent of teens owning a gaming console, and 90 percent of teens claiming that they play video games (Anderson and Jiang 2018). Esports provides a way to harness student interest and cultivate it into competitive and educational pathways leading to a vast array of university and industry opportunities.

Governing Structure

The high school esports structure is evolving each day. With many resources that provide differing information, navigating the world of high school esports can be a challenge when getting started. Currently three levels of implementation exist for high school esports programs: local, state, and national.

Local leagues and competitions are usually grassroots efforts that have been developed and implemented by innovative school districts, community centers, or gaming facilities that are making an effort to provide opportunities for students. These leagues are usually self-governed and select the games that are played at their discretion. These leagues, competitions, and tournaments can either be free of cost for players or paid entry depending on the event and who is hosting it. One example of a company that provides local esports opportunities is Game Arena, located

Esports teams in high school address student interests and provide potential career pathways in the growing esports industry.

in Hillard, Ohio. Game Arena has hourly, daily, and monthly passes. It hosts tournaments, sells food, and hosts birthday parties and other events (Game Arena 2019). Businesses such as this one are capitalizing on the interest in esports while providing teenagers a chance to socialize, compete in esports as a hobby, or hone their skills in a competitive manner.

State leagues and competitions are currently run by a number of different but similarly aligned grassroots organizations as well as national esports leagues. Most current state grassroots organizations are run as nonprofit organizations started by passionate school personnel with the goal of providing esports opportunities for all interested students. These organizations design rules, procedures, and game choices, they create competitive structuring for students and schools, and they also structure in-person tournaments at the state level.

Because these grassroots organizations often work with school districts, coaches, players, and stakeholders, they are frequently better positioned to serve their membership than a national body. For example, many coaches of the programs serve on governing boards and committees and are integral in the local decision-making process. Additionally, these state organizations are better suited to host competitions because of common and overlapping school or holiday breaks, time zones, and other geographic similarities. National governing bodies may be challenged to organize a common time across multiple time zones for players and teams to compete. Some states with grassroots organizations are Ohio, Illinois, Indiana, Wisconsin, Texas, Michigan, Missouri, Iowa, and Nebraska.

National organizations with large financial backing are able to create better software-based solutions for esports logistics in match scheduling, statistics tracking, and player and team ranking. However, the advantage that state organizations have over national bodies is that in addition to knowing their current state-level athletic governing bodies, they know their state or area well. They can easily structure competition to be fair based on the enrollment size of school districts. In addition, state-level organizations know how to structure competitive local and regional opportunities, especially those with traditional team or district rivalries that currently exist in traditional sports.

National organizations and competitions are handled by two types of organizations: scholastic and competitive. The most widely recognized national scholastic esports organization is the North American Scholastic Esports Federation (NASEF). NASEF is a nonprofit organization funded through the Samueli Foundation. It offers academic resources and esports league competitions to schools for free. National organizations also work with state-level organizations as affiliates to provide further outreach to students. There are a few widely recognized for-profit competitive high school esports organizations. PlayVS is a company that provides a digital platform for high school esports competitions. They work with the National Federation of State High School Associations (NFHS) and individual states in an effort to be recognized as the platform for varsity-level esports competitions. PlayVS also works with game publishers to enable school teams to play without the need for each tournament to go to the publisher to receive rights to host competitions. They also work to provide state championships for students in schools and states that adopt their program. As of 2020, the cost to participate in PlayVS is $64 per player per season. Another option is the High School Esports League (HSEL), a company that provides competitive high school esports opportunities and leagues. HSEL currently allows mature-rated games that may require more supervision (and school approval) and therefore might be hard to compete in within some school districts. HSEL also allows high school teams to compete without school district approval. As of 2020, HSEL charges $37 per year per student.

Growth

High school esports is growing exponentially and will continue to do so for the following key reasons:

- The cost of entry for schools is the lowest cost of any athletic sport. It requires little to no travel cost, and many school districts already have a computer lab that can support the game play needed to start esports.
- Esports brings a new opportunity to an unreached demographic of students. In Esports Ohio's first two seasons, they found that 80 percent of their nearly 1,000 students

were participating in their first-ever sport with esports (Esports Ohio 2020).

- Esports aligns well with multiple career pathways. Curriculum is currently being developed and aligned to Common Core and state standards that will help students graduate with industry-recognized credentials.

Given the current infrastructure of high school esports and how they are run at three different levels, along with the skewed marketing claims of commercial esports companies, it is challenging to gauge the actual number of students participating in high school esports. HSEL's website claims to have had an impact on 75,000 students, while PlayVS reported that it has 13,000 high schools on a waiting list to activate their programs (Ryan 2019), but the for-profit companies have released no definitive numbers. Through the grassroots study of Esports Ohio, their competitive player base in Ohio grew 317 percent in six months (during the 2019-2020 season), from 221 to 921 student participants (Esports Ohio 2020). It is clear that high school students are interested in esports and undertaking opportunities to play at both the casual or recreational and competitive levels.

Scholastic Connection

The educational and academic connection to esports in high school is one of the largest factors for the quick growth of high school esports. Aside from the competitive side of esports, engaging in esports activities provides numerous scholastic benefits. Students have the opportunity to learn and be educated about computer hardware, software management, how to build custom gaming computers, and how to configure the network to support play. These skills systematically can translate into the CompTIA A+ and Network+ industry-recognized credentials, which many schools count as eligible credit toward graduation requirements.

Aside from the obvious career fields related to **information technology (IT)**, several other industry-related skills go into running a successful high school program. These skills include social media management, marketing, branding, graphic design, broadcasting, **shoutcasting** (esports commentating), livestreaming, video editing, web design, coaching, and more. In addition to the specific industry skills, esports offers nontraditional athletes a way to develop soft skills that traditional athletes learn such as teamwork, communication, collaboration, strategic thinking, and giving and receiving constructive criticism.

Currently a number of curricular resources are available free of charge, most notably NASEF's high school and middle school esports curriculum (NASEF 2020) and the Gaming Concepts high school elective course designed in partnership with Microsoft and the HSEL (HSEL 2020).

Zoning

BUGHA'S $3 MILLION (AND COUNTING) JOURNEY

Roger M. Caramanica

Kyle "Bugha" Giersdorf is a recently minted industry icon in the game *Fortnite*, and his story is a tale of hard work and success that resonates within the esports industry. Even if someone is not familiar with esports, chances are they are familiar with the story of that one young man who won $3 million playing *Fortnite*.

A relatively unknown 16-year-old, Bugha spent time in the competitive space of *Fortnite* and livestreamed his game play on Twitch prior to 2019. He has played video games since the age of three and has a strong support system within his family. With relatively low viewership counts on Twitch and moderate success in the competitive space, Bugha appeared on the competitive scene in a big way when he won the *Fortnite* World Cup singles play in 2019 and a prize of $3 million. He earned 2019 Esports Player of the Year at the 2019 Esports Awards (Collins 2019), and is a member of the competitive *Fortnite* team of the esports organization Sentinels. This 16-year-old from Pennsylvania is one example of how a career as an esports player and professional can begin.

Future of High School Esports

The future of high school esports is bright. With colleges and universities investing millions of dollars into building new esports programs, just like traditional student-athletes, esports players have a direct pathway to college. High school scholastic esports resources are being developed to align with Common Core standards and other scholastic efforts. The competitive structure is gaining traction every day. The current coaches, participants, and stakeholders are seeing the esports ecosystem develop around them as they pave the way for the future of high school esports.

COLLEGIATE ESPORTS

The collegiate landscape of esports is fast moving, and colleges and universities are trying to keep pace its growing popularity. Colleges and universities use esports as a way to recruit students to their schools. To help with these recruiting efforts, a number of universities have started offering esports-related scholarships, similar to how top athletes are recruited for college football and basketball programs.

Organizing Esports at Colleges and Universities

Esports is not recognized as an NCAA sport. As a result, university esports teams are organized differently across university and college campuses. At some institutions, the esports team may be housed in their athletics department, while in others they may be located in their student life division, or within an academic major such as computer science or sport management. Adding to the list of challenges, depending on where the team is located within the university, rules and guidelines, funding sources, coaching structure, and more could quickly change. Parallels are often drawn between how high school and college esports programs are trying to find their ideal location. Without a recognized institution such as the NCAA as a governing body, numerous groups are competing to organize esports events, competitions, leagues, and championships.

The National Association of Collegiate Esports (NACE) was founded in 2016 and quickly grew into one of the best-known governing bodies for esports. On its website, the organization describes itself as follows:

> NACE is a member driven organization that focuses on the positive development of esports programs at the collegiate level, and advocates for members to create varsity programs that include scholarships for its participants and a strong institutional commitment to the sport. NACE is the only association of college and university sponsored esports programs that promotes the education and development of students through intercollegiate esports. (NACE 2020a, para. 2)

NACE and its member institutions have established eligibility requirements, guidelines for competition, and other resources in an effort to help ensure fair play. NACE has recently instituted recruiting rules and national letters of intent for college esports athletes, in very much the same way as the NCAA governs the same process for traditional sport athletes.

In 2020 NACE announced that it would hold *Counter-Strike: Global Offensive (CS:GO)* competitions. Within that press release, NACE touted a membership of over 200 schools and that over 90 percent of varsity programs are members (NACE 2020b). Other college conferences and loosely structured leagues exist, but NACE has the largest group of official member institutions.

Recruiting Esports Athletes

With the explosive growth of esports, schools are capitalizing on the national interest; they are trying not only to corner the market but also to compete with other schools for student-recruits. Universities are building esports facilities costing millions of dollars. While such an expenditure is not the norm, a number of facilities have been built around the half-million-dollar range. Even outfitting a current computer lab could cost over $100,000 to include a dozen gaming stations (computers, desks, chairs, keyboards, etc.) and a dedicated (or upgraded) Internet line. They are also hiring part-time and full-time esports coaches, assistant coaches, and directors to oversee these programs. Teams are competing in conferences, at regional competitions, and in national championship tournaments.

Substitute the word “esports” with any traditional sport (e.g., basketball, football, volleyball), and you see why it is easy to consider esports a true sport on college campuses. Similar to recruiting a high school senior to be a school’s quarterback because the roster needs an additional quarterback, esports teams can recruit for specific positions for certain game titles. Take a step back to examine an entire athletics department's recruiting activities, where basketball is recruiting a point guard, volleyball is recruiting a libero, baseball is recruiting a second baseman, softball is recruiting a pitcher, and rowing is recruiting a coxswain. Compared to a college's esports program, an esports coach or director could be recruiting a certain position player for each game title, and for specific team needs. Coaches might have a difficult time bringing a prospective esports student-athlete to visit campus (officially or unofficially). Thus, some coaches provide virtual campus tours, stream video showing esports games, have a top gamer contact a prospect, and send clips of matches, among other strategies to help recruit a top-level player. More important than just the visit is the scholarship offer, especially for private universities where the battle for prospective students is already intense.

Much like top sport recruits who visit campuses to see the stadia or arenas and training areas, esports athletes want to practice and play in state-of-the-art facilities. These athletes want the best and want to see that the university is actually investing in esports. They want coaches who will make them better players, they want the chance to compete, they want to pursue an academic major of interest, and they want their financial aid package (if available) to hit a certain affordable price point.

Collegiate Scholarships

One way schools are growing their esports programs is offering scholarships to esports recruits. Some schools offer somewhat modest amounts between $1,000 and $5,000 per year. Other schools offer upwards of $10,000 per year, all the way up to a full-tuition scholarship. Schools that can afford to give scholarships in high amounts could be more prone to getting the best high school players. Think of college recruiting and scholarships in the same way you think of valuable free agents getting signed to teams; those who can afford the best athletes, get the best athletes. Colleges and universities are currently considering these questions, among others:

- Given that currently esports is male dominated, do esports scholarship funds fall under Title IX or create an imbalance in Title IX equity?
- What amount of money is offered to entice a student to come? The more scholarship money a student gets, the less that student pays to attend the school, and the less revenue the school obtains to cover expenses.
- Do esports fall under the athletics department, recreation department, or student life?
- Should violent video games be one of the games played by the esports team?

Collegiate Competitions

Collegiate competitions are organized by various groups. They can be organized by a collegiate conference, an individual school, a publisher, governing bodies similar to NACE, and other groups. For example, Tespa has over 250 colleges and universities that are members, and it organizes competitions exclusively with games published by Activision Blizzard, such as *Overwatch*, *Hearthstone*, *Heroes of the Storm*, and *StarCraft* (Tespa 2020). Regardless of whether a school is a member of NACE or a member of an esports conference, in order to compete in an official *Overwatch* tournament, the school would also have to be a Tespa member.

Collegiate tournaments often reward players and teams with prize money if they win or finish as one of the top positions. Schools and their athletes are currently wrestling with how that money is received. Does it go directly to the esports program? Does it go to the esports athletes who competed as earned income or as scholarship money only? Does it go to the school? If a student receives any money, how does that payment affect that student's taxes and eligibility for financial aid? A common way this process is managed today is that the money is frequently put into some type of scholarship fund, often focused on paying for the recipients' education (Heilweil 2019).

COLLEGIATE CONFERENCES

In April 2019, after several months of review and consultation, the NCAA Board of Governors announced that they had decided to "table

Courtesy of St. Thomas Aquinas College Department of Athletics.

Collegiate esports teams can compete in events organized by various groups.

indefinitely" any plans to organize or offer a championship in intercollegiate esports, stating, instead, that they will continue to evaluate how it "can best support [their] members as they pursue and adopt esports programs" (Hayward 2019, para. 4). While no specifics were given on the decision to forgo involvement, several areas of concern seemed to be apparent, especially confusion over how gaming might fit in with the more traditional sports championships offered by the NCAA. Questions include the following:

- Are esports really a sport?
- How might current eligibility rules, including amateurism, be applied to esports team members?
- How would Title IX affect the predominantly male teams currently representing colleges and universities?
- How is it best to control game content to ensure overly violent or misogynistic games are not being endorsed by the organization (Smith and Fischer 2018)?

NCAA involvement had been rumored since NCAA President Mark Emmert had talked about that concept in his annual convention address in 2019. Some institutions had hoped for expanded NCAA involvement, thinking that it might bring a level of greater validity, organization, and resources to their programs. Some also hoped the NCAA involvement could lead to further esports growth, more organizations sponsoring collegiate tournaments, and higher athletic conference esports participation.

Independent organizations such as Collegiate StarLeague (CSL; founded in 2009) and Tespa (founded in 2012) serve as support networks for college gaming organizations and offer leagues and championships in several games to college clubs and teams as does the National Association of Collegiate Esports (NACE 2016), with new associations seeming to be in development each year. Specific leagues such as Riot Games' College League of Legends (LoL) and Collegiate Rocket League (CRL) have been created to be the main intercollegiate organizer for those games.

While the NCAA chose not to pursue esports at this time, in September of 2019 the National Junior College Athletic Association (NJCAA) announced plans to do just that for two-year institutions under their watch (Smith 2019). The Eastern College Athletic Conference (ECAC), which has existed since 1938, is a multidivisional conference with 220 members and offers championship opportunities in various sports. In 2016, the ECAC added esports while still offering other collegiate sports (Schaffhauser 2019).

In the spring of 2018, the Peach Belt Conference (PBC; NCAA Division II) became the first NCAA conference to offer an esports conference championship in the game *League of Legends* (Hendrickson 2018); it was quickly followed by Division II colleague the East Coast Conference (ECC) in 2019. The number of NCAA conferences expressing interest in esports has grown quickly. Unlike traditional NCAA sports that make conference membership almost mandatory to create schedules, earn postseason opportunities, and offer team and individual awards, esports at an institution could survive without league involvement through affiliations with organizations such as Tespa or NACE.

So, why should an athletic conference organize esports competitions? For sport conferences or leagues such as the PBC or ECC, the idea of bringing on this new sport was seen as an opportunity to help member schools grow and retain enrollment and to serve a population that may have been looked at differently than the traditional campus student-athlete. Esports has the potential to bring new attention and participation for the conferences. In addition, similar to the PBC, the ECC committed to treating esports in a similar manner to all other events with a well-organized regular season schedule and weekly honors, tournaments, online streaming, championships, and postseason awards. Also, the two conferences created a fall semester *League of Legends* crossover event between participating schools, which has added to interest and attention.

Those sentiments were echoed by leaders representing the Landmark Conference (NCAA Division III) and the Southern Collegiate Athletic Conference (SCAC; NCAA Division III). In explaining their decision to enter the esports space, conference leaders such as Dwayne Hanberry of the SCAC noted esports activities were fueled by school presidents who want their member institutions to be on the cutting edge of higher education. In addition, conferences not only serve to organize traditional intercollegiate sports but also can help expand into other activities that can serve their campus communities, not to mention that esports have the ability to provide excitement, camaraderie, and positive experiences to a new generation of esports athletes (Hendrickson 2019).

On the NCAA Division I level, the Metro Atlantic Athletic Conference (MAAC) began to offer esports events in 2016, formalizing it as an official MAAC sport in 2019. Kiernan Ensor noted that organizing competitions within traditional collegiate athletic conferences allows rivalries that have existed in traditional sports to cross over into esports (MAAC 2019). The MAAC also sees the opportunity to cross-promote activities; it is combining its 2020 esports championships with its MAAC basketball tournament because it has the potential to increase student attendance at both events.

The presidents of the NCAA Division I Mountain West Conference (MW) supported involvement in esports early on and the number of schools participating has quickly grown. MW's senior associate commissioner Carolayne Henry noted that institutions see esports as a recruiting tool, especially for schools focusing on students majoring in STEM programs (College AD 2018). Conference involvement has created branding and sponsorship opportunities as well as increased exposure. It has helped to build conference connections with a different group of students through promotion, recognition, and positive championship experiences.

Other NCAA Division I conferences have been a bit slower in establishing esports compared to the MAAC or MW, with challenges arising from different levels of support and expectations on various campuses. With a mix of campus departments taking the lead in managing the programs, challenges have involved varying levels of institutional support as well as game selection, funding, and management. At the same time, universities have recognized the value of engaging in esports and opportunities it provides (Schaffhauser 2020).

The NCAA boasts over 100 member conferences in its three divisions. Expectations are that other conferences and universities will also begin to offer and expand intercollegiate esports in the coming years. Conferences appear to be a viable option to handle operational concerns such as monitoring eligibility, sporting behavior, and game selection and can also be a key component in providing positive student experiences, even without NCAA governance or oversight. Michael Sherman, head of college at Riot Scholastic Association of America, has watched the growth of athletic conference involvement closely. He sees the value in aligning with leagues to help organize schools and team members, and assist them in providing resources and communication for efficient operations and quality championship events. Sherman notes that the role of Riot Games, the publisher of *League of Legends*, is to build the game competition platform, while each university can decide the level of resources to invest (Doran 2017).

Future of Conference Involvement in Esports

The growth of intercollegiate esports is expected to continue, and predictions are that more existing athletic conferences will choose to offer league play and championship events to match that expanding interest. As institutions see the value and importance of increased student recruitment and campus life that organized esports can offer, they will look to the conferences to provide a familiar home for those students. Growth, however, may bring additional concerns and increased efforts.

The major areas of concern mentioned regarding intercollegiate esports continues to be how to handle concerns such as game content and diversity. Game content relates to the choice of game titles universities may choose to support or reject. For example, some universities have purposefully chosen not to field teams or compete in game titles in which violent actions occur, such as FPS games (Kalinowski 2019). Another important concern involves diversity and the lack of female players competing. For example, some games and platforms, such as those involving shooting, racing, and sports games, skew toward male players (Yee 2017). In addition, female gamers may not outwardly discuss their game play due to fears of being singled out, treated differently, or not accepted (Phillips 2018).

In regard to expanding diversity and participation by underrepresented campus groups, conferences must make concerted efforts to encourage involvement, offer special events and programs, and build partnerships with students and high schools. The ECC has a partnership with the High School of Sport Management located in Coney Island, New York. The school, which has a predominantly African American and Hispanic student body, has created a growing esports program with hopes to open new higher education and career opportunities for its students.

As progress continues, the need to address how best to bring various groups together to better organize programs and, perhaps, to create national championships will most likely be considered again. Carolayne Henry from the MW, who also was selected as the inaugural chairperson of the Riot Scholastic Association of America in 2019, thinks the future of esports has great potential for athletic conferences, which already have expertise in running events and creating great experiences for students and fans. As the number of conferences supporting esports grows despite challenges such as new games coming to prominence every year or two, having a governing body that provides structure and rules can benefit all stakeholders (College AD 2018). Another challenge is the process and fees associated with licensing games (Stoller 2019). No fees need to be paid to organize a game of basketball, but in order to compete and broadcast esports, the rights holders (game developers) may require fees to be paid. As a result, this could lead to game publishers and third-party organizations creating real roadblocks for conferences and schools, adding to costs and confusion that could prohibit involvement and growth in collegiate esports.

PROFESSIONAL ESPORTS

As discussed previously in this chapter, esports has numerous levels, each slightly different than the next. Due to its notoriety, one of the most frequently discussed levels is professional esports. As the industry has evolved and grown, the idea of a career in esports is getting more attention.

Professional esports have taken the world by storm. Within the esports industry are many different professions. Playing is one of the most common professions in esports. Many professional esports players compete full-time while living in a team house so that they are able to be in a competitive setting around the clock. It is more than a career for players; it is also a lifestyle that they have to uphold and withstand. Professional players have to practice daily for a set number of hours and be able to compete at the highest level of a given season. This is why teams house players while also providing fitness trainers, chefs, and any necessary accommodations to improve the players' physical and mental being. The players are the greatest assets and the moving parts of a team.

Today, professional esports is mainstream. With popular esports titles such as *League of*

Legends, *CS:GO*, and *Fortnite* offering large prize pools through a competition, more people are willing to try esports full time professionally. Today, kids as young as 13 are pursuing professional esports as a career. Esports tournaments today are not only taking place in venues such as big stadiums or arenas; the industry has gotten so big and popular that many tournaments are taking place online with large prize pools.

Like other professional sports, players are required to sign contracts to play for a team for a set duration for a given salary. With the growing industry come more regulations. For example, the *Overwatch* League has regulations such as: Players must be guaranteed one-year contracts, minimum salary is $50,000, and the team must provide each player with health insurance and a retirement savings plan. Each league has different rules and regulations (Conditt 2017).

Professional teams aren't only made up of players, they require coaches and analysts to make sure the players have the knowledge and information they need to win. Coaches and analysts are most common with team-based games such as *League of Legends*, *Dota 2*, *Overwatch*, and *CS:GO*. These titles require intensive communication, and any miscommunication can lead to a major loss for a team. Similar to traditional sports, coaches provide guidance and training to improve the team's performance. They also provide both emotional and physical support so that the players are 100 percent ready for their matches. During matches, the coach is constantly communicating with the team, making sure that they're implementing what

Zoning

PROFILE OF JEFFREY AVILA RAMOS, CEO AND MANAGING DIRECTOR OF FATAL AMBITION

John McDermott

Jeffrey Avila Ramos is the 21-year-old CEO and managing director of the professional esports team Fatal Ambition. The Long Island organization fields competitive rosters in *Halo*, *Gears of War*, *Call of Duty*, *Paladins*, and *Smite*. He started his career in esports at the age of 13, when a group of friends formed a professional *Halo* team called Soulless Spartans. Like most esports teams, the team did not last, but as Jeffrey said, "I chose to continue with Fatal Ambition because of all the time and effort they put in. I saw potential there." This potential ultimately turned Jeffrey from player to manager.

Fatal Ambition quickly expanded into *Call of Duty*, and Jeffrey helped secure sponsorships that allowed the team to attend some events. He was able to secure these sponsorships thanks to the importance he placed on social media. One such event was AEL Dallas, where Fatal Ambition placed sixth, losing to the now tier one organization FaZe Clan.

As Fatal Ambition began to expand, Jeffrey naturally made the move from manager to CEO. He felt he was able to do this because he had the drive to succeed at the highest levels. However, he credits the mentors around him for supplying him with insight on the industry. These mentors became even more important when Jeffrey faced his toughest time as CEO.

At one point in the history of Fatal Ambition, Jeffrey started to focus on short-term success of the team instead of its long-term goals; he tried to buy his way into games and contracts. When the organization started to suffer as a result, he had to make the tough decision to take a step back and reorganize Fatal Ambition.

Jeffrey offers the key advice of getting experience. He believes that making it in the esports industry takes a lot of grit, determination, drive, and vision. Jeffrey believes future managers should find an area they are passionate about and stick with it. He also says that it doesn't hurt to be a little lucky.

Jeffrey believes that the future of esports is in mobile games. These games will continue to push further investments into the scene and create more mainstream media attention. This attention will also benefit the players as more player regulations will begin to occur. Sadly, all the investments will come at the cost of smaller esports companies.

they've done during practice and keeping them in check when misplays occur. Analysts are more active behind the scenes and are an integral part of a team. They help analyze the team's matches or even the opponent's matches to understand their play style. They are able to provide crucial statistics such as win–loss ratio against a certain team or even how many times a player has been eliminated by a certain character or player. These statistics are important in helping a team to decipher what they're doing right or wrong and how they can improve in future games.

The popularity of professional esports is at an all-time high. More people are starting to understand what esports is and how much of an impact it has on the economy and on society as a whole. With higher viewership and money within esports tournaments, it allows people to pursue esports professionally, thus growing the industry as a whole.

CONCLUSION

Esports has burst onto the global sports scene, and almost everyone is now paying attention to it. As more youth organizations, high schools, and colleges and universities create esports programs and teams, more opportunities will open. While challenges abound, such as who may be governing or managing esports, what types of games are played, and who is playing and participating, opportunities at all levels are also ripe for entrepreneurial-minded people. While each level of esports faces unique challenges, more and more people are learning the benefits and opportunities, such as helping to educate and train people at all levels. Esports represent both a challenge and opportunity. In order to identify ways to take advantage of the opportunities and mitigate the challenges, more about esports needs to be understood. The next chapter discusses many of the unique aspects of gaming culture.

DISCUSSION QUESTIONS

1. Should collegiate esports be treated as a traditional sport, such as with minimum practice hours, full-time head coaches and assistant coaches, and a travel schedule to play both home and away games?
2. As a college coach, how would you recruit an esports athlete to your school if you do not offer scholarships and the school has a mediocre facility? Do high school esports athletes expect state-of-the-art, multimillion dollar facilities, scholarship money, full-time head coaches, and other amenities as a minimum to come to a school? And if so, is it fair for high school esports athletes to expect these amenities, given that esports is new and the longevity of esports is unproven (e.g., if a game title stops being produced, it could end someone's collegiate or professional career)?
3. Should esports be organized to allow everyone to play, or should it be tryout based?

3

Esports Culture and Issues

Roger M. Caramanica | Aaron Colaiacomo | Rob Holub
Sang-ho Lee | John McDermott | Michael Newhouse-Bailey
Sheng Qiang | Ryan Rogers | Melissa Welby | Ashley Witt

INTRODUCTION

Esports (and gaming in general) has developed its own **culture**, norms, trends, and behavioral protocols for stakeholders. Through the years, gaming culture has evolved with changing technology and styles of games, broader cultural changes in the world, and especially with the move of game play to the Internet (Chikhani 2015). As with any sport, media, or pastime activity, a slew of social issues have arisen and gained media attention. Questions surrounding the violent nature of the games being played, gender and race equality within the player and talent bases, addiction, and the value of time spent on a sedentary pastime all permeate the public discourse on the topic of esports and gaming. These and other social issues have created varying perceptions of the industry depending on a wide array of factors. Defining all aspects of the esports and gaming culture is a monumental task and, given how quickly the industry is changing, it will be outdated by the time this text is printed. Therefore, this chapter will outline the various societal perspectives that exist around the globe as well as how they are similar and how they vary in different parts of the world. The chapter will also take a deep look at the potential for positive and negative outcomes in the competitive space of esports and gaming.

OBJECTIVES

- Understand different societal perspectives of gaming and esports.
- Identify areas where esports can have a positive impact.
- Identify areas where esports can have a negative impact.

SOCIETAL PERSPECTIVES OF GAMING IN THE EAST AND WEST

The way in which video games and those who play them socially and competitively are viewed is shifting. Competitive esports is not new, but awareness of the sport is higher than ever and increasing rapidly. The line between general gaming and esports is often blurred, and an increased awareness of concepts, stakeholders, and outcomes will help the industry continue to grow. Finally, the changing perspectives on the subject are dynamic and complicated with an international ecosystem of stakeholders around the globe. Depending on physical location or other demographics, these stakeholders have their own set of cultural norms, behavioral attributes, and social perspectives surrounding game play. This variation creates a complex environment of stakeholders to consider when discussing the topic of culture and perspectives. For example, it is impossible to divorce the culture of esports from the culture of South Korea, the country in which competitive video games first gained pop culture fame. However, esports have their own cultural heritage and dynamics that differ around the globe. Consider the following glimpses of esports culture in China and the United States as examples of how these cultures can differ in Eastern and Western nations.

Esports Culture in China

For game publishers, event organizers, and other practitioners in the esports industry, the Chinese market is attractive because of its large potential for growth. At the same time, it is essential that those wishing to enter the esports industry in China should also understand the complex policies, regulations, and cultural dynamics within the Chinese market. The Chinese esports industry started developing formally around 2010, and it continues to grow. In recent years, the government has recognized the value of esports based on numerous factors including potential economic benefits, opportunities for international publicity, opportunities for entertainment, and its appeal to young people. Therefore, both central and local governments have issued a series of policies to support the development of esports. At the national level, in April 2019, "esports athlete" and "esports operator" were listed as new professions by the Ministry of Human Resources and Social Security (MOHRSS 2019). In other words, the practitioners of these two professions can enjoy the benefits of the social insurance system. In the same month, the National Bureau of Statistics released a new version of the Sports Industry Statistical Classification; the esports classification was included in Category 02: Sports Competition Performance together with other traditional sports such as football, basketball, and volleyball (Ning 2019).

At the same time, a negative evaluation of video games and esports from a societal perspective also exists, especially in terms of their influence on minors. Although the electronic or "digital heroin" theories (i.e., gaming can affect players in a manner similar to addictive drugs, see Xia 2000) have ceased to be the mainstream attitude toward esports in Chinese education and society, it is believed that the indulgence in video games does affect the physical and mental health of minors (Hernández and Zhang 2019). As a result, the Chinese government is currently supervising the formalization of the esports industry through relevant policies. The main objective of these policies is to protect minors. All major streaming platforms in China strictly restrict the behavior of streamers to encourage underage audiences to donate in accordance with various government regulations. These measures are aimed at protecting the rights and interests of minors who do not have full civil capacity, so industries such as those involved in esports and video game streaming (where many practitioners and viewers are adolescents) will naturally be given special attention.

The deep-rooted cultural traditions and family heritage prevalent within Chinese society creates extreme sensitivity to anything that may be harmful to the growth of the next generation. In the past, many adolescents were neglecting their studies because of video game addiction (Huang 2018). Therefore, to prevent problems before they occur, the government-led standardization and normalization process was undertaken to meet the needs of mainstream public opinion. Only by improving its image and potential negative effects on society and young people in particular will the esports industry have the potential for further development in China.

Stereotypes and Stigma in the United States

Despite the widespread use of video games and the worldwide popularity of esports, players of these games are subject to **stereotypes** and **stigma** in the United States. These stereotypes are not only prevalent, they are detrimental to the players and to the development of esports as a legitimate activity or competition.

On his sports talk show, *The Herd*, Colin Cowherd (2015, 0:40) summarized many of the stereotypes of esports players in the Western world, all of which are negative. To begin, Cowherd claimed that he had "nothing against video games," then referred to esports players as "nerds" and "booger-eaters." While watching a pivotal moment at the EVO fighting game tournament, he asked, "How can you not make fun of that?" He also laughed derisively, shook his head dismissively, and pantomimed mock feelings of excitement. He then said the winner of the tournament will "go sit on a couch for months and we have to pick up the tab on Obamacare." Continuing his ridicule, he said that the winner "still lives at his mom's . . . goes to his room where a girl has never entered and goes to town on a Hot Pocket." He then turned from insulting the players to an attempt to delegitimize the activity itself by saying "it's video games, it shouldn't be on a sports network." The segment ended with Cowherd asking his female co-host if she would go on a date with someone who asked her to play a video game (Cowherd 2015). His words were an attempt to demonstrate that the players are not valued by women in society.

While Cowherd's stereotyping is particularly harsh, his comments over the five-minute video clip reflect media representations of video game players and the stereotypes broadly accepted in Western culture (Rogers 2016). Video game players are stereotyped as nerdy, loners, of little value, worthy of ridicule, failing to mature into adulthood, failing to contribute to society, and not taking care of themselves physically. Another stereotype perpetuated by media representations is that video game players are violent and mentally unstable because acts of violence are frequently linked to video game play (Rogers 2016). Given these stereotypes, at best, a video game player is a male, loner, loser, living with parents, has poor hygiene, and has a poor diet; at worst, a video game player is a male threat to the safety of those he is around.

Negative stereotypes can lead to stigma. Link and Phelan (2001) detailed this process. First, people see differences between one another and label them. Second, cultural norms (in this case, Western culture) attribute negative stereotypes to a labeled group. Third, distinct in and out groups are created, which manifests separation between "us" and "them." Finally, the stigmatized group is subject to discrimination. For example, John plays on his college *League of Legends* esports team. John's classmates associate him with all of the negative stereotypes of a video game player. These classmates do not want to be associated with these traits, so they decide to not invite John to an upcoming social gathering. This action denies John an opportunity for meaningful social interaction and any benefits therein. John's classmates have classified him as too different; he is viewed negatively, then stigmatized, and finally excluded.

These stereotypes serve to devalue individuals and groups of gamers broadly, but they also serve to remove legitimacy of the activity of gaming and esports. When a group is viewed negatively because of their participation in an activity, it demonstrates that cultural norms do not value this activity. Likewise, when a devalued group of people are attracted to an activity, by extension that activity becomes undesirable. Indeed, one of the most common questions about esports is whether or not it counts as a sport. This question is about legitimacy. While legitimacy is not the focus of this chapter, it is a factor in stereotypes of esports players. For someone who is invested in delegitimizing esports, negative stereotypes support their argument both on a personal and a cultural level. For someone invested in legitimizing esports, negative stereotypes are major obstacles to overcome.

POSITIVE IMPACTS OF GAMING

Although the positive impacts of video game play do not get the same level of media attention as the negative ones, competitive and social gaming positively impact individuals, groups, and society in a variety of ways. Gaming can increase a sense of connectedness among its participants, and it offers an avenue for collaborative social engagement. In addition, the industry has begun to self-regulate by creating programs and initiatives aimed at ensuring that positive behaviors, fair play, and general kindness become the cultural norm.

Shared Sense of Connection

One benefit of gaming and esports is that participants can share a sense of connection. Glanville and Bienenstock (2009) note that social capital (networks of interpersonal relationships within a societal context) is made up of network structure, trust and reciprocity, and resources. Gamers are building these shared connections through the social capital created in gaming and esports. Individuals are realizing these gains by playing games with others in person and online, engaging in video game streams and mobile gaming, and through organized esports.

Leon Neal/Getty Images

Gaming together can bring a sense of connectedness.

According to a Pew research report (Lenhart 2015), 84 percent of boys and 62 percent of girls who play games feel a stronger sense of connection to friends. According to the report, 91 percent of boys and 85 percent of girls play online games with friends they know in person, while 59 percent of boys and only 40 percent of girls play with friends they only know online. In addition to online gaming, more than 50 percent of boys and 35 percent of girls play games with friends in person.

Esports offer a viable social structure that allows for the creation of social capital through the shared connections in gaming that have existed for decades. Bruckman (1994) conducted some of the earliest research on this connection with her case study of multiuser dungeons (MUDs). MUDs were text-based VR environments that connected users in different physical locations in the early days of the Internet. Bruckman's case study found that users built an effective learning community in the MUDs and that strong friendships were formed in this supportive virtual environment.

As technology advanced and higher speeds of Internet access became more common, online gaming became more commercial and mainstream. Cole and Griffiths (2007) studied the social interactions of people who play massively multiplayer online role-playing games (MMORPGs). MMORPG players benefited from high levels of social engagement. In addition, it was found that these interactions enhanced the gaming experience and led to friendships outside of the game.

Hamilton, Garretson, and Kerne (2014) found that video game streams foster informal communities for gamers. These communities feature conversation as the main activity, and members develop an emotional connection with other members through a shared history and participation. These communities serve the emotional needs of the members. The attraction to interact with people who they view as similar to themselves is a large part of what shapes a stream. Individuals gain stronger connections within the community as they interact with the stream over time and develop a shared history with other members and the streamer.

In addition to increasing connections between people in disparate geophysical locations, augmented reality games such as *Pokémon Go* have allowed users to build shared connections within a shared physical space (Vella et al. 2019). The study found that the game's use of real-world mapping encouraged individual players to occupy the same public space. Gamers noted higher levels of social connectedness, including stronger social ties related to strangers within the community and a sense of place.

According to the North American Scholastic Esports Federation (NASEF; 2018), students have benefited from organized esports with the development of communities around shared interests, collaboration and enhanced communication, and overall engagement and connectedness to the school.

Organized esports at the collegiate and professional levels have been effective in developing and growing both in-person and online fan-based communities. Reysen and Branscombe (2010) categorized fan communities into music, media, sport, and hobby. Esports crosses over into both the sport and hobby categories, and Chadborn, Edwards, and Reysen (2018) found that these fan groups generally feel more connected to their fan groups than to their local community. Fans of esports who share the same online space are likely to feel more connected to other fans based on this shared connection, which can lead to an enhanced sense of belonging. Esports fans and players build these shared connections through video game streams, attending live events, interaction in group chat platforms, and through gaming together.

Building Diverse Communities

The gaming industry exhibits multiple instances where it is self-aware about its role in society, its duty to care for its stakeholders, and its willingness to create a positive environment for players, viewers, and fans. For example, AnyKey is an advocacy group that "supports diversity, inclusion and equity in competitive gaming. They amplify, connect and empower marginalized players and their allies through research and strategic initiatives" (AnyKey 2020a, para. 1). They are on a mission to collect 1,000,000 signatures from individuals to hold themselves ethically and socially to the tenets of the Good Luck Have Fun (GLHF) pledge. GLHF is a promise that gamers will follow the seven community guidelines that seek to ensure good sporting behavior and other positive behaviors, and that they follow a core set of antidiscriminatory standards in their interactions with others, whether competitively or socially.

The GLHF pledge asks participants to pledge to do the following (AnyKey 2020b, para. 2):

1. Be a good sport whether I win or lose.
2. Know that people online are real people and my words have real impact.
3. Set a positive example with my behavior.
4. Speak up against discrimination, hate speech, harassment, and abuse.
5. Show integrity by honoring the rules, my opponents, and my teammates.
6. Stop, listen, and reassess if I'm told that my words or actions are harmful.
7. Respect others, even if their sincere opinions are different from my own.

As of early 2020, the number of gamers who took the pledge was 421,197. Once a gamer has taken the pledge, they are given access to resources to help them move forward within the community in a positive manner. For example, pledge takers are given a Twitch badge that signals to other viewers that they have taken the GLHF pledge. They are also encouraged to add GLHF into their username or other naming indicators to signal their affiliation. Finally, AnyKey shares research on the positive impact of gaming, best practices, how to foster diversity and inclusion, and other topics to help drive the positive narrative of gaming from a quantitative and scholarly based perspective (AnyKey 2020).

Historically, **gender diversity** has been a cause for concern in the esports industry. Due to research and prescriptive initiatives, data show positive, albeit slow improvements in regard to including female gamers in the space. Advocacy groups such as Feminist Frequency and Girl Gamer Galaxy help to increase awareness of gender-equal gaming (Bian et al. 2019). In 2019, Gen.G and Bumble teamed up for an all-female esports partnership building a community around its female gamers. Although there is still quite a long road to travel in regard to gender diversity, this kind of prescriptive action toward gender equality within the gaming space enforces that esports (and game play in general) can get to a level playing field (Abrams and Settimi 2019).

Another example of building positive communities in the gaming space is a company called Gamers Outreach. A nonprofit organization that works with children in hospitals, Gamers Outreach seeks to use video game play and its positive impacts to help improve the patient experience. Gamers Outreach relies on the gaming community to help raise funds for their initiatives such as Project Go Kart (video game kiosks for use in the medical setting) and Player 2 (a volunteer

Rebeca Figueiredo Amorim/Getty Images

Advocacy groups are continuing to increase the presence of female gamers in the esports space.

initiative pairing gamers with those wishing to give back within a hospital setting). As of early 2020, Gamers Outreach had supported 1,250,000 children per year and had volunteers at 10 U.S. hospitals (Gamers Outreach 2020).

Dozens more organizations have a driving mission to improve the competitive and social gaming space. The sheer volume of organizations that exist in this relatively young industry bodes well for its culture and its potential for positive outcomes in the long term.

NEGATIVE IMPACTS OF GAMING

As any other industry, gaming has a dark side with potential for negative behaviors and outcomes. When you bring a group of people together, in the mix of personalities will be some bad actors with ulterior motives. The nature of competition in esports is subject to the same potential negative implications as any other competitive sport, possibly more so as the game media itself is often of a violent and aggressive nature. Finally, as has been seen within the sporting industry for decades, the feel-good brain chemicals a player receives during game play can lead to an increase in addiction or addictive behaviors.

Trolling and Toxicity

People choose to participate in sports for a variety of reasons; the same is true for esports and gaming. People may play for camaraderie, competition, and social interaction, which are considered positive. However, not all reasons people play sports and games are positive; some people play to annoy and harass others.

In the early 2000s, these types of esports players were called killers and griefers (Bartle 2004). Killers view the games as a chance to show their power because "Killers have fun acting on other players" (Bartle 2004, 132). These people also exist in esports, where they are called trolls; their behavior is known as **trolling**.

The term *troll* or *trolling* does not have one specific origin; it likely has the following three sources (theScore esports 2019). The most obscure origin of trolling comes from a war reference. During the Vietnam War, the U.S. Army used the term as slang for fighter planes entering enemy airspace to stir up opposition. Another origin is from fishing. Fishermen would use the term *trolling* to describe dragging bait through the water. This image pairs well with the idea that trolls often bait other gamers into reacting in a negative way. The most likely origin for modern trolling goes all the way back to fables. The mythical ogres known as trolls often are portrayed as living under bridges and harassing and badgering the people they encounter with annoying questions and riddles. Regardless of the term's origin, it has one overarching theme: maliciousness.

The most recent studies about trolling have shed light on this maliciousness. In two separate studies published by Buckels, Trapnell, and Paulhus (2014), a connection was found between trolling and what is known as the Dark Tetrad of personality—narcissism, Machiavellianism, psychopathy, and sadism. In these two studies the researchers used online surveys to delve into the minds of online commenters. In the first study, the researchers noticed that the time people spent commenting showed "lower conscientiousness scores" (p. 98). In contrast, these people showed higher than average scores on all parts of the Dark Tetrad except for narcissism. The second study showed similar results. As in the first study, a correlation seemed to exist "between The Dark Tetrad, commenting frequency, and rated enjoyment of various activities—including trolling" (p. 99). Also, the study reported a connection between sadism, Machiavellianism, and psychopathy in relation to trolling. Ultimately, these two studies concluded that the people who found enjoyment in trolling the most showed a positive association with sadism. Given this information, what are some signs an esports player is trolling?

In video games trolling can display itself in a multitude of ways. As previously discussed, a common version of trolling is commenting on the games themselves. Generally, people do it by discussing plays that occur during the game or over typing in the game's chat afterward. Often, it is also associated with players trying to get into arguments or generally being distracting in all chats. Another form of trolling in esports is known as bad mannering (BM). BM activity could be the spamming of emotes, taunting, or even the often talked about teabagging (i.e., standing over another player's in-game avatar and repeatedly moving up and down), which may all be seen in competitive FPS games.

On a more competitive level, trolling can take the shape of a player willingly playing their role in the game to suboptimal efficiency. It could be taking inappropriate items, playing characters they have not played before, or choosing not to execute simple strategies. In doing so, a troll can potentially cost their team the game and effectively ruin the enjoyment of their teammates. All of these versions of trolling do not cause lasting damage. However, one form of trolling that has recently increased in popularity is a criminal act that is dangerous and even deadly; it is called swatting. **Swatting** involves calling the police and claiming that a serious situation is occurring at the location of a player, resulting in an armed response (SWAT team) at the player's location. While it may seem difficult to do, tech savvy trolls can easily find another player's IP address and in turn know where they are located. This kind of trolling occurred when *Counter-Strike: Global Offensive* (*CS:GO*) professional Jordan "N0thing" Gilbert was swatted live on his stream (Anselimo 2014). Another devastating example of swatting occurred in 2017. In this instance, Kansas resident Andrew Finch was shot and killed during a swatting that was the result of an online argument during a competitive match of an esport (Almasy 2019). In the call to the police, Tyler Barris told dispatchers that a person in the house had "shot his dad in the head" and that "he was holding his mom and brother at gunpoint" (Almasy 2019, para. 9). Barris now serves 20 years in jail for the death of Andrew Finch.

The reason trolling is such a prevalent topic in the esports world is twofold. On a more casual level, most video games (and therefore esports) trap the players in situations with trolls. For example, if a player plays a game with someone who spams hate speech or attempts to ruin the game, a player is not able to leave the game without being punished. However, if this type of incident happened in a physical sport such as during a basketball game, a person could leave or stop the game. On the professional level, trolling can be a serious issue because it affects the professional esports athlete's ability to practice and earn money. This is because an extensive amount of esports athletes' practice comes from playing on the ladder. A ladder is a ranking system where one player moves up and down based on who they play and if they win. If a person ranked 10 on the ladder beats someone ranked 3, then they replace them and move up the ladder to the third spot. This situation leaves them open for people to troll them, preventing their practice.

Addiction

Participation in esports may begin as a fun and harmless diversion, but for some people it can transform into an obsession that has serious consequences. When esports use becomes an addiction, players experience negative consequences related to their gaming. They may forgo sleep, nutrition, exercise, self-care, involvement with family and friends, and neglect work and school.

Addiction is not determined by simply counting the hours a person plays esports. Serious gamers spend extensive time playing, but they may not have the same negative consequences and warning signs as a person struggling with an esports addiction. The difference between an addicted player and a healthy one can be characterized by the extent to which excessive gaming negatively impacts (and takes over) a person's life. **Addiction** is marked by compulsive playing and withdrawal from real life to the point that the person may lose their job or relationships.

The ability to lose oneself in an alternative reality can be a welcome relief from the stresses of everyday life. Esports can be an enjoyable and relaxing way to spend time. However, when esports become a person's primary coping strategy to escape real-life challenges, difficulties can develop. Most issues are not solved by avoidance, so problems are not resolved, yet the drive to escape continues.

For some players, participation in esports may satisfy unmet needs, such as being a substitute for lack of off-line friendships. Esports provides a virtual community and social interactions. If esports are depended on for social acceptance and self-esteem, then a person can become over reliant on gaming. They may spend increasing amounts of time trying to prove their worth through success in esports.

Warning signs of esports addiction include the following (American Psychiatric Association 2018):

- Increasing amounts of time spent playing esports despite negative consequences
- Preoccupation with the game when away from it
- Not prioritizing life outside of gaming, and neglecting responsibilities
- Ignoring negative consequences
- Lying to cover up time and money spent on esports
- Isolating oneself and withdrawing from activities that were previously enjoyed
- Irritability when trying to cut back on esports or when away from the game

In recognition of an emerging worldwide public health problem surrounding addiction and online gaming, the World Health Organization (WHO) added gaming disorder to the 11th Revision of the International Classification of Diseases (ICD-11) in 2018. The WHO (2018) defines gaming disorder as a pattern characterized by

> "impaired control over gaming, increasing priority given to gaming over other activities to the extent that gaming takes precedence over other interests and daily activities, and continuation or escalation of gaming despite the occurrence of negative consequences. For gaming disorder to be diagnosed, the behavior pattern must be of sufficient severity to result in significant impairment in personal, family, social, educational, occupational or other important areas of functioning and would normally have been evident for at least 12 months." (para. 1)

Official recognition of this addiction and clear diagnostic criteria for gaming disorder are keys to developing effective evidence-based treatment strategies and getting insurance to cover professional intervention if it is required.

Once an addiction has developed, professional support may be required. Anxiety, depression, and thoughts of suicide can overlap with (and be made worse by) a gaming addiction. Currently, several online self-help support forums help people with esports addiction (Naskar, Victor, Nath, and Sengupta 2016). The online programs are often modeled on the 12-step program Alcoholics Anonymous. Other treatment strategies with emerging data to support their use in gaming disorder include therapies focused on improving coping skills, increasing motivation for change, and identifying problematic ways of thinking and working to change them. Many of these treatments have been used successfully with substance-related addictions.

Another problematic area related to esports is the use of performance-enhancing drugs. It is not uncommon for players to use energy drinks and caffeinated pills to prolong the amount of time they can stay awake gaming. Unfortunately, some players also abuse prescription medications. It may be done in an effort to increase concentration, improve reaction time, and remain alert for long periods. Other misused medications are taken to stay calm under pressure or block the effects of increased adrenaline that can cause heart racing and shaking hands.

Most of the medications that are inappropriately used for esports performance enhancement have the potential to produce tolerance (the need to take more medication in order to produce the same effect), dependence (the body has physical withdrawal if the substance is abruptly stopped), and addiction (psychological dependence on the substance, often coupled with a physical dependence). Although developing an addiction to these substances is a separate issue from gaming, players experiencing esports addiction may be more likely to use performance-enhancing drugs as a way to extend the hours they can play. Once addicted to esports, a seemingly fun distraction is no longer harmless. Esports addiction may result in the same serious problems that are typically associated with substance-related addictions. Although the addiction is not to a drug, some similar physical changes and behaviors occur (Kuss, Pontes, and Griffiths 2018), and by definition, the person is experiencing negative consequences. With greater awareness of esports addiction, a person has a higher chance of receiving helpful intervention and treatment.

Violent Media

Violence in video games is nothing new to the industry, especially the links between violent acts and people's consumption of the media genre. In 1976, the game *Death Race*, a black-and-white game featuring a pixelated car running over pedestrians was touted as "Sick, Sick, Sick" (Blumenthal 1976, para. 5). In April 1999, Eric Harris and Dylan Klebold orchestrated the infamous shooting and attempted bombing at Columbine High School in Columbine, Colorado. Both Harris and Klebold were reported as enjoying the violence present in *Doom*, *Quake*, *Duke Nukem 3D*, and *Postal*; Harris wrote, "I will force myself to believe that everyone is just another monster from Doom" (Harris 1999, para. 12). However, no clear evidence has shown that video games have a direct cause in shaping people's thoughts for a prolonged period of time or that violence in video games leads to more violence in present society.

The two major types of video game violence are fantasy and realistic. Fantasy violence is the type of violence that cannot happen in present society. It includes games such as *League of Legends*, *Overwatch*, and *Rocket League*. Each of these types of fantasy violence is portrayed differently. In *Rocket League*, players can collide with and explode each other's vehicles, therefore it is considered a type of **realistic fantasy**. Events in realistic fantasy could technically happen, but they would need to meet the proper circumstances in order to occur. *League of Legends* includes characters such as Ryze, who can wield magical beams of plasma from his hands, and Volibear, a demi-god of thunder and talking polar bear. This type of game, in which events occur outside the realm of possibility, is considered **high fantasy**. In **futuristic fantasy** games, events have the potential to occur but not in the current realm of possibilities. *Overwatch* would fit into this category; Orisa, a large robot that can wield a gun and photon-based shield, could eventually exist in reality. Each game may contain certain elements that fit into different categories. For example, the character Hammond in *Overwatch* is an intelligent hamster that controls a large robotic suit, and *Pokémon* includes elements from all three fantasy pillars.

Realistic violence is usually based on a two-dimensional continuum rather than classified further into categories. On one axis of the continuum is a form of impermanence versus permanence. The violence caused to the person's character can be temporary, or the damage done to the character can have ramifications in future levels. An example of permanence is the *Fire Emblem* series, a medieval tactical, turn-based strategy game where the death of a character lasts for the entire game. On the other axis of the continuum is gory versus docile. Some games, such as *Counter-Strike* and *Call of Duty*, display realistic bloodshed; others, such as *Fortnite*, show little or no blood but still have a realistic form of violence.

Most video games come with a rating from the Entertainment Software Rating Board (ESRB). These ratings help determine whether a game is appropriate for a specific age group. The typical ratings include E for "everyone," E10+ for "everyone over 10 years old," T for "teens" (13+), M for "mature" (17+), and AO for "adults only over age 18." These ratings are guidelines that can help parents understand what may exist in games they are purchasing for their children. However, as more games become available online or include online content, it is difficult to rate and regulate the content available to the consumer. Most companies have labeled the online content as unrated, which has led to a further form of violence, bullying. Online bullying in certain games has been rising as more games move to online platforms or as more online games become available. Games begin to garner a reputation for their player base. For example, two infamous *League of Legends* players, Tyler1 and Dunkey, have taken separate paths following their violent comments toward other players. Because of his toxic comments, Tyler 1 was branded the most toxic player in North America and was banned from *League of Legends* for 20 months. Dunkey, who currently has over 5 million subscribers despite crude language, was once quoted typing to another player, "you are a . . . worthless brained . . . pile of trash . . . that should be gunned down in the street like the degenerate you are" (Dunkey 2015, 0:40). This type of toxicity and violence toward other players is frowned upon by both the video game publishers and the gaming community. Dunkey was permanently banned from *League of Legends*.

Colleges have taken strong stances against violent video games. In several collegiate esports programs, first-person shooter (FPS) games such as *CS:GO*, *Rainbow Six: Siege*, and *Call of Duty* are not allowed because the violence present in these games is not consistent with the mission or image these schools wish to portray. This topic has caused a severe divide between some colleges and within collegiate conferences, especially when some universities wish to compete in popular esports games that often include FPS titles, while others prefer to only compete in less or nonviolent games. Even though *CS:GO* is one of the five most popular games in the world, is popular on Twitch, and is one of the oldest esports, the college scene only has one major conference (NACE) that offers competitions in the game. In contrast, *Rocket League*, *Hearthstone*, and *Overwatch* are offered by most of the major esports conferences. These games are generally accepted across the industry and across colleges. At Johnson & Wales University in Providence, Rhode Island, the university has teams in 10 different games, including *Call of Duty*, *CS:GO*, *Rainbow Six: Siege*, and *Apex Legends*, but it does not market these games on the university's athletics website. The universities might feel that publicizing the official playing of the games might hurt the school's image so they might play some games, but not mention it on their websites. In other words, some universities may not want to draw attention to or publicize competing in perceived violent video games in order to maintain a certain image.

The stigma that follows some games labeled as violent has been apparent since the late 1970s, and it will not leave the industry until a fundamental shift occurs in society's approach to gaming. Violence in gaming will continue to be popular, not because of any deep-rooted thoughts that people develop when playing violent games, but because these games offer an opportunity for fantasy that does not exist in real life. The average gamer who consumes the violence in video games can normally separate the game action from their real activities. If gaming causes people to be violent in real life, then society would expect to see millions and millions of gamers being and acting in violent ways, which is something the world is just not seeing except in a few isolated instances.

CONCLUSION

This chapter outlined the various societal perspectives that exist in the space around the globe as well as how they are similar and how they vary in different parts of the world. The chapter also took a deep look at the potential for positive outcomes and the potential for negative outcomes in the competitive space of esports and within gaming in general. Although the positive impacts of video game play do not often get the same level of media attention as the perceived negative impacts, a wide range of areas exist where competitive and social play of video games positively affect individuals, groups, and society. One of the benefits of gaming and esports is the ability to create a shared connection with other people. Current insight signals that the industry is becoming far more self-aware about its role within society, its duty of care for its stakeholders, and a willingness to create a positive environment for players, viewers, and fans.

It is important to also acknowledge that competitive play and general gaming, as much as any industry, has a dark side fraught with potential negative behaviors and outcomes. In video games, trolling and toxicity can be observed in a multitude of behaviors and responses; it is often a malicious and damaging set of actions and behaviors. When esports use becomes an addiction, players will experience negative consequences related to their gaming. Finally, violence within game play and the implications of the consumption of said violence and potential to alter one's actions is something that will continue to remain a key area of research and concern.

The way in which video games and those who play them socially and competitively are viewed is complex and changing. The perceptions, cultural norms, and overall dynamics within the industry will continue to evolve as technology changes, viewpoints shift, and the credibility of esports as a viable sport grows with clear controls, regulations, and positively perceived norms.

DISCUSSION QUESTIONS

1. What are the effects of increasing diversity on gaming?
2. How are Western and Eastern cultural perspectives of esports similar and different?
3. What are some of the positive impacts of esports?
4. What are some of the negative impacts of esports?

4

Esports Stakeholders

Gil Friedⅼ | Aaron Castellan | Aaron Colaiacomo | Clint Kennedy | Michael Newhouse-Bailey | Sheng Qiang

INTRODUCTION

A **stakeholder** is someone who has an interest in a matter. Stakeholders are important because their perspective and ideas are critical for an organization to survive and grow. For example, if a local college were to contemplate building a recreation center, it would be important to know who the stakeholders are and what they want and need in a facility. Arguably the most important stakeholders will be the current students (however, if a major donor is giving most of the money, their say might override the perspective or desire of students). If you assume students are the most important stakeholders, then the recreation center architects might undertake various town hall meetings with students to learn what they want. Surveys might be undertaken to obtain additional information from stakeholders. The student stakeholders are a diverse group. They could include on-campus, commuter, international, and graduate students. Each might have a different idea or issue critical to them, and the recreation center developers need to understand each group.

Students are only one stakeholder group for this fictitious college campus recreation center. Other groups include the following:

- Faculty
- Administrators
- Employees
- Alumni
- Community leaders
- Local politicians
- Government officials at various levels
- Contracted third parties who might work on campus
- The recreation center architects, builders, and others

As is evident in this list, numerous individuals either have a direct say or will want to have some say in the recreation center.

The same diversity of stakeholders can be found in the esports industry. The esports space has many players—and not just those who play the games. The long list of players includes game developers, game players, coaches, leagues, facility managers, marketers, and many others. It would be very difficult to figure out who all the stakeholders are because some can be hard to identify.

OBJECTIVES

- Identify at least five different stakeholders with a stake in the esports space.
- Develop a map of the various esports players and how they interact with one another.
- Distinguish between major stakeholders and minor stakeholders.

For example, while it is easy to track those who play games, consider how fans are identified and their issues addressed. It might seem like an easy exercise, but when you dig deep you can find that it is actually very difficult. Can a fan be someone who likes one character in the game? Does a fan have to play the game? Does a fan need to watch a game? What if someone likes a game's story line but has never played or viewed the game? To be considered a fan, does someone need to be involved at a certain level (i.e., is there a difference between a casual fan and a raving fan)? When fans are being examined for a stakeholder analysis, it requires a little more depth and subtlety than simply grouping all fans into one homogeneous group. This process is also made more difficult when fans are **segmented** (divided into different groups) based on criteria such as age, gender, ethnicity, and nationality.

This chapter is designed to provide a broad perspective of the various primary stakeholders in the esports space. In chapter 1, numerous stakeholders were identified and briefly described. In this chapter, additional exploration and description of key stakeholders are provided. In addition, because some groups of stakeholders may be more integral, a tiered list (see figure 4.1) is provided in which the most important ones are listed in the first tier, with less important ones in the subsequent tiers.

Tier 1 stakeholders are the most important players in this space, and the examination begins with game publishers. Without publishers developing and updating games, the esports industry would not exist. This section then explores the various types of players. From there the chapter explores some of the teams that have jumped to prominence in some key games. This section then explores those who are operating various esports leagues as they are often the most visible sign for people exploring the esports business field. Finally, investors are the last element in Tier 1; they overlap with other Tier 1 entities. Investors can invest in publishers, start esports companies, or buy esports franchises.

Tier 2 stakeholders are important but not as critical as those entities in Tier 1 (see figure 4.1). The first Tier 2 stakeholders covered are event managers and promoters, such as ESL, who put on some of the major esports events. Next, the chapter explores some of the esports marketers who sell games, athletes, events, brands, and sponsorships. This section then covers those who broadcast esports over various media. Finally, this section covers educational institutions that host teams or events related to esports. These stakeholders will become more familiar to many readers who are college students.

When examining the business case for esports, Tier 3 stakeholders are not considered as critical as the other stakeholders (see figure 4.1). However, it does not mean these stakeholders are not important. The best way to examine the difference is

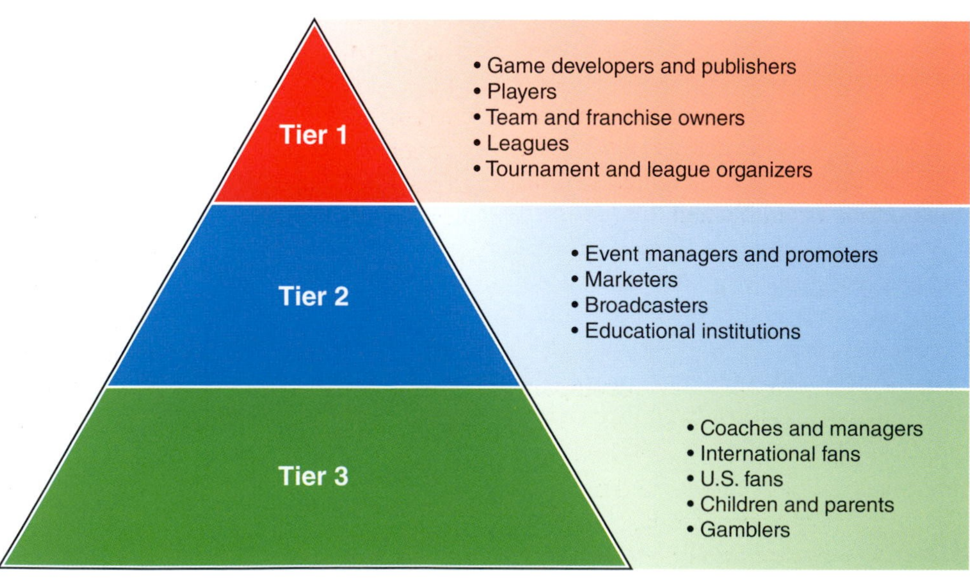

Figure 4.1 Three tiers of stakeholders.

to think about a high school. Those on the school board, the principal, faculty, and students could be top tier (Tier 1) stakeholders. Classroom aides, hall monitors, and coaches are all important for running programs at the school, so they could be classified as Tier 2 stakeholders. Tier 3 stakeholders could be people who work in the lunchroom or the library. They are important, but not as critical for operating the high school. Similarly, for esports the Tier 3 stakeholders include coaches, gamblers, fans, and parents. This section provides an opportunity to compare two different stakeholder groups in the same space. U.S. coaches and esports team managers are compared to their international counterparts. Different coaches use different styles and approaches for teams in different parts of the world. Next, the chapter explores gamblers who are having a significant impact on the esports space. The text then describes U.S. fans compared with international fans and what they want from esports games and events. The chapter concludes with an examination of the opportunities and concerns parents and children may have about esports.

TIER 1 STAKEHOLDERS

Tier 1 stakeholders are the most critical in esports. They include game publishers, teams, players, leagues, and investors. Critical stakeholders not covered in this text are phone and Internet companies. If a signal is lost, the game would end for a mobile gamer; the same holds true for gamers during a tournament. With the impact of so many people streaming and net neutrality (i.e., the idea and practice that all content on the Internet is treated equally by service providers), numerous issues will affect this stakeholder. Those issues are outside the scope of this text and are likely to change several times after this textbook is published.

Game Developers and Publishers

Esports would not exist without game developers and publishers. Several major publishers exist, and so do many small publishers. Anyone can become a publisher by coding a game and putting it out on the market. Some games might be sold (e.g., in stores or through download), while other games might be free to download. In other cases, some games may not become popular due to low publicity, poor quality, poor playability, or numerous other reasons. Building a popular game takes a lot of time and money. While different aspects of a game appeal to different people, in general, gamers are looking for both quality and depth. A simple game, such as *Pong*, might have been great 40 years ago. Today's audiences are more sophisticated and demanding, and that is why many of the most popular games require such high levels of investment in time and resources. As a result, well-funded and established publishers are more likely to survive the time and resource investments it takes to fully develop and build out ultimately successful games. Furthermore, if a small developer launches a game that becomes popular, larger publishers frequently attempt to (and often successfully) buy the developer in order to drive their own sales.

The largest publishers right now include Activision Blizzard, Capcom, Electronic Arts (EA), Epic Games, Valve, Ubisoft, Riot Games, and Nintendo. These publishers and many others do not simply create games. Some might develop and sell equipment. Some of these companies also own, host, and produce coverage for large competitions, such as Riot Games' *League of Legends* Championship Series (LCS) or Valve's "The International" *Dota 2* championship. Some also own or administer their own leagues and franchises. This deep involvement gives the publishers a lot of power in the esports space.

Publishers also license their games to external league organizers (such as PlayVS) and streaming platforms. To maximize revenue, publishers push to turn their video games into esports in order to generate additional revenue and exposure. Even free games can generate massive revenue through in-game sales, licensing agreements, establishing tournaments, and other strategies.

Publishers can spend significant resources to generate revenue with a popular game. In 2013, Rockstar Games released *Grand Theft Auto V*. Over five years, 250 people worked on developing the game. It was the most expensive game ever made at the time, costing a total of $115 million. The high-dollar investment was well worth it; the game had sales exceeding $1 billion in its first three days.

Players

Players such as Jian "Uzi" Zihao, Lee "Faker" Sang-hyeok, Michael "Shroud" Grzesiek, Turner "Tfue" Tenney, Tyler "Ninja" Blevins, and Katherine "Mystik" Gunn might not be household names for nongamers, but people in the esports space know them well. These and other players are not just famous, they are becoming rich. They are gaining their influence not just from playing games but from external activities as well. Thus, while someone might win thousands of dollars playing esports games, they can earn much more from donations from those watching their streams or from advertisers who want to be connected with their streams. Thus, someone who might not be a great player, but draws attention, can be important for a team or game as a star player. In recent years, influencers have grown considerably. The value of a player and their followers was apparent when EA paid Ninja a reported $1 million for playing *Apex Legends* for 24 hours (Thier 2019). Players can initially make their money from playing; then, some players can translate their earning potential to a postplaying career in various areas such as coaching and using their content creation skills to become commentators, analysts, and marketers for publishers and third-party tournament organizers.

Players often specialize in certain games that will maximize their skills and career ambitions. A player who loves and follows soccer might love playing *Fortnite* but realize their background knowledge in soccer (football) will allow them to do better in FIFA-based games. They might play a lot and get good. They then can start a stream and try to grow their following. This experience can lead them to winning more tournaments, focusing exclusively on this game, and then try to grab the attention of an esports team. That team could be affiliated with a larger esports organization or could be associated with a soccer team. Thus, through specialization, this player can take their passion, focus their efforts, and then become an employee of their favorite team—not as a front office person or as a player on the field, but as a gamer for the team that can help grow its influence and revenue generation.

Teams

While some individual players can grow and gain individual fame, the big money is often with teams. A number of well-known and well-funded teams exist, such as Cloud9, FaZe Clan, Team Liquid, Dignitas (formerly Team Dignitas), Evil Geniuses, and Ninjas in Pyjamas. Each team has its own strength and focus. Some teams are backed by larger corporations such as Comcast, which owns the *Overwatch* franchise, Philadelphia Fusion. In 2019, Comcast went all in through launching an effort to build a $50 million arena for the team; it will be called Fusion Arena. Other teams are just a group of friends who play together. Some of the players might be on the same team but have never met in person. Other teams live in houses dedicated to the team with paid coaches, nutritionists, and athletic trainers. While it might seem like an easy life, players on these teams know it is a job; they sometimes train for 10 to 15 hours a day. This rigorous training schedule can lead to burnout and early retirement. It is not unusual to hear about an esports star retiring in their mid-20s.

To maintain an image of integrity, teams must remain financially separate from tournament organizers. Teams that get too close to a publisher may be viewed as favorites, which could affect gamblers and others. No matter the connection, the key is how much a team and its players earn. While sponsors make up a majority of an esports' team revenue (e.g., **brand activations** on jerseys, **in-stream promotional content**, personal product endorsement, or other revenue streams), the public looks at the total won. It is similar to individual sports, such as golf and tennis, in which lifetime earnings is one of the key metrics for success.

One difference between esports teams and most professional sport leagues is the frequency of teams coming and going. While the franchise teams might be stronger (especially when backed by wealthy investors), smaller, independent teams are another story. Teams have come and gone over the years. Some of this turnover may occur because of internal rifts between players, rifts between owners, being kicked out of a league, and other related issues. However, just because one team no longer exists in one game does not mean they cannot come back. A great example is Team Dignitas. Originally, Team Dignitas competed in the LCS for four years, but the team never made the finals. The LCS team, which was based in Europe, was sold in 2016. Dignitas (the team modified its name) returned to the league in 2019 after merging with another LCS team, Clutch Gaming.

Zoning

EXAMINING ESPORTS PLAYERS' AND TEAMS' DATA

Gil Fried

Examining several teams by the numbers will help show the value and power of key teams. Similar to the Dallas Cowboys in football or the New York Yankees in baseball, some of the top esports teams are very valuable.

Team Liquid

Team Liquid began as a website for the gaming community. They initially sponsored a Dutch *StarCraft: Brood War* team in 2010. The team continued to grow, and in 2015 they merged with Team Curse. Shortly thereafter they became part of the entertainment and sports management company aXiomatic. In 2017, The Walt Disney Company chose Team Liquid to participate in the Disney Accelerator program. Team Liquid's greatest success was winning The International 2017, which brought the team $10,862,683 in prize money.

Through March 2019, the team had the following numbers:

- Total prize money earned: $24,448,847
- Total tournaments played: 1,430
- Top games and amounts won at each game:
    - *Dota*—$17,336,099
    - *Counter-Strike*—$1,772,175
    - *StarCraft*—$1,361,490.23

Top players on the team and how much they earned are as follows:

- Kuro "KuroKy" Takhasomi—$3,449,672
- Ivan "MinD_ContRoL" Ivanov—$3,433,172
- Lasse "Matumbaman" Urpalainen—$3,428,672 (Influencer Marketing 2019)

Fnatic

Fnatic is another major team. Based in London, many of its top players are of Swedish origin. Sam and Anne Mathews (son and mother) founded the team in 2004. They built the team using great players from all over the world. Their *League of Legends (LoL)* team won the first *LoL* World Championship back in 2011. The team has the most LCS split titles in the European LCS (EU LCS). Fnatic's *Counter-Strike* team is one of the best of all time, having won three *CS:GO* majors. The team has a broad base of games, including *Dota 2*, *Hearthstone*, and *LoL*.

Here are Fnatic's totals through March 2019:

- Total prize money earned: $11,908,332
- Total tournaments played: 788
- Top games and amounts won at each game:
    - *CS:GO*—$3,531,627
    - *Dota 2*—$3,089,323
    - *League of Legends*—$1,816,891

Top players on the team and how much they earned are as follows:

- Robin "flusha" Rönnquist—$687,864
- Jesper "JW" Wecksell—$679,188
- Freddy "KRIMZ" Johansson—$661,480 (Influencer Marketing 2019)

Teams can indeed come and go or, as in the case of Dignitas, they can buy their way back into a league (Esguerra 2019).

Tournament and League Organizers

Similar to game developers, various third-party companies operate their own competitions. These entities are not only hosting an event, they are focusing on all aspects of revenue generation associated with these events. Some of the largest tournaments include ESL One, *FIFA* Global Series, *Fortnite* World Cup, *LoL* World Championship, *Rocket League* Championship Series, and *Call of Duty* World League Championships. These tournaments entail finding appropriate locations, marketing, broadcasting, and all other elements associated with the events. For example, some smaller tournaments focus on attendance and trying to maximize ticket sales. Large tournaments might focus more on broadcasts or sponsorship rights and selling those rights to streaming platforms.

One problem with the tournament side of the industry is that everyone is trying to get into the game. When too many tournaments are associated with too many esports, significant **cannibalization** occurs. Both players and fans can only go to so many events; if a different event is scheduled every weekend, it is not sustainable. To deal with this issue, many tournament organizers negotiate for exclusivity rights, which would allow an organization or brand to be the only sponsor in a particular category (read more about this in chapter 7). For example, weekly viewership numbers for *CS:GO* on Twitch reduced dramatically after YouTube purchased the streaming rights to the ESL Pro League. Other streaming services such as Valve, Facebook, and Twitter have also entered into streaming deals with teams, tournaments, and league organizers.

As the industry grows, more techniques will be undertaken to generate additional revenue. For example, to lease a large arena similar to Madison Square Garden (MSG), a tournament might not be able to negotiate for a larger percentage of concession sales. As tournaments grow and draw bigger and more predictable crowds, arenas would be more inclined to negotiate better deals for tournament organizers. This negotiation occurs not only in esports but with any event. As events become bigger and more predictable in terms of attendance and **per capita** spending (how much money is spent by fans on a per capita basis for an event), the bargaining positions will change, allowing tournaments to negotiate from a position of strength. Of course, smaller tournaments might not have such bargaining strength, which could lead to many smaller tournaments losing money, and those who underwrite smaller tournaments might either fold or merge into a larger entity. In the case of too many events existing, another concern might be fan fatigue.

Investors

Another group of major stakeholders in esports, investors vary from star athletes to professional sports team owners and large telecommunication companies. In addition, a significant number of everyday people invest in esports; they may buy several shares of an esports company's stock or try to buy into a new team. One of the great characteristics of esports is that anyone can start a team; if they do well, the investors, founders, and players can all be successful. While the top investors generate a lot of publicity, numerous others have done well or lost. For example, one of the authors of this book did an exercise with his students to analyze the best publicly traded esports companies. Based on student analysis, the professor purchased shares in Activision Blizzard for $68 a share. The shares went up to close to $80, and the professor was very happy. Then the shares tanked and began trading for less than $60 per share. At the time of this writing, the shares had bounced back to trade at close to $75 per share. As in any other industry, investing in esports has risks. It offers both the potential to make a lot of money and the potential to lose it. Early investors might make more, but they also have a higher level of risk.

TIER 2 STAKEHOLDERS

Individuals and entities in the second tier are critical stakeholders, but the esports industry could still move forward without them. Given that esports started without tournaments, it can make progress without an event promoter. However, tournaments enhance and improve esports. The same holds true for marketers, broadcasters, and educational institutions. They all add value and are important.

Event Managers and Promoters

A number of small and large companies produce esports-related events and tournaments. A high school, college, and even a parks and recreation department could host a tournament. Small companies interested in making some money might try to put on a tournament or event. However, many small companies end up losing money; they often go out of business or put on one event and then stop. The idea of hosting a successful event is not the same as the reality of doing it. To host an event, you need a facility, which often means a rental agreement. Having a chosen game or games means getting licensing agreements with publishers. Among the many considerations are the marketing plan and budget, ticketing sales process, facility setup, and personnel. In other words, putting on a tournament takes time and money, and both can be underestimated.

Larger companies are usually equipped with more resources than smaller ones and thus have great potential for success. For example, consider Modern Times Group (MTG), a company that advertises itself as a world leader in esports entertainment. The company produces live events, professional leagues, and international tournaments, which are streamed live online and on television. MTG's esports companies run professional leagues, organize tournaments, and host mega-events for titles such as *CS:GO*, *Dota 2*, *Overwatch*, *StarCraft II*, and *FIFA*. According to the company's website:

> MTG's Turtle Entertainment, the world's largest esports company and operator of the leading esports brand ESL, covers a broad field of services in gaming technology, event management, advertising, and television production, fully catering to the needs of the esports ecosystem and offering numerous opportunities for brand activation. (MTG 2020, para. 3)

Turtle Entertainment is based in Cologne, Germany, with offices in the United States (ESL North America, Los Angeles), Australia (ESL Australia, Sydney), the United Kingdom (Leicester), China, Hong Kong, Singapore, the Philippines, Malaysia, France, Spain, Poland, Italy, Russia, Brazil, and partners in many other countries. In September 2018, MTG increased its ownership in Turtle Entertainment by 8.44 percent from 74.04 to 82.48 percent.

Each year, ESL runs 13 mega-events with thousands of attendees on five continents, and the number of locations is constantly expanding. ESL also produces world-class content from state-of-the-art broadcast facilities located in China, the Philippines, Australia, North America, the United Kingdom, Germany, and Poland.

MTG has a portfolio of companies such as ESL and DreamHack (a large gaming festival promoter). In January 2020, they announced a three-year agreement with Blizzard Entertainment to create new ESL Pro Tour formats for both *StarCraft II* and *Warcraft III: Reforged*. This description clearly shows the company's size and scope. The company is so large that they are publicly traded. The Nordic Entertainment Group AB (NENT-B.ST) is the publicly owned stock for MTG. Its shares are traded on the Stockholm Stock Exchange; in early 2020, they were selling for around $320 a share. The company was split, and Nordic Entertainment Group AB (NENTF) started operating independently of Modern Times Group Mtg AB (MTG-B.ST) as of March 2019. Those shares are for the esports division, and it was traded also on the Stockholm Stock Exchange for around $100 a share in early 2020. This example helps show how diverse companies can be in this segment. Some are larger broadcasting companies from which smaller versions evolve.

Marketers

Marketing takes on various rolls. For example, a marketer could be a publisher marketing a game and trying to sell it. Publishers can hire external companies or handle the marketing in house. Marketing can also be undertaken within a game, such as selling skins or other buying options that can occur automatically in a game, but often a prompt encourages the purchase. Significant marketing is undertaken by teams, franchises, and tournaments to generate interest. Through a blend of marketing and public relations, companies try to help grow revenue streams, **upsell** fans, market products, and generate as much revenue as possible.

Additional marketing can be undertaken by ancillary companies such as tournament organizers, broadcasters, esports venues, and law firms servicing the industry. They all are interested in selling their services to various entities, and marketing is critical for this effort. Some might buy a booth at a trade show to help sell their services. Others might take out advertisements whether in print, social media, or across broadcast platforms. Because it is a crowded field, standing out can be difficult, which is why having a unique message is critical. Branding is one way to stand out.

Corporate brands are by far the biggest source of revenue for every sector in esports, but the nature of a sponsorship or partnership depends on the deal and the parties involved. Teams can wear brand logos on their jerseys, use products and equipment, and produce social media content revolving around their sponsors. Streaming platforms can allocate screen space to a given team or sponsor. Furthermore, an influencer or even an entire channel can be dedicated to a single brand. Tournament organizers can add significant value to sponsors through providing name placement, showcasing sponsors on highlight reels, showing sponsors on video boards, announcing sponsors over the public address system, and numerous other approaches commonly seen with collegiate and professional sport tournaments.

Some of the most loyal esports buyers are those who are loyal to specific hardware manufacturers. Many hardware companies used to provide only trade-outs (equipment) rather than cash. Now that the industry has grown, these companies are forced to spend significant amounts of money to keep the attention of fans, customers, and players in a competitive marketplace. The push for the best equipment has created a niche market not only for esports companies but also for chip manufacturers and other companies providing goods for high-end systems.

Broadcasters

Esports currently has several large broadcasters over streaming services and over television or cable. South Korean television networks have been showing WCG tournaments for over 10 years. Sweden's TV6 broadcasting network airs DreamHack tournaments, The International (TI), and some *CS:GO* majors. The push into the United States market has taken longer. Major networks, such as NBC, ABC, CBS, and FOX, have all explored the space. They have struggled to find the right concept and approach. ESPN and Turner have done a deeper dive and will continue to have a huge impact. ESPN signed with ESL and Riot Games to broadcast ESL One events such as North American (NA) LCS matches, Intel Extreme Masters (IEM) events, and *Rainbow Six* Pro League competitions. ESPN is owned by Disney (which also owns ABC), and Disney XD has shown *Overwatch* League and the EVO Championship Series matches.

While traditional cable and television will continue to engage in the esports space, the larger broadcasters have been streamers. Main streaming sites and secondary sites are involved. The groundbreaker in this space was Twitch, but it is facing significant competition from various international and regional competitors. International competition comes from streaming sites such as YouTube, Smashcast, Steam.tv, and Facebook. Regional streaming sites include GoodGame in Russia, NimoTV in Southeast Asia, Japanese Openrec, Garena Live in Taiwan, and both DouYu and YY in China.

The key to success for any broadcaster will be having high-level content and production value to draw in viewers. Broadcasters now battle for exclusive contracts with top streamers, hoping that their followers will stay with them, and if they move to a different platform, that platform would be able to secure many of the followers. Broadcasters generate revenue from a percentage of tips, advertising revenue, and sponsorship packages.

Educational Institutions

A number of different educational institutions are involved in esports. High school teams and conferences are starting to pop up around the world. Organizations at lower levels than high school have been reluctant to engage in the space due to concerns about violence and screen time for young children. Colleges have been entering the esports space at breakneck speeds. While individual universities and colleges would probably be considered Tier 3 stakeholders, a large collegiate conference could be considered a Tier 2 stakeholder because they also may organize and broadcast competitions and championships among their member institutions. These entities are covered in greater detail in chapter 5.

High School Esports in the United States

As it stands in January 2020, high school esports exists nearly everywhere in the United States in one form or another. High school esports is defined as a team-based, coordinated competition in which students represent their schools. It is similar to definitions of other high school sports such as basketball or football, but the degree to which that competition structure closely resembles more traditional sports varies considerably. The student appetite for high school esports is undeniable, and the opportunity for the sport to grow is substantial, as evidenced by the 211 million Americans (67% of the population) who play video games (Crecente 2018).

A number of smaller organizations have implemented loosely structured competitions scattered throughout the country through after-school club-style programs. In addition, PlayVS has partnered with the National Federation of State High School Associations (NFHS) as well as numerous states to make esports an official high school sport activity on par with soccer or basketball.

Currently, the titles involved in high school esports depend largely on which of the two models schools choose. The more loosely organized, do-it-yourself models place minimal or no requirements on the titles in which students compete. This freedom comes from a lack of any sort of product or publisher partnership. Strictly speaking, these leagues are little more than a spreadsheet of schools interested in playing one another who are responsible for coordinating their own matches, recording their own results, and tracking their own statistics. They do it through a combination of Voice over Internet Protocol (VoIP) technology, email, text, and phone calls. This model, while maintaining independence from any sort of state association oversight, lacks the structures and institutional support many traditional sports rely on for stability and consistent fair play. Participation in these sorts of competitions is generally free and requires little more than the equipment to run the games. A crucial element in this structure is that it serves to keep esports in a separate category from other high school sports. These organizations accept the second-class status of esports as less than a sport and seek to continue esports as a niche club activity.

John J. Kim/Chicago Tribune/Tribune News Service via Getty Images

High school esports players have a number of competitive options.

Through its partnership with the NFHS, the PlayVS model establishes esports as a legitimate sport on par with any other high school sport or activity. It provides a full-stack platform that uses publisher integration to seamlessly coordinate matches and track statistics. While these features provide a more holistic experience, the platform limits the number of game titles based on the number of publishers currently partnering with PlayVS. The platform also handles leagues, scheduling, and much of the logistical support the previous model requires players to do themselves. For the benefit of these features, participation is currently $64 per player, per season.

While operating in all 50 U.S. states, as of 2020, PlayVS had partnered with 23 state associations to make esports an official sport or activity. Therefore, teams are required to have a coach, players must maintain academic eligibility, and competitions take place on school grounds. Early indications show that these structures prove useful for acquainting skeptics with the idea of esports as a legitimate sport.

Despite the appetite for esports at the high school level, numerous challenges remain on the path to widespread adoption. Beginning with generalities, a reality of most state associations (necessary stakeholders for nationwide adoption) is that their decision makers are often hesitant to trust or, in some instances, openly hostile to the idea of high school esports. The reason for this attitude may be generational. To people who did not grow up with a level of gaming ubiquity, video games themselves can seem foreign, niche, and antisocial. For some people, introducing games into a school setting is a nonstarter.

These ideas, as well as entrenched negative stereotypes about what a gamer is, work against the rising tide of esports growth. These sentiments are by no means unique to state associations. Administrators, athletic directors, parents, and teachers have also expressed apprehension about an esports program for these reasons. The answer to this problem, as with the numerous misconceptions surrounding esports and gaming in general, is education and exposure.

Education disarms skeptics with undeniable data; both quantitative numbers and qualitative anecdotes can be equally useful. The sheer size of the gaming industry often intrigues many skeptics because of its obvious link to future job opportunities. Individual accounts of esports being the key to unlocking engagement in a student on the fringes of dropping out are common. They convey a commonality between traditional sports and esports, namely, increased student engagement. In addition, schools are using esports to integrate soft skills into their curricula. Critical thinking, collaboration, communications, creativity, and other skills are essential to education in the 21st century. Leveraging an activity that students are inherently motivated to participate in (esports) while giving guided and reflective opportunities (through coaching) to build these soft skills is a huge opportunity for schools.

Concerns over privacy and IT also give pause to many in the educational community when adopting esports. The collection and use of personal data, particularly that of students, is of great concern. The fact is that the sorts of games in which students compete are large multimillion-dollar productions with plenty of resources devoted to upholding the integrity of user data. Concerns over these titles running on school servers do not hold up to significant scrutiny. The ability to whitelist specific IPs for competition keeps the narrow lane of external network access isolated to esports and nothing else. It is another instance of education leading to more widespread adoption. It is incumbent on any esports advocate to ensure that the apprehension decision makers feel at any level is not rooted in a lack of understanding.

After a year and a half of existence, PlayVS expanded its reach to 23 partnered states—nearly one-half of the country. A partnered state is an official partnership with and sanctioning by the governing state athletic association. It means that each individual state association has accepted esports as an official varsity sport or activity. Going from 0 to 18 partnered states in such a short time emphasizes the power of these arguments. However, the fact that two-thirds of the country are still without a partnership illustrates that resistance still exists to the adoption of esports.

While growth to date has yet to reach its full potential, the emergence of esports into the wider culture and in high schools appears imminent. From spring of 2019 to fall of 2019, PlayVS doubled the number of schools, students, and partnered states participating. The appetite for esports is ravenous. It is up to advocates to navigate institutional bureaucracies and help administrators see the value in bringing this sort of competition to their students. It may take longer than expected, but the number of high schools offering esports will rise substantially in the coming years.

TIER 3 STAKEHOLDERS

Tier 3 has the lowest impact for engaged stakeholders. The focus on stakeholder analysis is on those who have a current potential impact on the industry, which does not necessarily mean high level of interest or involvement. Therefore, this tier may include people who do not play esports or even those who are antagonistic toward it. For example, parents might not be interested in esports, but they can control the buying behavior of their minor children and as such could be a legitimate stakeholder for the industry. While parents, coaches, gamblers, and others all affect the industry, they have less of an impact than some of the higher-tier stakeholders discussed previously.

Esports Coaches and Managers Around the World

In addition to North America, Europe and East Asia (mainly China and South Korea) are regions with a developed esports industry. The selection and training mechanism, requirements for professionalism, working methods, and current situations of esports coaches and managers vary according to political, social, and cultural differences in these regions.

In Europe, traditional sports clubs (e.g., football clubs) have entered the esports industry. As a result, training and coaching programs of esports coaches are beginning to homogenize with programs of traditional sports coaches. Esports coaches start their career in small clubs in lower-tier leagues or youth teams that are associated with larger clubs, and they eventually climb to higher-end clubs and leagues. However, esports professionalism is still in the early stage of development. Hot esports titles are changing fast, so currently no qualification or license system is required for esports coaches to assume their position in a way that is similar to football and basketball.

In South Korea, esports is a major industry regulated by government. Training of esports players and coaches tends to occur in an official academy model such as the Game Coach Academy (Kim 2018), a Seoul-based government-accredited gaming camp. According to Lee Seung-hun, its director, the academy is dedicated to bringing clarity and structure to a fledgling industry that does not yet have a well-defined career trajectory (Kim and Bae 2018).

China has one of the biggest esports markets in the world. However, it does not have a mature professional sports model like those in North America and Europe, and it does not have the level of political support from the government that South Korea has. The selection and training mechanism of esports coaches in China at this stage depends on the esports clubs themselves.

No matter the environment, how the club performs in competition will dictate the interests and actions of other stakeholders such as managers, players, fans, and sponsors. It is inevitable for coaches to have contact with these colleagues during their daily work; assistance from others can take significant pressure off a coach. At the same time, it may be a good idea for coaches to maintain some distance from these stakeholders in order to carry out their job while avoiding any potential conflicts of interest or perception of favoritism toward any individual or group. Thus, an excellent esports coach should not only produce good player performance, daily training, developing and executing tactics, and competition results; the coach needs to exhibit great psychological qualities, leadership skills, interpersonal relationships, communication, and teaching skills. Coaches continually balance their skills and style with numerous stakeholders, often with competing interests (read more about this in chapter 13).

In Asia, where the attitude of *winning is everything* dominates the esports environment, generally the threshold of becoming an esports coach is very low; game knowledge is the only requirement. Because of the potentially high number of games being played, many teams are staffed with multiple coaches. The size of a coaching staff depends on the size of the club and the type and popularity of the esports title. A standard esports coaching team is usually composed of a head coach, an assistant coach, and an analyst. Currently, no special attention is given to esports coaching segmentation. Budget limitations, lack of effective systems for dividing coaching responsibilities, and ignorance from managers can interfere with a coaching staff's success. This leads to an extremely high-intensity work environment for coaches, especially the head coach. In China and South Korea, a head coach may work 10 to 12 hours a day; during major events, they may work more than 18 hours a day.

Another major concern for many esports coaches is poor broader academic or business knowledge. Some coaches are not equipped to deal with problems outside the realm of games, which tend to be their main focus. Coaches need to be more than just experts in a game; they need marketing, publicity, and financial skills. Their lack of training in these areas can result in passive avoidance and silence when faced with questions and criticism. Coaches also have lower social media exposure and fan support compared with their players, potentially leading to ego-based conflicts. In South Korea, a society with a strict social code (in terms of formality used in young–old and superior–subordinate relationships), public opinion can restrict noise from fans, help coaches maintain their authority, and minimize some of the coaches' weaknesses. China does not have the same social environment, so when a conflict arises between a coach and a player, usually public opinion supports the latter. As a result, the coach may become a victim of the club that is interested in stabilizing fans and ensuring positive social media coverage.

Income for esports coaches is currently not stable worldwide. The exception is coaches in clubs who compete in top leagues or big clubs with multiple esports title departments. Within smaller, amateur-level clubs, coaches may hold unpaid positions (British Esports Association 2019). A robust social welfare system such as those in Canada and many European countries (or a strong internal recultivation and reemployment system in esports industry similar to that of South Korea) can help coaches solve their financial worries to a certain extent and allow them to concentrate on coaching. China generally does not have these two conditions, so if coaches cannot be reemployed in the industry or develop their own business with accumulated personal resources, it is more difficult for Chinese esports coaches to reintegrate into society and find a suitable job in other industries. Inability to obtain professional respect, high work pressure, unstable income, difficult career transition after retirement, and other concerns harm the ability for Chinese coaches to thrive even though China has millions of esports athletes and many professional players.

Some former coaches have reentered the field as esports club managers. Management tasks for an esports club are primarily divided into these two parts:

- Logistic support around players and coaches including training, travelling, competition, and health protection
- External work related to player transactions, advertising sponsorship, livestreaming contracts, ticket sales, media promotion, fan and community outreach, and the like

Each club has a different focus based on its operating strategies. When it involves player trading and daily activities, managers must communicate with the head coach, so a manager who was a former player or has prior coaching experience can facilitate the execution of works. However, the professional competence and ethics of managers are not consistent at this stage. In South Korea's social environment, excessive power-endowed managers can easily lead to their abuse. In China, where clubs are operated like family businesses, money and nepotism help drive decision making for clubs. Some managers get their positions with inadequate playing or coaching experience, minimal professional management knowledge, and little ethics. As a result, in several cases, managers have been able to succeed on their own. However, in other cases, often due to public pressure, they have undertaken activities that undercut the coaches in order to keep or save their own jobs.

In addition, given the wide range of formal education of many professional esports players and coaches, a professional management team should also take responsibility for their continued educational growth and career transition planning after retirement from esports. Because of the esports industry's unique structure and because differences exist in culture, policies, and club operating models, coaching varies in different regions. Many esports regions are still in development; as the industry matures, it will experience significant growth in standardizing professional coaching.

Gamblers

Gambling is a major component of the sport industry. A recent U.S. Supreme Court decision has allowed more states to offer sport-related gambling. Both live and mobile gambling are fixtures in Las Vegas and Atlantic City, but these

Zoning

CAN A GOVERNMENT BE A STAKEHOLDER?

Gil Fried

Many people have no interest or direct involvement in esports but may still be considered stakeholders. For example, numerous government officials all over the world might not be esports players and might know very little about esports, but they could make policy decisions or develop government offices that support esports. As such, they are potential advocates for esports, and those involved in esports would be wise to cultivate positive relationships with them. In fact, five Asian governments have significantly backed the esports movement.

The most supportive national government so far has been South Korea. In the 1990s, the country tried to boost its broadband capabilities and esports gained popularity. Soon thereafter, South Korean television networks (with government support) began broadcasting esports. The Korea e-Sports Association (KeSPA) was then established by the South Korean government to help develop esports. The government worked with game publishers (e.g., Blizzard) to help promote tournaments. Esports blossomed in South Korea, with many parents paying over $1,000 a month for their children to attend prestigious esports training schools. Professional gaming has become a dream job in South Korea. Some professional gamers are treated similarly to major actors or K-pop stars. These examples show the value that can be generated from government support. The South Korean government is still aggressively supporting esports and gaming, including implementing new laws to help prevent abuse.

China became an early adopter of esports. The country hosted major international tournaments such as the Esports World Convention (formerly known as the Electronic Sports World Cup) and the World Cyber Games (WCG). In 2003, China's General Administration of Sport (GAS) declared esports as an official sport. In 2012 and 2013, the GAS helped host the WCG. While government has the power to promote esports, it also has the power to create restrictions. In 2019, the Chinese government cracked down on esports publisher Tencent, demanding they limit the number of hours people could play in China.

In 2014, the Indonesian government officially recognized and supported esports by creating the Indonesia Esports Association (IESPA), which became a formal entity under the State Ministry of Youth and Sports Affairs. The Indonesian government threw more support behind esports in 2018 when it hosted the Asian Games and included esports as a demonstration event.

The Philippines is one of the few countries in the world where top-tier esports players are considered as bona fide athletes under the country's legislation. This recognition helps ease the players' struggles in getting visas to local area network (LAN) events in other countries, which is a perennial problem for esports players in the region.

The Philippines established the National Sports Association (NSA) and the Esports National Association of the Philippines (ESNAP) to promote esports in the country. The Philippines also classified esports athletes as legitimate athletes under the law, allowing them to more easily obtain visas to travel to tournaments.

Malaysia appointed an avid *Dota 2* player (Syed Saddiq Abdul Rahman) as the Minister for Sports, and he promised significant support to develop esports in Malaysia. This support included receiving significant funding ($2.4 million) from the central government (Raghuram 2018).

While government involvement can be beneficial, it can also lead to challenges. For example, a major dispute erupted between KeSPA and Blizzard Entertainment (and GOMTV, a Korean streaming service and a broadcasting channel) over KeSPA's decision to prevent its players from competing in the 2012 Global *StarCraft II* League (GSL) Season 4. In a relatively new industry, a dispute over which players are allowed to compete could cause significant damage. Government regulation will also continue to be a major concern for esports, especially in the areas of net neutrality and Internet transfer speed. Net neutrality refers to the fact that Internet providers need to treat everyone on the Internet the same and governments can demand such behavior from Internet service providers (ISPs). Governments can also demand that Internet transfer speeds meet certain criteria, such as not slowing down at certain times or after certain amounts of usage. Such speed changes can significantly impact gamers.

cities pale in comparison to the global sport betting experience. Some estimate that Macau and Hong Kong, with their position in Asia, might represent almost half of all sport-related gambling. Soccer (football) and basketball have numerous dedicated gambling sites and companies where a fan can bet on almost anything associated with a game, including elements associated with nonsport activities such as who might win a coin flip to start a game.

No reliable numbers exist as to the size of the sport betting industry, primarily because the legal sport betting market is significantly lower than the illegal sport betting market. The same concerns apply to esports betting. Esports gambling is similar to sport gambling. Some estimates predicted that esports betting would reach around $13 billion by 2020. Unfortunately, COVID-19 had a significant impact on esports-related events and gambling, so it is impossible to know whether $13 billion was reached, but it is estimated once things return to "normal" the total handle should far surpass $13 billion (Everett 2019). Major betting houses in esports include Betway, Lootbet, Cyberbet, and GG.bet. Betway, which was founded in 2006, is a relatively newer company that has leveraged the Internet to allow online wagering (compared with in-person betting). The company boasts a large number of games people can bet on, including *CS:GO*, *League of Legends*, *Dota 2*, *Overwatch*, *Hearthstone*, *World of Tanks*, and *StarCraft II*. They carry not only the major tournaments but also smaller events. Bettors can bet on a variety of options besides whether a team will win a match, such as win–draw–win, correct score, outright, to win, double chance, handicap, and totals. For more information, sources such as Betwayesports (2020) provide detailed information about different betting choices and options.

With so much money at stake, a significant amount of organized crime is involved in sport. Esports is no exception. The concern related to organized crime and possible money laundering and match fixing was seen in 2019 in Australia. An Australian *Overwatch* team was being investigated over suspicions of match fixing. It was part of a bigger investigation into esports and crime, and several Australian *CS:GO* players were served with warrants over match fixing claims. Victoria Police's Sporting Integrity Intelligence Unit was also investigating organized crime links to the ownership of an Australian team that played in the *Overwatch* Contenders league (Henry 2019).

International Fans

Esports fans are generally people who admire or support an esports player, an esports title, or an esports club. They are also people who watch or participate in esports events (including professional and amateur events) or frequently play esports games (iResearch Center 2019). Participation in traditional sports is subject to time, venue, equipment, number of people, and physical conditions. In contrast, esports has more flexible and diverse participation methods. Therefore, esports fans are more practical than traditional sports fans, reflected in the fact that the number of players only is much higher than the number of viewers only of the main esports titles in the market (Pannekeet 2019). However, traditional sports and esports are similar in some ways, such as fan classification based on behavioral segments (Wragg 2017, p. 8), and fan habits or behaviors affected by regional and cultural diversity.

For example, Asian fans pay a lot of attention to the group and social nature of esports activities. According to Nielsen esports data surveys titled "Influences in becoming an eSports fan" in 2017 (Pike and Master 2017, para. 11) and "Where fans are being introduced to eSports" in 2018 (Pike and Port 2018, para. 6), 47 percent of fans in South Korea and 45 percent of fans in China indicated that friends and family members introduced them to esports. In contrast, among the major European and American countries, 46 percent of fans in France, 38 percent of fans in Germany, 37 percent of fans in the United States, and 35 percent of fans in the United Kingdom indicated that friends and family members introduced them to the genre. In the words of Sebastian Radu (former CEO of ESL Asia), "The Asian markets, specifically China, Japan and South Korea, share common cultural values and behavioral patterns. Unlike the more individualistic centered cultures, such as the US or Europe, for Asians the group cohesion and harmony is extremely valuable" (Pike and Master 2017, p. 15).

Meanwhile, female esports fans in China and South Korea (the two biggest esports markets in Asia) account for 39 percent (China) and 38 percent (South Korea) of the fan base (Pike and Port 2018, p. 7). Those percentages are much higher than the world average of 29 percent and very close to the percentage of female fans in traditional sports, which is 39 percent (Pike and Master 2017, para. 5).

In recent years, female fans have significantly contributed to the global esports market. There are two main reasons. First, compared with male fans, female fans tend to pay more attention to the social nature of games, are more willing to share their gaming experience, and are also more easily affected by hot topics in social media (Xinhua 2019). The most popular esports genres in the market (MOBA, battle royale, FPS, and survival) provide real-time interaction in the game and endless game-related topics on social media platforms, which resonate with female fans. In 2018, the most popular esports title in China was the MOBA mobile game *Wangzhe Rongyao* (meaning "Honor of Kings" and known in English as *King of Glory*), developed and published by Tencent Games. With a portable gaming platform (mobile phone), fragmented time utilization (15 to 20 minutes per round), and convenient registration methods (QQ or WeChat account), the popularity of *King of Glory* in China and particularly with female fans around the world far exceeded other titles such as *League of Legends* (developed by Riot Games, a wholly owned subsidiary of Tencent) (Pike and Port 2018, p. 13).

Second, in recent years, the esports industry has connected with other entertainment industries. Fan groups who were originally active in other entertainment industries (such as music and movies) have gotten involved in esports activities. In Asia, idol culture, which is similar to when star players in traditional sports have a group of devoted die-hard fans, significantly affects the esports industry. In the past couple years and with a stronger economy, the consumption habits of younger Asians have become closer to the habits of European and U.S. fans. Esports fans (usually young people under 30) are more avant-garde, are more aggressive, pay more attention to customized service and sense of belonging (compared with price performance in consumption), and enjoy sharing their consumption experience in their social circle. Therefore, regardless of direct revenue or benefits from indirect Internet traffic, esports clubs need to establish and maintain a fan community and produce content that fans want. In recent years, led by game publishers and local government support, a significant number of international esports clubs have begun to imitate the home-and-away system used by professional sports leagues, hoping to develop a more stable local fan base.

Currently, most esports clubs are still unable to maintain their daily expenses with tickets,

Hannah Foslien/Getty Images

Fans at esports events are a lot like fans at sports events.

merchandises, broadcasting, and sponsorship income similar to traditional professional sports clubs. Therefore, the fan economy will play an important role in the esports market. "Fandom is a harbinger of cultural phenomena to come" (Baym 2007, p. 2). All esports practitioners, including game publishers, event producers, clubs, players, coaches, streamers, etc., need to improve their ability to connect with fans and to meet the needs of diverse fan groups.

U.S. Fans

Imagine you are attending a major traditional sporting event such as basketball, baseball, or football. You look to your left and see a wave of fans wearing team jerseys or other paraphernalia associated with the organization. You look at the field and see the team's mascots on the sidelines cheering on your favorite team. Then, you look to your right and see an obnoxious drunk man with his shirt misplaced while yelling his team's name or chant. His body is covered from head to toe with body paint in the team's colors, and he's wearing a foam object on his head in the team's honor. Each person in this scenario is expressing a different level of fandom. Esports fans are analogous; the casual fan may be wearing their team's jersey while hardcore fans have their face painted, signs with witty sayings, or merchandise associated with the game. The major difference between esports and traditional sports fans is the prevalence of **cosplayers**, people who are dressed and act like the character they are portraying from their game. The pool of fans at every major esports event includes casual fans, hardcore fans, and cosplayers.

Casual Fans

Casual fans represent the majority of esports fans. They typically know the names of their favorite players and own a piece of their favorite team's merchandise. In 2018, Riot Games added all LCS team jerseys to their merchandising online store; teams could sell the same official jersey that the teams wore for $60. Fans could also purchase items directly from the team stores if they wanted a custom jersey with their in-game names printed on the back. Riot Games has also had team icons available to fans since 2013. The purchase of these icons, which display as the players load into their game, typically cost between $1 and $2, with some of the proceeds directly benefiting the teams. In 2019, Riot Games also added an in-game team pass, which allowed fans to purchase and complete in-game missions in order to unlock special team-related skins for Braum, a popular character in *League of Legends*. These items are often purchased by casual fans.

Hardcore Fans

Hardcore fans are more extreme in terms of their commitment to supporting their team. These fans have purchased most of the previously mentioned merchandise and in-game content as well as doing more to show their commitment. These fans are known to tattoo their favorite team's logos, dye their hair, or purchase more merchandise to support the game. Hardcore fans are also passionate about the general game in addition to an LCS team. Riot Games has a full merchandising store dedicated to in-game characters in the form of small statues, plush dolls, T-shirts, onesies, and even an award-winning board game. One Reddit user, u/SitoSama, owns one of every item available at riotmerch.com; items range from $10 to $100 each. Some items are available only to those who have visited LCS events, especially in the earlier days of *League of Legends*. These items included the coveted stress balls thrown into the stands by Riot Games' staff and LCS players as well as lanyards handed out depicting various characters on the front and back. These items, which are now considered rare, can sell for hundreds of dollars on third-party sites. These items have also created a secondary and counterfeit market selling products to collectors at a reasonable price.

Cosplayers

Cosplayers are sometimes a middle ground between hardcore and casual fans. A cosplayer can be a casual fan of the game who plays for only a few hours each week, or even a casual fan of the professional teams who barely watches any games on the weekends. Cosplayers are more likely to immerse themselves in the world and lore of the games. They have been featured in several short Riot Games documentaries and have gathered large followings on social media platforms like Twitter and Instagram. A short film titled *Thresh: Making a Monster* was released in July of 2016. It depicted a studio creating a 7-foot (2.13 m) replica of the character, Thresh. The replica was supposed to be a scale model of the character in game. It was operational as a large puppet and engineered to be worn by a single person. The costume was displayed during the 2016 LCS finals at Madison Square Garden. Other content creators have made replica weapons, jewelry, merchandise, or other paraphernalia associated with *League of Legends*.

Riot Games has also sanctioned fan meet-and-greets before or after major events as well as attendee-only experiences for those present at the events. Fans can always view major events on all major streaming platforms, but the true fans attend these events in person. In 2016, Riot Games created a full, in-depth experience for fans to see not only cosplayers from across the United States but also fan art and the history behind the sights and sounds of the LCS. The exhibit spanned the entire interior of the Pennsylvania Hotel ballroom and lounge, located across the street from Madison Square Garden. Fans could also meet with their favorite players or content creators before the finals, and many fans were willing to pay for these individuals to sign various articles of clothing or other items. Team Liquid, one of the teams playing in the third-place match, had their own analyst signing posters announcing an event that would be held in Washington Park the next evening. So many fans came to the event that the New York State Police closed the event 20 minutes after it began due to public safety concerns. Once the team began to leave, fans continued to follow the players and staff until the team asked police to prevent them from following the members.

Fans make the games more enjoyable, and U.S. fans are always willing to show up to events. U.S. fans of esports are similar to those of traditional sports; they are passionate and willing to express why their team is the best team in the region. They are even willing to put aside their own dignity to show their unbridled support for their teams and games, a commitment that others may find exuberant or inappropriate. Casual fans, hardcore fans, and cosplayers alike are not only passionate about the teams and players but also the sport.

Parents and Children

The rapid growth of esports has led to a large volume of minors who have had success playing games and a large volume of children who are interested in esports. It is important for parents to understand how they can get their children involved, understand the concerns with online video games, and understand the benefits of participating in esports. According to Pew Research, 92 percent of teen boys and 75 percent of teen girls have access to a video game console in the United States (Perrin 2018).

Children have multiple avenues to begin competing in esports. They can begin with informal individual competitions at home, join organized leagues or tournaments in a recreation setting, or start in a high school club setting or a high school team that is part of an esports league.

Zoning

PROFESSIONAL SPORTS STAKEHOLDERS

Gil Fried

An increasing number of connections exist between traditional sports and esports. From esports and video game versions of traditional sports (e.g., *FIFA*, *Madden*, *NBA 2K*) to professional athletes of traditional sports playing esports and video games to these players using games to scout opponents or practice tactics and techniques, traditional sports and esports have a strong relationship. Another growing and important connection is based on opportunities for professional athletes of traditional sports to invest in esports companies or franchises.

One such example is the video game discovery platform Skillz. In November of 2019, the National Football League's (NFL's) investment arm, 32 Equity, invested in the platform (Cohen 2019). Skillz has more than 30 million players, manages more than 4 million daily tournament entries, distributes $60 million in monthly prizes, and is currently ranked as the fastest growing company in the United States on the Inc. 5000 list (Skillz 2020).

Opportunities for Informal Competition

Children are able to compete in esports on mobile devices, home consoles, or home computers. The easiest way to begin competing on an informal level is to identify what game and gaming device the child wants to try, and to purchase or download the appropriate game. Parents should ensure that the appropriate parental controls have been set prior to allowing a child to engage in online gaming. Online safety is addressed in detail later in the chapter.

Young players often learn about certain games from their friends. Then, they try to develop a basic knowledge of these games at home in order to share a common language and experience with their peers.

Opportunities for Recreational Competition

Children also have the opportunity to get involved with more structured and organized events. There are multiple private recreational opportunities and some city recreational departments have starting hosting esports events (Bhatt 2019). Various private recreational opportunities are available in many communities across the globe. In 2019, Evolve Youth Sports hosted esports events for kids in *Fortnite*, *Super Smash Bros. Ultimate*, and *Rocket League* on their website. The cost for participating was $150 for an eight-week session. Kids received a jersey for signing up and had the chance to win additional prizes. They had four players per team, one weekly practice, and one weekly match. The format closely resembled the format of traditional youth sport leagues.

In 2019, the National Recreation and Park Association (NRPA) discussed the growth in esports and encouraged local departments to consider adding esports programming to their upcoming schedules. The reasons behind wanting to expand into esports were to target teens and young adults, a demographic that is currently difficult for parks and recreation departments to attract. In addition to attracting a new audience, parks and recreation departments view esports as a way to better use city facilities and generate revenue.

Opportunities for High School Competition

Many U.S. high schools field esports teams. The NFHS partnered with PlayVS to govern most competitive esports teams on the high school level. Typically a small fee is associated with competing, and teams are open to both male and female competitors. At the time of this writing, 23 state high school associations offered competitive programs through PlayVS.

Concerns About Esports Opportunities

A number of concerns exist for children and young adults playing esports online. Cyberbullying, or the bullying of others online, is one of the larger concerns. It may take place over voice chat or within chat channels. These channels often exist in the game itself but may also exist in third-party platforms such as Discord or on streaming platforms such as Twitch.

In January 2020, an important article was published in *The New York Times* highlighting how esports and other types of electronic games have turned into a breeding ground for sexual predators (Bowles and Keller 2019). The article explored how sexual abuse and stalking were a major concern for parents and the industry. Sexual predators created an easy access point into the lives of young people by meeting them online through multiplayer video games and various chat apps. These bad actors strike up a conversation and try to gradually build trust through the common language of esports. These nefarious individuals often pose as children who are confiding in others, pretend to be victims, and spin false stories of hardship. The eventual goal is to trick others (primarily children) into sharing sexually explicit photos and videos. The bad actors will then try to blackmail the victim for more imagery, much of it increasingly graphic and violent.

Unfortunately, the nefarious use of online activities for potentially criminal reasons is not an unusual occurrence. In online environments, it is challenging for many people to identify potential perpetrators. As a result, predators use gaming activities and social media platforms to identify targets. While the environment is ripe for those wishing to conceal their identity and true motives, numerous examples exist of law enforcement intervening and arresting predators. For example, the authors of a *New York Times* article stated,

> In May, a California man was sentenced to 14 years in prison for coercing an 11-year-old girl into producing child pornography after meeting her through the online game

> *Clash of Clans*. A man in suburban Seattle got a 15-year sentence in 2015 for soliciting explicit imagery from 3 boys after posing as a teenager while playing *Minecraft* and *League of Legends*. An Illinois man received a 15-year sentence in 2017 after threatening to rape 2 boys in Massachusetts—adding that he would kill one of them—whom he had met over Xbox Live. (Bowles and Keller 2019, p. 3)

Educating children of these risks, imposing specific rules, and setting and enforcing appropriate privacy and parental control settings for the video games are strategies to help mitigate these risks. Similar to other new technologies that can raise concerns (e.g., social media), parental supervision and child education are crucial.

In addition to some of the safety risks is a growing increase in awareness of video game addiction. In 2018, the World Health Organization (WHO) recognized gaming disorder as a disease. In order to be diagnosed with gaming disorder, the gaming habit must result in "significant impairment in personal, family, social, education, occupation or other important areas of functioning" for at least 12 months (World Health Organization 2018, para. 2). In a 2018 survey from Pew Research, 41 percent of teenage boys stated they spend too much time playing video games.

Benefits of Esports Opportunities

All is not bad for esports and video games. Playing video games has been shown to have numerous cognitive benefits (Granic, Lobel, and Engels 2013). Shooting games have been shown to have a positive impact on **spatial resolution** and **visual processing**. In addition to these benefits, scientists have found that video games are a good medium for developing problem-solving skills. In a study of over 500 12-year-olds, Jackson et al. (2012) found that creativity had a positive association with video games.

Seen particularly in multiplayer games where communication and teamwork between players are needed, social skills can be gained and new friendships can be made through gaming. Players need to make decisions on who they can trust and who to cooperate with in a relatively short period of time. Prosocial video games have been shown to enhance prosocial skills in the real world (Ewoldsen et al. 2012).

CONCLUSION

Esports has a number of different stakeholders. Sometimes they have congruent plans and goals, and other times they can be at odds with each other. The publishers want game rules, the players want rules for fairness, the tournaments want rules for continuity, and teams want rules to help with preparation. They can all be on the same page for certain elements. In contrast, the marketing and revenue desires of some publishers might come in sharp contrast to what broadcasters, tournaments, and players might want to pursue as goals. Money is often the sticking point for many stakeholders.

There is no one way to resolve the potential conflicts between various stakeholders except to talk with one another. Since esports is still in its infancy, discussions to resolve common issues are ongoing. As more players enter the sector, the conflicts and competition between stakeholders are expected to grow.

DISCUSSION QUESTIONS

1. Who are the most important stakeholders in the esports industry?
2. What strategies and tactics can be used to improve the relationship between game publishers and other stakeholders?
3. Do you think government and Internet companies will play a major role in the future of esports? Explain.
4. What are the similarities and differences in esports between Asian countries and those in Europe or North America?
5. How can parents and coaches take on stronger roles as stakeholders in the esports environment?

5

Esports Governance

Gil Fried | Tobias M. Scholz | Jason Batzofin | Clint Kennedy
Sang-ho Lee | Lance Mudd | Michael Newhouse-Bailey
Colin Webster

INTRODUCTION

Imagine you wanted to play a basketball game. What rules would you follow? Would you use schoolyard rules, high school rules, collegiate rules, women's or men's rules, or FIBA or NBA rules? For a game to be fair and fun, someone has to develop and enforce rules.

The same concept applies to esports. While everyone may be playing the same game, is it the same if one person is a beginner and the other a professional player? Would it be fair if one person had an older operating system and poor peripheral equipment compared with someone who had the highest-quality equipment? Would it be fair if a coach abused a player, cheated at events, or plied players with drugs? Those questions drive the push for a strong governance system that esports players, coaches, fans, gamblers, sponsors, and other stakeholders can respect and support.

This chapter starts with an overview of governance that defines this important concept and explores its types and forms. It then presents a more specific discussion of governance in esports. That section leads into a specific analysis of various governance entities that is written mostly by people who are leading or are intimately involved with various governing bodies. Given the high turnover of esports organizations, covering them all would be impossible. However, care was taken to cover a range of esports governance organizations, including international, national, amateur, and professional organizations. The chapter concludes with a discussion and examination of governing esports in the same or similar ways as sports.

OBJECTIVES

- Identify the role governance plays in esports.
- Compare and contrast the different organizational styles that different esports organizations use.
- Explain the differences between the various esports organizations in the professional and collegiate esports space.
- Identify the similarities and differences between federations and associations.

DEFINING GOVERNANCE

The term **governance** refers to the rules, accountability, fairness, and similar issues between various members (people or entities) of an organization. The focus of governance is on establishing, monitoring, and enforcing policies created by the organization's governing body. Typically, a governing body is formed to balance the powers of the organization's members so that everyone can participate in a fair way. Fairness is a major driving force behind many organizations.

Imagine two race car drivers who finish a race only a few milliseconds apart; they need to decide who won. A neutral third party could be created to help monitor events, make sure they run smoothly, and develop rules for when someone is allowed to start and what constitutes a win. After some rules are developed and other racers see the value of them, more racers may join the organization to protect each other and give some legitimacy and fairness to racing. The organization could hold increasingly more events and develop a reputation for providing a fair environment for all participants. Having more events could encourage the organization to add rules for preventing cheating, setting an age minimum for drivers, determining what engines are appropriate for a given class of racing, and requiring specific safety gear for cars. These rules are often developed after an exception is raised. For example, perhaps a rule didn't exist regarding changing tires during a race, but after one racer engaged in that conduct, the organization had to develop rules to cover that conduct in future races. Organizations spend a lot of time dealing with exceptions in order to make sure events are as fair as possible.

Many governing organizations start with a few members and rules, then they expand both in membership and documentation. Growth could include officially operating as a nonprofit or a for-profit organization. Board members are usually elected to help run the organization. It could hold annual meetings during which the members vote on rules. Many organizations develop educational material to supplement rules. Sometimes several organizations in a similar field might unite to form a larger organization.

For example, the United States Olympic Committee (USOC) is the governing body for Olympic sports in the United States and is chartered by the U.S. federal government. The USOC membership is composed of U.S. national governing bodies for sports approved by the International Olympic Committee (IOC). Thus, if esports wanted to join the USOC, they would need the IOC to approve esports as an official Olympic sport. Then they would need to decide who is the official representative for esports in the United States and have a majority of esports entities agree to this representation. This complex process is one reason for so few occurrences of preliminary discussions to include esports in the Olympics. Esports does not have one overarching organization. In fact, a number of esports organizations could be considered in competition with each other, which can be a challenge for obtaining broader acceptance by the Olympic family.

The previous example is the typical process by which an organization is developed. People or organizations identify a need, then they work together to develop a governing body. Several issues affect the ability of esports to launch governing bodies, including the following:

- Traditional sports normally have one governing body for a given type/level of play. While the predominant professional basketball league is the National Basketball Association (NBA), the international governing body is the International Basketball Federation (FIBA). Between different levels of basketball (e.g., high school, college, professional), there are minor differences (e.g., the difference in the location of the three-point line). However, in most respects, basketball is nearly identical around the world. In contrast, every esports game is different, with different rules and different goals. As a result, creating a single international governing body to oversee all esports would require bringing together a multitude of different genres (first-person shooter, multiplayer online battle arena, sports, digital card games, etc.) of games.
- The vast number of publishers and games presents difficult decisions such as which publishers would be involved, which titles would be used, and which format would be followed.
- The big variety of stakeholders in esports presents challenges in developing a consensus.
- Esports is a rapidly growing industry that is still changing.
- Esports is played without a field, but online and Internet speed in different parts of the world can limit competition.
- The truly global nature of esports can create challenges such as governments limiting what games could be played in a given country.

One similarity between traditional sport and esports organizations is that both are often defined and stratified by geographical boundaries (e.g., New York Athletic Club), physical markets (e.g., Senior Games), weight divisions (heavyweight boxing), levels (e.g., high school, collegiate), and other criteria. Each group or level could create their own rules. For example, if a sport or esports organization is formed to represent athletes with disabilities, the organization could define what constitutes a disability. An organization could develop detailed approaches to identifying, testing, and vetting participants to ensure they meet the organization's definition of a given disability.

The difficulties associated with forming an esports organization have not stopped a number of entities from entering the space. While some esports organizations are interested in generating revenue, others might be interested in solving a problem in the industry. One example is the World Esports Association (WESA). WESA was founded in 2016 by the Electronic Sports League (now simply called ESL) and a number of leading esports teams. The organization was founded to help promote and professionalize esports through protecting players. That protection included an effort to represent players' interests and to allow players to share revenue. Advocating for additional player funding is not a problem, but if game publishers do not want to agree to any arrangement, then WESA may have only a limited number of options or actions it can use. To date, WESA has undertaken a number of important actions including outlining its jurisdiction, addressing the need for neutrality, addressing corruption, analyzing potential conflicts of interest, and dealing with other similar issues when they have arisen and action(s) need to be taken.

Once an organization interested in governing is formed, what specifically do they do? Multiple esports-related governing bodies exist, and they all have different agendas, but most have a primary focus, namely, solving an issue that will make the sport better for all stakeholders. The Esports Integrity Commission (ESIC) was formed in 2016 with a set of principles that examined integrity, fairness, enforcement of codes, recognizing sanctions, sharing appropriate information, and confidentiality. The ESIC is a membership-based organization representing publishers, leagues, media platforms, tournament organizers, various gambling authorities, and gaming regulation entities. It is the ideal type of governing organization because it identified an issue, developed broad support to address that issue, then implemented a program to benefit the industry.

Only a limited number of organizations can focus primarily on competitive integrity and preventing cheating. However, esports organizations could try to provide guidance in other areas, including the following:

- Rules of play
- Players' rights (avoiding player exploitation)
- Age-related protections
- League rules
- Intellectual property rights
- Doping
- Gambling

No matter what areas an esports organization might try to address, in order to succeed, it needs to be transparent with everything it does. When organizations operate in the dark, they lose credibility and eventually fail with stakeholders.

TYPES OF GOVERNANCE

Regardless of their organizational structure and level, it is important to know the differences between various organizations and the scope of what they can do. A **federation** is an organization composed of a set of smaller organizations, individuals, groups, and companies that join because they want to bring attention to issues important to its members. A key element of a federation is that each individual entity maintains control over its own operations and does not let the federation determine its direction or actions. A great example is the IOC. Each of its member nations has a vote. Whether a country is the size or population of China or India or a small island nation, each one has a say. Similarly, each country has its own national governing body that can control its own policies and procedures as long as they are consistent with the IOC rules. Thus, a country can have its own drug detection and monitoring program, and that program needs to be consistent with IOC requirements. A country may try to skirt IOC rules and work to pursue its own strategies, and the consequence of getting caught is punishment by the IOC. The key to success is that the federation members have agreed to abide by specific rules as part of their membership. The same holds true for the NCAA in terms of college athletics. In esports, the same holds true for an organization such as IESF and the ECAC.

Federations might start with a certain number of members, and then other members can join. Membership can be extended to others who adopt the federation's governing rules and regulations.

Thus, an external entity can decide to create its own organization and get others to join, and this organization can become a federation. Each organization can decide to join if they wish. However, if they want to be part of the federation, they must follow its rules.

An **association** differs from a federation in that it is a group of individuals or organizations gathered together for a joint effort or purpose. They do not need to be equal parties joined together to form a federation. Thus, an association can have different forms of membership such as corporations, academic institutions, or individuals. In order to maintain membership in the association, members only have to follow certain minimal rules such as paying a yearly fee.

Associations can be created for any reason; members can find like-minded entities, individuals, or others who might want to join to pursue a common goal. For example, a group of individual esports athletes can form a club focused on a specific game. This group is an association of like-minded players who enjoy that game. At any time, a player can decide they no longer want to play the game or be part of the association. In contrast, it is much harder to leave a federation, which may have contractual obligations that impose significant penalties. For example, if a major college wants to leave their current athletic conference to join another conference, they can. However, they have to pay millions of dollars to leave their old conference and millions more to join another conference. The cost is determined by the parties to the conference (which is a federation). It might be that no other federation is available to join, so if an esports team leaves one league, it might not be able to join another.

The distinction might seem minimal, but it is significant because governance helps determine how an organization will operate. Esports has seen both federations and associations. Each type has faced challenges. A university interested in starting an esports team could decide to launch an esports club. That club would need to follow rules and regulations that apply to all other clubs on campus. The university could also decide to launch a varsity esports team, which raises a number of questions. For example, how would the university define *varsity*? Does that mean it is part of the athletics department? Will it be subject to NCAA rules? If so, how can they be enforced given that the NCAA does not have a division associated with esports? The university's team can compete in informal scrimmages and might join a number of associations such as a regional group of like-minded universities. Several associations may exist, each associated with a different game. Joining these associations can be a simple step, such as agreeing to play other schools. If the university wants to drop out and not play a given game, it can do so without any repercussions. If the team will join an esports organization, the process might be significantly different. The university might have to complete an application, and part of that application process might include agreeing to specific terms such as what constitutes eligibility, the number of hours esports athletes can train, when athletes can be coached, and when tournaments are held.

This federation would be a more formal process and organization. Similar to NACE, schools can be part of a more exclusive organization. However, the university can choose which federation to join, whether a federation might accept it, and whether it might want to maintain a more informal path going forward. Thus, the university would need to pursue a choice based on what it hopes to accomplish with the esports team. A formal approach (federation) might provide significant structure and legitimacy from the beginning. A less-structured approach (association) allows more flexibility as the team tries to find its way and determine what it might want to do.

What separates esports from other sport federations is that a publisher can change a game. Thus, a federation established to play *League of Legends* would need to have the involvement of the publisher in order to be effective. Without the publisher, a federation can make as many rules as it wants, but it would not necessarily affect the game and a publisher would not need to follow the rules or recommendations. Associations can partner with a publisher, but they can also partner with multiple publishers or none at all.

Esports governance occurs at many levels. Although few definitive organizations exist at this point, one can consider organizations that are attempting to govern at the international, national, high school, college, and professional levels.

INTERNATIONAL ESPORTS FEDERATION (IESF)

Established in 2008 and based in Busan, South Korea, the International Esports Federation (IESF) is a nonprofit organization made up of 72 national esports member federations. The IESF works consistently to promote esports as a true sport transcending language, gender, race, and cultural barriers. The organization has established robust policies that ensure the welfare of its participants and protect the integrity of esports. Structurally, it comprises a board whose members usually serve a four-year term and are duly elected by member federations.

As an international federation for esports, the IESF's charge includes hosting international esports tournaments; expanding the range of member nations; and establishing standards for referees, players, certifications, titles, and competitions. The IESF has these four primary directives:

1. Increase the number of member nations.
2. Advocate for international esports standardization in which the IESF can help develop statutes and regulation for professional esports.
3. Raise the level of training for esports referees through the creation and operation of the International Esports Referee Academy.
4. Host world esports tournaments such as the Esports World Championship.

The Esports World Championship is one of the only international esports events where players compete while representing their country. IESF aims to broaden the opportunities for amateur players and enlarge the global esports foundation, which would ultimately lead to the final goal of building a comprehensive global esports structure for cooperation, collaboration, and competition. IESF holds its annual Global Executive Esports Summit (GEES) to share ideas between key stakeholders in different esports industries to align understandings and ensure esports develops in the right direction and manner. The summit also involves the international traditional sport community in an open discussion about the potential of esports and the potential synergy between esports and traditional sports.

In 2018, through the launch of the Global Esports R&D Center, the IESF created three initiatives to help accomplish their stated directives: the creation of the Esports Academic Research Center, the International Training Center, and the International Esports Referee Academy. The Esports Academic Research Center supports and conducts esports-focused research; the International Training Center is focused on providing a location for esports training, research, demonstrations, and education; and the International Esports Referee Academy will develop and provide education, training, and certification for international esports referees. The IESF also supports career transitions for retired professional players and provides opportunities for people outside the esports industry to join and engage with the industry.

UNITED STATES ESPORTS FEDERATION (USEF)

The United States Esports Federation (USEF) is a nonprofit national federation and is the governing body for esports in the United States, as recognized by the IESF. As a national federation, the USEF runs qualifiers and other events in the United States to promote safe gaming and participation. Athletes who qualify for USEF events compete domestically and globally among the members of the IESF.

The USEF's mission is to promote, grow, and develop the quality, diversity, and beauty of esports as part of the fabric of American communities for generations to come. The organization seeks to nurture, inspire, and protect athletes and esports culture and to unite all esports stakeholders, including athletes, event organizers, technology producers, innovators and inventors, IP holders, parents, sponsors, and fans.

As it continues to develop internationally and among the traditional sports movement, esports presents an opportunity to athletes, fans, and countries that currently doesn't exist in typical sports. Traditionally, events such as the Fédération Internationale de Football Association (FIFA) World Cup, the Olympics, and the Pan-American Games bring the best athletes from around the world together. These events are major cultural experiences in which each athlete from their respective country can have the opportunity to

Zoning

INTRODUCTION TO THE INTERNATIONAL ESPORTS FEDERATION (IESF)

Colin Webster

Founded in 2008, the IESF was the first international federation for esports. Although it started with only 8 original members, it quickly grew to a membership of 72 national federations as of June 2020. The purpose of IESF is highlighted in its statutes. In essence, the mission is to help foster the growth of national federations and promote every aspect of esports as a full-fledged sport governing body. Thus, every move made by IESF has been to solidify esports as a sport. Realizing that this huge task could not be done alone, IESF has embarked on partnerships with many other institutions, summarized here:

- 2013—Became a signatory of World Anti-Doping Agency (WADA)
- 2014—Affiliated with The Association for International Sport for All (TAFISA)
- 2015—Signed a memorandum of understanding (MOU) with International Amateur Athletics Federation (IAAF)
- 2016—Signed a MOU with AliSports
- 2016—Began a partnership with World Cyber Arena (WCA)
- 2017—Signed a MOU with International University Sports Federation (FISU)
- 2017—Signed a MOU with International Table Tennis Federation (ITTF)
- 2019—Signed a MOU with City of Busan
- 2019—Signed a MOU with Dubai Sports Council

The IESF also negotiates constantly with publishers in order to encourage a greater sense of community and shared vision and values.

IESF ran its first World Championship in 2009. Since then, tournaments have evolved not only by making use of the latest developments in equipment but also by making use of the various methods to broadcast the event. Change has not been limited to technological advances; it has also occurred in the systems used in the championships in order to create a better event for all the participants.

The first IESF World Championship was held in South Korea. After significant changes were made to IESF's statutes, a democratic process was developed to allow any member to bid for the tournament. Thus in 2013, it was held outside of South Korea for the first time; Romania proved to be a successful and competent host. Although the tournament has returned to South Korea many times, it has been held successfully at other venues, too.

- 2009—Taebaek, South Korea
- 2010—Daegu, South Korea
- 2011—Andong, South Korea
- 2012—Cheonan, South Korea
- 2013—Bucharest, Romania
- 2014—Baku, Azerbaijan
- 2015—Seoul, South Korea
- 2016—Jakarta, Indonesia
- 2017—Busan, South Korea
- 2018—Kaohsiung, Chinese Taipei
- 2019—Seoul, South Korea

IESF also governs test matches held between its member federations. Due to the nature of esports, such test matches may be held online or face-to-face. Because face-to-face matches are both time consuming and expensive, many members opt to hold online test matches. It should be noted that such test matches, whether online or face-to-face, are governed by regulations to ensure a fair competition.

From the beginning, IESF has held a symposium at its general meeting. The symposium increased in popularity as industry leaders began to attend in order to better understand IESF's view of the

(continued)

INTRODUCTION TO THE INTERNATIONAL ESPORTS FEDERATION (IESF) *(CONTINUED)*

trajectory of esports. In 2016 IESF began holding its symposium separately from its general meeting and rebranded the symposium as Global Esports Executive Summit (GEES). The 2016 summit was held in Shanghai, China, and from 2017 through 2019 it was held in Busan, South Korea.

Esports finds itself in a fractious environment where many people seem to be in it for themselves. IESF is a community of national federations and other interested parties that seek to provide unity and stable growth. The biggest future challenge will be for IESF to fully convey its message of unity among the entire esports community, so that esports can be considered for inclusion in major sporting events such as the Olympic Games. To that end, IESF began an initiative to become a full-fledged member of the Global Association of International Sports Federations (GAISF) in 2017. At the end of 2019, IESF established a solid relationship with GAISF.

IESF also promotes standardization in esports in order to provide esports-oriented human resource training and to continually promote esports and its values. Initiatives such as the establishment of the Global Esports R&D Center, the Esports Academic Research Center, the International Training Center, and the International Esports Referee Academy have all been supported by IESF's national federation members. In addition, the importance of and emphasis on creating employment opportunities for esports athletes after their esports careers ended have also been widely supported.

IESF's structure closely resembles that of traditional sport organizations. All full members are national esports federations who are tasked with developing esports in their own countries. Such member national federations are also tasked to produce national teams.

proudly declare, "We won gold!" and be part of the most dominant country in their sport. This feeling is the foundation for building national pride in many countries, and it fosters an atmosphere for developing the best possible athletes.

Sport continues to include large staged events that cost and earn millions or even billions of dollars. Major sporting events help show the world how strong sports can be. Sports break down borders; people come together to watch and cheer for a team or country, sometimes paying very high prices to attend these events live. However, esports epitomizes an opportunity traditional sport does not offer; sports may break down borders, but esports has no borders. Esports is truly global, with participants from multiple countries competing in real time. Online and live esports events can be operated significantly below the cost of traditional sporting events, reducing the costs for fans and inviting more fan engagement. This opportunity poses a threat to traditional sports at a time when more viewers are turning away from them. For example, Formula 1 racing and Formula 1 sim racing (video simulated racing) are complimentary toward developing drivers and growing audiences across generations for live racing. The traditional sport world continues to embrace the competitive gaming version based on their live sporting events (e.g., *Madden*, *NBA 2K*, *Formula 1*, *FIFA*, *Pro Evolution Soccer*). During the COVID-19 global pandemic in 2020, several professional sport leagues and organizations turned to esports when their own events and games were cancelled. NASCAR was one of the first to turn their drivers into esports racers and keep fans engaged.

COLLEGIATE ORGANIZATIONS

While a significant focus of esports governance has been on the biggest international and national esports federations, other organizations have been filling the governance needs at lower levels. The larger organizations are needed to deal with international organizations such as the IOC and national governing bodies or governments. Other organizations are needed to deal with issues closer to the players. That is where collegiate and high school organizations come into play.

A number of collegiate esports leagues exist. The Collegiate StarLeague (CSL) is the oldest collegiate esports organization; it began in 2009.

It started with 25 schools participating in the inaugural competition of the game *StarCraft: Brood War*, which the University of California, Berkeley won. CSL expanded into a variety of games. By 2019, it had 15 titles being played in various tournaments, it hosted a total of over 1,800 universities across the globe, and it had over 55,000 total players who have competed in the league.

The National Association of Collegiate Esports (NACE) is a nonprofit membership association organized by and on behalf of its member institutions. It is the only governing body of varsity college esports in North America. NACE currently has over 200 varsity esports programs as members, accounting for 90 percent of varsity programs in North America. NACE teams compete in *Overwatch*, *Paladins*: *Champions of the Realm*, *Rocket League*, and *Smite: Battleground of the Gods*; all four are fall leagues. The spring leagues include *Counter-Strike*, *Fortnite*, *League of Legends*, and *Rocket League*.

Another large collegiate esports organization is Tespa, which is a network of students, competitors, and collegiate esports club leaders. Tespa is not designed to be a conference similar to NACE, but it is a grassroots group of gamers at the college level that has over 270 chapters in North America and with over 120,000 individual Tespa members and alumni. Over 1,350 schools have competed in Tespa tournaments. Also, over 40,000 players have competed in Tespa tournaments, and they have already won over $3.3 million in prizes and scholarships. Tespa membership is free for students, so its business model is significantly different from that of NACE, which has paid membership by school-based teams. Tespa hosts a number of key tournaments, including the following:

- *Call of Duty* Collegiate Series: Varsity Invitational
- *Call of Duty* Collegiate Series: Ladder
- *Call of Duty* Collegiate Series: Duos
- *Hearthstone* Varsity Invitational
- *Hearthstone* Collegiate Championship Open
- *Overwatch* Collegiate Championship

While both NACE and Tespa are collegiate esports organizations that play at least one of the same publisher's games, that is where the similarities end. NACE generates revenue and has grown with colleges who want to enter into the esports space and need a structure to compete with other schools. The fee to join as a college is significant, but NACE provides an opportunity to compete in tournaments without a need to engage the publishers (those agreements have already been negotiated between NACE and publishers). NACE also generates revenue through national partner programs with different companies such as athlete recruiting companies, Twitch Student, and

Josh Lefkowitz/Getty Images

Collegiate esports leagues provide competitive opportunities.

various equipment-related providers. In contrast, Tespa does not charge a membership fee; they are focused on drawing in students and expanding their base of players. This structure exists partly because Tespa is headquartered in the offices of Blizzard Entertainment in Irvine, California. Thus, Tespa is a way for a publisher to help upsell their product and develop strong leagues for their titles. It is evident in how protective Tespa is about using its name and logo (as also evidenced by its game list using the registered trademark symbol after every game title). Tespa has an entire web page focused on rules and regulations for using the Tespa name in promoting a tournament.

Another collegiate organization is the American Collegiate Esports League (ACEL), a student-formed nonprofit organization made up of colleges and universities throughout the United States. ACEL grew from a group of gamers from West Virginia University who started networking with other college esports athletes. Schools were gathered from West Virginia, Virginia, Maryland, Kentucky, Ohio, and the surrounding areas to create the Eastern Esports Conference (EEC). That organization morphed into the ACEL.

The collegiate governance landscape is and will continue to be turbulent as publishers, colleges, students, those who want a better system, and those seeking profit and power are all fighting for space in this sector. An example of this turbulence is Riot Games' College League of Legends (LoL). In 2011 Riot Games partnered with CSL in their first collegiate tournament season, and this relationship continued for several years until Riot launched their official North American Collegiate Championship (NACC) effort. The NACC was operated by several organizations including CSL, IvyLoL, and North American Challenger League (NACL). This effort did not last long as in 2016 the NACC became the University League of Legends (uLoL) Campus Series run exclusively by CSL (both IvyLoL and NACL ceased operating). The following year, Riot Games rebranded NACC as the College League of Legends and partnered with Battlefy. The league evolved once again in 2019 when Riot Scholastic Association of America (RSAA) was formed as the collegiate and high school governing body for *League of Legends*.

Combined together into one space, the multiple organizations operating in the collegiate space show how chaotic leagues and organizations in general can be. It also shows how much power the game publishers have and why conferences, leagues, or whatever other formation is undertaken will always fall in line behind the publishers. Game publishers want to work with others who will promote their titles, but when all is said and done, they control the game. This model is significantly different from traditional sport where several collegiate sport organizations (ranging from NCAA and other national bodies to individual conferences such as the Big East Conference, Big Ten Conference, Atlantic Coast Conference [ACC], Peach Belt Conference [PBC], or East Coast Conference [ECC]) exist, but they all follow the same rules for the sport.

That is not to say collegiate conferences or the NCAA might not enter the realm of esports. Similar to IESF's effort to get the IOC to adopt esports, some schools will try to explore whether esports can be added to the list of NCAA approved sports. For example, the Eastern College Athletics Conference (ECAC) has endorsed collegiate esports. The ECAC is over 80 years old and has over 200 member schools across all three NCAA Divisions. Most of the ECAC's members also belong to another conference but participate in various ECAC events such as sponsored championships, leagues, bowl games, tournaments, and other competitions throughout the Northeast region. Besides traditional sports, the ECAC also hosts a comprehensive esports program. In 2020, the ECAC is expecting to organize esports competitions among more than 50 member schools and 200 teams in eight different game titles (ECAC 2020).

HIGH SCHOOL ORGANIZATIONS

After Robert Morris College organized the first collegiate esports team in 2014, it was only a matter of time before organized competitions found their way into high schools. What started as school clubs driven by students has grown and is supported by multiple governing bodies. In 2018, Munster High in Indiana was the first school in the United States that allowed students to letter in varsity esports (Gardner 2018).

In 2012, Mason Mullenioux and Charles Reilly launched the High School Esports League (HSEL) (Gardner 2018). Its inaugural season featured 20 schools; by 2014 that number grew to 300. As of 2019, the HSEL continued its growth and represented over 1,200 high schools in the United States and around the world. Even during the COVID-19 pandemic, HSEL's number continued to explode and by June 2020 their website highlighted over 3,000 schools involved with over 80,000 players.

In 2018, Delane Parnell founded PlayVS after raising $15 million in startup funds (Takahashi 2019). Since its launch, PlayVS has raised an additional $80.5 million and has partnered with the NFHS. Through its partnership with the NFHS, PlayVS has programs in all 50 states. As of 2019, over 13,000 schools were on a waiting list to start an esports program through PlayVS and the NFHS. In 2019, students paid $16 per month to play on an esports team and competed in *Smite*, *League of Legends*, and *Rocket League*. As part of its partnership with the NFHS, games that feature shooting are banned.

The North American Scholastic Esports Federation (NASEF) supports club-based esports programs at high schools that do not offer varsity teams. Beyond offering tournament support and organizing competitions, NASEF offers training, webinars, clinics, and workshops for affiliated schools. Schools that are affiliated with other governing bodies are allowed to join NASEF. In 2019, NASEF partnered with Japan High School Esports Federation (JHSEF) to coordinate international activities and information exchange (Geracie 2019).

GOVERNING PROFESSIONAL ESPORTS

While a collegiate or high school association can try to galvanize players across multiple games for various reasons, the professional ranks are different because associations are controlled by game publishers. The publisher can always change a game even if an organization might protest such a change. An organization might want to keep a current version of a game as the primary competitive version to assist players, but the publisher can

Zoning

STARTING A HIGH SCHOOL ESPORTS PROGRAM

Clint Kennedy

In general, starting an esports program requires support from administration, teachers, technology staff, and parents (Kennedy 2019). This support ensures that the program will adhere to the numerous rules and regulations that are unique to individual school districts. Schools also need to have the appropriate technology suite to support online gaming. Some programs already have the appropriate technology, while others need large upgrades in order to compete. Depending on the financial impact on technology investment, programs often engage in various fundraising efforts to launch and sustain a program.

It is critical to be able to make the case for the value of esports to administrators. Comparing esports to traditional sports in terms of the ability to develop students' health, teamwork, and skill, and connecting esports with a traditional physical education curriculum can help. Esports has been considered a way to engage students in learning, but it is increasingly considered a learning tool in and of itself. Some, including myself, have argued that esports can improve social, teamwork, and other "soft" skills. While seen as valuable skills to build in school, these skills did not neatly fit into traditional high school curricula. The NFHS notes multiple benefits of high school esports, including a sense of community, character development, and other educational benefits. Students who participated in esports noted increased engagement, higher academic achievement, developing critical thinking skills, enhanced communication, strong collaboration, and greater creativity. Many schools across the U.S. are working on integrating these skills into their programs currently and it is expected that this trend will continue for the foreseeable future. It should also be noted that high school esports are inclusive and open to all students on coed teams, and often represent the first extracurricular opportunity that many students have embraced at their school.

get significant revenue when a new title is released or an old version is revised.

Some have tried to develop an organization or association for professional esports. The benefit of developing such an entity can be to generate power, provide employment opportunities, generate revenue, or even help others. While altruistic motivation does exist, often new associations or organizations are formed strictly as a means to generate more money for someone. With that caveat, the following section explores some professional esports associations.

The Professional Esports Association (PEA) was formed in 2016. PEA defines itself as a collective of team organizations working as equals to advance the industry and mature the business of esports. The web page looks impressive, but when digging deeper, one can find that the stories are from 2018 with no updates. This is an example of an organization that had some great ambitions but was not able to actually move forward in a meaningful manner. The PEA was supposed to offer a minimum $1 million prize pool its first year, with its first event scheduled to be a *CS:GO* league in January 2017. The PEA was hoping to offer a so-called revolutionary profit-sharing system not seen elsewhere in the esports environment. The PEA was also supposedly owned and run by its teams, but the commissioner was relieved of his duties only a few months after the organization launched (Beck 2016).

The PEA is one of a number of organizations attempting to work with professional esports athletes. Some are associated with specific publishers. Others are trying to work with the teams in the hopes that publishers will cooperate. Without a union, and then a collective bargaining agreement (CBA), publishers are not required to change their behavior. As discussed earlier in the chapter, the World Esports Association (WESA) is trying to solve that problem. WESA is a joint effort between some high-profile professional esports teams (such as Fnatic, Team Envy [formerly known as Team EnVyUs], and Ninjas in Pyjamas) and ESL. It is not a union with a contract, but it is an agreement between teams and a major esports tournament organizer. The goal is to further professionalize esports through introducing elements of player representation, standardized regulations, and team revenue sharing. Another WESA goal is creating a predictable schedule for fans, players, organizers, and broadcasters. WESA started with the ESL Pro League for *CS:GO* and hopes to expand from there.

WESA is not alone in its activities. In 2019, 16 star *Fortnite* players came together to form the *Fortnite* Professional Players' Association (FNPPA). Some of the founders included World Cup champion Kyle "Bugha" Giersdorf and Benjy "Benjyfishy" Fish. The FNPPA is attempting to create a platform for productive dialogue between competitive players and game publishers. The objective is similar to the WESA—developing better relationships. It is not to say that they can really influence the publishers; the publishers will do what is in the best interest of the company and their titles. Players can come and go, and their demands will be addressed if they make sense financially and politically. Thus, the timing of tournaments and the amount of rest time for players are easy topics to cover. Giving the player equity ownership in teams would be a much more difficult ask.

These organizations are not without controversy. For example, FNPPA was started with eight North American players and eight European players. They were scheduled to grow from there, but the controversy was who picks the people involved? The potential conflict could be significant and even who starts an organization can be controversial if people are chosen for the wrong reason or who might have a political agenda. Such questions are where power struggles can occur and organizations start taking shots at one another. Another question is who is behind every organization (and what are their agendas)? These types of issues occur with every type of organization and can be characterized as normal growing pains.

SHOULD ESPORTS BE GOVERNED THE WAY SPORT IS GOVERNED?

Esports is often perceived as something new and different. As a result, esports is often compared to the Wild West. However, being new and different does not necessarily mean you have no governance. Esports cannot be compared to one distinct sport such as football or baseball, because it encompasses numerous esports titles, genres, and regional approaches depending on where one is located. In other words, every country and every game is unique and potentially has its own unique ecosystem and system of governance. Furthermore, game developers such as Activision

Blizzard, Riot Games, and Valve Software, which own the intellectual property of their respective games, play a vital role in any governance of their esports ecosystem. Specifically, because they own the intellectual property of their games, they have the right to govern the games in any way they want (subject to any existing contract laws such as user agreements). Still, developers are interested in creating an environment in which the game can thrive, generate revenues, and become sustainable. Having said that, it is not always possible for developers to oversee every aspect of the game in every geographic region, so it is in their best interest to share power with other stakeholders. Many game developers have sought to create an ecosystem that combines grassroots development with the professional competitions, while others have taken a different approach and regulated the whole ecosystem from the top down (Scholz 2019a). A negative side effect of overregulation is that the grassroots and amateur base may not fully develop because of the manifest focus on only the most important or profitable aspects of the game. When organizations focus only on certain aspects of the top level of their ecosystem and potentially ignore the grassroots user base, the result can be a lack of talent development and decrease in size of the user base (Partin 2019).

Figure 5.1 illustrates an esports governance model in which the top-level stakeholders are linked to the grassroots movement in esports. At the top level exist powerful stakeholders such as international governments, national and international governing bodies, game developers, and professional teams. At the bottom are the grassroots local stakeholders that typically represent amateur players and fans. The middle area between the top level and grassroots stakeholders represents efforts focused on mediating between both groups while also attempting to identify legitimate sources of authority in both levels. Even though top-level and grassroots stakeholders share

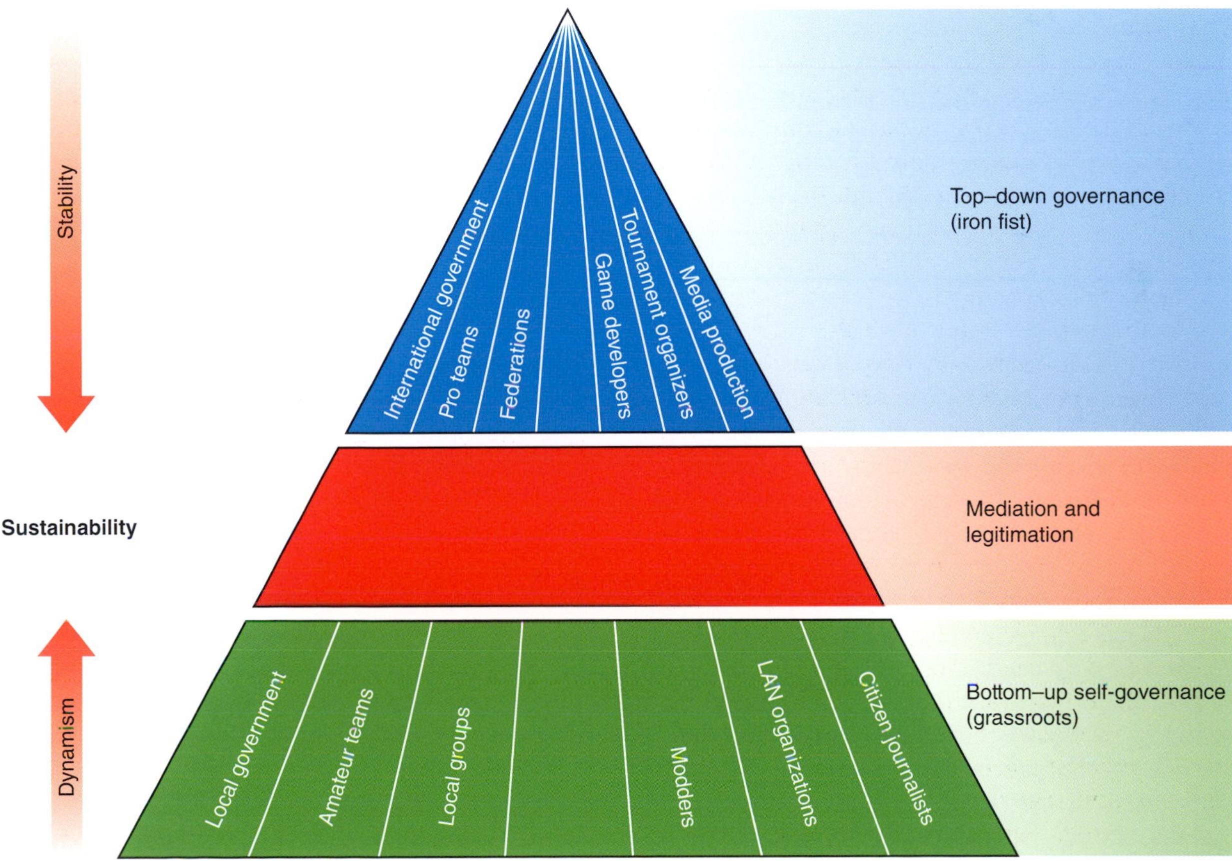

Figure 5.1 Esports governance ecosystem.
Adapted by permission from Tobias Scholz (2019a).

Zoning

THE INTERNATIONAL ESPORTS FEDERATION PLAYERS' COMMISSION

Jason Batzofin

The IESF Players' Commission was founded at the 2016 IESF Global Esports Summit. Athletes from six different countries founded the commission in order to represent athletes at the highest level of the IESF.

The purpose of the IESF Players' Commission is to "represent the views of athletes to the International Esports Federation ('IESF') Board" (International Esports Federation 2019, p. 2). The role of the IESF Players' Commission is to protect all athletes involved in IESF championships, tournaments, and any other events that IESF may host. The Players' Commission also serves to advise the IESF board on all matters but specifically those that involve esports athletes; they include matters involving the IESF, international federations, National Olympic Committees, doping, athlete eligibility, event accommodation, IESF ceremonies, sports, politics, and anything else that the Players' Commission deems fit. The overarching goal of the IESF Players' Commission is to create a better future for esports athletes.

The Players' Commission is led by athletes to look after athletes. In order to be eligible for election to the Players' Commission, the athlete is required to

- have represented their country in an IESF event
- have reached the age of majority
- have a seat on the board for their own member federation
- be no more than 30 years of age

These requirements exist to create good governance and keep all athletes that serve in the commission relevant. The Players' Commission is composed of six members; three are female, and three are male. Only one representative per country may sit on the board.

The Players' Commission strives to create a brighter future for esports athletes. In this future, all athletes are free from anything that could prevent their pathway to success; all can perform to the best of their ability without barriers. Thus, the role of the Players' Commission is to uphold the IESF and their member federations to a higher standard that puts athletes at the forefront. It creates an environment that furthers the development, competition, and sportsmanship of all athletes and officials.

many traits in common, the middle level may be different for every game, genre, and region. This middle area balances the interests of both levels and contributes to a sustainable ecosystem. Top–down governance may lead to instability and conflict between stakeholders, while bottom–up self-governance may not be realistic or financially viable. At the same time, however, it is essential that esports games have a dynamic and involved grassroots user base. The dynamism of the user base helps to maintain the long-term viability of the players' ecosystem and support continued growth of the game. Games such as *Counter-Strike* are a prime example of dynamism and the linking of grassroots stakeholders with top-level governance. Many tournament operators (e.g., ESL) have regional and amateur tournaments (e.g., the DreamHack Open), which empower players to participate while also linking grassroots stakeholders with professional teams, event operators, and tournament organizers.

Counter-Strike is also a compelling case to explore. The players' union (*Counter-Strike* Professional Players' Association [CSPPA]) has helped to advance the rights of players. For example, CSPPA has focused on improving working conditions and giving players a unified voice when communicating with top-level governance. Many professional esports teams are also linked to WESA. The purpose of WESA is to assist in the creating of rules and regulations of esports. Furthermore, in times of dispute, organizations like CSPPA and WESA work with outside partners such as the Esports Integrity Commission (ESIC) to solve gaming conflicts. For example, at the behest of WESA, ESIC undertook an investigation into a controversy surrounding player allegations against the professional team Ninjas in Pyjamas (NiP) regarding reported mismanagement and the engagement in malicious activities toward players (WESA 2019a). The resulting ESIC report provided to WESA was published in full and noted no consequences were merited for NiP management (WESA 2019b). This process and actions undertaken by WESA and ESIC provide an example of effective governance.

Counter-Strike continues to be a good example of the game developer, Valve, following a laissez-faire governance approach to the game. Furthermore, the game is a tactical shooter, and consequently many sports associations distance themselves from associating with such games. The laissez-faire approach combined with little external intervention from sport associations allowed governance for *Counter-Strike* to emerge and evolve its structure to fit the game and stakeholders. For example, even after 20 years, the stakeholder-created associations continue to foster an environment in which the game is still popular.

Nevertheless, this open approach of governance makes the game susceptible to influential stakeholders, which happened during the *Counter-Strike* Championship Gaming Series in the late 2000s. At that time, influential stakeholders were able to concentrate most of the talented players in one single league. Ironically, however, the league was not profitable and went bankrupt (Scholz 2019b).

In the early years, before the emergence of more organized governance in the game, the *Counter-Strike* scene struggled, notably because Valve had two games on the market: *Counter-Strike 1.6* and *Counter-Strike: Source*. When *Counter-Strike: Global Offensive* (*CS:GO*) was released, stakeholders were reunited and worked together. Without one preeminent stakeholder, the scene flourished, because a diversity of stakeholders shared governance. While some governance-related friction still exists in *Counter-Strike*, today the ecosystem seems to be stable, and the evolving governance structures have resulted in distinct yet successful regulation. It will be interesting to observe whether this stability will hold in the future.

Governance in esports is all about power; no model for legitimate governance is available. Few believe that one stakeholder should be the sole caretaker of any one particular game. The game developer must be involved, because it must support and update the game; at the same time, the developer can shut down the game at will. Most game developers are business driven, and they have financial interest in ensuring the game is profitable. If other stakeholders are supporting them and helping their bottom line, most are willing to share power.

Several associations have attempted to become *the* legitimate entity to organize, govern, and oversee esports, which has often led to friction between game developers and esports associations. Esports associations continue to develop in many countries, and they sometimes claim to be the legitimate top-level organization responsible for esports in their country. The legitimation often derives from simply attempting to grab power, leading to a competition between rival associations in some countries. This competition has led to a rush of people trying to create different governing bodies to obtain **first-mover advantage**. Creating the first esports organization does not give them legitimacy, and there will be a culling or combining of regional associations as the industry and ecosystem continue to develop.

In some cases, the governance of some esports games mirrors that of traditional sport; in other cases, it is more comparable to business governance. Some countries follow a more public governance approach, while others maintain a focus on professional competitions. Still, similar to traditional sports, professional esports competitions have their own rules and regulations. Governance in Major League Baseball (MLB) is business driven, while recreational baseball activities are governed with more of a public focus on health and wellness activities. The challenge, however, is that esports governance on the grassroots level consists of a multitude of approaches and stakeholders. Furthermore, without a general understanding of the politics associated with esports in a country, rules and regulations are often governed by the most influential stakeholder. Sometimes, this stakeholder could be a large government agency; other times it could be the one with the most money or political clout.

Governance requires legal certainty, and to a large extent it may come down to the definition of esports. If esports is considered to be a sport in one country, there the governance structures will shift because legal claim exists for a sport association to be in charge. If esports is not considered a sport, the governance power may reside with the game developers. In the case of governance emanating from game developers, be it a laissez-faire approach in which they allow participation in governance by many stakeholders or overregulation where smaller or less important stakeholders can be oppressed, governance in esports widely varies. The key challenge is connecting the top-level stakeholders with grassroots esports movements. One stakeholder cannot create this connection; it requires the cooperation of many stakeholders in the ecosystem. Governance is shared within the ecosystem. Strong governance can be observed in successful games such as *Counter-Strike*, *Dota 2*, and *League of Legends*, all of which include shared governance.

The esports industry is relatively young, and just like traditional sports, it will take time to create effective governance that satisfies all stakeholders. Furthermore, because esports consists of many different esports titles, stakeholders also perceive esports and various games in different ways. Therefore, it may be presumptuous to make the case for one governance model for esports, especially because no one governance model exists for all sports. While FIFA attempts to organize soccer (football) around the world, national and local associations may have different rules and governance. While recent history has shown that a sole focus on top–down governance structure might be less successful than a mix of both top–down and bottom–up self-governance structures, a mixed governance structure may make it difficult for traditional sports associations such as FIFA or the IOC to understand and work with the diverse stakeholders that may represent entities within the esports industry. The esports industry is dynamic and evolving. Therefore, top–down governance in the style of the iron fist may be very harmful. In the coming years, undoubtedly a variety of governance models will exist in esports, and many ecosystems may shift over time as newer games, such as *PUBG* or *Rainbow Six*, are more fully developed. Governance in esports is dynamic and will continue to be vibrant moving forward, because it consists of hundreds of unique ecosystems, all interacting with each other based on numerous, often overlapping stakeholders. Therefore, the main goal of governance should be to link the grassroots movement with the stakeholders powerful enough to support them. This interaction may lead to a sustainable ecosystem in esports.

CONCLUSION

This chapter covered a variety of esports federations and associations at multiple levels. These organizations are meant to benefit the various members and partners. The industry is still very young, so some groups have come and gone and will continue in this manner as the industry grows. No formal government regulations exist, so anyone can make any rules or regulations they wish as long as they are not violating any contracts and user agreements. Publishers are in the best position to control any federations or strongly move them in a given direction. As players strive to gain more power, some battles are inevitable. At the present time publishers have the upper hand, but if players can unionize, they might be able to negotiate more beneficial terms for themselves rather than simply nice gestures. However, this process of unionization is not without challenges, because players currently have multiple groups that could be considered their employer (e.g., publishers, teams, leagues).

DISCUSSION QUESTIONS

1. What are the similarities and differences between the ways different organizations govern their respective esports areas?
2. How can governing bodies grow and improve their activities?
3. What should be the ideal structure for an esports organization?

6

Esports Marketing

David P. Hedlund | Anthony Palomba | Lisa Cosmas Hanson
Michael L. Naraine | Henry Wear

INTRODUCTION

From commercials and advertisements shown on Twitch to influencers promoting products on social media, marketing has been central to the efforts to introduce, increase, and enhance the consumption of esports and gaming goods and services. Based on estimates of as many as 2.7 billion gamers around the world, in 2019, $152.1 billion was expected to be spent on gaming-related activities, with respective figures of $68.5 billion, $47.9 billion, and $35.7 billion in mobile-, console-, and personal computer (PC)–related revenues (Wijman 2019). One of the key factors fueling growth in gaming and esports is the marketing of new and existing goods and services. This chapter examines the principles and practices underpinning marketing activities, with an emphasis on exploring topics not often discussed in mainstream marketing.

OBJECTIVES

- Identify important marketing principles affecting esports consumers.
- Describe how the five Ps of marketing are used to influence esports consumer behaviors.
- Explain unique esports marketing strategies and how they can be leveraged in marketing activities.
- Compare and contrast strategies and tactics used by esports marketers to influence potential consumers' behaviors.
- Summarize how esports marketing activities focused on players, spectators, and fans are similar and different.

THE FIVE PS OF ESPORTS MARKETING

According to the American Marketing Association (AMA), **marketing** is defined as "the activity, set of institutions, and processes for creating, communicating, delivering, and exchanging offerings that have value for customers, clients, partners, and society at large" (2017, para. 2). In practice, esports marketing includes, but is not limited to, promotional, advertising, public relations, and sales activities intended to influence individuals' cognition and behaviors. As noted in gaming consumer research published by Newzoo (2019), a large overlap exists between those who play esports (gamers) and those who watch esports (spectators). Based on aggregate data from fans of the game *League of Legends*, 32 percent are only players, 26 percent are only spectators, and 42 percent are both players and spectators (Pannekeet 2019). Because of the large percentage of overlap between players and spectators, game publishers focus on marketing activities intended to motivate consumers to play their games, while a growing focus in esports is motivating attendance at in-person esports events, consumption of streamed content, and purchase of other related goods and services. Whether through creating commercial advertisements for their game shown on television, streaming gaming competitions live on Twitch, or contracting with influencers to promote the game on social media, today's marketing of esports is diverse and continues to evolve with technology and creativity.

A number of concepts and activities underpin marketing of any good or service and therefore are relevant to esports marketing. In addition, more specific esports-related marketing applications are useful. In traditional marketing discourse, the four Ps of marketing (product, price, place, and promotion) often form the basis of the strategies and tactics marketers use to influence consumers' cognition and behavior. Because sports marketing involves large amounts of media attention, public relations was added to the four Ps, resulting in the five Ps of marketing (Mullin, Hardy, and Sutton 2014). In practical terms, the five Ps represent factors that can be considered and leveraged by marketers during the marketing process. The five Ps are also applicable to esports and will now be discussed in turn.

Product

Product marketing focuses on how the product (good or service) is positioned in the marketplace and the attributes associated with it. When *Apex Legends* burst onto the gaming scene in February of 2019, developers positioned the game as an improvement over other games in the battle royale category (e.g., *Fortnite*, *PlayerUnknown's Battlegrounds* [*PUBG*]). For example, players noted unique attributes and improvements in the *Apex Legends* game, such as how players could communicate with others on their team through the innovative ping system; the attention to detail the developers paid to the graphics, sounds, and player controller action; and how the game was delivered through paid influencer partners (e.g., Tyler "Ninja" Blevins, Michael "Shroud" Grzesiek) during the initial launch (Gilbert 2019).

Price

Sellers can manipulate the price charged to consumers or quantity of goods and/or services received. Often price is combined with marketing promotions, such as "buy three games for the price of one" or "buy a game and get a free game controller." In recent years, **loot boxes**, which provide opportunities for gamers to use real money to buy or win virtual items in game, have become popular for players to purchase to enhance and improve their game play or in-game experience. In the game *Clash of Clans*, game publisher Supercell introduced a monthly Gold Pass at the beginning of each month for USD $4.99; it consisted of opportunities to earn more in-game upgrades. During the first week of sales, Supercell netted approximately $27 million worldwide in the App Store and Google Play (Nelson 2019). To increase revenues, game developers can leverage other types of battle passes, in-game upgrades, loot boxes, and other opportunities for virtual sales.

Place

Often described as the means of distributing goods and services, place is a multifaceted concept in the esports industry. The games themselves can be instantly downloaded or purchased for one or more platforms; some games (e.g., *Fortnite*, *PUBG*) are offered on mobile devices, consoles, and personal computers. Often other peripheral goods and services can be purchased online or through brick-and-mortar locations. Cloud gaming (e.g., Google Stadia, Microsoft xCloud) allows gamers to play their favorite games any place and any time, and as a result, has pushed game developers to increase the number of partially or fully cross-platform games. Moving forward, in order to leverage the opportunity for gamers to play without any restrictions, game developers and platforms will need to improve how games are distributed and how play is facilitated.

Promotion

Promotions are the strategies and tactics used to motivate increased consumption of goods and services. In esports, promotions can include any activities intended to introduce or increase knowledge of goods or services; the ultimate objective is increasing interest and demand. Examples of unique esports promotions are diverse and extensive. For instance, when Activision Blizzard launched the *WWII* version of their $15 billion *Call of Duty* video game franchise in 2017, five billboards were simultaneously unveiled around the world, and each billboard contained hidden codes

(Chen 2017). Upon deciphering and combining the codes, players could unlock exclusive game content. In another example of unique promotions, for the 2014 *League of Legends* World Championship, upstart band Imagine Dragons and game publisher Riot Games collaborated on the creation of the song "Warriors" and produced an accompanying animated music video about *League of Legends* gamers, gaming, and competing in esports competitions. As of early 2020, the animated music video "Warriors" published on the *League of Legends* YouTube site had been viewed almost 243 million times (YouTube 2014).

Public Relations

Public relations is the practice of communicating with the public. As the esports industry experienced highs and lows during its recent history, firms focused on esports communications and public relations started to grow; one such firm is The Story Mob. Based on their Seven Commandments of Esports Communications, The Story Mob (2020) note the importance for organizations involved in esports to do the following:

1. Create value.
2. Be authentic.

Zoning

INTERNATIONAL ESPORTS CONSUMER BEHAVIOR

Lisa Cosmas Hanson

Asia is the heart of global esports. The market in Asia is more than half of the total world, and global esports activities often follow the path set in Asia. For example, the streaming video viewership in China alone is more than 90 percent of global streaming video viewership for many tournaments, such as *Dota 2* and *League of Legends*. Another example is the infrastructure of esports events. In Malaysia, pop-up esports tournaments in retail malls have inspired U.S. malls to follow suit and organize spaces for esports activities and tournaments.

The rise of prominence of esports in South Korea is due in part to the Internet café culture (e.g., PC bangs), opportunities for socializing with others, and cost (gaming is one of the least expensive forms of entertainment). Similar factors also play an important role elsewhere in Asia. Consumers in the Philippines, China, and Vietnam generally do not have as much disposable income for entertainment as do consumers in the West. In part, playing digital games and socializing at Internet cafés have filled the void and created new opportunities for socialization, all priced within one's budget. In addition, since the advent of mobile gaming, and because almost everyone in Asia has a smartphone, digital games and esports are now the collective social activity many people are doing.

Japan is the last major Asian country to fully embrace esports. Around the world today, multiplayer online battle arena (MOBA), first-person shooter (FPS), and battle royale games tend to be the most popular. However, historically, Japanese gamers preferred playing fighting games and sports games. Preferences are beginning to change in Japan as streaming video, consumer product sponsorships, and infrastructure for esports venues are all becoming more popular. Because Japan has not had an avid fan base for MOBA and FPS or battle royale games, they have not needed to establish regulatory systems supportive of esports. The development of the esports and gaming industry in Japan has much in common with that of Western nations.

Currently, Asia leads the world in the number of esports participants, fans, venues, tournaments, and even in developing regulations that support this growing industry. Esports organizations based in Western countries may have established well-organized teams and professional events, but Asian gamers and fans passionately underpin much of the global audience for esports. Esports can be a great global peacemaker. Gaming is international, it is nonjudgmental, and it is welcoming to all types of participants. I hope Asia can be the leader of the world for the youth to embrace esports and facilitate global understanding among all those that participate as players, fans, and spectators.

3. Be timely.
4. Be media savvy.
5. Be transparent.
6. Be truthful about who you are.
7. Be bold.

The esports industry has tremendous opportunities for growth in players, communities, and revenues, all while facing challenges including concerns about players' health, wellness, and addiction. As a result, multiple aspects of it are unique to esports.

UNIQUE ASPECTS OF ESPORTS MARKETING

From the beginning, sport marketers for traditional sports have debated with business marketers about whether anything unique existed in their marketing activities or whether sport marketing was simply an application of traditional marketing principles in sport settings. One area of difference is the existence of these two types of sport marketing:

- Marketing *of* sport
- Marketing *through* sport

Simply put, the marketing of sport consists of sport marketers who market aspects such as players, teams, and leagues. Marketing through sport includes marketing goods and services through communications and activities centered on and produced by the team and its partners.

In the video game industry, the marketing of esports and marketing through esports also both occur. In January 2020, Activision Blizzard's new esports league for the game *Call of Duty* began with a three-day event held in Minneapolis. As noted earlier by Reuters (2019), "the event will feature all 12 professional *Call of Duty* League teams as well as fan and player experiences to celebrate the launch of the new city-based league, including the first Challengers Open where amateur players can compete as teams in an open bracket tournament format" (para. 2). During the two and a half months between the announcement introducing the new league and the inaugural event itself, Activision Blizzard marketed numerous aspects of the league, including the 12 teams, some of the most talented players, the new version of the game *Modern Warfare*, the 28-week schedule, and the amateur Challenger events (Takahashi 2019). Prior to and during the start of the *Call of Duty* League season, sponsors and partners also began to market their goods and services through the teams and events. For example, YouTube was announced as the exclusive streaming partner for the *Call of Duty* League (Grubb 2020). During the inaugural event streams, league partners and sponsors such as the U.S. Army and Air Force, MTN DEW AMP GAME FUEL (energy drinks), ASTRO Gaming (headsets), SCUF Gaming (controllers), Sony PlayStation (consoles), in addition to team sponsors such as Jack in the Box (restaurant), Monster (energy drinks), Corsair (hardware and peripherals), Turtle Beach (headsets), and GameStop (games and accessories), all marketed their goods and services through activities such as on-screen graphics, commercials, branding on uniforms and clothing, and in-game use (YouTube 2020). All of these activities used the *Call of Duty* League and YouTube to broadcast and communicate marketing information, messages, and branding to consumers and spectators.

Another area where the marketing of traditional sports and esports have diverged from those used in business is the strategies and tactics used by marketers. The six most important and frequently used esports marketing strategies and tactics are identified as follows:

1. Use digital marketing.
2. Consider diverse types of gamers, and avoid stereotypes.
3. Use influencers.
4. Be authentic.
5. Provide opportunities for experiential marketing.
6. Engage and activate through activities and events.

Each one is examined next.

Use of Digital Marketing

One of the most important and unique aspects of esports is its electronic underpinnings. While traditional board and card games such as Dungeons and Dragons (D&D) continue to provide entertainment for legions of fans, there are now popular online or digital collectible card games (CCGs) using similar types of characters, rules, and structure, such as *Hearthstone* and *Magic: The Gathering Online*. Like traditional video games, these digital card games all exist today in electronic form. In order to distribute electronic content, Internet-based platforms such Twitch, YouTube, DouYu TV, and Huya are all used by individuals and organizations to stream their content directly to consumers. While the production of content (e.g., a person playing a video game title on a computer) is often done in person, most other aspects, from the game being played to the distribution and consumption platforms, are completed digitally. As noted by the marketing firm Engine Group (2019), gaming and esports have transformed the marketplace; to reach digital natives (i.e., [young] people born and raised with access to digital technology), companies and brands should invest in digital marketing strategies. Recall the Activision Blizzard billboard example from the Promotion discussion earlier in this chapter. While it was a unique tactic in 2017, today's marketers would be wise to consider promoting their products through digital methods. Moreover, Stream Hatchet noted in September of 2019 that "sports live streaming across all platforms including Twitch, YouTube Gaming . . . increased by more than 41 percent over the past 12 months – an incredible 746 million more hours watched compared to the previous year" (Millennial Esports 2019, para. 2). Because esports consumers are found online, companies seeking to reach esports consumers should use digital marketing campaigns through internet-based mediums.

Gamer Diversity and Avoidance of Stereotypes

Building on the first strategy of creating digital marketing, the second strategy is to be inclusive of all types of gamers while also avoiding the perpetuation and potential use of stereotypes. A frequently used phrase for describing today's esports players, spectators, and consumers is something to the effect of "not just nerds anymore." According to the Entertainment Software Association (ESA 2019), the average age of a gamer is 33 years old, 65 percent of American adults play video games, the gender ratio of male to female gamers is 54 percent to 46 percent, and they include members from every generation. Further, gamers are diverse and play on PCs, consoles, and mobile and multiple platforms (Westcott, Loucks, Ciampa, and Srivastava 2019). In terms of consumption behavior, casual, core, and hardcore gamers exist for different platforms (Niko Partners 2019). In short, because all types of people play video games and esports, it is essential that organizations and their marketers endeavor to understand the unique types of consumers existing in the marketplace and to not judge or stereotype based on preconceived notions. For example, only creating esports marketing campaigns focused on men may limit the reach of these activities to just over half of those participating.

Influencer Marketing

According to the American Marketing Association (AMA) and the Association of National Advertisers (ANA), **influencer marketing** is defined as "leveraging individuals who have influence over potential buyers and orienting marketing activities around these individuals to drive a brand message to the larger market" (AMA 2017, para. 6). In other words, organizations may identify celebrities or other well-known people in the industry and ask for or provide compensation in return for the individual promoting or advocating the use of particular goods or services. As described by Duran (2019), when Tyler "Ninja" Blevins left Twitch and moved to Mixer in mid-2019, within one week he added more than 100,000 followers on Facebook, Twitter, and Instagram, and he gained more than 700,000 followers and over 1 million subscribers on the new platform. While it is difficult to measure the promotional effect of a marketing campaign offering a one-month free subscription to Ninja's channel (Duran 2019), it can be speculated that many, if not most of those that followed or subscribed to his new channel on Mixer, were influenced to do so by Ninja. As of the writing of this textbook, Mixer is set to close in July of 2020, and Ninja has not yet announced on which platforms he will stream in the future. Further research by Duran (2017a) indicates fans frequently have a deep and personal connection to esports influencers and their content. Because of the personal connection and perceived importance of the relationship, fans may be strongly affected by the suggestions of influencers they follow. Due to the connections developed, organizations and their brands may also attempt to use **relationship marketing** tactics in order to build and enhance loyalty toward their goods and services among those who follow the influencer. In summary, organizations wishing to market their goods and services to esports players, spectators, and consumers would be well advised to consider creating marketing campaigns and activities involving popular influencers in their target market. Having said that, organizations would also be well advised to vet influencers and ensure there are no obvious past issues that may affect future activities and collaboration (e.g., sexist, racist, or otherwise discriminatory words or actions).

Authenticity

The next tactic in esports marketing is to be authentic in one's orientation toward players, fans, spectators, and other consumers. According to Joseph (2016), seven characteristics of authentic people exist, and eight exist for those that are inauthentic. Table 6.1 displays the characteristics of authentic and inauthentic people.

In esports, fans, spectators, and consumers respond positively to people and organizations they perceive as authentic (Arkenberg, Van Dyke, Tengberg, and Baltuskonis 2018). When explaining how to influence the esports fan base to those that might be otherwise unfamiliar, staff from companies such as Code Red Esports and Intel noted "ultimately the most important thing is to do things in an authentic way . . . If you're not authentic they will let you know. They are able to get onto Facebook, Twitch and Twitter and voice their opinions. They're very happy with putting their gaming and their lives online, and expressing their opinions" (Rogers 2018, para. 42 and 44). Further, platforms such as Twitch have helped organizations to authentically market to gamers. As noted in Nielsen's (2019) *Esports Playbook for Brands*, "Gamers are not a niche audience, and watching others play video games is neither a new nor niche activity. Twitch has successfully explained to brands (through case studies, research insights, and other means) precisely how their brand messaging can authentically connect with such an engaged and influential audience" (p. 24). As an example of authentic esports marketing, the Coca-Cola Company worked with Electronic Arts (EA) Sports to create a fictional digital character within the game *FIFA 17* named Alex Hunter. Alex can be accessed in *FIFA 17* (and future editions *FIFA 18* and *FIFA 19*) through the journey mode of the game. As documented by Duran (2017b), within *FIFA 18*, players can "go behind the scenes of the endorsement deal as well as shooting a commercial. The virtual TV spot re-imagines a classic Coca-Cola commercial from 1979 in which a young fan offers 'Mean' Joe Greene a Coke, which lifts his spirits" (para. 5). Despite some fans of the real-life team Real Madrid expressing some negative sentiments about digital player Alex Hunter being signed by Real Madrid in *FIFA 19* and selling his jersey in real life (Griffin 2018), staff from Coca-Cola noted the importance and outcomes related to engaging with real-world content within virtual gaming worlds (Wong 2017). In addition, Coca-Cola produced and sold limited edition custom cans that also included both Hunter's image and codes that could be used in game to download exclusive content (Liffreing 2017).

Experiential Marketing

Another important principle in esports marketing is the opportunity to facilitate the creation of connections and relationships between

Table 6.1 Characteristics of Authentic and Inauthentic People

Authentic people	Inauthentic people
1. Have realistic perceptions of reality	1. Are self-deceptive and unrealistic in their perceptions of reality
2. Are accepting of themselves and of other people	2. Look to others for approval and to feel valued
3. Are thoughtful	3. Are judgmental of other people
4. Have a nonhostile sense of humor	4. Do not think things through clearly
5. Are able to express their emotions freely and clearly	5. Have a hostile sense of humor
6. Are open to learning from their mistakes	6. Are unable to express their emotions freely and clearly
7. Understand their motivations	7. Are not open to learning from their mistakes
	8. Do not understand their motivations

Based on Joseph (2016).

players through experiential marketing and related hands-on activities. According to the Common Language Marketing Dictionary, a project of the Marketing Accountability Standards Board (MASB), experiential marketing is "a marketing approach that directly engages consumers and invites and encourages them to participate in a branded experience" (MASB n.d., para. 1). Further, as the Association of National Advertisers (ANA) noted, experiential marketing "includes events and more individual experiences, such as a demonstration of a product's performance, extra care/personal connection, and grassroots events" (ANA 2020, para. 5). Experiential marketing provides an important opportunity for organizations to connect and create relationships with consumers through activities in which they can directly interact with the goods and services of a brand. If a person attends almost any esports event, it will likely be rife with opportunities for attendees to be subject and party to experiential marketing activities. For example, when competition organizers host esports events and viewing parties, they often provide experiential marketing opportunities for attendees. During these marketing activities, attendees have the opportunity to play games and try technology such as virtual reality (VR), augmented reality (AR), or mixed reality (MR). Sometimes organizers also create cosplay activities, where attendees can dress up in costumes and look like their favorite video game or anime characters. Through these experiences, attendees can interact with various goods, services, or people, resulting in possible future consumption.

Another important benefit of experiential marketing has to do with inclusion. One of the biggest challenges facing traditional sports is the opportunity to facilitate everyone playing, regardless of factors such as gender, disability, size, or height. In video games and esports, adaptive controllers allow people who are able bodied and those who are non–able bodied to play and compete with and against one another without limitation. In other words, gamers are empowered to play video games and esports regardless of many physical limitations. As detailed by Bailey (2019), "to support gamers with physical disabilities, an industrious community has for years modified existing controllers or devised new ones altogether. And now those efforts, by organizations like Warfighter Engaged, the AbleGamers Charity and SpecialEffect, have been amplified by Microsoft, which in September [of 2018] released an adaptive controller for the Xbox One" (para. 3). As a result, video games and esports can be marketed to all types of consumers regardless of differences that might prevent such collaborative consumption and activity in traditional sports and other activities.

David P. Hedlund

Experiential marketing allows people to try esports products they might eventually buy.

Event Engagement and Activities

While more fans have the opportunity to watch esports events through online streaming rather than in person, given the previously described principle of experiential marketing, it is important that event organizers create opportunities for spectators to engage with each other and those competing in the event in as many ways as possible. Through engaging with others online or in person, players, teams, and organizers can activate fan behaviors that are important to various stakeholders. Beyond simply hosting an event that may hold esports games and competitions, organizations have the opportunity to create additional activities for spectators and fans. For example, the esports event currently with the largest prize pool is the International *Dota 2* Championships, also known as The International (TI). In 2011, TI prize pool was $1.6 million; by 2019, that amount had grown to in excess of $34.3 million (Liquipedia 2019). The prize pool and the event itself include multiple opportunities for fans and spectators to feel connected to the experience. The prize pool is crowdfunded primarily through in-game sales of the Battle Pass, and 25 percent of those sales are then earmarked for TI's prize pool (Valve n.d.). As detailed by both Valve (n.d.) and Gamepedia (2019), the Battle Pass is both a tournament pass and a bundle of quests, achievements, rewards, opportunities to play unique game modes, equipment, items, features, and other in-game enhancements and effects players can buy or earn. The game publisher (Valve) also offers weekly challenges and player, team, and coaching activities in the lead-up to the event. In addition to the 2019 Battle Pass, prize pool activities and events held at Mercedes-Benz Arena in Shanghai, China, four additional activities occurred through which spectators and fans could watch and connect to TI. These activities included livestreams of the tournament competitions on Twitch and SteamTV platforms, multicast streams during the early stages of the competition where the highlights of various matches could all be simultaneously watched, in-game streams through the game itself where spectators could see what professional players were actually seeing during the competition, and related events in 145 local venues on six continents (Barcraft n.d.). As a result, no matter where fans were located, they had opportunities to watch and connect with others in game, via streaming platforms, and at live events around the world.

An Esports Marketing Example

All six esports marketing tactics are apparent in the following example from 2018, in which global courier and logistics company DHL created a marketing campaign featuring *Dota 2* game personality Jake "SirActionSlacks" Kanner. In the marketing activities, Kanner acts as an employee of DHL. He is overseeing the company's automated warehouse robot, EffiBOT. In the initial video for the event ESL One Birmingham, Kanner prepared and used EffiBOT to deliver packages to *Dota 2* players. In the follow-up video for ESL One Hamburg later that year, Kanner used EffiBOT to transport supplies needed by players in the digital *Dota 2* game from a real-world DHL warehouse. As the video morphs from the real world to the animated digital world, EffiBOT finds itself inside the *Dota 2* game being attacked by various in-game characters and overcoming numerous common *Dota 2* obstacles and challenges throughout its digital journey, in the same way those playing the game might experience. At the end of the video, EffiBOT successfully delivers its contents to an in-game character that ordered and needed them. Also at the 2018 ESL One Hamburg event, DHL hosted a web page with information about the event, created the hashtag #MomentsThatDeliver where the videos and in-game *Dota 2* highlights of each day of competitions were shown, provided a real EffiBOT with which event attendees could take photographs, and provided an opportunity for attendees to play DHL's virtual reality game *BoxStacker Pro*.

DHL's engagement opportunities at the ESL One Birmingham and Hamburg events and its online videos and activities epitomize all six important marketing practices. DHL used *digital* marketing online through the creation of videos and other marketing materials. DHL also found a unique way to connect the logistics and courier purposes of the company to most consumers without using stereotypes and in authentic and natural ways while also connecting to the game itself.

Zoning

THE ESPORTS EVENT CONSUMER EXPERIENCE: THE CASE OF IEM SYDNEY

Henry Wear and Michael L. Naraine

From May 3 through May 5, 2019, the Intel Extreme Masters (IEM) event was held in Sydney, Australia for the third straight year. Owned by ESL, a major player in the esports ecosystem, the event is part of the Intel Grand Slam, with other events hosted in Katowice, Poland; Dallas, Texas; Montpellier, France; and Cologne, Germany. As a result of its international reach, the profile of this type of esports event is quite large; it has international teams, large prize purses, and high production value (Scholz 2019). The size of the event means hosting it in a larger facility, Qudos Bank Arena, with the capability of broadcasting to millions of fans around the world, and concurrently exercising significant sponsorship activations (Cunningham et al. 2018). What does this esports event actually look like for the thousands of fans who physically attend? The case of IEM Sydney reveals key elements of the consumer experience.

At its core, IEM Sydney and other IEM major events are staged for professional esports teams to compete in a playoff-style format in an attempt to win a prize and be crowned champions. These events operate on a season-based schedule and range from staging competitions for one game (e.g., IEM Sydney and *CS:GO*) or several games (e.g., IEM Katowice and *CS:GO*, *Dota 2*, and *StarCraft II*). To compete in these events, teams must be directly invited or must qualify as representatives of their geographic region. Most often, high-profile and high-performing teams are awarded the direct invitee spots at the event; lower-profile teams have to work through the qualifying stages. Teams often qualify for these global events in IEM sanctioned qualifier matches held in the months and weeks before the IEM major event and are usually located offsite in smaller venues or offline qualifier tournaments.

Once the field is set, the onsite tournament begins. As mentioned previously, most IEM events take place in large cities using existing stadiums or arenas. For example, IEM Sydney has now been held in the Australian city for three consecutive ESL seasons, using the Qudos Bank Arena in Sydney Olympic Park. The arena has a capacity of 21,000 and has been used for concerts and sporting events since it was built for the 2000 Summer Olympic Games. In other cities hosting IEM majors, similar spaces are used for the events, including traditional spaces used for professional sport teams (e.g., United Center in Chicago and Lanxess Arena in Cologne). From a consumer experience perspective, holding esports events in traditional sport arenas may frame the event experience for consumers in a particular way. For example, esports consumers may be prompted to attend an event or engage with the space because the facility has a relationship with traditional sports (Funk, Pizzo, and Baker 2018; Rovell 2017).

While these events may take place in traditional sport venues, the consumer's experience in the venue is quite unique to esports (Seo 2013). In the case of IEM Sydney, attendees walk into the arena and are immediately greeted by a large on-site sponsorship activation space where ESL and IEM partners have created experiential product engagement opportunities for consumers. Demonstration tables, kiosks, and competition spaces featuring the latest and greatest gaming hardware by major esports brands Predator, Intel, HyperX, and HP are dispersed throughout the arena's foyer (Naraine and Wear 2019). This provides fans and consumers with the opportunity to not only engage with new products, but also compete against one another in a variety of esports at the event (Seo and Jung 2016). This sense of consumer-focused experience is particularly unique when the esports event is compared to a more traditional large-scale sporting event such as a professional basketball game or intercollegiate football game. Fans in attendance at these events are not usually given the opportunity to participate in a basketball or gridiron football game staged by the major sponsors of the event. This unique atmosphere at esports events also allows for physical spaces to facilitate interaction among attendees.

Attendees are also presented with the opportunity to engage with the arena in both traditional and unique ways. Many of these events are taking place in sport and concert venues, and so traditional concession options are available for consumption. At IEM Sydney, this meant traditional Australian sporting food staples such as sausage rolls, meat pies, chips (French fries), beer, and cider. Additionally, much

(*continued*)

THE ESPORTS EVENT CONSUMER EXPERIENCE: THE CASE OF IEM SYDNEY *(CONTINUED)*

like at traditional sporting events, team and licensed merchandise is available for purchase. However, unique to the esports space from a fan consumption perspective is the relative scarcity and availability of esports team merchandise outside of major events. While ESL and other high-profile teams have online stores, it can often be difficult to purchase merchandise in a timely and cost-effective manner outside of esports events. In the case of IEM Sydney, this difficulty has led to heavily trafficked merchandise store fronts every year, with jerseys, T-shirts, and other ESL and team licensed merchandise being sold out over the course of the three-day event (Naraine and Wear 2019).

An additional key component of IEM majors and ESL events is the presence of core gaming hardware and software brands, vendors, and exhibitors showcasing and selling their products. It draws a unique distinction from traditional sporting events. Sporting goods companies such as Spalding, Rawlings, or Easton are not regular exhibitors at major sporting events and do not use these events as opportunities to sell their products. At esports events, doors open several hours in advance of the onstage competition. This time provides ample opportunity for attendees to wander in between sections of the venue and engage with sponsorship activation stations, event exhibitors, concessionaires, and merchandisers.

The core event product at an IEM major tournament is the onstage competitions between esports teams. Similar to the previous descriptions of the spaces within the concourse of the facility, the core competition has both similarities and differences when compared to the traditional sport product usually found in an arena. Most often, the arena is curtained off and only half of the seating bowl is ticketed and occupied. An ESL-branded competition stage is constructed on the middle of the arena floor, with large video screens and floor seating installed in front and to the sides of the stage. Events are hosted and emceed by well-known commentators or personalities, and they often attempt to engage the crowd through giveaways, trivia, fan participation, and other activities. The numerous large video screens are not simply used to show individual players' live views from game play; in the case of *CS:GO*, a specialized video feed overlays a player's video with actual positions of hidden opponents. This perspective gives the crowd an unprecedented view of the competition and adds a considerable amount of drama to the viewing experience. The escalation of this cat-and-mouse type of drama between opposing players is something that is not often seen in traditional sport competitions (Hamari and Sjöblom 2017). During competition, fans in the stands regularly cheer for their favorite teams and players and engage in traditional sport fan behavior including starting and organizing cheers, holding and crafting signs, and celebrating big-play moments with the people around them. Team introductions and trophy presentations are similar to those found in professional sports and encapsulate and encourage a great deal of fanfare (Naraine and Wear 2019).

While esports events have a multitude of unique aspects and intricacies, it is also important to recognize the many commonalities attendees at esports events share with those attending traditional sports. If one were to remove the on-stage competition at an IEM master's event and focus entirely on the behavior of the crowd, it would have many similar qualities of a professional sporting event. This allows these large-scale events to have a broad appeal to both traditional and esports consumers (Naraine and Wear 2019). With audience metrics for esports and traditional consumers trending in the direction of overlap rather than isolation (Newzoo 2019), it will be interesting to see how event professionals in esports and traditional sporting events can learn from one another and build events that appeal to a wide variety of consumer interests and opportunities. Traditional sporting events have also played host to esports events before, during halftime or intermission, or after the event. For example, the day when consumers will be able to attend a professional basketball event between two teams, then watch the esports players from both of the same teams competing in a game such as *NBA 2K*, is not too far away. Marketers will not only learn from each other, they will need to work together. Perhaps one day the sport marketer and esports marketer will even be the same person.

DHL hired a well-known and respected commentator to appear in their marketing activities. At the ESL One events, DHL facilitated opportunities for attendees to experience the company through both the EffiBOT and the VR box stacking game. Additional engagement and activation activities occurred online and were touted throughout social and digital media. In the end, the combination of DHL's marketing activities resulted in positive feelings and sentiments toward the company; in fact, they were so positive that at one point attendees within the ESL One Birmingham event began chanting "D-H-L, D-H-L" (Hayward 2018).

MARKETING ESPORTS TO PLAYERS, SPECTATORS, AND FANS

Another important aspect of esports marketing is understanding what types of factors motivate players, spectators, and fans to engage in various types of consumption behaviors. Because partial (but not complete) overlap exists between esports players, spectators, and fans (i.e., not all players are spectators and fans, and not all fans and spectators play esports or video games), the motivations of both groups are discussed separately. In terms of why players play esports, Hedlund (2019) identified these six unique factors:

- Socialization
- Positive affect
- Competition
- Fantasy or escape
- Coping
- Passing or wasting time

Socialization

Socialization refers to the opportunity for players to meet new people, make new connections, and feel a **sense of community** with others. Anyone who organizes esports competitions or activities would be well advised to provide opportunities for players to socialize and communicate with one another and to market these opportunities to players. Unlike traditional sports, where many of these activities occur face-to-face, many esports players feel a sense of community and kinship with other players of the same game regardless of location or team affiliation. Even in situations

Ben McCanna/Portland Press Herald via Getty Images

Socialization is an important motivation for esports players.

where players are competing against one another today, they may wish to connect with each other at some future time for scrimmages, friendly games, and opportunities to learn from one another. As noted earlier in this chapter, the communication system built in to the game *Apex Legends* that allows players to ping and communicate easily with each other in game can facilitate more connections and communication among players (i.e., making friends), which is an outcome that many players desire.

Positive Affect

Another way to use marketing to motivate player consumption is through providing ways for players to experience fun, enjoyment, and relaxation during their games, inducing positive affect. Positive affect is another way of describing beneficial or good emotions. While the process of playing games may in itself be relaxing, fun, and enjoyable, game developers can offer opportunities for in-game achievements, often called badging (see Schau, Muñiz, and Arnould 2009). For example, in the game *Clash of Clans*, after a player wins enough matches and earns 400 trophies, they automatically earn a badge for the corresponding level of trophies (e.g., Bronze III=400-499 trophies). As they win more matches and trophies, they can move up in the league levels or down if they lose too many matches. In total, there are 22 levels, with the highest being Legend (which equates to 5,000+ trophies). In many aspects of the game, these levels and badges are essential, because they determine everything from whom one is matched to attack or defend against, resource bonuses one receives when they win a match, and more. Competition organizers can also undertake similar activities during which players who have played or won a certain amount can be promoted to a higher level. In addition, they can segment players and take actions to ensure that players are grouped according to experience or skill; top players are rarely matched to compete against novice players. In this way, players have a chance to enjoy the games; they avoid the frustration of being matched with more-skilled players who might be using **smurf accounts**, or intentionally low-level separate accounts. For example, *League of Legends* has nine tiers of players (Iron, Bronze, Silver, Gold, Platinum, Diamond, Master, GrandMaster, and Challenger), most with sub-ranks (I-IV). Over time, *League of Legends* players gain in-game playing experience and can **level up** to a higher rank and tier. Many players feel positive emotions when they accomplish in-game achievements or level up. As players move up, they may strive for more and more success, so providing opportunities for players to earn an enhanced title or badge can reinforce the pride they feel and the desire and motivation to continue to play.

Competition

Another motivation for players is the opportunity to compete. Similar to traditional sports, esports has opportunities for players to play both recreationally and competitively. Underlying the motivation to compete is the opportunity to show one's abilities to others, provide evidence that one knows how to play the game well, and in a competitive situation, defeat one's opponents. Players may be motivated based on pride or confidence in themselves and their teammates, not to mention the desire to represent themselves and an organization (if they have an affiliation). As a result, game developers and organizers should provide a wide range of opportunities for players to compete with and against others; these opportunities can be included in marketing activities focused on encouraging more people to play and compete. For example, in North American collegiate esports, organizations such as Collegiate StarLeague (CSL), Tespa, the National Association of Collegiate Esports (NACE), and the Electronic Gaming Federation (EGF) work with game developers to create, host, and manage esports competitions for college students. In recent years, Riot Games (2019), developer of *League of Legends*, created the Riot Scholastic Association of America (RSAA) as the governing body of both its high school and college esports activities. These types of organizations can organize and manage esports competitions, thus providing opportunities for players to compete at a high level and potentially create a career in gaming while also fueling younger players' motivations to learn how to play. As a result, the opportunity to play and compete can become a marketing tool for future players and competitions.

Zoning

MAKING A DIFFERENCE THROUGH GAMING

David P. Hedlund

Over the last few decades, organizations around the world have increasingly taken part in corporate social responsibility (CSR) activities; this concept is also called corporate citizenship. When they take part in CSR, organizations and their employees engage in activities that positively influence the world and give back to it; simply taking resources has a potential negative effect. According to a 2019 U.S. Chamber of Commerce Foundation report on CSR in the gaming industry, corporate members undertake the following:

- Employee and community engagement activities
- Responsible gaming activities
- Diversity and inclusion efforts
- Workforce development activities
- Charitable giving and the establishment and operations of charitable foundations
- Employee volunteering and matching activities
- The establishment of community partnerships
- Sustainability activities (e.g., recycling, water efficiency, food waste, carbon emissions, energy efficiency, green building certification, supply chain)

Specifically, the authors of the report note that industry members have spent more than $275 million a year on supporting responsible gaming activities, and they have provided more than 64,000 staff with training in this area (U.S. Chamber of Commerce 2019). In addition, 69 percent of industry members use diversity and inclusion hiring practices. Employees of these industry members average 14 volunteer hours per year, and over $367 million in direct charitable giving was reported in 2017. In summary, corporate members of the gaming industry are very active in CSR-related activities.

As an example of CSR activities in esports, during early 2020, wildfires razed large portions of land in Australia. Infinity War, the game developer of *Call of Duty: Modern Warfare*, created downloadable content that players could buy called the Outback Relief Pack. As a result of players purchasing this content, $1.6 million in proceeds were raised and donated to the charity group Direct Relief, which sent breathing masks to areas in which the air was poisonous to breath (Van Boom 2020).

Another example of CSR from the gaming community is seen through the organization Extra Life. The purpose of Extra Life is to organize gamers globally to play esports and video games in support of local children's hospitals. Since 2008, Extra Life has raised over $50 million for children's health care services, treatments, medical equipment, and care (Extra Life n.d.). The best-known activity is an annual gaming marathon, typically held in early November, during which gamers play and oftentimes stream esports play and competition.

In today's world, being active in the community is a strategy organizations and their employees can use to generate positive goodwill and counterbalance any current or future negative stories or perceptions consumers might have. Esports players and organizations can use CSR and corporate citizenship activities to market the ways they are giving back in an attempt to sway consumer gratitude toward their organization and brand. When negative information or activities are reported, organizations can leverage consumer goodwill and gratitude in activities focused on mitigating any fallout. As a result, engaging in good deeds now can help to build up positive associations, and in the event something bad happens in the future, minimize any negative effects.

Fantasy or Escape

Opportunities for fantasy and escape are frequently used in the creation and marketing of esports and video games. Because in-game characters can be imbued with magical powers, abilities, and special skills that are unrealistic for human beings, playing esports and video games can be marketed as opportunities to be someone different or as the ability to do things only possible in one's dreams. Alternatively, games can also be marketed as an escape from daily life. For example, game developers may emphasize in commercials and marketing messages how playing esports and video games can help players to live out their fantasies or dreams in the game. In fact, the premise of the Oasis (a VR world in the year 2045) in the 2018 movie *Ready Player One* epitomizes this motivation. In the movie, citizens are faced with numerous challenges such as overpopulation, energy and resource shortages, poor infrastructure, low-quality housing, and unemployment. As a result, citizens regularly use VR and related to technology to go to the Oasis in order to escape their otherwise unhappy and mundane lives. While still a fantasy world in the movie, many of today's esports and video games are attempting to create and market the same type of opportunity for people to play games and escape anything they do not want to think about in their real lives.

Coping

Another opportunity is the chance for players to use esports to cope with problems or challenges. Sometimes known as catharsis, this motivation epitomizes how consumers cope and seek opportunities to feel a release of pressure from life. When people face challenges in life, the opportunity to cope by playing esports and video games is a frequently marketed strategy. For example, at any hour of the day or any day of the week, players can quickly log in to a game such as *Fortnite*, and within a few minutes they can be playing the game instead of dealing with their problems or challenges. Some games offer an opportunity for coping without the escape from reality. For example, *That Dragon, Cancer* is an autobiographical story in which the game developers chronicle how their family dealt with a cancer diagnosis, treatment, and eventual death of their young son (CBS News 2017). Undoubtedly, both the developers of *That Dragon, Cancer* and its players may take the opportunity to face their own challenges through the game. The opportunity to cope with problems, challenges, or unfortunate circumstances is a potential benefit that could be leveraged through marketing to assist others who are facing similar obstacles.

Passing or Wasting Time

One of the most common motivators for playing esports, especially mobile games, is simply to pass the time. With 3.5 billion smartphones currently in operation globally (Turner 2020), users may pass the time by playing esports and mobile games on their devices. According to the results from the Mobile Gamer Insights Report, 55 percent of American smartphone users play mobile games to pass the time (Tobin 2019). From a marketing perspective, the results suggest an important opportunity for cell phone manufacturers and mobile game developers to market their products to consumers as something to do when they have nothing else to do. The next section examines and discusses the motivations of esports spectators and marketing tactics that can be leveraged with these individuals.

SPECTATOR MOTIVATIONS TO WATCH ESPORTS

The second area of esports marketing examines factors influencing people to watch esports either online or in person. While many player motivations are similar to those of spectators and fans, numerous additional factors influence why people might want to watch or attend an esports event or competition. First are the context-related factors such as the attractiveness of the event, event schedule, teams competing, features of the commentators, qualities of the online chat room, and quality of the online stream (Qian, Zhang, Wang, and Hulland 2019). When examining spectator motives, additional considerations such as the player, game, and commentator qualities (e.g., physical attractiveness, knowledge of the game); the opportunity to learn in-game strategies and tactics; the novelty of the game and event experience; and vicarious achievement (When a player or team I like wins, I also win) also can be leveraged in marketing activities (Hamari and Sjöblom 2017; Pizzo, Baker, Na, Lee, Kin, and Funk 2018; Qian, Wang, Zhang, and Lu 2019).

Player, Game, and Commentator Qualities

This motivator is perhaps the most obvious. In the same way traditional sports teams and broadcasting companies market their players and employees, esports similarly leverages these individuals. Whether it includes marketing physical attractiveness (good-looking players) or knowledge of the game (expert commentators), both of these example characteristics can be leveraged to motivate fans, spectators, and consumers to watch esports. Commentators (often called casters or **shoutcasters** for online streams) help spectators understand both what and why in-game activities are happening. For example, Hamilton (2018) details these characteristics of successful esports shoutcasters: They are entertaining, are able to tell compelling stories, bring energy and passion to their work, and build momentum and excitement in their voice as in-game play reaches its peak. Commentators and casters keep spectators interested and engaged. As a result, broadcasters and event organizers can market their commentators and casters with highlight videos and other types of promotional **sizzle reels** of high-quality in-game action accompanied by knowledgeable and entertaining personnel.

Learning How to Play Esports

A popular motivation of esports spectators is the opportunity to learn new and different in-game strategies and tactics. While traditional sports rarely change (except for an occasional rule change or update), when a new or updated version of a game is published, players may need to learn new ways to play the esports game. Toward that end, an efficient way to learn how to play is watching how others, especially experts, play the game. Game developers and event organizers can market the opportunity to learn how to play the esports game and pick up new strategies and tactics from spectator opportunities.

Novelty of Esports

Another important spectator motive is the uniqueness and novelty of some aspect of the game or event experience. While large numbers of people play esports and video games, much smaller numbers of people attend in person or watch esports competitions and events online. The scant experience many consumers have with attending esports events leaves room for an opportunity to market how novel and unique it is. Large-scale (mega) esports events are still relatively uncommon. As a result, the rarity of such events and possibility for consumers to experience something new is a good opportunity for marketers to leverage.

Opportunities for Vicarious Achievement

The final important spectator motive is the opportunity for people to feel a sense of vicarious achievement. While perhaps most likely when spectators identify with or have some connection to the esports players and teams, if people perceive themselves as related to those they may be watching, then they may be more likely to consume those events in person or online. For example, at international esports tournaments such as the *Fortnite* World Cup, The International (*Dota 2*), or *League of Legends* World Championship, players not only represent the teams on which they play but also the nation they are from. For example, when China's FunPlus Phoenix battled Europe's G2 Esports in the 2019 *League of Legends* World Championship, the pride of both regions was on the line (Pe 2019). After FunPlus Phoenix defeated G2, news stories from China heralded the team and its fans basked in the reflected glory of the team's victory (Futian 2019). As a result, when marketing esports events to potential spectators, leveraging information about teams and players in an effort to find connections and give people reasons to watch can be effective marketing strategies.

CONCLUSION

This chapter discussed and provided examples of the basic concepts of esports marketing, such as the five Ps (product, price, place, promotion, and public relations). It explained the unique aspects of marketing both of and through esports. Further, it described the six most important and frequently used marketing strategies and tactics (using digital marketing, considering diverse types of gamers while avoiding stereotypes, using influencers, being authentic in marketing activities, providing opportunities for experiential marketing, and engaging and activating consumers through activities and events). Finally, the chapter provided further information and examples about how organizations can use various tactics to motivate esports players, spectators, and fans to engage in consumption behaviors. The next chapter explains sponsorship, one of the most important and growing areas of esports marketing.

DISCUSSION QUESTIONS

1. What are the five Ps of esports marketing? Explain the five Ps, explain how each is leveraged in marketing activities, and give examples of marketing in which each is used.
2. What are the two unique aspects of esports marketing? Compare and contrast their similarities and differences, and give examples of how each may be undertaken.
3. What are the six important esports marketing strategies and tactics discussed in this chapter? List, explain, and give examples of all six strategies.
4. How is marketing to esports players similar and different to esports spectators? List, explain, and give examples of marketing tactics and strategies that can be used to influence behaviors of players and spectators.

7

Esports Sponsorship

David P. Hedlund | Daniel Liang

OBJECTIVES

- Explain the sponsorship process.
- Identify and differentiate esports rights-holding properties and endemic and non-endemic sponsors.
- Identify esports sponsorship opportunities in the industry.
- Explain issues facing esports rights-holding properties and sponsors.
- Summarize the sponsorship evaluation process.

INTRODUCTION

One of the most profitable marketing opportunities in esports is engaging in and leveraging sponsorship activities. Esports consumers may ignore many traditional marketing tactics (e.g., advertising) and thus render them ineffective. Therefore, esports marketers explore alternative opportunities through which they can still create awareness of their goods and services and motivate consumers' behaviors—while simultaneously disguising these actions. In other words, in order to market goods and services to esports consumers who might be oblivious to or ignorant of traditional marketing, marketers can camouflage and integrate their activities into the normal routines of games, competitions, and events. One of the most popular ways to convey marketing messages and attempt to influence the behavior of esports consumers is through the use of sponsorship. This chapter introduces the subject of sponsorship in the esports industry. It provides information and examples that focus on various types of esports sponsors, sponsorship opportunities, issues faced by properties and sponsors, and methods of sponsorship evaluation.

UNDERSTANDING SPONSORSHIP

According to IEG, **sponsorship** is "a cash and/or in-kind fee paid to a property (typically in sports, arts, entertainment, or causes) in return for access to the exploitable commercial potential associated with that property" (2017a, p. V). Sponsorship activities create opportunities for organizations and their brands to generate positive associations and influence the behaviors of esports consumers. For example, in order to compete in esports, players need to use electronic devices (e.g., personal computers [PCs], consoles, mobile devices). Therefore, companies that manufacture or assemble the hardware needed to play esports are likely to have an interest in marketing their products to esports fans, players, teams, franchises, leagues, and competition organizers. One tool that organizations and their marketers may choose to use is sponsorship. Through sponsorship, the property (the group being sponsored, also called the **rights holder**) can sell access or rights to any number of its **assets** (e.g., naming rights, event tickets, VIP experiences). In return, the **sponsor** pays cash or provides an in-kind trade (e.g., provides PCs to the sponsored property at a low or no cost) to the sponsored property. The sponsor can then

leverage the rights it receives in support of its marketing, sales, hospitality, and customer relations activities.

When we examine the esports and gaming industry, companies such as Dell (Alienware), HP (Omen), iBUYPOWER, Acer, CORSAIR, Republic of Gamers (ASUS), and MSI all compete for a share of the PC gaming market. Such companies may consider sponsorship opportunities as an effective activity to help increase their market share and revenues. If a potential sponsor would like consumers to perceive their products as high in quality, then they may explore sponsoring championship-winning players or teams with the hope that consumers will connect both in their minds, gain and maintain positive associations of the products, and when they need to buy a product in this category, purchase the sponsors' goods and services. For example, in 2019, Dell's Alienware gaming hardware group became a sponsor for Riot Games' *League of Legends* events (Dell n.d.). As described by Naz Aletaha, Riot Games' Head of Esports Partnerships, "As our official PC and display partner, Dell and Alienware, with their extensive expertise in hardware and technology services, will help us continue to level-up the sport — setting a global performance standard for the hardware that powers it" (LoL Esports Staff 2019, para. 2). While the complete terms of the sponsorship agreement are not known, Alienware provided Aurora R8 computers, 240-hertz monitors, and various types of support to *League of Legends* events around the world. In return, Dell and Alienware received opportunities to activate and leverage their sponsorship at *League of Legends* events, including displaying the use of their products at the event, accessing VIP seating at the events, and related marketing and branding activities (LoL Esports Staff 2019).

In this example, Dell and its Alienware brand had at least two sponsorship goals. The goals were to show consumers the high performance of their gaming PCs and monitors in an attempt to (1) impact consumers' image of Alienware and (2) influence consumers' purchasing preferences toward Alienware gaming hardware. Effective sponsorship, in this case, would result in consumers perceiving the Alienware brand and its performance as high quality and purchasing the brand when they are shopping for gaming hardware. One could measure the results of this sponsorship in numerous ways, including how positively or negatively consumers perceive the sponsor, what positive or negative messages consumers are telling others about the sponsor and its brands, and how much of an increase or decrease in the interest and purchase of the sponsor's goods and services occurred.

TYPES OF ESPORTS SPONSORS

The two major types of sponsors are endemic and non-endemic. **Endemic sponsors** produce goods and services used in the actual playing or production of esports competitions and events. Examples of endemic sponsors include computer, console, and mobile device software and hardware manufacturers; broadcasting and streaming technology; and other products that players, teams, or event organizers might need or use during the process of competition. **Non-endemic sponsors** produce goods and services not directly used in the playing of the game or production of esports competitions and events. Examples include credit card companies, transportation (e.g., automobile companies, airline companies), telecom companies, insurance companies, and food and beverage companies (e.g., those selling energy drinks, snacks and foods, and vitamins and supplements). According to IEG (2019), after surveying more than 300 brands representing more than 40 industry categories (e.g., consumer electronics, telecom, retail) engaged in esports sponsorship, 53 percent of sponsors are endemic and 47 percent are non-endemic. In addition, IEG (2019) identified the 12 most active endemic and non-endemic sponsors (see figure 7.1). Because both endemic and non-endemic sponsors may be easily linked to esports activities, sometimes confusion exists about the endemic/non-endemic category in which a particular sponsor may be categorized. For example, because of their pervasive use by many players, some might consider energy drinks to be endemic sponsors. However, because an esports event can occur without such drinks, by definition they would be classified as non-endemic sponsors. Esports competitions require PCs, consoles, or mobile devices, in addition to numerous other types of peripheral computer technology, so any company selling or marketing these types of hardware would be defined as an endemic sponsor.

Top endemic esports sponsors	Top non-endemic esports sponsors
• Alienware (Dell)	• adidas
• CORSAIR	• Anheuser-Busch
• DXRacer	• Betway
• HyperX	• Boost Mobile
• Intel	• GEICO
• Logitech	• Gillette
• Omen (HP)	• McDonald's
• Razer	• Mercedes-Benz
• Republic of Gamers (ASUS)	• Monster Energy
• SCUF Gaming	• Mountain Dew
• SteelSeries	• Red Bull
• Turtle Beach	• Vodafone

Figure 7.1 Top endemic and non-endemic sponsor brands.
Based on IEG Esport Sector (2019).

Sponsors are now seeing the growth and impact of the esports industry. More companies are looking for ways to enter the marketplace, create awareness among consumers, position their goods and services in positive ways, and influence consumers' behaviors. Within the esports industry, Nielsen (2019a) notes how organizations and their brands can engage in sponsorship and form partnerships with players and personalities from various teams, franchises, leagues, event operators, broadcasters and distributors, and game publishers. Through these relationships, brands can activate and leverage their sponsorship activities in attempts to gain more awareness and increasing shares of consumer resource allocations (e.g., purchases, attendance).

Within the industry, many esports players and teams are interested in becoming a sponsored property. Sponsorship opportunities are perceived as a means of providing financial stability and performance incentives for players and teams. In ideal situations, many of the largest costs (e.g., hardware, peripherals [e.g., headset, keyboard, mouse], chairs, travel and transportation, accommodations, and gear [e.g., clothing, shoes]) facing esports players, teams, franchises, leagues, and competition organizers can be provided free or at a low cost from sponsors. In turn, sponsors want to associate themselves with well-known and impactful influencers (see chapter 6) and organizations with the power to motivate consumer behaviors. In return for sponsors' support, sponsored players and teams can use the products in authentic ways and help to raise awareness for the sponsors and their brands.

Because well-chosen and effective sponsorship can drive sales, attendance, and other positive consumer behaviors, especially with young consumers, many endemic and non-endemic sponsors have sponsored players, teams, and other properties in the esports ecosystem. However, as Fischer (2018) noted, esports players and consumers desire authentic relationships with sponsors and brands (see chapter 6). As a result, sponsors may need to forgo traditional marketing activities until they are well known and trusted by esports consumers. Instead, sponsors may need to focus on brand building, increasing name recognition and **brand equity**, and developing positive associations such as consumers' feelings of gratitude toward the sponsors for helping the esports community. Sponsors still have numerous opportunities for activities in which they can engage and leverage. The next section details the different types of sponsorship opportunities.

WHO IS SPONSORING TEAMS AND LEAGUES?

David P. Hedlund

In recent years, sponsorship by endemic and non-endemic brands has been growing in esports. Given this fact, important differences exist between the types of sponsors that engage in team-based sponsorship and those that engage in league-based sponsorship. Based on data published by Nichols (2017), figure 7.2, *a* and *b*, shows how much companies based in different industry sectors sponsor top esports leagues and top teams. For example, sponsors from the computers and software and consumer electronics areas, many of whom are endemic, lead both types of sponsorship, while mostly non-endemic sponsors from categories such as energy and soft drinks, financial services, television, Internet broadcasting, office products and services, and others round out the top sponsors for leagues and teams.

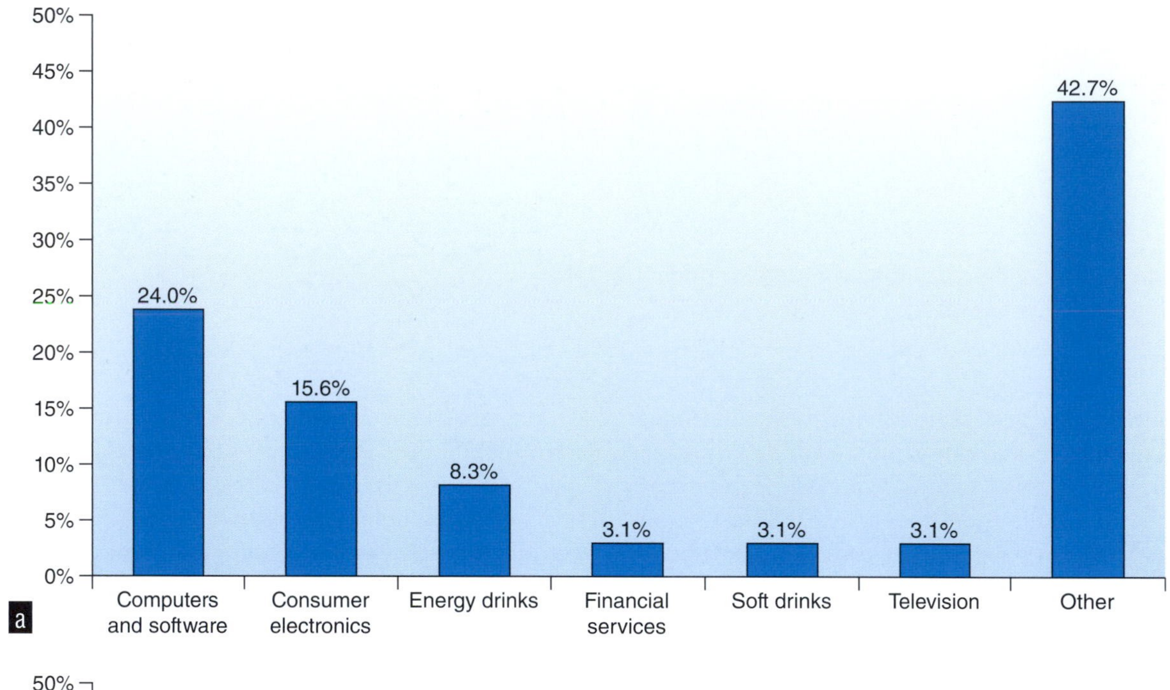

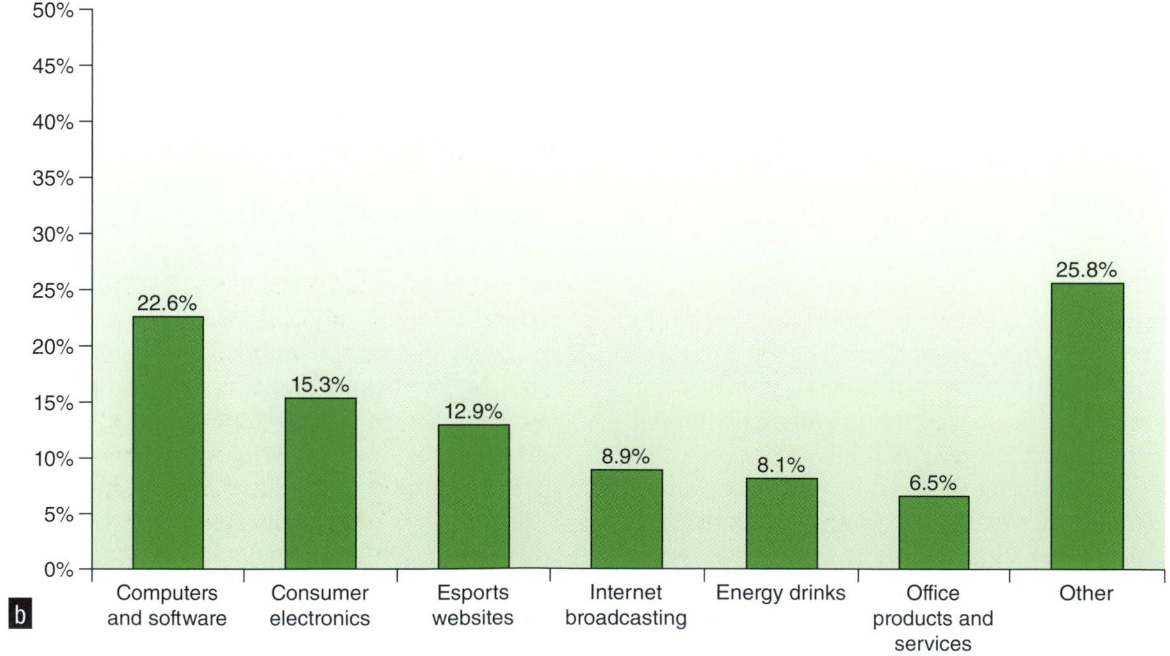

Figure 7.2 Top areas of (*a*) league sponsorship and (*b*) team sponsorship by industry segment.

Based on Nichols (2017).

SPONSORSHIP OPPORTUNITIES

When considering different types of sponsorship for esports players, teams, leagues, and events, six common opportunities exist (Nielsen 2019a):

- Apparel
- Equipment
- Signage
- Digital overlays on the broadcast or stream
- Content included during the digital broadcast or stream
- Digital content on social media

These sponsorship opportunities (often called assets) are available for sponsors and partners to negotiate rights fees to purchase and use. Later, it is the responsibility of the sponsor to leverage the opportunities they purchased to affect consumer behavior toward their organization and brand(s).

Apparel

Sponsorship of apparel is one of the most frequently sold assets in esports around the globe. Examples include Nike's apparel and footwear sponsorship of all 16 teams in China's *League of Legends* Pro League (LPL), Puma's sponsorship of the Cloud9 franchise to provide official gameday shirts and pants, and adidas' sponsorship of Tyler "Ninja" Blevins through its adidas Originals brand (Fanelli 2019; Holland and Al-Ali 2019; Russ 2019). Usually esports players, teams, and leagues receive free personalized apparel from the sponsor; in return, the sponsor has their logo prominently located in one or more places on the merchandise. The sponsor and the property can both sell the same branded apparel. In addition, sponsors frequently receive supplementary assets as part of their sponsorship, such as signage, print and digital advertisement opportunities, and complimentary event tickets.

Equipment

As was briefly described earlier in this chapter, endemic hardware and equipment sponsorship is also common in the esports industry. For example, in 2020, hardware and peripherals manufacturer CORSAIR sponsors eight esports franchises around the world with hardware, support, and innovation (CORSAIR n.d.). Alienware sponsors Team Liquid, providing gaming PCs, monitors, and other types of hardware. In addition, it purchased the naming rights to the team's state-of-the-art training facility (the Alienware Training Facility) in Santa Monica, California (Takahashi 2018). As of 2020, Logitech sponsors 27 teams around the world with their hardware and peripherals, it sponsors and owns the naming rights to the Logitech G Challenge eRacing competition, and the company also sponsors individual players and esports events around the world (Logitech G n.d.). Sponsors might provide hardware and equipment such as the following:

- Gaming PCs
- Chairs
- PC cases
- Keyboards
- Streaming or web cameras
- PC memory chips
- Mice
- PC processor chips
- Mouse pads
- Tables
- PC fans and cooling systems
- Headsets
- Lighting
- Accessories, wiring, and parts
- Speakers
- Power supply
- Apparel and gear

Signage

Another important asset sponsors may purchase is the right to have their marketing and branding displayed on signage. In recent years, properties have expanded opportunities to include not only signage within a facility or at an event (e.g., video boards; LED screens and displays; casting, commentating, and broadcasting desks; programs and informational booklets), but also at their training center, on the backdrop used for press conferences and interviews, and as naming rights for a facility. Earlier Team Liquid's Alienware Training Facility was provided as an example, although larger facilities such as the HyperX Esports Arena Las Vegas (located at the Luxor Hotel and Casino in Las Vegas, Nevada) have also sold their naming rights. The sponsorship and partnership between HyperX and Allied Esports, the arena's owner and operator, includes "co-branded experiences and events, including opportunities and activations with HyperX's plethora of personalities, esports athletes and influencers" (Ring 2018, para. 3).

Through putting marketing and branding words and messages in front of consumers on signage, sponsors hope to create awareness and provide information that will influence consumers' opinions and actions.

Digital Overlays on the Broadcast or Stream

Now that competitive esports are broadcast on both television and Internet platforms, sponsors have the opportunity to create overlays or digital frames for the broadcast or stream. They can frame the content and provide information on other parts of the screen while allowing consumers to continue watching their chosen programming. While consumers may not always notice it, sponsors may want to have their marketing and branding content and messages located in this digital space. Sponsors can activate their sponsorship and continue to create associations while consumers watch esports content.

Content Included During Digital Broadcast or Stream

A related yet unique sponsorship activity is the opportunity to include marketing and branding within the content of the digital esports broadcast or stream. These types of activities could be well-described as product placement. In 2018, energy drink company Red Bull signed Tyler "Ninja" Blevins as an endorser. Almost immediately, Red Bull and Blevins began to leverage this sponsorship with the announcement and activation of an all-night *Fortnite* tournament called Red Bull Rise Till Dawn, which was held in Chicago and streamed on Twitch (Miceli 2018a). Red Bull also created a customized headband on which both parties' logos were displayed. In addition, the company provided Blevins with a Red Bull–branded refrigerator, clothing, and other products with brand marks for on-air display in his streaming room (Red Bull Gaming 2018). Since then, Red Bull and Blevins have continued to expand their relationship with numerous activities, including adorning limited-edition cans of Red Bull with photos of Blevins, delivering the limited-edition can to Blevins via drone and posting a video of the activity on Twitter, and creating opportunities for those that purchase the limited-edition cans to win a chance to have a gaming session with Blevins (Muncy 2019; Red Bull 2019; Sweeney 2019). As of February of 2020, according to Blevins' website, "It is estimated that more than 6.8 billion ninja Red Bull cans have been consumed in two years all over the world. While 2 billion ninja Red Bull cans have been used in the US only" (Ali 2020, para. 9).

David P. Hedlund

Setup for a collegiate esports event with participants' and sponsors' signage.

Hanna Lassen - Gran Turismo/Gran Turismo via Getty Images

Sponsorship can be integrated into events and broadcasts.

Digital Content on Social Media

In line with how Red Bull and Blevins used social media to leverage and activate their sponsorship relationship, the eMLS League (an official partner of the EA SPORTS FIFA 20 Global Series) and sponsor PlayStation also have engaged in numerous social media activities through which they have promoted digital content, often on social media. For example, in 2018, PlayStation became the presenting sponsor of the inaugural eMLS Cup; the competition was promoted on social media and streamed on both Twitch and the official MLS website (MLS Communications 2018). During 2019, eMLS tweeted about how followers could win a PlayStation 4 by retweeting and replying to a post about which MLS player they use most when competing in FIFA (Major League Soccer 2019). In 2020, the eMLS Cup, presented by PlayStation, was scheduled to be held at the South by Southwest (SXSW) conference, and again, promotions and matches were scheduled to be shown on Twitch, Twitter, and other social media sites. Unfortunately, the 2020 events did not occur due to COVID-19 and the cancelling of the conference. With a separate sponsor, Scuf Gaming (provider of customized controllers), eMLS hosted a 24-hour stream of FIFA 20 in support of the sixth annual Kick Childhood Cancer campaign benefitting the Children's Oncology Group Foundation (MLS Communications 2019). The streaming was promoted and shown on multiple social media platforms. Due to these and numerous other activities, digital research firm Zoomph found that (1) the top eMLS team, FC Cincinnati, generated 15.6 million impressions (i.e., how much individuals read, hear, or learn about something in the media) valued at $83,612; (2) the top eMLS player, Gordon "Fiddle" Thornsberry, received 34.3 million impressions with a value of $183,717; and (3) due to their sponsorship activations, PlayStation generated 46.1 million impressions valued at $247,770, while Scuf Gaming received 25.5 million impressions with a value of $136,358 (Lindner 2020). Often combined, digital content and sponsorship **activations** have become an integral and useful aspect of the marketing mix.

Examples of Sponsorship Activation

Finally, in addition to the examples listed earlier in this chapter, countless unique sponsorship activations exist. For example, in addition to sponsoring multiple activities at the event, Mastercard created an experiential marketing opportunity (the Mastercard Nexus) for the 2018 *League of Legends* World Championship (Mastercard 2018). The purpose of the Mastercard Nexus was to allow fans to experience what it is like to become a champion through augmented reality; to become educated about streaming and hear from a panel of experts; and to meet professional players, teams, and cosplayers (Mastercard 2018). In 2019, while launching Game Fuel, their newest beverage, Mountain Dew (MTN DEW) provided players in the *Call of Duty* World League with samples in advance of its release (Miceli 2018b). In addition to *Call of Duty* branding, the new Game Fuel container has a unique resealable cap and no-slip coating about which many in the media have reported (Giammona 2019; Hayward 2019; Wallace 2018). In 2020, the U.S. Air Force became a sponsor of the *Call of Duty* League and activated their relationship at the inaugural event by providing fans experiential opportunities in flight simulators (Martin 2020). As a final example, Mastercard is the exclusive financial services partner of Riot Games' *League of Legends* Championship Series (LCS), and it sponsors the LCS Player of the Week Award (Hitt 2020a). The goal of this activity is likely to associate a top player in the financial services industry (Mastercard) with the top players in *League of Legends*. However, one of the challenges many of the sponsors listed in this chapter face is with measuring the effectiveness of the sponsorship resource allocations and ensuring a return on their investment. The next two sections discuss sponsorship effectiveness and other issues.

ISSUES FACING PROPERTIES AND SPONSORS

Properties and sponsors are faced with many issues. For rights-holding properties, a cluttered marketplace of endemic sponsors, a lack of activation on the part of sponsors, inauthentic activities of sponsors, and ineffective insights and results of sponsorship all provide cautionary notes.

Saturation and a Cluttered Marketplace

First, literally hundreds of companies are selling computer and electronic hardware. With a saturated marketplace, it is often a challenge for endemic brands to stand out, especially those with weak brand equity and little awareness by consumers. Therefore, it may take a long period of time and many resources on the part of sponsors before esports consumers will recognize and develop positive associations. Impatient sponsors looking for near-immediate returns may be disappointed by the amount of brand-building activities required.

Lack of Activation Activities

Another related issue focuses on the lack of activation, which often may not occur. According to IEG (2017b, 2018), sponsors will spend an average $2.20 on sponsorship activation for every $1.00 they spend on rights fees. In other words, if a sponsor spends $100,000 on the title sponsorship of an event, it will spend $220,000 on activities focused on making people aware of their sponsorship and leveraging the sponsorship for beneficial outcomes. However, while 24 percent of respondents to IEG's survey indicated a ratio of money spent on activation to rights fees, 19 percent of respondents noted an intended spending ratio of zero to one. In the case of those that may have responded with zero, the only way consumers would be aware of the existence of a sponsor is by the actions and rights sold by the property. Not undertaking activities focused on leveraging or activating sponsorship could be a recipe for underperformance and a lack of return on investment in the sponsorship activity. Properties may want to consider stipulating in sponsorship contracts that sponsors must also spend a matching amount of resources, equal to the cost of the rights fee, on activating their sponsorship in order to help ensure value is produced through the activities.

Perceptions of Inauthenticity

The purpose of marketing and sponsorships is to facilitate future sales and behaviors that may benefit the bottom line of the company. As a result, consumers may be inherently suspicious of the true motives of any organization or persons engaged in any type of marketing activities. This phenomenon even extends to organizational behaviors and activities such as engaging in corporate social responsibility programs, when consumers question the purpose behind company support. In esports, players and consumers are even more suspicious of the motives of companies involved throughout the industry. Esports is about more than just playing video games, it is also a way of life to which many people devote large amounts of their time. Because so many players and consumers take esports very seriously, the expectation is that others in the community share the same passion and genuine love for gaming. Esports players and consumers are hesitant to support organizations and people that are not authentic and genuinely passionate toward esports. Therefore, sponsors need to do everything possible to engage in authentic marketing and sponsorship activities. Moreover, properties would also be wise to educate sponsors on the importance of creating authentic activities, not to mention holding sponsors accountable and assist them if they fail or struggle to create genuine relationships with consumers. For example, in 2016, fast-food chain Arby's partnered with the U.S.-based television show and esports competition series *ELEAGUE* to create a series of commercials around the game *Counter-Strike: Global Offensive* (*CS:GO*). In one of the commercials, a lineup of Arby's sandwiches are unexpectedly blown up one by one, and the narrator is heard yelling the oft-used *CS:GO* phrase "Rush B," which refers to a tactic for team members in the game to quickly change to position B (Berzen 2019; iSpot.tv 2016). According to Berzen (2019), these types of authentic commercials are effective, and "Arby's has seen this come to life for their brand as social, earned media and attribution results around their campaign have been incredibly positive" (para. 11).

Ineffective Insights and Targeting of Consumers

Another challenge facing properties is the ineffective insights and results that can be associated with targeting young consumers. McKinsey analysts Singer and Chi (2019) expressed the challenges of imprecise measurements and understanding of target markets when they noted that "we still can't segment esports viewers: How many are in the United States? Male? Thirteen to 18 versus 18 to 35 years old? How many watch less than an hour versus 10+ hours per week? As with other forms of digital advertising, brands also have concerns about ad viewability, viewing by bots and fake accounts, and targetability" (para. 19). According to Nielsen's (2019b) Games 360 U.S. Report, 66 percent of the U.S. population ages 13 and older are gamers, and the average age of esports fans is 25 years old. However, because many young people do not earn a salary or have disposable income at a young age (13-16 years), the insights that can be generated about this important segment of the gaming population is extremely limited. As a result, sponsoring companies may exercise extreme caution when targeting and creating relationships with young gamers.

Sponsors face a number of important issues, including exclusivity in sponsorship categories, identifying properties that match their own consumer demographics, and finding properties that share similar values and goals.

Exclusivity

Confronting exclusivity in sponsorship can be a challenge. While many sponsorship categories can easily have one exclusive sponsor (e.g., keyboard, mouse, headset, chair), an overlap in exclusivity can exist in some popular sponsorship categories. For example, in the case of many esports events, consumers can watch online streams on any one of various streaming platforms such as Twitch, YouTube, Facebook, Caffeine, DouYu, Huya, and the organization's own website. While the industry has slowly eliminated the overlap (e.g., popular streamers generally broadcast on only one platform; esports leagues such as *Overwatch* League [OWL], *Call of Duty* League, and *Hearthstone* esports competitions also have exclusive streaming deals), exclusivity in the use of a single broadcasting platform is still not universal. Another area where exclusivity is challenging is in competition and event organizers. Due to the holding of intellectual property rights by game developers, they have the right to license their games to others as they see fit. However, conflict can arise when multiple game licensors overlap in their target player and user markets (e.g., high school, college, professional). Sometimes, two competing organizations both have licenses to host competitions for the same game. Because exclusivity does not exist in this case, organizers must identify alternative ways to differentiate what they offer. As the industry continues to develop and mature, more sponsors and partners may expect exclusivity to be included in the esports sponsorship contracts they sign.

Identifying Properties With Matching Consumer Demographics

As noted earlier, properties face a related challenge of ineffective insights and results associated with targeting young consumers. In a well-publicized article titled "Shady Numbers and Bad Business: Inside the Esports Bubble," D'Anastasio (2019) reported on numerous challenges and inconsistencies faced by the industry. Many of the issues stemmed from questions about the reliability and validity of data and reported results on topics ranging from how many and what types of people watch streamed esports events to how much revenue leagues, teams, and players generate to what the value and **return on investment (ROI)** are from buying in or sponsoring esports. To counter these potential concerns and produce more standardized and comparable information and results, beginning in 2019, ESL, DreamHack, Riot Games, and a growing number of sponsors and stakeholders partnered with Nielsen to measure multiple aspects of the industry including data on fans, viewership, and sponsorship impact (Rolander 2019; Swant 2019; Takahashi 2019). As Modern Times Group's (owner of ESL Gaming and DreamHack) CEO Jørgen Madsen Lindemann noted, "Standardized reliable data measured by an independent company like Nielsen is something that has been widely requested from brand partners, advertisers and broadcasters as we have worked to increase monetization of media and sponsorship rights in esports . . . the introduction of [**key performance indicators (KPIs)**] . . . like **Average Minute Audience (AMA)**, is something that traditional sports have provided for years" (Sinclair 2019, para. 3). KPIs, such as AMA, are quantitative metrics used to determine whether or not organizational objectives are being achieved. KPIs can also be compared between different offerings. For example, a broadcasted esports event with a higher AMA might be more appealing to certain sponsors interested in advertising and marketing their goods and services to the same target audience.

Identifying Properties With Matching Values

Another issue facing sponsors is a question of fit—in other words, how well or how much in common the rights holder and the sponsor share. One of the manifest goals of many sponsors is to partner with people or organizations that share a similar vision, values, and goals. Many sponsors raise an important question that focuses on support of first-person shooter (FPS) games. Stern (2019a) noted the importance of sponsorship to esports rights holders. However, sponsors whose values do not align with games in which in-game human avatars try to shoot and kill one another may be dissuaded from sponsoring FPS players, teams, leagues, and competitions. Another issue is related to a lack of overlap between consumer segments. Nielsen's (2019b) Games 360 U.S. Report provides extensive information about esports consumers. In their profile of U.S. esports fans aged 13 to 40, 75 percent are men, they average 3 hours and 5 minutes of weekly esports playing and 7 hours and 35 minutes of weekly video game playing, and 75 percent are classified as millennials (aged 18-34 in 2019). If a business targets their goods and services to female consumers ages 40 and over, utilizing esports sponsorship may be less effective than alternative opportunities because esports has a smaller base of older female consumers compared to other sponsorship channels.

In summary, rights-holding properties and sponsors face a number of challenges when it comes to creating win–win relationships for all parties involved. However, based on near-universal growth across the esports industry and with improved understanding of who esports consumers are and how they consume, sponsorship will undoubtedly increase, especially in the area of non-endemic sponsors entering the space. The overall knowledge base and learned experiences from all stakeholders will help mitigate many of the issues noted in this section. Additionally, the added knowledge and experience will also likely assist with properly managing both expectations and evaluations of the industry.

SPONSORSHIP EVALUATION

Within the sponsorship industry, many organizations offer opportunities to evaluate the value generated and received after the conclusion of the activities or agreement. Many companies also use external marketing research or media firms to calculate the benefits and costs and determine the value received based on the costs paid. These types of analyses are often described as examinations of ROI. In esports, recently a movement

Zoning

UNDERSTANDING WHY SPONSORS ENGAGE IN SPONSORSHIP AND WHAT THEY WANT

David P. Hedlund

With every sponsor, rights-holding property, and stakeholder having unique goals, decision makers are faced with considering a multitude of benefits, evaluation objectives, channels, services expected, and evaluation metrics. In the 17th annual ESP Properties Sponsorship Decision-Makers Survey, the leading responses were tallied (IEG 2017b). While not specific to esports, the insights from the results can provide esports sponsors, rights-holding properties, and stakeholders with useful information that can inform their activities.

Here are the top 10 benefits that sponsors want:

1. Category exclusivity
2. Presence in digital, social, mobile, and media
3. Tickets and hospitality
4. Rights to property content for digital and other uses
5. Rights to property marks and logos
6. On-site signage
7. Right to promote co-branded products and services
8. Spokespersons or access to personalities
9. Access to property's audience or fan data
10. Broadcast ad opportunities

Here are the top 10 channels that sponsors use to leverage their sponsorships:

1. Social media
2. Public relations
3. Hospitality
4. On-site or experiential
5. Internal communications
6. Digital or mobile promotions
7. Traditional advertising
8. Business to business
9. Sales promotion offers
10. Direct marketing

Here are the top 10 objectives used to evaluate properties:

1. Create awareness and visibility.
2. Increase brand loyalty.
3. Change or reinforce image.
4. Entertain clients or prospects.
5. Stimulate sales, trial, and usage.
6. Obtain or develop content to use in digital, social, and other media.
7. Showcase community/social responsibility.
8. Capture database (lead generation).
9. Sell products and services to sponsored property.
10. Access platform for experiential branding.

Here are the top 10 property-provided services that are important to sponsors:

1. Assistance measuring return on investment
2. Postevent report/fulfillment audit
3. Audience research on attitude/image
4. Leveraging ideas
5. Assistance developing relevant content
6. Audience research on recognition/recall
7. Audience research on propensity to purchase
8. Third-party valuation statement
9. Assistance earning internal buy-in at sponsoring organization
10. Tracking of promotional offers

(*continued*)

UNDERSTANDING WHY SPONSORS ENGAGE IN SPONSORSHIP AND WHAT THEY WANT *(CONTINUED)*

Finally, here are the top 10 sponsorship evaluation metrics:

1. Attitudes toward brand
2. Amount of position social media activity
3. Awareness of products, services, and brand
4. Awareness of company's and brand's sponsorship
5. Product service sales
6. Response to customer or prospect entertainment
7. Response to sponsorship-related promotions and content
8. Amount of media exposure generated
9. Television logo exposure
10. Lead generation

has begun toward standardizing the (e)valuation of sponsorship activities through (1) using experienced and impartial firms such as Nielsen to collect data and provide results and (2) measuring viewership and value through the use of common and standardized metrics such as average minute audience (AMA). Nielsen defines AMA as "the average number of individuals or (homes or target group) viewing a TV channel, which is calculated per minute during a specified period of time over the program duration" (Ashton 2019, para. 4). For example, after the conclusion of the 2019 *Overwatch* League (OWL) season, Nielsen released AMA viewership figures for both digital streaming and linear broadcasts, with some year-over-year (YOY) comparisons. According to Stern (2019b), the key findings were as follows:

- OWL averaged 95,000 U.S. viewers (34% YOY growth), with 55,000 from the 18- to 34-year-old demographic. These results indicated OWL is the fastest growing league in the 18 to 34 demographic in the United States.
- OWL averaged 313,000 global viewers (18% YOY growth).
- The median age of OWL viewers is 24 years old. These results indicated the average OWL viewer is younger than those for traditional sports (both professional and college) leagues.

For comparison, regular-season viewership in 2019 for National Football League (NFL) games averaged 16.5 million viewers and 5 percent YOY growth (Young 2019). During the 2019 Major League Baseball (MLB) season, FOX averaged over 2.4 million viewers (more than 8% YOY growth), ESPN averaged over 1.6 million viewers (more than 2% YOY growth), and average viewership on TBS increased by over 10 percent YOY (MLB 2019). As a result, while OWL viewership is growing and is notably strong with the 18 to 34 demographic, substantial growth is required to match traditional sports viewership. In early 2020, Nielsen announced the implementation of their new metric called live+. It has the capability to measure viewers watching both the live event and later on-demand views (Hitt 2020b). As a result, this new metric will take into consideration both live and on-demand future views, perhaps by updating or projecting future viewership. As the industry progresses, sponsors will need to decide for themselves how much they are willing to pay to sponsor and partner with esports groups and how they want to evaluate their ROI.

CONCLUSION

This chapter introduced sponsorship in the esports industry. It discussed various types of sponsors, sponsorship opportunities, issues faced by properties and sponsors, and methods of sponsorship evaluation. Sponsorship in the esports industry has grown in recent years as new insights, such as the year-over-year (YOY) growth and comparatively young age (18-34 demographic) of esports consumers, have fueled interest by both endemic and non-endemic sponsors. As the esports industry continues to develop, sponsors are likely to remain important partners for players and rights-holding properties such as game developers, teams, franchises, leagues, competitions, and events. One of the most popular areas where sponsorship activities are seen is at or through the broadcasting of esports events. The next chapter provides information about the organization and management of esports events.

DISCUSSION QUESTIONS

1. What are the two different categories of sponsors? Give examples of both, and explain them.
2. What are the six types of sponsorship opportunities organizations have to sell? Explain, giving examples of each one.
3. What are the different types of goods or services available for esports sponsorship? If you work for the rights holder, which ones would you prioritize when seeking to sell sponsorship opportunities to companies and their brands? Explain your answer.
4. What are some of the most important issues facing both rights-holding properties and sponsors? Explain, and give examples of the issues you identify.
5. How can both rights-holding properties and sponsors evaluate sponsorships? Give examples of different types of information or data you would like to collect or see in order to properly undertake sponsorship evaluation.

8

Esports Events

R.C. Smith III | Gil Fried | Jide Osipitan | David P. Hedlund

OBJECTIVES

- Outline areas of event management to consider when planning an event.
- Understand the role of event security as part of the event planning process.
- Explain the steps involved in organizing esports events.
- Summarize important considerations and issues facing esports event organizers.

INTRODUCTION

Planning an esports event takes careful attention to detail, foreseeing what could happen in best- and worst-case scenarios, and clear communication with all stakeholders. Esports event planning is much like planning traditional sporting events. Think of the steps you would need to take in order to host a sporting event. First, you would need to secure a location and players or teams. For those unfamiliar with the process it may seem to be a straightforward and easy task, but it isn't always as simple as it sounds; numerous concerns could subsequently arise. Consider the following factors:

- Choosing an optimal date
- Availability of the facility
- Conflicting events (either events in the same facility or similar events that would compete against your event during the same day and time)
- The time required to set up the facility
- The cost and number of resources needed to host the event, such as financial, human, and equipment
- Availability of facility personnel to work that date
- Adequate storage space and loading docks
- Size of the facility
- Ability to leverage concessions, parking, and other elements

This list represents only some of the facility-related issues that require consideration. Numerous other concerns may arise, such as how to price, sell, and distribute tickets; how to market the event; which group(s) or sponsors are paying for event operations costs; and who will suffer the financial loss if the event is not successful. All these issues need to be analyzed and considered for every type of event. Esports-specific events have additional considerations, including the quality of Internet connection available at the facility, the layout of the facility (e.g., seating and stage) and feasibility of setting up large video screens in different positions, and the ability to broadcast the event through the Internet (e.g., streaming) or traditional media.

Creating an esports event has similarities to and differences from creating a traditional sporting event. A major difference is that you can host an esports event entirely online. Players, teams, and fans may not have to physically travel to a location in order to compete. Instead, all activities can take place online, and all participants can be located anywhere in the world. Another difference is that depending on the level of competition and how the competition is organized, organizers may not know who is really playing the game; competitors could fabricate or be untruthful about who they are in real life. This scenario could be especially harmful if an event is designed for college students but nonstudent professional players are able to join the competition.

Events come in many shapes and sizes, so there are many ways to plan them. This chapter provides a general overview of esports events and some issues to consider when planning an event, including brainstorming, setting goals and objectives, things to consider when planning an event (e.g., budgeting, marketing, target markets, registrations), what to consider when reviewing venues, and postevent evaluations. The chapter also explains communication and run of show (creating a timeline of events that happen during the event).

BRAINSTORMING AND SETTING GOALS AND OBJECTIVES

An event usually stems from an initial idea or concept, no matter the size and scope. Then, having a **brainstorming** session (or sessions) gets the process started. The event organizers should take part in the brainstorming session. During the session, people come up with ideas, note potential challenges, decide who else to include in the event planning process, and discuss anything else that comes to mind. The brainstorming session itself can be organized in a variety of ways. For example, a trained facilitator or someone from an internal or external group may lead the session. One of the first goals to pursue at the start of this process is getting all the appropriate people involved. The group can work together to develop ideas through brainstorming, but some individual organizers who are involved in the process may be able to leverage their knowledge, experience, and professional network/connections for the betterment of the event. For example, consider an internal university group that wants to hold an esports event. While brainstorming the basic issues (e.g., who, what, where, when, how, why), the group as a whole might express interest in hosting an event for a first-person shooter (FPS) game title. Because of these individuals' experience all might vigorously support this idea; as far as they might know, FPS titles are one of the most popular titles their target audience (students) plays. However, if no one in this group is a university administrator who is involved in the process, they may not realize that the person or people (e.g., athletic director, facility or arena manager) overseeing the prospective facility (e.g., the on-campus arena) will not support the hosting of FPS events and would withdraw funding or support if such an event proceeded. Without understanding and appreciating the perspectives of all possible stakeholders, those involved in brainstorming might work for months putting an event together only to find out later that their plans and work were all for naught.

During brainstorming sessions, consider these additional basic questions among others: Who is the target audience or market for the event? What is the purpose or intended outcome of the event? Do any logistical challenges exist? If the goal of a group of friends is to have a fun Friday night hosting *League of Legends* competitions, then they would communicate information to each other about a time and place, the rules of competition, and any competition or tournament structure. These individuals may take into account factors such as who can host the event and where to host it, who has the best and more reliable computer hardware and Internet connection, how participants will travel to the event location, what restaurants might provide food, and whether any reward will be given for the winner(s) of the championship. These casual questions and activities among friends are another example of the brainstorming phase. This same type of process is undertaken during the brainstorming phase of planning international esports competitions, but it is on a much larger scale. For a small-scale event, this process might take a couple minutes during a single meeting; a major international event might take years of planning and development before it comes to fruition. Countries often have 5 to 10 years to plan and build facilities for mega sporting events such as the Olympic Games or FIFA World Cup.

Keeping in mind a company's or organization's mission and vision are important in the event planning process; or, one of the goals of brainstorming might be to develop a mission and vision if it's a new company or a new event. A **mission** explains a company's customers, product, and future growth. A **vision** explains what the company wants to become. Both the mission and vision help formulate goals and objectives, while keeping in mind the reason(s) the organization exists and the population it serves.

Setting goals and objectives is the next logical step in event planning. Goals should be SMART (specific, measurable, attainable, realistic, and timely). **Goals** are overarching statements about what one wants to achieve, while **objectives** are statements, often about topics that can be measured, about how one knows if they are on track to achieve the goal. For example, the statement "Let's create a tournament with friends for fun" is not a SMART goal, because it is impossible to measure fun. Each person has a unique perception of what constitutes fun. A better-framed goal is "Host a collegiate esports tournament for all 25 college-level *Rocket League* teams based in Ohio by April 1, 2021." This goal is specific (e.g., all 25 college teams in Ohio and specific about the date by which it should occur [April 1, 2021]), measurable (e.g., which and how many teams will have the opportunity to compete [25 teams] and a specific end date [April 1, 2021]), achievable and realistic (because the organizers hail from Ohio, it is more achievable and realistic to host it in state than host a tournament for all college teams in all possible games in the United States), and timely (a date by which the event should be completed is provided); in other words, it is a SMART goal.

Goals, objectives, and tactics have these important distinctions: Goals are high-level things to achieve; and objectives can help identify, when completed, how the goals have been reached; while **tactics** provide detailed steps that need to be undertaken in order to accomplish the objectives (and which would also help accomplish the goals). For an example of all aspects of this step in the process, see table 8.1.

The goals and objectives for an event should be communicated to the entire staff so that everyone can work together to achieve them. Simply stating goals and objectives is not enough; they also need to be widely communicated, and the tactics must be clearly outlined. Finally, keep in mind that different groups may use different words to express the same idea. For example, some may use words such as *strategies*, *approaches*, and *methods* to describe similar activities. The words themselves are not as important as the ideas they express about what will be accomplished, when, why, and how.

CREATING THE FRAMEWORK OF THE EVENT

After goals and objectives are set, the next step is putting the proverbial pencil to paper to create the framework for the esports event. Although an event planner may have a positive feeling about their plans at this stage, they must realize that it

Table 8.1 Examples of Vision, Mission, Goal, Objectives, and Tactics

	Examples
Vision	Provide exceptional esports entertainment.
Mission	Produce a high-quality esports event that showcases the university and its students in a positive light.
Goal	Host a *League of Legends* event during the 2021 fall semester with 12 teams, and broadcast it to an audience of at least 10,000 people.
Objectives	1. Partner with Riot Games or another tournament hosting group to provide the platform for the event. 2. Recruit six college-level teams and six semiprofessional teams to participate. 3. Partner with a streaming company to record and broadcast or stream the event. 4. Identify interested alumni and celebrities with strong followings on social media to promote and attend the event.
Tactics	1. Use personal and professional connections to contact Riot Games or other tournament hosts. 2. Offer opportunities for competition and prize money to teams in return for their participation. 3. Use personal and professional connections to contact streaming companies. 4. Ask the alumni relations or development office to contact alumni and other individuals and groups who have donated to or taken an interest in esports. 5. Secure a venue. 6. Develop marketing and advertising materials. 7. Identify students or groups that can satisfy staffing needs.

may be too early to know whether enough people also like or love the idea enough to make it successful. Sometimes it is helpful for event planners to take a step back from the process and look at their idea objectively or ask others for feedback; and oftentimes, positive results occur, such as better defining the target markets and the tactics used to motivate people to attend the event. A **target market** is a defined group of people to whom your product will appeal the most.

The next step is defining who the event organizers want to target to participate in or consume the event. The proposed target market helps to frame the event and identify goals and objectives. If an organization's goal is to host a high school esports tournament, then their target market would include inviting students who are currently in high school. While it is a very broad demographic, further consideration about whether this event is for a specific game title or for a specific region or state would help better define the proper target markets.

If an organization wants to host an in-person event, target markets may be defined on a more local or regional level. For example, if a high school esports tournament is being planned to take place in Dallas, Texas, then the first target market question might be: Would people from the state of Washington, Florida, Maine, California, or Michigan travel to Dallas to compete? Perhaps they would travel if the prize money, scholarship opportunities, or prestige associated with winning the event is lucrative enough. However, because the event is targeted for high school students, many may not be able to rent cars and hotel rooms on their own, so their coaches or parents may travel with them as well. Also, assuming the students cannot miss too many days of school, the time frame for the event is now defined as when schools most likely have a vacation or break from school, such as over a holiday weekend or during the summer. If the event is held during a three-day weekend, the target market would likely be any high school players or teams living within a reasonable half-day drive of Dallas, Texas.

The venue selection process is also very important, and the final choice will affect a number of additional aspects of the event planning process. When choosing a venue, consider the impact of the following and how any changes might affect the event itself:

- *Location*: In what city, state, or country will this event be hosted?
- *Seating*: If hosting a live event, what is the shape of the venue, and is it conducive to hosting an esports event? What is the seating capacity? Can spectators see the activities well from all seating locations?
- *Parking and accessibility for patrons*: Do on-site parking and public transportation exist near the venue?
- *Concessions (food and beverage)*: Is a concession contract (e.g., **pouring rights**) already in place? What, if any, percentage of concession revenue will the event organizers receive?
- *Ticket sales*: Are tickets being sold for the event? What distributors are used to sell tickets? Can the event organizer sell tickets? What ticket cost is reasonable?
- *Technical capabilities*: Does the venue have appropriate technical capabilities and in-house staff who can assist with any issues arising during an esports event? What are the exact technical specifications (e.g., power, speed) for the facility?
- *Staffing*: How many staff members are needed to manage all aspects of the event? Does the venue provide staff, such as ushers and security, or do the organizers need to hire external groups for these responsibilities?

For esports events, it is important for event goers to see the action on a scoreboard or large-scale video board. Unlike a football game, where most seats in a large venue can see the live action, without a direct video (and perhaps audio) feed of the esports event, fans will have difficulty seeing it. As a result, understanding what hardware may exist or be built into a facility (and thus what may need to be rented or shipped to the venue) are also important considerations.

Perhaps one of the biggest questions esports event organizers have is: Do they want to livestream the competition? If the competition is livestreamed for free, then an obvious consideration would be: Why would people purchase tickets to attend the event in person? On the surface, it makes sense to stream the competition; more people will be able to see the event, thus expanding the reach of the event. However, livestreaming can also negatively affect event attendance,

David P. Hedlund

Identifying venues with areas for setting up experiential activities for consumers can benefit organizers, sponsors, and attendees.

thus an important source of revenue may be lost. Of course, event organizers can put the stream behind a **paywall** and force would-be viewers to pay a fee to watch the stream. This tactic might recoup some lost revenue from in-person sales. Each of these decisions surrounding the organizing and management of events comes with both costs and benefits.

EVENT BIDDING

Event bidding is a process by which an organizer sets minimum expectations for their event and then sells the rights to host the event to one or more organizations such as a sports commission, a venue, a city, or some other entity. For example, the National Football League (NFL) and the International Olympic Committee (IOC) both allow cities to bid to host their respective events. Alternatively, Major League Baseball (MLB), the National Basketball Association (NBA), and the National Hockey League (NHL) hold their championship games at the home facilities of the two teams competing.

If an event draws enough attention, it could mean a significant positive economic impact for a city to host a large tournament. In a 2019 article published in *The Esports Observer*, Duran cited a report from Riot Games noting that when the *League of Legends* European Championship was hosted in the city of Rotterdam in the Netherlands, the event generated a $2.6 million economic impact for the city. This economic impact occurred partly because over 87 percent of attendees came from outside of the city (Duran 2019). In order to earn possible economic benefits, a number of facilities or organizing bodies might bid to host an event. When multiple bids are received, the event organizer or rights holder has the ability to choose the best potential host with the largest number of benefits. A potential negative outcome of this process could be a bidding war between possible hosts trying to lure the event by offering more rewards. For example, a venue could reduce how much they charge for use of the facility, reduce the load-in and load-out costs, or forgo any concession- or parking-related revenue. The bidding process is usually associated with larger (mega) events, so many smaller high school and college esports events would not be subject to this process.

EVENT BUDGETING

Even if an organization's goal is not to make money from an event, resources are still needed to advertise the event, organize it, and host it. Event sponsorships are a great way to offset costs and raise revenue for the event, but organizers cannot rely on sponsorships as the sole source of funding for an esports event. Furthermore, the ability to receive cash from sponsorship deals is difficult and tenuous because many potential partners would prefer to provide goods and services in exchange for the sponsorship rights and benefits. For this reason, it is important to prepare a realistic budget.

Building a Budget and Managing Cash Flow

Organizers should build a **budget** for the event that includes all known expenses and a realistic view of what revenues may be produced. In general, it is best to overestimate expenses and underestimate revenues. Furthermore, an organization must include expectations of cash flow to ensure that invoices are paid on time. For example, a 50 percent deposit for the venue may be due before the event takes place. The event organizer cannot rely on day-of-event revenues to cover the deposit. Thus, an event might need revenue from sponsors, a broadcast contract, or a line of credit from a bank to help pay these up-front expenses. Knowing when money comes in and out is critical. A **cash-flow statement** is essential for tracking transactions. Numerous businesses are in a situation where they have significant sales, but because the in-flow of cash cannot keep up with the outflow, they have cash-flow problems and are at risk for bankruptcy. Typical **line item** expenses found in an esports event budget include the following:

- Licensing (What does it cost in royalties or licensing fees to use a game title for competition?)
- Venue rental
- Streaming costs
- Security and staffing (e.g., ticket takers, ushers, cashiers, cleaning staff)
- Cost of goods sold (How much does it cost to buy the food and beverages?)
- Event-specific costs (e.g., staging, hardware and software, audiovisual equipment)
- Prize money (What is the total cost of all prizes?)
- Hospitality and lodging (What is the cost of hospitality, food, transportation, and lodging for staff, officials, VIPs, and other groups?)
- Insurance
- Marketing
- Salaries and wages

Typical line item revenues include the following:

- Ticket sales
- Streaming sales
- Sponsorship
- Concessions
- Parking
- Merchandise
- Event registrations

Event Marketing

Depending on the type of event that is hosted, event marketing widely varies. Marketing can take place in a variety of forms, such as commercials on television or radio; advertisements in newspapers or magazines; messages pushed through social media, billboards, and other outdoor advertising; and word of mouth. The following section discusses some of the basics of marketing esports events. For a more robust discussion of esports marketing principles and practices, see chapter 6.

Depending on your target market, the cost of marketing activities varies to a large degree. For example, if an organization is hosting a college esports tournament and inviting varsity college esports teams from within a 100-mile (about 160 km) radius, few marketing expenses are likely. Direct outreach to the institutions and their leaders may be the only requirement. In this case, the cost of marketing can also be shared; it would likely benefit the institution if it leveraged its own participation in the event through its own marketing activities. Alternatively, if an organization is hosting a tournament that has a much larger target market, more marketing activities should be done to generate the highest level of interest in the event. Sample marketing activities include paying for advertising on television, social media, and other digital locations with heavy traffic from those in the target market. Often these types of marketing require professional production if attempting to create engaging video content, so they can become very expensive. Moreover, identifying proper placement in tangible and digital media to reach the target market can take extensive resources. In addition, many organizations must hire external groups to provide a specific, often local knowledge base to aid in identifying appropriate marketing messages.

In the past (and to some extent today) in localized communities (e.g., college campuses), many groups post paper flyers in central locations, because this activity is low in cost. However, the old adage *You get what you pay for* may be appropriate in this case. Often many different flyers are posted in a given space, making it difficult to give any one of them full attention. Consequently, few people see them unless they are posted in a unique way or place.

In recent years, email advertising has become a popular form of marketing. However, as with posting paper flyers, it is often ineffective because of the high volume received; users delete the message before reading it, or it may be directly sent to a spam folder. For event organizers who use marketing email services that track recipients' actions (e.g., Constant Contact, Mailchimp, Sendinblue), data such as how many people receive the email, how many people open it, and whether people clicked on any links can be useful information. It helps organizers to understand what types of people are engaging with their content and what content is interesting for recipients.

One challenge facing both sports and esports event organizers is that sometimes they don't know which players and teams may be participating in a given event. For example, most (if not all) championship events are planned many months and even years in advance. Knowledge of which players or teams are competing in championship events is often not known until the days or weeks immediately preceding the event. In this type of situation, the marketing of the event may take on a different form or style. For example, the marketing messages may focus on the importance of the event itself (e.g., "Come and watch the champions play in the most important event of the year") rather than the players or teams who are competing. In addition, certain aspects of the event itself such as the location and activities planned and announced to occur at the event (with optional messages included, such as "Subject to change" in cases where planned events have a high level of uncertainty) can also be marketed. As in traditional sports, organizing esports events in destinations popular with tourists can facilitate **esports tourism** (travel to a particular destination in order to attend or participate in an esports event in combination with tourist activities).

After all the details of the event (including the participants) are finalized, oftentimes ticket prices may increase, especially when popular players and teams will compete. When engaging in marketing during the last days before an event commences, make sure to always include information such as (1) the date, time, and location of the event; (2) the URL with more information, including contact information of event organizers; (3) social media account names; (4) information about how to purchase tickets; and (5) words or images that showcase the event. In today's digital world, where most people own smartphones, more and more groups are replacing all of that information with Quick Response (QR) codes. People simply use the camera function on their phone to scan the QR code, and they are redirected to a digital resource or website that provides all of the same type of information.

EVENT REGISTRATION

Organizers can manage the registration process for esports events in many ways, such as online, by email, by phone, by mail, or in person. Depending on the event, some processes may be easier and more effective to operate than others. Generally, the most popular ways for event participants to confirm their participation in events is through an online registration process, because it is likely to be the most cost-effective and efficient mechanism available to event organizers.

The online registration process for event participants is generally straightforward. Event organizers can create a digital registration website, form, or survey where participants can confirm their attendance, pay any registration fees, and provide any required information. Organizers can also ask participants for pertinent information such as names, shirt sizes, travel plans, accommodation information, medical information, and more. Such information can be stored and used for future marketing efforts. One important concern that organizers face is they might need to collect important personal information about participants (e.g., contact information, birth date, and credit card information), and such information needs to be protected and secure. While many registration form websites are free and can integrate with Internet-based email systems, these tools may not provide the same level of security as digital event management platforms (e.g., Eventbrite). Moreover, if fees are being collected, the organizer may still need to use a service to process payments (e.g., PayPal, Venmo, Zelle). In recent years, a number of esports-focused websites have also begun operations (e.g., Battlefy, Challengermode, Toornament, WorldGaming) that combine event registration, tournament management, and other important tools.

EVENT MANAGEMENT

Planning an event is not the same as actually executing it, but the two tasks are connected. The attention to detail in the planning process helps shape how the event will actually run. For example, if you combine a shortage of staff with a line of attendees waiting to enter the venue becoming longer when people can't find their seats (too few ushers are there) and the ticket-taking process taking longer than expected (too few ticket takers), the event is off to a bad start. How would the organizers deal with a situation where fans waiting in line become irate? What if attendees miss some of the action because they couldn't enter the facility and find their seats on time? This example of staffing shortages is not uncommon and it is the reason so many experienced event organizers schedule extra personnel to work. A prevailing philosophy is that it is better to pay for someone to work and perhaps do a different task or go home early than to avoid the cost and not have enough staff. This example also highlights how event organizers need to consider every possible detail in advance.

Various additional considerations exist in managing an esports event, and many of the variables differ based on the size and scope of the event. Ticketing, crowd management, communication and run of show, security, concessions, and parking are some key areas for event managers to consider. Each area is discussed next.

Ticketing

The first ticketing question for many event organizers is whether the event will be free or do attendees need to buy tickets. In general, three types of ticketing platforms exist; they vary depending on the size, scale, and whether or not tickets are initially being sold or resold. For smaller events, especially those that are self-organized and self-managed, websites (e.g., Eventbrite, Ticketleap) provide a wide range of tools and resources. For larger events, keep in mind that many venues may be contractually obligated to sell tickets through specific platforms. A number of companies service these events, including Ticketmaster/Live Nation (merged in 2010), Brown Paper Tickets, Ticket Tailor, Vendini, and Paciolan (Datanyze 2020). Some of these companies charge a processing fee, thus increasing the cost of the ticket for the consumer. The third group of ticketing companies consists of groups that originated as ticket resellers (the **secondary ticket market**), including StubHub, SeatGeek, and Vivid Seats.

If tickets are sold to an event, then event organizers should prepare for the maximum number of ticket sales in everything else they plan. For example, if a venue seats 5,000 patrons and the event organizer does not put a limit on how many tickets can be sold (not to exceed capacity), then event components such as staffing, security, parking, food, communication, and emergency operations should all be planned and budgeted for 5,000 attendees. Of course, some events may not sell out. As the day of the event approaches, organizers can modify plans based on ticket sales. Often, there are multiple plans, such as a 25 percent capacity, 50 percent capacity, 75 percent capacity, and fully sold-out facility. This allows event organizers to have preset numbers and/or benchmarks of when to hire additional security, provide additional concession, etc.

Consider an example of a collegiate sporting event. Imagine planning and organizing for a college basketball game in an arena that has a maximum capacity of 6,000 people. At some universities, because students can attend sporting events at no cost and only need their student identification for entrance, organizers should plan for the maximum number of attendees. Even though only 1,000 tickets may have been sold, plans need to be in place in case 5,000 students arrive and enter the event. Many experienced event managers may also have useful data from prior events to plan for staffing and other event necessities.

Event organizers should carefully weigh the pros and cons of presale tickets and walk-up ticket sales. Presale ticket sales are sometimes not as high as walk-up ticket sales, because people wait

Zoning

HOSTING AN ESPORTS EVENT

Jide Osipitan

You have learned that esports means competitive gaming. You are passionate about esports. You live and breathe the industry. What happens when you finally decide to take a leap and not only be a fan but also a host, an organizer, and an engine behind competitive gaming activities and events? Where do you begin, what factors need consideration, how do you prepare, and how do you run an event? The following text outlines the important considerations Gaming Insomniacs (GI) follows when managing an esports event.

When planning an esports event, you should consider these three stages:

1. Framing
2. Administering
3. Hot wash and debriefing

You will spend the most amount of time, energy, and money in the framing stage, somewhat less during the administration stage, and even less during the hot wash and debriefing stage.

Framing the Event

Framing is the brainstorming stage to any successful event, which is discussed in this chapter. Think of it as the architectural phase of running an esports event. Consider the following eight factors during this phase:

1. *What is the goal?* Is the goal of the event based on scholarships, cash prizes and incentives, status, and credits? If numerous goals exist, one primary goal should be decided on during the early stages of the framing process. Depending on your goal, the event might be by invitation (only selective participants can register) or open registration (any individual or group can register).
2. *What is the style?* Choose the style that best supports your goal(s) for the event.
    - *Tournament style* is an effective tool when considering an esports event that is designed to maximize a limited amount of days for competitive play.
    - *Leagues* are almost always used as prerequisites for tournament (sometimes known as championship events) play. They are designed to extract the most competitive teams that will eventually compete against one another in a tournament setting.
3. *Who is the target market?* Consider the demographic. Is the level middle school, high school, collegiate, semiprofessional, or professional? The chosen demographic will impact the size, scale, and goal for the event.
4. *What game title(s) would you like to play?* When deciding on a game title, the first thing to consider is licensing. Do you need (and will you be able) to obtain license from the publisher? Because many games can be played on multiple platforms (PC, console), it is wise to decide which platform to use. Consoles are a cheaper route to go than PCs, but PCs do operate at a higher processing power for most games and are widely considered the standard for competitive play.
5. *What venue type/style is needed?* Choose a place for your event that can hold the number of participants you expect and has sufficient Internet capability.
6. *What staff will you need?* It does not have to be an exact number, but you should estimate how many people you will need. You should have a core management team in place and assign responsibilities for which they must be held accountable. It is crucial that you hire an adequate number of security personnel with a plan in place for any given situation. When you hire a security firm to provide such services, it may limit your liability. Check with the venue for different options they might recommend.

7. *How will you market the event?* Will you use traditional means of marketing such as advertisements or word of mouth? Do you plan to use social media as a marketing vehicle? It is important to partner with organizations that bring valuable resources or capabilities you might not already have to the table. Through those partnerships, you may have access to resources that will improve your marketing reach and strategy with little to no cost to you.
8. *What is your budget and funding source?*
   - *Loans* are one way to generate funds to get the process started. They can buy you time and credibility to attract partners and sponsors. On the flip side, loans can bankrupt you should you fail to reach your financial goals. Maxing out credit cards/lines of credit from a bank is one example.
   - *Investors* are a great option because they can offer you benefits of loans without the liability if the event fails. Some investors require that they be involved in every step of the process, which can result in slowing down progress.
   - *Self-funding* an event can be exhilarating because you are liable only to yourself and you set your own expectations. The downside is that an unsuccessful event will most likely result in personal financial loss.
   - *Sponsorships and partnerships* are one of the most attractive forms of producing revenue for the event, but they cannot be solely relied on to provide funding to create the event. They have some potential limitations, but those limitations are rarely crippling. You can enjoy all benefits that come with access to funds, but the financial consequences of a failed event are shared among everyone.

Framing need not follow this chronological order. For example, you might have to frame the event before you determine the cost of operations, which could affect your decision on fundraising sources. On the other hand, you could decide on a maximum budget you are willing to spend and then frame the event around that amount of money.

Administering the Event

Event days are usually the most exciting and nerve-racking stage of your journey of hosting a successful esports event. Keep the following advice in mind during this phase:

1. *Manage registration effectively.* The smoother this process is, the more enthusiastic all will be for your event.
2. *Communicate with participants, customers, and staff.* It is important to communicate any changes or updates to everyone involved. Make everyone feel invested in helping the event be a success. The more vested everyone feels, the more productive they will be.
3. *Put out as many fires as possible.* Events will always include both anticipated and unforeseen issues. Make sure you have contingency plans to manage those issues and follow up on them if needed. Becoming a reliable, trusted, and successful esports event host is related to your ability to manage issues that arise.
4. *Capture content.* As the event manager or host, you are a content creator. Content is everything; it is your product, marketing, promotion, credibility, advertising platform, and many other things, all wrapped up in the event experience. You should capture as much of the content you will inevitably create during the event through video, photos, and other experiential activities.
5. *Manage time efficiently.* Begin and end the event at the scheduled times. Ensure you are strict with time management because it can affect your overall event performance. For example, some vendors (e.g., security/police) are billed in blocks of time, so if time is not managed effectively and the vendors spend one minute extra, they may bill for an entire hour, or another block of time (e.g., four hours).
6. *Thank everyone.* Be sure to thank sponsors, partners, participants, staff, patrons, and everyone else that played a role. Showing gratitude and appreciation adds to your credibility.

(*continued*)

HOSTING AN ESPORTS EVENT *(CONTINUED)*

Hot Wash and Debrief

The hot wash and debriefing stage is critical to the success of future events. It is just as important as the framing stage because it provides feedback to help you improve future events. During this stage, consider the following:

1. *How do you and your team feel about the event?* You should have goals and parameters set for defining success. The success of the event should be determined by you and your team and not by what everyone else thinks.
2. *Did you have an adequate amount of resources at your disposal?*
   - *Staff:* Did you have enough or too many staff members for the event? Too small of a team can result in work overload and burnout, so you may need to adjust staffing levels for future events. Too many staff members can result in negative outcomes as well. Some people may compare and question the workload and value they and others brought to the event.
   - *Equipment:* You should always have extra equipment just in case any issue arises with the equipment being used. However, storage is a common concern, so too much equipment is not good. That said, no organization has unlimited funds to spend, so do your best to determine whether you will need more or less equipment at future events.
   - *Funds:* How is the bottom line? Did you overspend or underspend in any areas? Could an in-kind partnership and sponsorship (partners or sponsors provide the goods and services being used at the event and can cover future costs for those same products) be an option in the future?
3. *How effective was the marketing?* Was your marketing effective, partially effective, or ineffective? Your answer to this question determines how you move forward with marketing this and other events in the future. If specific marketing campaigns were successful, then more resources could be allocated to these activities in the future.
4. *Decide what to improve, eliminate, or leave alone.* This stage is critical for creating a successful event series or franchise. You and your team must decide on what needs improvement, what needs to be eliminated or removed, and what must be carried over to the next event because it was successfully executed and contributed to the success of the event.

The overall message is that you should think of the three GI stages of (1) framing, (2) administering, and (3) undertaking a hot wash and debriefing as a set of tools you can use as you create and manage esports events. As you complete your event and acquire more knowledge and experience, your skills and ability to apply the three principles will also improve.

until the day before or day of the event to commit to attending it. Because consumers may not buy tickets in advance of the event, organizers should plan for a sold-out venue despite any related cost increases. If event organizers allow only presale tickets and no walk-up sales, they may decrease the opportunity for additional revenue. However, they can also increase the likelihood of lowering their expenses, because they will only have to plan for the number of tickets sold.

Parking

For event patrons, the event experience starts when they seek information about an event. The process continues through purchasing the ticket to the day of the event, when they travel to the venue, find parking (if they drive), and then walk into the venue. Parking is sometimes overlooked as part of the event experience, because some venues may be more conducive to event patrons using public transportation. That said, for many event organizers, parking is an essential consideration.

Charging patrons to park their vehicle at the venue is an additional source of potential revenue, but it takes planning to manage this effort. Patrons may expect that if they pay for parking, someone will be monitoring the parking area throughout the event. They may also expect that their vehicle would not be blocked by other vehicles; blocking the vehicle means they would be unable to depart whenever they chose. Depending on the venue, some parking areas may or may not allow for tailgating, alcohol consumption, and other types of pre- or postevent activities. Event organizers and venue owners or managers should agree on parking fees and rules when deciding whether or not the event will take place.

Another important consideration is that if parking is not free, then event organizers should have cash on hand and provide it to the parking supervisors in order to make change for patrons. Alternatively, some venues have installed portable and wireless credit card machines to receive parking payments. However, security staff may still be needed to monitor the facility. If security is not an option, then a "Park at your own risk" notation may be required. In addition, event organizers should think through how to move vehicles off main roads and into parking lots in the safest manner. For example, staff working the parking lot may not want to stand at the very front entrance of the lot because a line of cars could form in an active roadway, thus making traffic worse. Some facilities have dedicated security groups that are mandated to hire, while others may require a minimum quantity of people to hire but from no specific firm.

While it may be beyond the control of the event organizer, depending on the size and scope of the event, they should take into account factors such as spaces for handicapped-accessible parking and staff parking, and special parking for sponsors, event participants, special guests, taxis, buses, limos, and large vehicles used to transport patrons to the event. A more recent consideration is ride sharing. Ride-sharing companies may need designated areas for dropping off and picking up patrons. Having dedicated areas for ride-sharing pickup and drop-off help patrons get in and out of the facility faster, while also maintaining a good traffic flow and not causing additional congestion. While it is usually beyond the scope of event organizers to control parking, because the transportation of patrons to and from an event can cause significant congestion concerns, and because patrons may blame the event organizer (not the venue) for any related issues that might arise, it is wise to consider how parking and transportation may affect the event.

Security and Crowd Management

Depending on the size of the event, specific rules or regulations may dictate how many police, ushers, and other security officials are required to be present. Some large sporting events go into a venue lockdown 48 hours before the venue is open; no one, sometimes not even staff, can enter while a complete security sweep of the venue is completed. As a result, event organizers should work closely with the venue managers to create appropriate security plans.

Creating a security action plan in case of an emergency is an important part of any event, especially one that is expected to have a large crowd. A venue may already have an existing plan or protocol that an event organizer may be able to use, thus they would not be required to create their own. When hosting an event, consider these security and crowd management questions:

- Will you have or are you required to have armed police officers at the event? If so, how many, and where should they be located?
- How often is cash at parking lots, merchandise tents, concession, and ticketing areas taken from the point of sale to a secure location such as an armored safe? Where is the safe located? What types of security are required to safeguard the transportation of the money?
- Will alcohol be served at the event? What is the alcohol management plan that staff should follow? If they believe someone may be overly intoxicated, what steps should they take?
- Do event participants (e.g., the esports athletes) need a security escort?
- Does the facility have an on-site trained emergency medical response service, or should one be hired?

- Will **magnetometers** (metal detectors) be used at the ticket entrances? How and with what types of devices will patrons and their personal belongings be checked? Are clear bags required for personal belongings?
- Who creates and writes incident reports for security concerns, injuries, or anything else that the organization considers an incident? Where are these records kept? Who should keep copies of any records?

The most important part of security is having a plan that is thorough, is focused on keeping patrons safe, and considers every possible scenario that could impact safety of anyone at the event. For some events, it may even be wise to practice emergency drills with staff members to ensure they properly understand how to deal with situations that might arise, perhaps multiple times, much like grade school fire drills.

To prepare for the event, security officials and others involved with security should go through pre-event meetings and trainings, including tabletop exercises and walk-throughs. Tabletop exercises are discussions involving potential security scenarios, allowing participants to talk through the action they would take. A security walk-through includes a physical walk through the space to identify any issues discussed during security trainings and meetings.

Crowd management plays a large part in the overall event management strategy and crowd satisfaction. Event organizers should think through where concession lines will form and whether lines block access to restrooms and exits. Event organizers should also consider the line of sight for patrons and if any seats do not offer a full view of the event, such as a bench seat that is blocked by a pole or offers some other type of obstructed view. Event organizers should ensure a minimum number of reserved seats for compliance with the Americans with Disabilities Act (ADA), along with specific restrooms (or toilets within a restroom) and reserved parking. Having a plan and knowing the emergency evacuation procedures, having knowledgeable and trained ushers in the aisles, and allowing fans ease of access to and from their seats to restrooms and concessions all go into making the event experience a positive one for patrons while also managing the safety of the crowd.

Concessions

Food and beverage sales can be a great source of revenue for event organizers. If alcohol is being sold, an alcohol management plan must be put in place. Key components of the alcohol management plan can include how staff will ensure legal consumption (e.g., checking IDs), a policy on the maximum number of drinks served (e.g., two per transaction), when to not serve someone (e.g., drunken behavior), what time sales of alcohol are stopped (e.g., at baseball games, some teams discontinue selling alcohol after the sixth or seventh inning), and how staff will engage in the process of monitoring fan behavior and identifying risks).

With food and beverage sales also comes the need for health inspections and sales permits. In many cases the permitting, inspection, and sale of food and beverages are overseen by the facility managers; as a result, event organizers may only need to discuss how revenues will be split. In the case where event organizers have oversight over food and beverage operations, although they would not make as much revenue, they may choose to transfer the food and beverage operations to a third party (or multiple third parties) and negotiate a **percentage of sales** or a **flat rate**. A percentage of sales would take the form of the vendor (or vendors) splitting profits with the venue host and event organizer. A flat rate would allow the venue to collect a set dollar amount from the vendor (or vendors) regardless of sale volume. In the case of small esports events, organizers can take a do-it-yourself approach and either purchase food and beverages on their own, have food delivered to the event, or find a group that can be paid to cater the event.

Communication and Run of Show

Running an event requires undertaking multiple types of communications-related activities, including communication with staff, communication with participants, and communication with event patrons. In addition, the **run of show**, which details the plan for the entire event, should be shared with everyone involved. The run of show outlines what takes place and when, and who is in charge; and it is timed to the minute (sometimes to the second). This is sometimes also called an event script or a production schedule. Ensuring

Zoning

HOW SAFE ARE ESPORTS EVENTS?

Gil Fried

The popular saying is that it is all fun and games until someone is hurt. Will esports follow that adage? For many, the smaller esports tournaments were off their radar as a major security concern. Yes, security was present for the large events at major arenas, but what about a small tournament at a school or esports venue? That question was unfortunately answered on August 26, 2018 in Jacksonville, Florida, when a gunman opened fire on fellow contestants after he was eliminated from a *Madden NFL 19* tournament.

The tournament took place at an esports bar in the Jacksonville Landing outdoor mall. It was hosted by Electronic Arts (EA), the publisher of the Madden video game franchise. The event was the first of four regional qualifiers for the Madden Championship event, which was to run later that year in Las Vegas. The tournament featured both amateur and several professional players. Similar to other larger events, this tournament was being aired on Twitch. Airing an event on a local or national platform can generate significant security concerns. For example, people might try to gain publicity by jumping in front of the cameras. Such antics can represent a potential for injuries to some, but usually they would be smaller injuries from people being jostled. Moreover, organizers of small events did not necessarily consider violence against others. One of the lasting results of this shooting is that event organizers know they need to consider the prospect for violence at events of all sizes, and they need to plan accordingly for this type of activity to happen again.

In 2015, two gamers were arrested after travelling from Iowa to a *Pokémon* tournament in Boston equipped with both a shotgun and an assault rifle. Neither man was licensed to own the assault rifle (which also had a large capacity magazine to hold bullets), the shotgun, or the 300 rounds of ammunition police found in their vehicle. Both men allegedly posted on private social media groups making reference to the Columbine school shooting, Boston Marathon bombing, and specific threats against several tournament players. One post supposedly read: "MY AR-15 says you lose." The social media group monitor was alarmed enough that he contacted security at the *Pokémon* World Championship in Boston, where the two men were headed to play. Security was able to intercept the men before they could cause any harm (Sweet 2015).

The prospect for possible violence is increased when the event has potential for significant prize money or event publicity. For example, the Evolution Championship Series (formerly Battle by the Bay), an esports event held in Las Vegas that focuses on fighting games, has drawn around 15,000 people for past tournaments. In March 2018 organizers called the FBI when someone wrote this message online: "mass shooting @EVO18 see you there" (Lush and Bynum 2018). The event went off without any major incidents, but the tournament organizers used a significant amount of undercover law enforcement personnel to ensure the safety of all participants (Lush and Bynum 2018). Such an effort costs a significant amount of money. Most security personnel cost at least $20 an hour, but undercover officers can cost over $75 an hour. Imagine needing to hire five undercover officers for 10 hours a day for a two-day tournament. It would be 100 hours of officer pay totaling an added $7,500 in expenses. Such an amount can turn a once possibly profitable event into a loss. But the cost is necessary not only for safety reasons; event insurance might be cancelled if adequate security is not provided. Shootings are not the only risk of potential concern. In December 2017, the *Call of Duty* World League tournament held in Dallas had to be evacuated twice because of multiple bomb threats. Despite the high cost, the importance of being proactive about security measures at events is clear.

From a risk management perspective, developing and implementing a robust security plan is necessary for large and small events. Typically the NFL produces a comprehensive security plan for each game, and each plan barely fits into a three-ring binder. Every detail is identified and documented, such as who is in charge of security, what communication channels are used, where security personnel will be deployed, where metal detectors will be positioned, and which event rules participants have to follow. These details represent some of the questions that will be raised in the planning process; given

(*continued*)

HOW SAFE ARE ESPORTS EVENTS *(CONTINUED)*

the level of detail to consider, the process could take months. In fact, major events often start planning over a year in advance to address various safety-related issues. The process begins with identifying all the potential risks and then developing strategies to address each one of those risks.

The risks are diverse. They could include strikes by local employees, protests outside a venue, protests against a participant, global political turmoil, natural disasters (e.g., earthquakes, hurricanes, tornadoes), threats of violence, theft, and data breaches. Clearly a number of things can go wrong, and an event is judged by how well organizers have prepared for these potential issues. Organizers can prepare by having the right people in the right place at the right time, and with the necessary resources. To accomplish this goal, they can use security plans, communicate with all stakeholders about security concerns, train employees and security personnel, and show a security presence both inside and outside facilities so that everyone knows security is being taken seriously.

The tragedy in Jacksonville was a wake-up call that violence will not spare esports. Esports event organizers need to prepare for the worst. It is up to facility and event executives to show they are up for the challenge because the likelihood of it happening is high.

that communication is streamlined, efficient, and clear is important to the success of any event.

As discussed earlier in this chapter, communication with the staff before, during, and after the event must be effective and efficient. Before the event, communication begins with sharing information about timelines, schedules of events, and duties and responsibilities through face-to-face meetings, emails, conference calls, and other communication tools. On-site communication is often done face-to-face, through the organizational structure (i.e., venue managers give information to area supervisors who then communicate to **front-line employees**), and through two-way radios, as opposed to communicating with staff publicly, such as over a loudspeaker. Because communication often needs to be secure, such as to coordinate employees in the event of an incident response, two-way radios are a good way for employees to communicate with one another.

Communicating with fans is often done prior to an event through website messages, social media posts, and emails. Once on site, patrons receive messages through signage, face-to-face communication, and public address announcements. Directional signage in parking lots and venues helps fans find what they need, such as entrances and exits, restrooms, seating sections, concessions, and first aid. Posting or handing out a schedule to the fans is an effective way to communicate competition start times and any event-related activities. Public address announcements are used to convey important information, but they can also be filled with **sponsor reads**, introductions, speeches, commentary, and more. Sponsor reads are verbal advertisements for organizations that gave money to the event in exchange for advertising. Sponsor reads are a good opportunity for the event organizer to provide value to sponsors. However, the longer the message, the more chance fans will not retain or will ignore the content of the message.

Prior to the event, organizers need to communicate additional information to participants, including arrival times, parking locations, specific things to bring or not bring, rules, and any other information deemed necessary. Depending on the event, communication with the participants during an event can be done in a variety of ways, such as face-to-face communication to the participants or team directly, communicating through a team captain or manager, or posting messages in a predetermined location (e.g., a digital communication platform such as email or a messaging application on mobile devices), so that all participants receive the same message at the same time.

Finally, perhaps the most important activity involves communication of the run of show, in which the timeline of events is provided. Sometimes referred to as a script or a rundown, a run of show lists, second by second and minute by

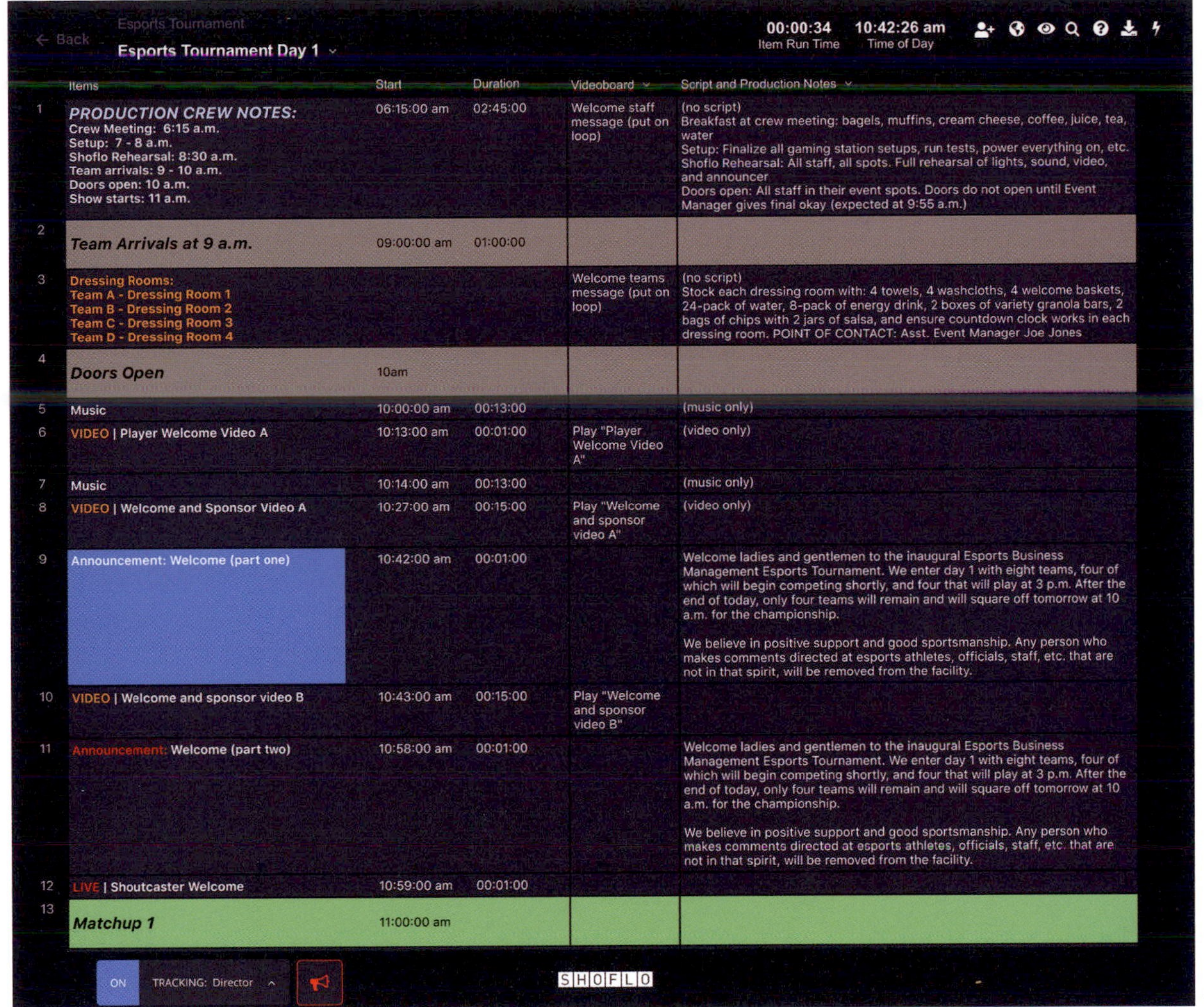

Shoflo is an example of specialized software used for the run of show.

minute, the order of activities at the event. A run of show also attempts to ensure that the event and participants stay on schedule. In its most detailed form, it usually includes the action items for certain staff, such as when activities should begin, when public address announcements should occur, when audio and video activities should commence and finish, and when sponsor reads should appear, and more. The run of show can be created using a word processing or spreadsheet program, or using specialized software (e.g., Shoflo). Because esports games and competitions often do not have time limits or end at precise moments, event organizers need to be flexible when planning and implementing the run of show, not to mention creating plans for how different types of activities can be added if time needs to be filled or removed if games are running late.

Communicating during an esports event is important not only to ensure the safety of all involved but also to make any changes necessary to the timeline of activities, event structure, or any other revisions that may be needed. Even the best-laid plans can go awry, so event organizers must use clear and concise communication through multiple platforms in order to effectively reach all stakeholders and patrons. Esports event organizers also need to work closely with venue managers and staff in order to leverage their knowledge and experience and create the best event possible.

POSTEVENT EVALUATION

After the event has concluded, the evaluation stage begins. Most organizations evaluate an event using a number of potential metrics, the most important of which are often based on finances (Was there a profit?), event attendance (How many people attended?), streaming or viewership (How many people viewed the stream or broadcast?), website users (How many unique users viewed the website?), social media followers (How many new people are following on social media?), number of incidents (How safe was the event?), and how patrons evaluate different aspects of the event experience (e.g., perceptions of value received, venue, amenities, concessions, staffing, parking, website, and ticketing). For larger events in which sponsors and partners are involved, useful data include additional information and evaluations about how patrons perceive sponsors, information posted on social media, and media or news stories in which any aspect of the event was discussed.

Organizers can evaluate an event in multiple ways. One of the best ways to initiate the evaluation process is to provide places at the venue where patrons can answer a short survey or provide immediate feedback to staff. Another popular evaluation opportunity would be to send electronic surveys to all those people who registered for or bought tickets to the event. Finally, market research firms can undertake even more detailed evaluations in addition to collecting accessible data from traditional media, social media, and other digital sources.

Surveys

Surveys are popular for soliciting feedback. They can be administered online, in person, or a combination of both. Surveys can be administered to participants, event attendees, staff, sponsors, and vendors. One way to administer a survey is for staff members to ask questions to event patrons as they are leaving the venue. Because they may be in a hurry to leave the event and get to their cars or public transportation as quickly as possible, these surveys should be brief (one or two questions). If available, staff members could implement digital surveys using portable devices.

Numerous types of questions could appear on a survey. Beyond some of the questions outlined earlier, event organizers may be interested in information such as the following:

- How did patrons hear about this event?
- What was the major factor that motivated patrons to attend the event?
- How far did patrons travel to get to the event?
- What aspect of the event experience was the most memorable?

The respondent can answer the questions verbally while a staff member quickly writes them down. Answers to these types of questions may help determine your event success:

- What type of advertising worked?
- What motivated people to attend?
- Did people travel from out of town to attend?

Another way to conduct a survey is posting it online after the event or sending a survey link directly to attendees and participants. These questions can be more thought provoking and detailed, and the responses can be longer and more informative. In addition, patrons who may have had unsatisfactory experiences or encountered problems during the event can also use these evaluation opportunities to communicate with event organizers. At future events, these types of feedback can be used to improve patrons' experiences.

If an event organizer wants to solicit feedback through the Internet or email, their questions should pertain to the exact group they are targeting; in other words, specific survey questions should be created only for participants versus fans who attended the event. For example, surveying staff, vendors, and sponsors is also an important part of the process. Receiving feedback from those who worked at the event can shed important light on what they may have experienced. Especially in cases when these individuals may have helped plan the event, feedback based on their experiences and insights can be extremely valuable and used when planning future events. Concurrently, receiving feedback from sponsors and vendors is also important because their sponsorship (funding) or their assistance (as a vendor) is vital to an event's success. These surveys perhaps are best conducted one on one or in small groups so that they are more personable and the interviewer can ask follow-up questions.

Thanking Patrons and Participants

At the end of each event, it is common to have a message thanking patrons, viewers, and event participants. Thanking patrons is extremely important whether delivered through a public address system announcement; on screens or televisions; by staff members at the exits of the facility; or through follow-ups by email, social media, or otherwise. This time is also an opportunity to inform and market future events to patrons. Messages such as "Join us next month for our next event . . . Tickets available now . . . Check out our website" are a great way to promote the next event to a target market that already has shown interest in the product.

CONCLUSION

Putting on an esports event can be a fun and exciting challenge. Many types of questions will arise during the planning process, and it is important to undertake extensive efforts toward creating a successful event. These efforts entail creating planning documents in which the event organizer's vision, mission, goals, objectives, and tactics are clearly stated. The planning process can take days, months, or years, all depending on the size and scope of the event.

The planning process requires sufficient amounts of time and energy, resulting in the holding of the event. When the event is actually held, the event organizers and their staff need to be prepared for any number of possible positive or negative activities and outcomes. Numerous problems can arise during the event. What if a pipe in the building breaks? What if the concessions area runs out of food? What if participants do not show up? Planning for esports events can be an ongoing activity consisting of "what if," "what if," and more what-ifs. The planning process should address as many of these issues as possible so that everyone is prepared to effectively handle them while making sure the event runs as smoothly as possible.

DISCUSSION QUESTIONS

1. When creating an event, what would be your top two goals or objectives? Explain why.
2. Describe a time when you went to an esports event. What do you remember about it? Are those memories based on what you experienced (e.g., fandom, a win for your favorite team, an amazing play), or was your memory based on your overall fan experience (e.g., parking, seating, food)? How can your own event experiences shape your event management and event planning?
3. Is it possible to sell tickets to an event and have free event streaming of the same event? How could doing so benefit the organization? How could it hinder the organization?

9

Esports Venues

Gil Fried | Alexander Champlin | Katelyn Chapin | Matt McGivern

OBJECTIVES

- Identify the ideal characteristics of an esports venue.
- Explore different types of esports venues around the world.
- Design an esports facility addressing the various technical requirements.
- Identify different pricing models used for various esports facilities.

INTRODUCTION

Esports used to be played exclusively in people's homes. As the sport evolved over the years, Internet cafés around the world became a hotbed for esports players to complement home playing. Then mobile gaming became popular and esports could take place almost anywhere a signal was available. Thus, Wi-Fi and stronger cell phone service changed where esports were played. The growth of large-scale events changed the future of esports. With esports viewership morphing from only streaming services to live events, the entire esports venue landscape changed. While many people still play at home, on their phones, in cafés, and in clubs, specialty locations are now available for play. Esports playing locations can take the form of dedicated locations inside big-box stores (e.g., Walmart), Internet cafés, or large events held at Madison Square Garden (MSG). Not all esports facilities are huge. In fact, many of the best esports venues are more intimate. Esports venues often work best when they can be easily converted and used for other purposes. In most places, dedicated esports events are not abundant enough to fill a facility and generate revenue during downtimes. Similar to large sport arenas, they make a profit when they are running nonstop with different events. Thus, an arena that has both National Basketball League (NBA) and National Hockey League (NHL) teams as tenants and also hosts numerous concerts, ice shows, truck rallies, circus performances, and related events would do much better than a facility that is used for a limited number of events.

Architects designing esports venues must determine the best layout for hosting esports tournaments while also considering where the industry might go in the future. That is a difficult task given that the industry is still so new and everyone is learning from a host of unanticipated challenges. For example, having elevated screens is great, but what if fans can then communicate strategies and movement to give an unfair advantage? That is why at new facilities, playing areas are being situated such that they minimize the chance of fans providing coaching assistance. As more large dedicated esports facilities are designed and built, the attention to detail will continue to evolve along with the industry.

Existing facilities may be renovated to serve as revenue generators, but not all older facilities will serve as good esports venues. Maybe these older venues do not have the necessary power, Internet, technological (i.e., scoreboards and video screens), and other amenities that would be required for hosting esports events. More modern arenas are usually better because wider concourses are needed to help with all the brand activation activities.

This chapter explores both smaller and larger esports facilities and how they are built and operated. The focus is on how quickly facilities are being designed and how quickly they can become outdated. As new revenue streams are developed, facilities will need to change. This situation is similar to stadiums and arenas in the 1980s. They evolved from cookie-cutter models to venues with significant **personal seat licenses (PSLs)**, areas, and luxury or corporate suites. Around the 2010s they further evolved into facilities where large, open **loge seats** and more intimate seating bowls were the fad of the day. Esports will also similarly evolve over the coming years. Besides high-speed Internet, they now need all the necessary infrastructure such as sound, lighting, kitchens, sales areas, scoreboards, and more.

Although sport venues are a model for esports venues in some ways, esports events differ from sporting events in ways that influence facility design. A typical basketball game or hockey game might last four hours from opening until the event ends. In contrast, a *League of Legends* or *Dota 2* tournament can last 10 to 12 hours. It is a completely different type of event with significantly different demands. For example, while a basketball game might need one meal (e.g., hot dogs, hamburgers), a large esports championship might require two or three meals. That means larger kitchens, more storage, more trash receptacles, and more sale points.

This chapter first explores large esports venues that are emerging onto the scene. Then the chapter explores some of the smaller facilities, especially the PC bangs in South Korea. The chapter then explores what is required to actually manage a facility. The chapter provides a perspective on media- and broadcasting-related issues for esports facilities. Lastly, it provides the perspective of a specific facility owner and how they launched their virtual reality (VR) business.

LARGE-SCALE ESPORTS VENUES

Large-scale esports venues are a new phenomenon. Several years ago, no dedicated esports venues existed; now, they are starting to pop up. Initially, large esports venues were traditional sport arenas that were converted for use in large esports events. Smaller events were held in larger rooms and theaters. The problem with such an arrangement is that the facilities were not ideal for esports, and it was very expensive to prepare a facility for an esports tournament. A larger esports event needs stages built, screens set up, lights installed, cooling systems installed, and the cabling needed for the Internet (for both games and broadcasting), among numerous other elements. To help reduce the need for facility conversions and the expense associated with constantly installing and removing equipment, specially designed esports facilities were developed.

Esports facilities are relatively small, and their seating capacity has usually ranged from 300 to 1,000 seats. One drawback to some of the early facilities is that they were more focused on the team (players and coaches) and broadcasting side than on the spectator experience. Some facilities are owned by the game publishers, such as LCS Battle Arena and Blizzard Arena. Both these facilities can hold 1,000 spectators. These facilities are so esports focused that they do not provide ancillary and additional revenue-producing options. In the sports realm, many modern stadiums and arenas have focused on being destination locations. Patriot Place (Foxborough, Massachusetts, home of the NFL's New England Patriots and MLS' New England Revolution) and AT&T Stadium (Dallas, Texas, home of the NFL's Dallas Cowboys) have much more than just a sport field on which games are played; a person can spend an entire day at these types of venues without ever seeing a game, such as dining and shopping. Most esports facilities do not yet follow that model, but the OGN E-Stadium in Seoul, South Korea, with numerous large screens, seating close to the stage, and other amenities, provides a more tailored experience than most esports venues. More options are available in part because a publisher does not own the facility; a facility operator owns it, and they understand that in order to keep the doors open, they need more revenue streams.

The following section discusses several large facilities in greater detail. A variety of different dedicated esports facilities are now being built on a regular basis. Some are smaller training lounges, while others are larger arenas. The following represent some of the iconic facilities built to date.

UC Irvine (UCI) Esports Arena

One of the earliest esports facilities was the esports arena built at the University of California,

Irvine (UCI). Opening in September of 2016, it was the first dedicated esports facility on a college campus. The 3,500-square-foot (325.16 m^2) facility cost $250,000 to build. The facility has 72 computer stations for players along with areas for screens and coaches. Thus, it is not a typical arena in which the esports athletes are on a stage; it is more of a training center. The arena was backed by iBUYPOWER, which provided all the gaming PCs for the facility. Another major donor was Riot Games.

The facility was built in the UCI Student Center, which is conveniently located in the middle of campus. The arena is open not only to students; people in the community can also play there. The facility is open seven days a week from noon to midnight, except for holidays when the campus is closed. The cost to play at the facility is $4.50 per hour; people can purchase a 10-hour pass for $40.00.

According to the arena's website, it supports the following games: *League of Legends*, *Overwatch*, *Apex Legends*, *Fortnite*, *Legends of Runeterra*, *Counter-Strike: Global Offensive* (*CS:GO*), *Rainbow Six: Siege*, *Call of Duty: Modern Warfare*, *PlayerUnknown's Battlegrounds* (*PUBG*), *Dota 2*, *Path of Exile* (on Steam), *Minecraft*, *Hearthstone*, *MTG Arena*, *World of Warcraft* (Retail and Classic), *Diablo III*, *StarCraft*, *StarCraft II*, *Heroes of the Storm*, *Final Fantasy XIV*, *Rocket League*, and *Team Fortress 2* (UCI Esports 2020). UCI Esports (2020) also provides these rules of conduct for users to follow at their facility (para. 8):

> We welcome and respect gamers of all types, from all places and backgrounds.
>
> 1. Harassment based on any aspect of a person's identity will not be tolerated.
> 2. No "toxicity" allowed. Behaviors that create an intolerable environment such as bullying, threats of violence, stalking, or other forms of intimidation will not be tolerated.
> 3. No cheating or illegal activity allowed.
> 4. If you see something, say something.

One element for marketing an esports facility, especially when it is just as easy to play games in the comfort of a student's dorm room, is having great equipment. UCI Esports (2020) also highlights the equipment provided to help sell how powerful the gaming experience is in the facility. As of early 2020, the facility provided the following equipment:

- Windows 10 operating system
- Intel Core i7-9700K processor
- ASUS Prime Z390-P motherboard
- ASUS GeForce RTX 2070 8GB video card
- ADATA 16GB XPG memory
- Intel 512GB 600p SSD

Zoning

EQUIPMENT MAKES THE FACILITY BETTER

Gil Fried

Technology is the key to any facility. In late 2019, AT&T announced that North America's first-ever 5G-enabled esports event live coverage would occur at DreamHack in Atlanta (AT&T 2019). At the event itself, fans watched the *Counter-Strike* Twitch channel livestream the tournament via AT&T, which used a deployable dedicated 5G network provided by Ericsson. AT&T hopes to show how 5G will eventually enable content creators to capture higher-quality livestreaming video at a faster rate and get it to the end user more quickly, thus creating new fan and event experiences (AT&T 2019). The network is just one of many technological necessities. The facility will have many advances, but the gaming equipment will also be critical. For example, keyboards are an essential piece of equipment. They can be examined in a manner similar to a bat or glove for a baseball player. Some keys can be pressed as many as 10 times per second. To handle such speed, some keyboards use lasers that pass through a switch to an optical sensor on the other side, which registers the button being pushed. As the speed at which consumers can access the Internet increases, so too will the need to improve the technology and how it responds when used.

- Thermaltake 750W power supply
- 240mm liquid CPU cooler
- ASUS ROG 24 in. 180Hz 1080p 1ms G-SYNC monitor [PG248Q]

Blizzard Arena Los Angeles

The Blizzard Arena Los Angeles opened in Burbank, California, in 2017. The facility was the home court to many Blizzard championships in 2018 and 2019, so one might expect it to be large. However, it was a relatively small location. The arena had a seating capacity of 450 people to watch the playoffs for *Overwatch* Contenders, Season 1. Similar to the UCI Arena, Blizzard repurposed an existing facility space for esports. However, instead of taking space from a student center, Blizzard found a local broadcasting studio. The old television (TV) studio was built in the 1950s and used to be the home of Johnny Carson's *The Tonight Show*. As a former TV studio, it already had numerous amenities critical for broadcasting esports tournaments. It had hair and makeup rooms, green rooms for celebrities, rooms for training and lower-level match play, a broadcasting control room, a large sound stage, and audience seating. This overlap helped reduce construction costs. Some additions included a luxury box in the back for Blizzard executives to help promote esports to future franchise owners. One element that needs updating is food. The initial food offerings included casual snacks, grab-and-go food, prepacked sandwiches, candy bars, and soft drinks. After the first year, the arena started offering hot food items such as nachos, pizza, and hot dogs. Such food options would need to expand over time, because fans are often at tournaments from 4 p.m. to 10 p.m. If fans arrive an hour before a tournament begins, they likely will want a full meal and not only snacks that evening.

The Blizzard Arena became the second dedicated esports stadium built for hosting events. The first was a 200-seat esports arena in Taipei that Blizzard opened in April 2017. The Blizzard Arena had traditional amenities often found in sport venues. From having to pass metal detectors in order to enter the facility to numerous concession points (merchandise, food, and beverage), fans were greeted to a familiar type of environment seen at other esports events and sport events. In the first season, the venue tried to sell merchandise by having fans write down what they wanted and then hand the slip to the person working the cash register. Over time, they improved the experience; to further engage the fans, they created events and activities outside the facility. The publisher had never been in the facility management industry before their doors opened, so it was a learning experience for them.

DAVID MCNEW/AFP via Getty Images

Blizzard Arena.

Esports Stadium Arlington.

Esports Stadium Arlington

The Esports Stadium Arlington is located in Arlington, Texas. With a 100,000-square-foot (9,290 m^2) area, it is the largest dedicated esports venue in North America. While the venues discussed previously could hold several hundred fans, the Arlington venue holds 2,500. Plans to build the venue were announced in March 2016, and it opened in November 2017. This time frame is an exceptionally fast turnaround to build a facility; most professional sport stadiums and arenas take around two years to complete. It was not a complete build from scratch but a renovation of an existing facility, which helped reduce the construction time. The project was a joint venture between the city of Arlington and Esports Venues LLC (owned by Texas Rangers co-owner Neil Leibman). The facility was designed by architecture firm Populous and is managed by NGAGE Esports.

The venue cost $10 million to construct and was specifically built to meet the needs of esports events. Broadcasting and concession amenities are customized for esports events, which is one reason that so many esports events are scheduled for the facility. In February 2020, before the global COVID-19 pandemic hit the United States in large numbers, the venue had 13 scheduled esports tournaments; that number is in addition to the esports gaming center on the property. The gaming center is open every day of the week, with hours on Monday through Friday from 2 p.m. to 2 a.m. and on the weekends from 12 p.m. to 2 a.m. The facility offers gaming on NVIDIA-powered gaming PCs with 240-Hz G-SYNC monitors; or PlayStation 4, Nintendo Switch, and Xbox One consoles. Players can bring their own controllers and headsets, or they can rent them. As of early 2020, the facility offered the following cutting-edge equipment:

- Case: iBUYPOWER
- Motherboard: ASRock Z370 Pro4
- CPU: Intel 8700K 3.70 GHz
- GPU: Titan XP
- Memory: XPG 16GB DDR4
- Monitor: Acer Predator XB272 (Refresh rate: 240Hz—Using display port and response time: 1 ms)

Everyday fans can play at the gaming center. The cost for one hour is $6. Special discounts are available for those who purchase packages, such as 5 hours for $25, 10 hours for $40, and 100 hours for $100. Players also have the opportunity to purchase food and merchandise from concession stands and the team store.

Gabe Ginsberg/Getty Images

HyperX Esports Arena Las Vegas.

HyperX Esports Arena Las Vegas

The 30,000-square-foot (2,787 m^2), multilevel HyperX Esports Arena in Las Vegas, Nevada, is designed to host various forms of competitive gaming. The arena has a 1,400-square-foot (130 m^2) stage and can hold up to 1,000 people. Unlike Blizzard's first attempt at an esports arena, HyperX has a full-service kitchen (it is attached to a major hotel in Las Vegas), two full-service bars, three private VIP rooms, and one VIP lounge. The arena hosts both daily play to the public and high-stakes esports tournaments. The arena features a competition stage, a 50-foot (15.24 m) LED video wall, telescopic spectator seating, PC and console gaming stations, and a network TV-quality production studio. The hourly prices for playing at the venue are as follows: One hour: $15, two hours: $25, four hours: $40, a day pass is $50, and a weekend warrior pass is $125. Las Vegas residents receive double time with valid identification. The arena provides a military discount of 15 percent with valid identification. This type of pricing structure is designed to push foot traffic into the facility. The arena is located near a casino, and people visiting the casino may also want to play esports. Along similar lines, the facility can also serve as a spot for young people to play while their parents or guardians are elsewhere. The facility has been used for other purposes as well, such as the staging area for a 2020 World Poker Tour event.

HyperX Esports Arena is part of the Allied Esports Property Network (also known as Allied Network). The Allied Network is the first esports venue affiliate program created for operators around the world who are interested in participating in their global event programming and licensing deals, design expertise, development experience, and operational knowledge for dedicated esports venues. Allied properties include HyperX Esports Arena Las Vegas, HyperX Esports Studio, HyperX Esports Truck - North America, and HyperX Esports Truck - Europe. Affiliated Allied properties include Waynoo, Fortress Esports, Mall of Georgia, Esports Arena Oakland, and Esports Arena Orange County. The company went public in 2019 (NASDAQ: AESE) and the 52-week range of prices for the share fluctuated widely from 40 cents to $10.56 per share.

Fusion Arena Philadelphia

The Esports Stadium Arlington was built in an old convention center, and the HyperX was built in an existing casino. In 2020, the first purposely built stand-alone esports arena is being built in Philadelphia for the Philadelphia Fusion. The building is expected to cost more than $50 million and is scheduled to open in 2021. The difference between the first esports stadium and the first esports arena is a matter of semantics. The stadium in Taipei was designed mainly for players with a minimal focus on fans. In contrast, the Philadelphia arena is being built more for spectators and less for the players. The 3,500-seat arena will be the largest dedicated esports venue with a large seating capacity. The Philadelphia Fusion ownership group knows how to run and manage sport venues. They are owned by Comcast, one of the largest cable companies in the world, which owns several professional teams in Philadelphia and has a facility management division that owns and manages sport facilities. In fact, the Fusion Arena is being built in the Philadelphia Sports Complex, which leverages Comcast's other sport facilities. In 2019, Comcast announced it would partner with Korean phone company SK Telecom to create a new esports organization (T1 Entertainment & Sports) that would field teams in esports games such as *Fortnite*, *League of Legends*, and *Super Smash Bros.*

Fortress Melbourne

When Fortress Melbourne opened in early 2020, it was the largest esports venue in the southern hemisphere. Designed by one of the world's most influential sport architects (Populous), the 29,000-square-foot (2,694 m^2) venue has a 1,000-person capacity. It includes 160 gaming PCs, console gaming suites, two bars, a restaurant, and a multilevel, 200-seat esports arena. Fortress Melbourne is not only an esports arena; it is a place to celebrate gaming. The facility features retro arcade games, the latest LAN games, and VR activities. Besides being large, it has all the latest technology, including audiovisual (AV) technology, digital screens, and LED lighting to enhance the space. The goal was to create a sensory experience so that guests could immerse themselves in the various games and events (Malone 2019). As of June 2020, the facility had opened, but was not open to the public yet due to the global pandemic. The facility was offering online events and delivering food to people through services such as DoorDash to help generate some revenue.

Zoning

POPULOUS: THE CUTTING EDGE OF ESPORTS ARCHITECTURE

Gil Fried

What do Fusion Arena, Fortress Melbourne, and Esports Stadium Arlington have in common? They all were designed by Populous. Populous is a well-known sport architectural company. They have designed many of the top stadiums and arenas around the world. They are also aggressively assisting the esports industry. Here is how Populous describes some of the elements included in the Fusion Arena:

> Once inside, visitors pass through a captivating 6,000-square-foot [557.41 m^2] lobby with 2,000 square feet [185.80 m^2] of interactive media surface displaying overhead. The heart of the facility is a 25,000-square-foot [2,322 m^2], theatre-style event space, one flanked by bird's-eye social areas on each side and dynamic views back to the stage. Other viewing experiences include two balcony bars, club seats with USB ports, flexible loge boxes and exclusive suites. Nearly 10,000 square feet [929 m^2] of behind-the-scenes space acts as the central nervous system of the venue, housing a training facility, state-of-the-art broadcast studio and offices, among other areas. Taken all together, Fusion Arena's design sets a new standard for the sport. The high-tech hub will power the Fusion's continued rise through year-round recruiting, training and competing. (Populous 2020, para. 4)

As early as November 2018, Populous released a design for the Gaming House of the Future (Populous 2018). This structure was designed on paper to help show what could be the future for a holistic facility with living and training space, natural lighting, playing pods, health areas, and a host of other ideas. An architectural firm such as Populous can be as creative as it is practical, and the esports industry needs as much creativity as possible.

SMALL-SCALE ESPORTS VENUES

While large esports facilities attract a lot of media attention, small facilities still serve as the backbone for the industry. For example, during the *Overwatch* League's first season (2018), all regular-season matches were held at the Blizzard Arena Los Angeles (see earlier section on Blizzard Arena). However, in 2019, the league added three events that were held at smaller venues in Atlanta, Dallas, and Los Angeles (although most matches were played at Blizzard Arena). This addition was a test to see how the local market responds to these events. The organizers hope that local esports fans can be groomed to help support a local team rather than rooting for an individual esports player regardless of where they might be from or where they might play. The 2020 *Overwatch* League season (which started in February of 2020) is attempting to leverage the home-and-away format seen in most traditional sports in order to further this emphasis on building local support for esports teams. The league's 20 teams will each host at least two home stands in 2020, and some might host up to five matches. The *Overwatch* League also requires each host city or team to host three additional events that can range from viewing parties to gaming tournaments. As an incentive to motivate local teams, teams can keep 100 percent of any local revenue earned from ticket sales, concession sales, advertising revenue, and local partnership agreements. During the first week of league play, *Overwatch* team New York Excelsior held its match at the Hammerstein Ballroom. Built in 1906, Hammerstein Ballroom is a 12,000-square-foot (1,114.83 m^2) facility able to seat 3,500 people in New York City. One-day tickets for the back of the house were being sold for $78; tickets closer to the stage were initially priced at $123. A two-day pass for the back of the house and stage area was $145 and $235, respectively (New York Excelsior 2020). In contrast, the Dallas Fuel hosted their home stands at the Esports Stadium Arlington. The Fuel's second home match for 2020 was scheduled for April 4 and 5, 2020. Due to the COVID-19 global pandemic, events were moved online. The team was to take over the Toyota Music Factory (Irving, Texas) for a weekend full of music and matches where the Fuel was to battle the Chengdu Hunters and Hangzhou Spark (both based in China). The Toyota Music Factory is a 45,000-square-foot (4,180.63 m^2) flexible event space that is also home to a state-of-the-art 8,000-person capacity live music venue. The venue is managed by entertainment juggernaut Live Nation. Concerts were also scheduled for the same weekend. Tickets for a weekend pass were priced from $65 to $295 (Dallas Fuel 2020). The Toyota Music Factory is a larger venue and represents a push by some to move from the smaller venues to the larger venues. However, most of the venues that have been planned or started for individual franchises have been smaller venues. After the COVID-19 pandemic of 2020, it is uncertain whether future larger facilities will be built or smaller venues become the best investment based on government regulations and spectator fears.

Teams are examining the possibility of using existing facilities unless they have a dedicated facility (often owned by the team's owner). However, numerous smaller facilities exist around the world. The most popular small esports facilities are **PC bangs** in South Korea. South Korea has an estimated 20,000 PC bangs, and many of them are open 24 hours. The PC bang charges vary; some can charge rates as low as 333 won per hour ($0.28) to around 1,500 won ($1.30). If you prepurchase time, it can be as low as 10,000 won ($8.45) at a time to purchase 30 hours of gaming time. This arrangement buys you time on relatively new computers, SSD drives, 30-inch (76.2 cm) monitors, gaming mice, keyboards, and gaming chairs. If a PC bang with over 90 computers was using its computers for 12 hours per day, one computer could generate about 3 million won ($2,300) a year. Based on 90 stations, this facility could have gross yearly revenue of around $200,000. While usage would decline in the early morning hours and during the day, peak usage pricing could help drive income. Further income could be generated by selling drinks and some food. The costs are primarily the equipment (which needs frequent updating to stay competitive), facility rental, marketing, and several employees. It does not mean the owner is making a fortune, but enough demand and usage exist that 20,000 facilities are doing well enough.

PC lounges (the equivalent of PC bangs in South Korea but are located in other parts of the world) can be found in areas where reliable home Internet access is less common. A facility with a dedicated line would be a much better option for gamers than locations that experience sporadic connectivity issues. If the Internet were not reliable in a facility, it would be difficult to operate and the business would develop a poor reputation. Such facilities are not as popular in the United States and other highly developed countries with strong and reliable Internet. While South Korea is generally a high-technology country, its PC bangs have developed their own culture and have survived because they are also a social hangout.

In the mornings, users tend to be adult males, usually between 30 and 50 years old. Afternoon users are primarily young males who flood in after school. Dinner time brings in teenagers and young adults who are still primarily male. Competitive gamers over the age of 18 arrive around 8 p.m. and play for a number of hours or through the night until morning.

DESIGNING ESPORTS SPACES FOR UNIVERSITIES AND ATHLETES OF THE FUTURE

In 2019, the University of New Haven (UNH) announced it was developing a first-of-its-kind academic program focused on esports management. The curriculum would launch as a concentration within the University's bachelor's degree in business management program, then expand to an interdisciplinary undergraduate program and a companion master's program in esports, the first such graduate program in the United States. Simultaneously, the university was already in the final stretch of constructing a new 55,000-square-foot (5,109.66 m^2) multidisciplinary academic and collaboration facility. Administrators recognized that the premier program needed a premier space within this facility. Thus, a 1,400-square-foot (130.06 m^2) esports training and competition center became a feature of the new Bergami Center for Science, Technology, and Innovation. Working with Svigals + Partners architects in New Haven, Connecticut, the team of 10 stakeholders from across campus observed the ever-growing esports industry to study its growth, dynamics, and best practices in facilities, technology, furnishings, and operations. The development and construction of this facility offers a case study in the questions and considerations that go into designing esports facilities in the academic space. Figure 9.1 shows the blueprint for the facility, and figure 9.2 shows two artists' renderings of the facility.

Understanding Facility Use and Users' Needs

Early on, the UNH facility design team knew esports were expanding and bringing attention to a new type of athlete. On the academic side, the team understood that esports has many synergies with other university departments, such as athletics, business, and health sciences. They also understood that esports competitions are very popular; they attract over 400 million viewers annually, and that number is growing. With a background understanding of the esports landscape, the team established the project timeline, budget, and location. By using the university's Bergami Center, which was under construction at the time, the team decided this central location on campus aligned with the esports interdisciplinary framework. Others who are considering developing such a space should note that retrofitting an esports facility into an existing campus building can present some challenges and opportunities. The location needs to be visible, have enough space, not adversely affect other activities in adjacent spaces, and have easy access to food and campus recreational facilities.

Equally important to the scope is identifying the specific end users. In addition, knowing what games the facility will need to accommodate and how many athletes will play each game affect the plans for the facility. Because requirements for academic, club, and varsity team play differ significantly, it is critical to understand the differences and resolve usage issues early on to inform design decisions.

Instructional Space

Equipped for academic use, an esports lab must accommodate target class sizes in alignment with the optimal number of gaming stations and related room functions. Academic gaming spaces should also be designed to focus on the professors' instructional preference, whether from a designated area with a writable wall surface or from a mobile podium with various writable surfaces around the perimeter of the room. How students will engage with the professor should also be predetermined. Will they interact from their gaming stations or from a designated gathering spot in the room?

Club Versus Varsity Usage

For club team use, esports environments often integrate casual areas for students to observe and socialize. This soft seating area can also be used by a coach to review game strategy with players. Will the esports lab also feature a Nintendo gaming area; if so, can the varsity coach use this area to review previously recorded content with the players? For varsity team use, designers must consider the competitive nature of the sport and find ways to create visual separations between rows of competing teams.

Technology Needs

Architectural solutions must consider technological capacity, adaptability, and requirements for the specific game play at hand. Working with academic leaders, the university IT department, and expert consultants, the UNH facility was designed to meet the needs of the university,

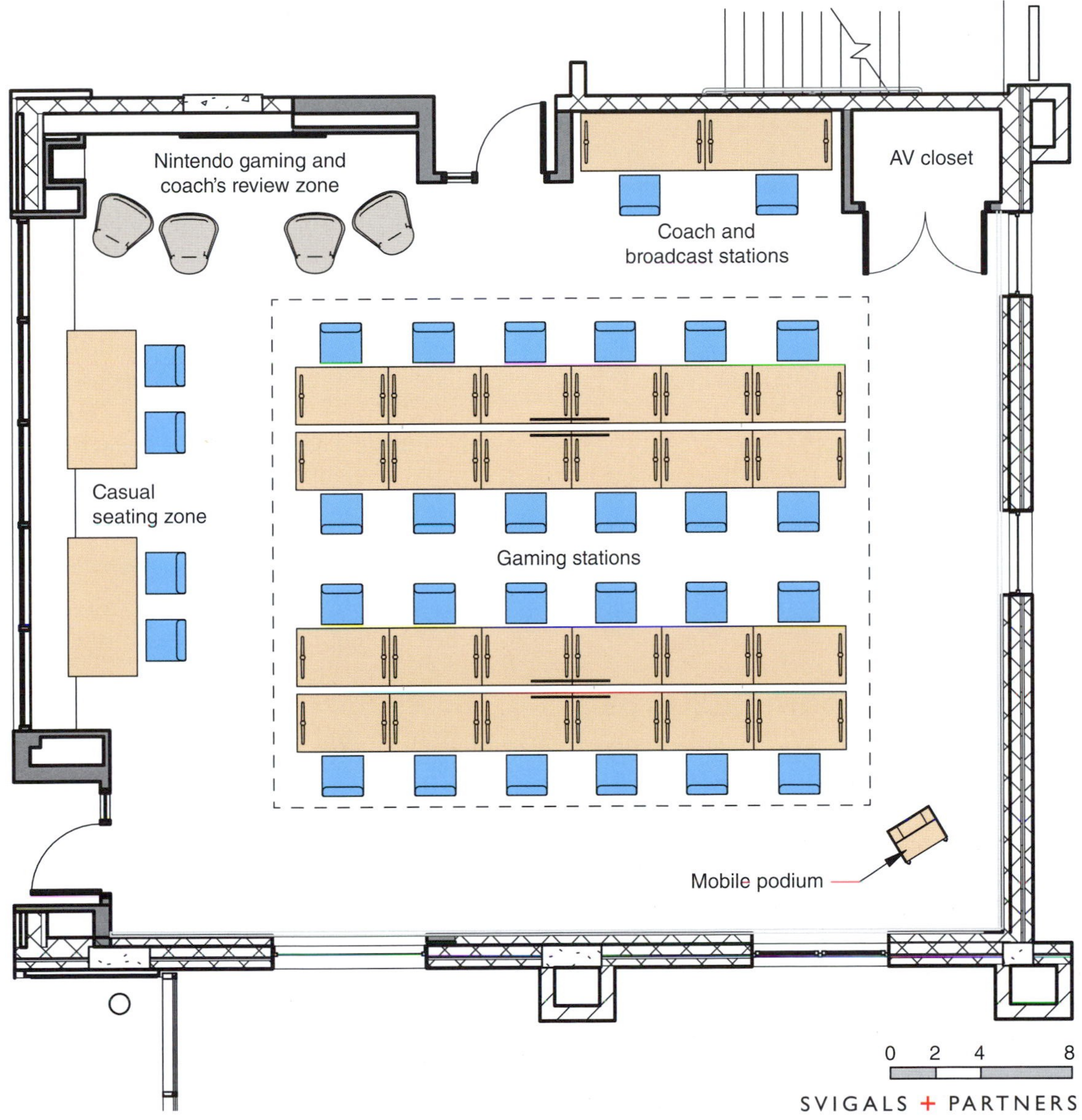

Figure 9.1 Blueprint of UNH esports facility.
Reprinted by permission from Svigals + Partners.

Reprinted by permission from Svigals + Partners.

Figure 9.2 Artists' renderings of UNH esports facility.

students, and athletes. Each station is equipped with ample power, data, and bandwidth. Large LCD screens are located above each row of gameplay monitors for instructors and coaches to view play. To accommodate this configuration, ceilings may be designed to be higher than those in traditional academic settings. Other technology-related features include ceiling-mounted speakers, audiovisual (AV) equipment for broadcast ability, and wall-mounted cameras for both security and broadcasting. A broadcast station is required in the room in order to edit and disseminate content. The location of server racks for the AV equipment needs to be determined, potentially in a nearby closet dedicated to information technology.

Aesthetics and Room Features

Successful esports venues use space efficiently and are equipped for comfort, a design imperative that directly benefits the athlete's playing style. Specialized technology and esports manufacturers produce furnishings uniquely suited to specific gaming needs. Unlike standard office and academic furniture, the ergonomics of these unique solutions reflect how tournament players often sit for extended periods.

Work surface sizes are typically 30 inches (76.2 cm) deep by 48 inches (121.9 cm) wide. Players need as much accessible and unobstructed work surface as possible for maximum flexibility to accommodate their play preferences. CPU towers, and any other gaming consoles, can be stored either below or above the workstations, but if located on the workstation, they need to be outside the area of play. Ergonomic solutions include customized game play surfaces as well as adjustable chairs with lumbar and neck support, height-adjustable seat ranges, and height-adjustable arms. Cleanable surfaces such as polyurethane, vinyl, or simulated leather materials help ease maintenance needs and allow administrators to keep the facility fresh and ready for high-level competition.

To keep the work surfaces clear of personal belongings, custom solutions such as millwork can be integrated into the room layout to accommodate backpacks, jackets, and extra equipment. Coaches' belongings can be stored in an office or designated coaches' station.

Overall aesthetics and lighting affect both athlete mindset and performance. Dimmable LED fixtures can offer functionality as well as mood-setting capabilities. Design consideration should be given to window shades and the arrangement of the light fixtures in order to prevent glare on the monitors.

End-user interviews and surveys can help determine the overall look and feel of rooms for esports gaming and instruction. As in many university settings, using integrated artwork, sculptural lighting, and university-branded elements can enliven walls and furniture systems. For the esports lab, users value aesthetics and overall feel. Is the room a magnetic, inviting, and comfortable place to work, study, and game? Time will tell.

BASICS OF ESPORTS FACILITY MANAGEMENT

Building an esports facility is not the same as operating it. Facility management is the art and science of operating a facility. It encompasses a range of problem solving with direct, measurable answers as well as solutions based on wisdom and instinct. For example, what should be the temperature of a facility? All indoor facilities have some type of heating, ventilation, and air conditioning (HVAC) system. It could be as simple as opening a window to let air in. It could be more advanced such as changing a filter, changing the airflow intake, or increasing the temperature through a passive airflow system. The key is that an HVAC system is needed, and it needs to operate effectively. It is as critical for an arena with an ice rink as an esports arena where computers are producing a significant amount of heat.

Facility management begins before a facility is even built. The number one concern for most facility managers is the lack of storage space. An esports facility must have the capacity to store computers, screens, cameras, and similar items when a stage might be transformed. Other issues that arise during the planning process include what zoning and topographical elements could affect the facility. Some cities may not want to have certain entertainment facilities in a given area. Also, some land might seem ideal, but it may end up being inappropriate. What if a great site has no parking or very limited Internet options? It could destroy the ability to use a piece of land. Thus, significant research on management issues needs to be undertaken before, during, and after the planning and construction phases of a new or renovated facility. Facility-related concerns can also include whether to build a new facility, renovate an existing facility, have the owner finance the facility, or lease a facility. Each option has its pluses and minuses, and a careful overview is needed to determine the best option. Once a decision is made, it is very difficult to change that decision without incurring significant financial setbacks.

People often examine facility management for sport facilities with an outside-in approach; that means first examining the parking lot and answering these questions before even exploring the facility structure or interior: Does enough space exist for parking? What types of parking spots are available? How many handicapped parking spots exist? Has public transportation been considered? Are safe walking paths available for pedestrians? Is the parking lot fenced in? All elements of the facility need to be considered, from the smallest details outside through the details inside the facility.

Zoning

GOING OLD SCHOOL FOR GAMING

Gil Fried

Numerous facilities are opening around the world and trying to take advantage of the latest trends, whatever they might be. Trampoline parks have sprung up over the past 10 years. Then Topgolf became the newest popular thing. Several years ago, axe throwing shot to prominence with numerous facilities opening all over the country. While new facilities are constantly opening, just as many close after several years. They close for numerous reasons such as legal issues, state regulations, or financial stress. Sometimes the best business models entail going old school.

Harkening back to activities common in yesteryear is happening around the United States. Instead of focusing on the latest trends, some bars and other establishments are bringing back old technology. For example, GameCraft Arcade is a craft beer bar and video game center that opened in 2020 in Southington, Connecticut (GameCraft Arcade and Bar 2020). While some contemporary games are available on consoles (e.g., Nintendo, Nintendo Switch, and Xbox), most of the games are original arcade games in new cabinets. The games include *Asteroids, Donkey Kong, Double Dragon, Ms. Pac-Man,* and *Teenage Mutant Ninja Turtles*, just to name a few. The 2,700-square-foot (250.83 m^2) space has 35 freestanding vintage arcade machines. Some of the funds needed to open the bar were raised on the funding platform Kickstarter.

The same concerns arise for an esports facility when examining the structure itself. Will the facility's exterior envelope (or skin, similar to a character's skin during a game) be metal, glass, brick, or some other material? This decision will have an impact on the construction cost and also on the need for maintenance. A steel exterior might not be as expensive to maintain as glass. The same concern is evident with what material is used for the concourse floor and arena floor. Carpeting (whether rolled or carpet tile squares) has different cost and maintenance concerns than polished cement or tiles. The same goes for what types of seats are being used. While upholstered seats are more comfortable, they are more expensive than molded plastic seats. Careful analysis of other similar facilities can show what has worked and what has not worked and why.

After looking at the facility's skin, the discussion moves to what is inside. Issues include the type of plumbing system (imagine 300 toilets being flushed at the same time), the type of lighting, the type and location of speakers, the type and location of scoreboards and video displays, and where the stage will be located. These small details make a facility pop with excitement. These elements are called **furniture, fixtures, and equipment (FFE)**. Specialty designers can be hired to help identify the FFE that can work. While some unusual concepts might be proposed and may even fit into the budget, designers must make sure that these elements are not too difficult to operate or replace. Imagine installing a great lighting system using neon light. Some might be upset with such lights not being environmentally friendly LED lights. Others might be concerned about the environmental impact of disposing of such lights when their useful life ends. Others might be concerned about the maintenance or replacement costs associated with such lights. Yet others might be concerned with how much electricity the lights use and the total operational costs over the light's lifetime. These types of issues need to be explored for numerous facility elements.

The key is research and communication to determine what is needed and how to keep the facility in as great a shape as possible. Some video screens or scoreboards can cost several hundred thousand dollars, so they represent a huge investment and they need to be properly maintained. Savvy facility managers spend a lot of time learning about the industry and trying to find the best possible solutions. For example, what is the best concession equipment and configuration? How many points of purchase spots are needed to handle the rush of fans (or is there a typical rush similar to what is seen at points during other sport events)? Because so many differences exist between traditional sport and esports, some of the examples seen in esports might not apply to concession stands for traditional sport venues and vice versa. For example, how strong are alcohol sales at an esports event? Will the facility have enough alcohol distribution areas to meet the perceived demand? Some sport facilities have wide concourses. Will esports facilities generate the same type of crowd, crowd flow, and crowd dynamic that will require wider concourses? Even if the answers may not yet be clear, these facility planning questions need to be asked and analyzed.

After all the information is gathered to make informed decisions concerning the facility structure and layout, the discussion will shift to how to manage these facilities. The most significant costs over the life of a facility are the people who work in it. The next significant cost is the debt service to repay any bonds or bank loans required to construct the facility. The next major cost will be the facility upkeep. Similar to a house, facilities always need repair. Elements within a building eventually break. Regular maintenance is required from floor cleaning to restocking soap and toilet paper in the bathrooms. Maintenance requires vigilance in terms of analyzing stock on hand, ordering appropriate amounts, and making sure workers are properly trained.

Most larger facilities employ an **incident management system (IMS)** and a **computer maintenance management system (CMMS)** to help manage facilities. In years past, managing a facility was done manually. Incidents were written down and analyzed to determine which areas were more dangerous. Similarly, any maintenance or repairs to equipment might have been written down on index cards and stored away. Now, all that information is maintained online. It can be immediately accessed from smartphones to learn what repairs are needed and where areas of concerns might be located—all in real time. This way of maintaining information helps operate a facility more effectively.

To summarize, thinking about a great esports venue is a fun and constructive process. However, facing reality is imperative for examining the

Zoning

INTERNATIONAL PERSPECTIVES ON ESPORTS FACILITIES

Alexander Champlin

I started researching esports venues in 2013 in Seoul, South Korea. My focus turned to Riot's NA LCS Arena and the Blizzard Arena, both in Los Angeles. However, given that it is the birthplace of modern esports, Korea was an excellent place to begin. The changes I saw in the design and implementation of studios offered an excellent case study in the shifting scale, scope, and understanding of esports as a media commodity. Specifically, what I saw take place over the course of five years was a transformation of esports venues from minimalistic, utilitarian spaces into spectacular, immersive theaters.

Korea famously pioneered a large-scale esports industry in the early 2000s. The small size of the country, the incubation of gaming culture in PC bangs, an economic climate that favored gaming, and a cable industry that was quick to adopt gaming competitions made Korea fertile soil for esports growth. The first esports matches to appear on TV appeared alongside children's programming on cable channels dedicated to this niche. Later, sports channels would also feature esports. The process of turning esports into regular cable productions called for infrastructure in the form of smaller studios where matches could be recorded on a weekly basis. Larger events still took place in event venues, but serialized esports could be produced most efficiently out of simple permanent soundstages. This process was the genesis of the modern esports arena.

In the month I spent in Seoul, I visited three permanent esports studios that produced content both for Korean cable TV and for streaming distribution. By 2013 esports had become a Korean media export, and streaming video was key to globalizing esports distribution. The broadcast/production studios I visited were operated by GOM, Nexon, and OGN. Each of them was in essence a very small TV studio. Two were tucked into basements of office buildings, and the third was in an auditorium on the top floor of an electronics mall. Admission to events was free. Inside, the audience would sit on plastic patio chairs and watch the games unfold on a central screen. A handful of cameras would cover the action in the studio, alternating between the players, the shoutcasters, and the audience. These setups were minimalist in their approach to translating game play for the studio audience. It was generally understood that the studio audience was there as a point of reference for people watching the broadcast from home, thus not much fanfare or immersion was inside the studio itself.

As esports have grown, the concept of the studio and the studio audience has changed. Esports studios have become destinations, ticketing has become a part of esports revenue stream, and the experience of watching in an arena has grown from utilitarian to immersive. When I returned from Seoul, I started following the development of the North American *League of Legends* Championship Series (NA LCS) Arena, Riot Games' proprietary esports venue for North American *League of Legends* competitions.

In December of 2013, the NA LCS moved out of a tiny studio in Culver City, California, into a larger soundstage with room for a studio audience; a sister studio for the European *League of Legends* Championship Series (EU LCS) was opened in Cologne, Germany at the same time. The NA LCS Arena was the first arena of its kind in the United States. It was permanent and designed to house LCS matches weekly, and it gave *League of Legends* fans a place to watch competition. It had more cameras and screens than the studios I visited in Korea, but the emphasis was still on creating an esports media product as efficiently as possible.

In 2015 the studio moved into a larger venue. It contained two theaters, a gift shop, and a host of secondary production spaces for all kinds of ancillary *League of Legends* and LCS promotion. The studio was becoming a destination, and the number of screens began to grow. Besides screens that showed players' reactions, the arena added screens that annotated game play; they echoed in-game announcements such as "First Blood" or "Pentakill." Eventually, these screens began to add more subtle touches, such as ambient backdrops of the game's flora. The esports arena morphed from a broadcast studio to a destination that could attract and engage a paying live audience.

Perhaps the best illustration of the changing function of the esports arena came in late 2017 when Los Angeles got its second esports venue, the Blizzard Arena. Launched alongside the inaugural season

(*continued*)

INTERNATIONAL PERSPECTIVES ON ESPORTS FACILITIES *(CONTINUED)*

of Blizzard's *Overwatch* League, the Blizzard Arena's most outstanding feature is a massive LED screen that wraps around the front of the arena like a gigantic U. It is easily two stories tall and four times as wide, and it is complemented by an LED halo that sits above the players and audience. In fact, the entire stage and first six rows of the audience are completely surrounded by these screens. This arena is designed to give the audience the sense that they are immersed in the game. This design coincided with Blizzard's plan for the future of the *Overwatch* League. The league planned to eventually create city-based regional arenas so that each team could host matches in its home city.

As esports grows, these changes take place all over the globe. Proprietary and independent esports venues are opening at a record rate. In the United States, Korea, and China, esports teams are piloting regionalized competition, and some are even opening home arenas. As esports revenue diversifies, the esports arena is no longer just a modified TV studio. The arena is a destination for fans, and it is enmeshed in the growing complexity of esports revenue streams.

cost, determining feasibility, exploring the actual construction process (and what will be included), and what would be required to keep the facility running and in great shape.

VIRTUAL REALITY (VR) ARCADES

Virtual reality (VR) has been an exciting technology for decades, but it was not easily accessible to consumers until recent years. The first round of high-end VR certainly came with challenges. Not only was the required hardware expensive, but gaming also required a significant amount of space in order to create a great experience. The new VR wave brought about the rise of room-scale gaming, the ability to physically move around a large space while wearing a VR headset. The experience was incredible, but it was not conducive to gaming at home. Enter VR arcades.

VR arcades present a fresh take on the classic arcades of the 1970s and 1980s. Rather than lining up rows of gaming cabinets side by side, VR arcades offer access to a multitude of games from each headset. From miniature golf to underwater experiences to zombie shooters, you can do just about anything in VR. In order to keep spectators engaged outside the headset, most VR arcades have TV screens showing the in-headset footage, creating a group experience whether you are in the headset or not.

Since 2017, VR arcades multiplied throughout the United States and Canada. Companies such as CTRL V and VR Junkies quickly started franchising, peaking at 19 and 12 stores, respectively. Spark VR joined the fray and launched in May 2017 with a 1,600-square-foot (148.64 m^2) location in Vernon, Connecticut. This location was a proof-of-concept store with four gaming stations and giant projection screens showing in-headset footage. Customers showed up in large numbers, so the owners of Spark VR quickly negotiated a new lease and built a larger store. A larger 3,200-square-foot (2,972.89 m^2) store opened in December 2018. This larger store features five gaming stations, contains five full-motion professional racing simulators, and serves beer and wine.

After watching the industry for the past few years, a concerning trend has emerged. VR arcades are failing in large numbers. A Connecticut-based competitor quickly opened three stores in close proximity to Spark VR, then quickly closed all of them. VR Junkies peaked at 12 stores in early 2019 and has closed all but 5 locations as of early 2020. CTRL V quickly scaled to 18 stores by early 2019 but has added just 1 location in the past year—in Costa Rica. Aside from the chains, independent VR arcades continue to open and close in quick cycles. For VR arcades in their current form, the outlook is dim.

The gaming experience is incredible. It is fun for all ages, and the technology is on the cutting edge. However, the industry is facing numerous challenges. The team at Spark VR has identified a few of the top reasons for industry failure. The primary challenge facing VR arcades is that revenue per square foot (m^2) is very low. As an industry average, each gaming station takes up about 150

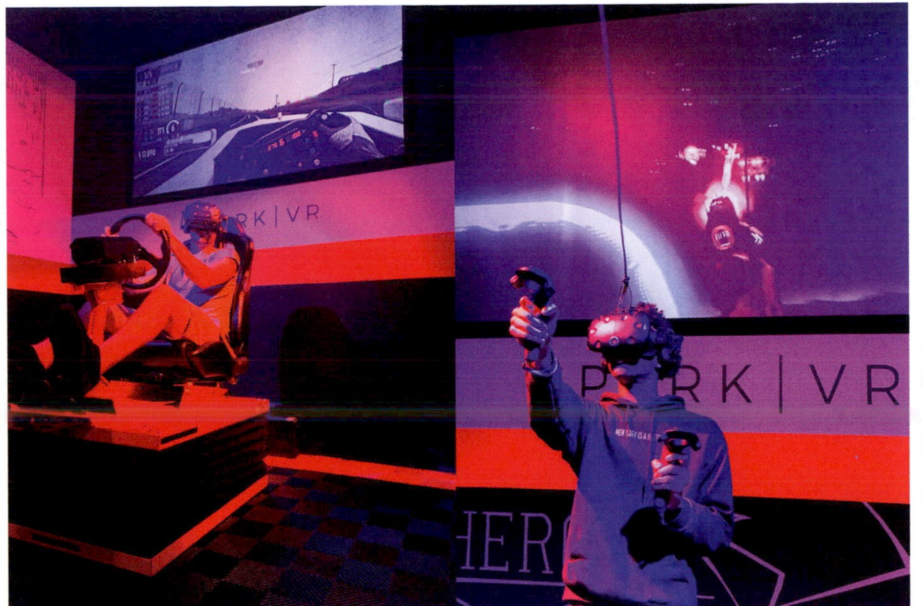

Courtesy of SparkVirtualReality.

Each headset in a VR arcade offers a multitude of games.

square feet (13.93 m^2). The hourly revenue per gaming station ranges from $25 to $45. By contrast, a restaurant could place multiple tables in a 150-square-foot (13.93 m^2) space and generate several hundred dollars per hour. Similarly, bars can accommodate a significant number of people in that area, generating very high revenue per square foot. A common argument for improving revenue per square foot in VR arcades is to install VR treadmills that allow gamers to play within a much smaller space. Treadmills may be great for hardcore gamers playing advanced shooting games, but for the average consumer looking for a fun VR experience, current treadmills are much too cumbersome and less immersive than physically moving around a large space.

Location selection is another major challenge affecting the industry. Indoor shopping malls are a dying breed in North America. A Forbes magazine article written in late 2018 predicts that 30 percent of shopping malls will close or be repurposed over the next decade (Danziger 2018). To combat this decline, shopping malls are offering favorable terms to attract exciting new businesses. Despite the decline of shopping malls, VR arcade owners are jumping at the favorable rent and financing terms being offered. However, many malls end up closing anyway. Spark VR has received numerous requests to open additional locations in shopping malls; to date, they have passed on each offer for specific reasons. The requirement that store hours match the open hours of the mall, combined with the reliance on walk-by traffic for revenue, make shopping malls a poor bet for entertainment centers.

The third major challenge is educating consumers on the VR arcade experience. Are VR arcades for kids? Are they for adults, teenagers, or families? Numerous questions about the target market and usage patterns by various demographics are pervasive. Because high-end VR is such a new phenomenon, the public does not have a strong understanding of what VR entails. At Spark VR, they do not focus on being a location that hosts children's birthday parties, because these types of activities run in cycles (e.g., high traffic only on weekends and holidays). From Chuck E. Cheese to inflatables to trampoline parks to Ninja Warrior locations, it is very difficult to find **staying power** as a birthday party location. Spark VR has found that most VR arcades primarily target families with young kids. To differentiate the Spark VR brand, they designed a VR arcade specifically geared toward adults, with beer and wine available for purchase and bar-height tables throughout. However, Spark VR has still had trouble convincing consumers that VR is not just for kids but for consumers of all ages.

Educating consumers who do not know about VR arcades presents a significant hurdle. In taking the path of least resistance, it is much easier for consumers to visit their local bowling alley or movie theater, because they know exactly what to expect. That same notion holds for bars, trampoline parks, and miniature golf. They are all established methods of entertainment that require no explanation. It will take time and resources to educate consumers on the VR experience. Moreover, because VR and related technologies (e.g., augmented reality [AR], mixed reality [MR]) will improve during the coming years, ongoing education will be needed and will take extensive resources.

CONCLUSION

This chapter provided information about esports facilities of all sizes and types, including insights into how they are built and operated. It discussed examples of large-scale arenas, smaller-scale venues, college facilities, and virtual reality (VR) and other types of arcades. In addition, the chapter provided insights into many of the challenges and opportunities facing people who manage and operate these facilities. As the industry progresses, individuals and organizations in charge of building and managing esports facilities (both dedicated esports facilities and venues used by event organizers, managers, and operators) will continue to be challenged with opportunities and innovations in both design and management. In addition, as esports operations expand and new revenue streams are identified, venue and facility managers and operators will need to explore new technology and opportunities in order to provide the best possible experience for all customers and stakeholders.

DISCUSSION QUESTIONS

1. What are the different types of esports venues and facilities? What are some of the considerations stakeholders should consider when building and developing esports venues and facilities?
2. Do you think PC bangs could be successful in any country other than South Korea? Explain your answer.
3. Based on the pricing structure used by several American esports venues (compared to PC bangs), do you think they are overpriced? How would you go about determining the appropriate price to charge for using a gaming PC?
4. What type of existing facility (e.g., warehouse, office, sport complex) do you think could be easily turned into an esports facility? Explore spaces on your campus and try to determine what elements might be required to convert it from its current use to an esports arena. How much do you think it will cost to transform the facility?
5. If you were to design your ideal esports playing space, what would you include? Price out the optimum system that you think would meet your needs.

10

Esports Communications

Anthony Palomba | Ryan Rogers | Aaron Colaiacomo
David P. Hedlund

OBJECTIVES

- Identify similarities and differences between the broadcasting of traditional sports and esports.
- Understand the tools available for esports communication professionals to use.
- Explain the process of streaming esports content.
- Summarize how esports communication overlaps with business topics such as sponsorship, analytics, and consumer behavior.
- Explain how social media is used in esports communication.
- Explain how public relations and crisis communications are used in esports.
- Identify employment opportunities and skills needed for those seeking employment in esports communications.

INTRODUCTION

Esports relies on fanfare, energy, and communication between partners, stakeholders, broadcasters, and fans. Similar to live sports, esports is mostly viewed in real time, and these live events have tremendous urgency embedded within them. This type of demand taps into audience needs, compelling them to watch live competitions and stay up to date on esports activities. For fans, the fear of missing a match in which a dramatic plotline unfolds or the opportunity to see two prolific streamers locked in a sweat-inducing final round of competition provides impactful and satisfying theater. The ingredients necessary to create these heightened experiences (including proper lighting, camera direction, stage setup, broadcasters, shoutcasters, producers, sponsors, and rabid fans) inform and communicate the gravity and significance behind each live event. Further, competitions between rivals can take spectators on a roller-coaster ride encompassing numerous positive and negative emotions. The narrative arc that players and spectators move through together is fueled by the unpredictability of game play and competition. In many ways, a live esports match is similar to an orchestra or symphony in which numerous instruments are playing. At certain times, some instruments must play louder and come to the forefront while others are silent. Because the goal of any live sport or esports match is to hold the attention spans of audience members across multiple matches, commercials, commentary, streamer interviews, and other segments, it is essential that all those participating in the production and communication of the event add energy and intrigue to it.

As noted throughout this book, esports is one of the most dynamic and fastest-growing sports. In order to increase and improve consumption, numerous essential communication tools are available to and frequently used by advertisers, broadcasters, streamers, public relations staff, and other professionals. For example, fans are eager to follow, learn, and engage with esports streamers. As a result, communication channels must be in place for these interactions to occur. Moreover, many esports matches are executed with tremendous energy and speed. This heightened pace places pressures on numerous stakeholders, including broadcasters and shoutcasters who are responsible for explaining to and educating spectators. This chapter describes several essential areas of communication in esports. They include broadcasting, shoutcasting, social media, streaming platforms, and other communication technologies.

SHOUTCASTING AND BROADCASTING IN ESPORTS

Tony Romo, a retired quarterback for the Dallas Cowboys, currently serves as an analyst for National Football League (NFL) games, where he provides in-depth **color commentary** for fans. Romo's experience as a player allows him to convey important insights to the audience. Today, much of the broadcasting of traditional sports is provided by expert sport journalists and those who have extensive insights and experiences with the game itself (e.g., former players). Similar to traditional sports, the broadcasting of esports competitions includes parallel types of broadcasting techniques, which all require a deep understanding of the game and how it is played.

Shoutcasting, which is popular in gaming and streaming, is distinct from traditional sportscasting in several ways. The task of a *shoutcaster* is to galvanize audiences and drive fan fervor during the experience. This goal of explaining what is happening during any game can be particularly difficult to accomplish during long, drawn-out esports competitions. In professional sports, often a ball is involved; as a result, audiences largely pay attention to where the ball is and where the players in its immediate vicinity are. In an esports competition, multiple players perform numerous competitive tasks every minute, but technology limits the visibility of some actions. As a result, broadcasters and shoutcasters may need to discuss actions that are happening both on- and off-screen, all while paying attention to the activities of multiple competitors. These types of commentary require energy and precision from the broadcasters, not just about understanding and explaining where the action is, but also where the subsequent activities may be and what it might take for each group of competitors to achieve success or avoid failure.

Similar to traditional sports, most professionally broadcast esports competitions have two main types of broadcast personnel: a **colorcaster** and a **play-by-play analyst**. These casters generally broadcast together and play off each other's strengths to provide insightful information and analysis of the game play. A colorcaster explains player story lines, in-game character strategy, and rules, or talks about the overall strengths and weaknesses of the teams. For example, in *League of Legends*, characters (generally known as *champions*) have certain strengths and weaknesses that make them vulnerable or extraordinary at certain points during a match. The colorcaster's job is to point out these differences in the characters as well as the items the players choose, their position, their levels of health and resources, or even their runes (enhanced abilities players may equip themselves with before a match).

In contrast, a play-by-play analyst breaks down the on-screen action for the audience. These analysts are frequently compared to sports broadcasters and are responsible for expeditiously describing each player's moves during the game. One of the most renowned play-by-play casters for the game *League of Legends* is Clayton "CaptainFlowers" Raines, who has been called a rap god because of his ability to speak at a rapid pace (Geracie 2019). In *League of Legends*, many actions can occur in just a few seconds. For example, the in-game heroes Fiddlesticks and Rammus previously had abilities that could be used to prevent opponents from taking action for three seconds. These characters' abilities have since been reduced to 2.75 or fewer seconds because 3 seconds was considered too powerful (Gamepedia 2019a, 2019b). Explaining in-game actions by multiple players, followed immediately by certain players being unable to complete any action due to the use of Fiddlesticks and Rammus' abilities, and then having actions being quickly restored, all while

Kyle Miller/ESPAT Media/Getty Images

Broadcasters and shoutcasters in esports serve essentially the same functions as broadcasters in traditional sports.

trying to explain what's happening and why to spectators who may be unfamiliar with all of these activities is a challenging task. Moreover, because the colorcaster and play-by-play analyst work in tandem to bring the games to life for fans, they often have even less time to provide information and explain the nuances of the game to viewers and spectators.

In terms of shoutcasting, the "shout" portion of the title also indicates their secondary role, which is to get the crowd excited. When a player does something particularly impressive or unanticipated during a game, the casters will frequently raise their voices and shout to express their surprise and note the importance of the actions that just occurred. For example, David "Phreak" Turley frequently uses his well-known catchphrase and battle cry, "Get on my level," to urge opponents to step up and improve their game, especially after his in-game hero kills an opponent first (Riot Games n.d.). A shoutcaster may then repeat or shout the phrase and explain its importance, all while the exciting action and drama continues in the game. The use of catchphrases is meant to highlight particular plays, create drama, and encourage fans to become active spectators.

One of the most important jobs of the casters is to develop and push story lines for players and various teams. It helps the viewer understand the importance of the action, game, or event. During the 2019 Spring *League of Legends* Championship Series (LCS), the colorcasters emphasized the stories of long-time veterans Doublelift and Bjergsen, who were competing against one another on different teams. They were both chasing their sixth LCS title, and both were attempting to earn the title of the greatest LCS player of all time (Chiu 2019). Fans were reminded during the entire five-game series that the winner could become the undisputed best player in history. Other story lines from the same event included Sven and Jensen, who were both esports veterans and considered exceptional players even though neither had ever won a title (Zaidi 2019). During the 2019 LCS Summer Split (also known as a season), Counter Logic Gaming and Team SoloMid (two of the four original organizations that competed in *League of Legends*) were about to play a game of moderate importance. However, the fact that Counter Logic Gaming had been outperforming Team SoloMid for most of the season meant that Counter Logic Gaming was possibly in a position to defeat Team SoloMid for the first time in three years. On social media and through news stories, casters and players constantly reminded the fans about the 1,176 days that had passed since Counter Logic Gaming had defeated Team SoloMid (Moncav 2019).

Shoutcasting is not only important to viewers, it is also significant for the legitimacy of esports. Without shoutcasting, little else connects the analysts, teams, and viewers. As a result, shoutcasting has become an essential form of communication in esports. It also allows those outside of the game's fan base to understand the basics of what is happening during these games. Casters can play an important role in bridging the gap between spectators who may know everything about the game and those who might be otherwise unfamiliar (McCormick 2014).

Shoutcasting is also an appealing element to the esports experience. It helps create commercially desirable perceptions surrounding the game itself. Moreover, it offers a window into the inner workings of a team. It may be difficult for fans to discern what strategy is being employed or what players may be saying to one another at some important moment in time. Shoutcasters are able to dissect and deconstruct the action going on in front of fans and explain it so that even those that are unfamiliar can have a basic understanding. Furthermore, because many spectators may not understand the nuances of the esports competition they are watching, shoutcasters play an important role in educating the audience and giving insight that only the most experienced players might see. Without colorcasters, play-by-play analysts, and shoutcasters, much of what happens during esports games might not be understood, so these people fill an essential role.

TOOLS IN ESPORTS COMMUNICATION

All industries rely on numerous tools that facilitate communication among employees and team members. For example, NFL coaches rely on headsets and microphones that allow for constant contact with other coaches who watch the game from above and discern distinct patterns of game play. While the use of technology by coaches of other sports such as baseball, basketball, and soccer is not as widespread (or in some cases allowed), teams also use hand and body signals to surreptitiously communicate with one another during games. Since its inception, the esports community has worked diligently to further this concept, creating digital communication applications that allow team members to speak to each other. Through these different types of technology, gamers are able to communicate in real time, discuss strategy as it unfolds, and closely work with each other. Effective team communication helps cultivate trust and often fuels high-quality performance.

In May of 2015, the mobile application and website Discord was launched as a free **Voice over Internet Protocol (VoIP)** service (Marks 2016). It allows for an all-in-one voice and text chat that works across multiple platforms, including desktop computers and mobile devices, and has become one of the most popular tools for voice and text chat for gamers. Discord boasts over 250 million unique users who have used its platform (Discord 2020), and as of the beginning of 2020, more than 10 million people daily (56 million people monthly) send an average of 963 million messages (Discord 2020). Each user has a four-digit number after the username, which allows for multiple iterations of the same username while still allowing for members to be searched for by other users (Discord 2020). As Lorenz (2019) noted, Discord has not only become an indispensable tool for gamers, it has also become a place where a community of fans of an influencer, player, team, league, or group can come together in the digital world, interact, and connect with other like-minded people who share the same interest.

Another platform, TeamSpeak, also provides high-quality VoIP communication systems for gamers and consumers. TeamSpeak markets their advantages as utilizing military-grade security, having numerous built-in privacy features, and providing clear and lag-free communications, among a number of listed benefits (TeamSpeak 2020). This software debuted in October 2001, making it one of the oldest VoIP softwares on the market. Different from its competitors, it maintains its user data and does not sell it to third parties. In addition, it empowers its members to host their own private servers. Users are able to customize their interface, and they have control over unlimited subchannels and file transfer alongside game pad and joystick hot-key support. Together, these value propositions that have been laid out for its users help separate TeamSpeak from its other competitors.

Mumble is another open-source VoIP service. It boasts a low-latency voice communication and has worked to create greater security for gamers

Zoning

USING DISCORD WITH THE MOBILE GAME *CLASH OF CLANS*

David P. Hedlund

On August 2, 2012, Finnish game developer Supercell globally launched the downloadable and free-to-play mobile game *Clash of Clans*. Due in large part to the in-game purchases players can make (e.g., buying gems that can be used in game to speed up or finish the construction or development of buildings, troops, spells, etc.), within three months of its launch, *Clash of Clans* became the top-grossing game in the United States (Supercell 2020). In 2013, Supercell earned $892 million in revenue (Tweedie 2014). After several years of ups and downs, in 2019, the game experienced resurgence through the advent of a monthly pass users could buy for USD $4.99. As a result, player spending soared by more than 26 percent year-over-year (YOY) to $722 million (Koczwara 2020). Because *Clash of Clans* is a mobile game, Supercell has been able to periodically improve and enhance the game, with updates being made available and pushed directly to the device(s) on which users play.

After downloading the game and establishing their profile, players can begin the task of building their in-game base, increasing the levels of their troops and spells, attacking randomly assigned opponents and gaining loot from those bases, and having their base defend against opponents' attacks and losing loot as a result. Players also have an option to establish their own or join someone else's clan. Clans are composed of up to 50 members, and they are led by a single Leader (an official in-game title) who has the ability to assign other in-game titles such as Co-Leader and Elder to members of the clan. Leaders and Co-Leaders can write and edit a description of the clan in addition to adding requirements that incoming players should meet. Within the game, players have the ability to search for and read about different clans and their members. Further, players also have the ability to request to join clans, and they may be accepted by the existing leadership if a slot is available and they meet the clan's requirements.

The U.S.A Family of Clans

During the final months of 2012, a user with the handle "Joecomotive" established and organized the "U.S.A" (spelled with only two periods) clan (logo shown in figure 10.1). Because of its name, when searching for a clan to join, many high-level players (mostly from America) flocked to the clan. Shortly thereafter, with the addition of numerous high-level players, the U.S.A clan became the top-ranked (by performance) clan in the United States and regularly one of the top 10 globally ranked clans. Due to the high ranking of the U.S.A clan, many of the most skilled players frequently were accepted into the clan. Later, when in-game rewards were distributed at the end of each in-game season, jockeying for a place within the clan became the norm among many of the best players in the United States. To combat the challenge of how to consistently fill the U.S.A clan with the most highly ranked members and to also provide a proving ground for up-and-coming players, so-called farm clans were created in order to house members that were either waiting to enter the U.S.A clan or developing the skills and experience necessary to be accepted into the top clan. Over the years, this process was repeated again and again as the interest in joining one of the top U.S.-branded

Figure 10.1 U.S.A family clan logo.

Logo courtesy of Michael Scott.

(continued)

USING DISCORD WITH THE MOBILE GAME *CLASH OF CLANS (CONTINUED)*

clans increased. As of 2020, the family has 10 U.S.A-branded clans (e.g., U.S.A; U.S.A 2, 3, and 4; U.S.A Freedom, U.S.A Honor, U.S.A Valor, etc.) and 7 Farm4USA numbered clans, totaling more than 700 total members. Periodically, as the U.S.A clans fill, new clans are created and added to the family. In order to organize all of the members of the U.S.A family of clans, the leadership decided to use the Discord mobile application to organize, communicate with, and build the community.

Using Discord for Organization and Communication

The Discord application has numerous functions and capabilities. For example, it has the ability to create channels for different groups (clans), assign membership in one or more clans to members, assign roles, and provide direct and indirect lines of communication among members through public and private text and voice chat capabilities. In addition to the fact many gamers already have profiles on Discord that they use with other organizations, the leadership of the U.S.A family of clans began officially using the mobile application and website around 2015. Moreover, because the *Clash of Clans* game does not facilitate private communication among players, and because the U.S.A family of clans wanted to provide a universal platform in order to assist in communication and the organizing of activities (such as the movement of players between different clans within the family), the decision to use Discord was met without hesitation. Since the establishment of the official Discord channel for all of the U.S.A family of clans, frequent communication and activities such as inter-U.S.A games and competitions have resulted in numerous benefits, such as a greater sense of community among members; opportunities for recognition, achievement, and advancement within the clan; opportunities to learn from and share in-game and real-world knowledge with other members; opportunities to promote and engage in social responsibility and charity activities; and even national pride and celebration activities. Despite the natural coming and going of players and leaders as they level up in game, choose to move to other clans to have new in-game experiences, and even when they retire from the game, the U.S.A community on Discord has become the backbone of support for many of its most important activities.

Undoubtedly, the members of the U.S.A family of clans are not unique to using Discord (or other communication platforms) to organize and promote positive outcomes among their members. Multiple leaders within the U.S.A Discord community (known as the Oval Office) actively work to ensure positive experiences for users and deal with any issues that arise. For example, the leaders post and remind users about appropriate behaviors, and they also keep an eye out for concerns raised about player behavior, toxicity, or other Discord-related issues (see Brewster 2019; Jargon 2019; Menegus 2017). As a result, information about rules and requirements are posted in places within the community. Albeit rare, players and even leaders who have run afoul have found themselves relegated or removed depending on the transgressions.

In the end, creating opportunities for connections among players is an ideal outcome for any PC-based, console, or mobile esports and video games. While using third-party tools such as Discord has costs associated with it, in addition to the built-in functions of the games, opportunities exist to further facilitate and advance the benefits of gaming through these tools. Esports and video game players, especially when they find themselves playing and competing on or for the same team or in the same group as others, are often looking for ways to facilitate good communication. The U.S.A family of clans from the game *Clash of Clans* has taken their use of the Discord application to the next level, whereas they are now using it for many positive activities and achieving positive outcomes. In the future, as technology and esports continue to evolve, tools such as Discord, appropriately used and managed, can continue to facilitate and improve community and comradery among people who otherwise might never meet face-to-face.

(Mumble n.d.). The low-latency voice communication allows for quicker dissemination of voice and hearing reception. Among web interfaces, channel views, and authenticators, Mumble works to provide a safe environment for its users.

Esports communication is the bedrock of the business itself. When video game play is competitive, teamwork is an inextricable element of the game play experience. Team players who can speak in terse and precise sentences are able to convey directions, guidelines, strategies, and other mechanics of game play to their constituents with ease. For example, over the years, sponsors have frequently taken advantage of opportunities to consistently communicate the same message across disparate platforms. Across broadcasts, branded content, signage in venues, gaming equipment, social media, and apparel, the manners in which to communicate to fans and stakeholders are unlimited (Nielsen 2020).

Shoutcasting, streaming, and other communication tools have become essential components of the esports experience. These tools have fueled the rise of many esports personalities, including individual influencers such as Tyler "Ninja" Blevins, and esports team players such as Kuro "KuroKy" Salehi Takhasomi (from Team Liquid) and Johan "N0tail" Sundstein (player and coach of the team OG). Effective communication of personal and team brand messages helps ensure that particular traits, characteristics, and images are reinforced in the memory of fans. In addition, the dispersion of communication tools and technology allows fans to use the same implements that professionals use. These strategies are critical not only to the success of the esports experience but to creating overarching, seasonal, or career narratives that consumers have interest in and desire to follow. These exploits may also influence consumers' behaviors to subscribe to a streaming service, watch linear or online content and competitions, and purchase event tickets or products being sold by or marketed through the influencers, players, and teams they follow. A large amount of the consumption process would likely not be as effective without the communication tools currently being used.

STREAMING

A myriad of **streaming services** are available for players to use to broadcast various activities. Streaming services allow for portability and the ability for users to access the same service (e.g., Twitch, YouTube) on different platforms (e.g., Microsoft, Apple, PC, mobile). As a result, audiences are able to stream live video game feeds from almost any device. In addition, streaming services are able to capture the data footprints of the audience while creating unprecedented levels of interaction between streamers, broadcasters, and fans. Unbounded streaming experiences manifest opportunities for further granular data collections, which has pushed data analytics into uncharted territory. As more and more users create streaming content and increasing numbers of people consume it, multiple opportunities and threats are present. For example, are there ways in which streaming and any associated activities can be monetized? What types of content do users want to watch and avoid? These types of questions are critical to consider when examining how streaming services have been rapidly moving to the forefront of broadcasting esports. For example, according to Esports Charts (2020a), in 2019, the top 10 categories of streamed content on Twitch, in order of highest to lowest total number of hours watched, were as follows:

1. 1.08 billion hours of the game *League of Legends*
2. 1.02 billion hours of the game *Fortnite*
3. 734 million hours of users chatting
4. 564 million hours of the game *Grand Theft Auto*
5. 492 million hours of the game *Dota 2*
6. 441 million hours of the game *Counter-Strike*
7. 404 million hours of the game *World of Warcraft*
8. 338 million hours of the game *Apex Legends*
9. 277 million hours of the game *Overwatch*
10. 244 million hours of the game *Hearthstone*

While many fans undoubtedly want to watch and learn from others who play and stream content, many may be interested in livestreaming in order to meet new people, have opportunities for social interaction, join existing communities of like-minded fans, and perhaps also seek out opportunities to receive social or emotional support (Hilvert-Bruce et al. 2018). Here is a list of 20 of the top streaming platforms used around the world (Esports Charts 2020b):

1. Afreeca TV
2. Bilibili
3. DouYu
4. EGame
5. Facebook
6. Garena
7. GoodGame
8. Huomao
9. Huya
10. KingKong
11. Longzhu
12. OPENREC
13. Quanmin
14. Smashcast
15. Steam
16. Twitch
17. VK
18. YouTube
19. YY
20. Zhanqi

Twitch currently is one of the most popular ways for consumers to watch esports (Alexander 2020). Because it is owned by Amazon, Twitch allows gamers to receive free games and connect with other assets and opportunities (Amazon 2020). Twitch has also curated partners across multiple mediums, including Turner Sports. The platform created a gaming show titled *ELEAGUE Super Punch*, which debuted on both digital (Twitch) and linear platforms (TBS) in February 2020 (Stern 2020). With streamers at the helm, the show provides a recap of esports around the world in a late-night talk show format.

In 2020, YouTube Gaming made a big splash when it partnered with game publisher Activision Blizzard to exclusively stream matches for the *Overwatch* League, *Call of Duty* League, and *Hearthstone* competitions. From the fourth quarter of 2018 to the fourth quarter of 2019, esports viewership on YouTube Gaming grew almost 14 percent (from 293 million to 334 million viewers; Alexander 2020). To bolster their stable of esports influencers and content creators, YouTube has also signed Jack "CouRage" Dunlop, Rachell "Valkyrae" Hofstetter, Elliott "Muselk" Watkins, and Lannan "LazarBeam" Eacott (Alexander 2020). YouTube Gaming has also helped push the boundaries of streaming technology by allowing viewers to rewind and pause during a live broadcast (Brathwaite 2018).

Traditional social media firms are also increasingly involved in esports. Facebook Gaming has a program known as Level Up, which allows game developers and livestreamers to build communities around the games they build and play (Imah and Miller 2018). Facebook Gaming has also partnered with ESL to provide access to streams of Intel Extreme Masters (IEM) events, ESL One events, and *Counter-Strike: Global Offensive* (*CS:GO*) Pro League competitions (Olebe 2019). Steam, developed by the game publisher Valve (the company behind *CS:GO* and *Dota 2*), also offers live broadcasts of games hosted on its platform. To differentiate themselves, viewers on the Steam platform can engage in public chatting, private chatting, and limited voice chatting features to go along with their video streaming technology (Brathwaite 2018).

ESPORTS COMMUNICATION AND SPONSORSHIP

As first discussed in chapter 7, sponsorship is a major asset esports organizations can leverage for numerous benefits. For example, esports organizations can help to strengthen attachment between fans and their games. In addition, brands may be able to refine their reputations and increase sales of products by partnering with esports organizations. Moreover, fans who subscribe to a team's newsletter, streaming service, or organization's email list may become leaders and evangelists for the organizations they follow.

However, like most branding strategies, attempts to create awareness, interest, and future behaviors can become muddled. Therefore, it is necessary for brand managers to carefully consider appropriate brand partnerships, and most importantly, how to effectively create relationships and communicate with fans. Insightful, passionate, and quick to criticize, esports fans frequently possess strong brand loyalty toward the video games they play. As such, sponsorship activities should include the creation of meaningful connections between fans and the brand. If fans cannot connect to a brand, then regardless of the communication activities used, the market-

© Photo by (Drew Amato, Estars LLC)

Sponsorship can be used to communicate messages to consumers.

ing and sponsorship campaign will struggle from the outset.

In both traditional sports and esports, fans are an active part of the product, because they simultaneously produce and consume events and activities (Napoli 2011). Attending live events in person is attractive to fans, because the experience allows them to meet like-minded people and share experiences while watching skilled players compete (Taylor 2016). Interwoven in the sports–business mix, sponsorship is a critical element that creates revenue for esports organizations. For these activities to achieve success, information must be effectively communicated. In esports, finding suitable messages for diverse stakeholders is often challenging.

Across the esports industry, the measurement of sponsorship effectiveness is often based on how much communication consumers and the media undertake. For example, online sponsorship may take the form of an advertisement placed on an Internet page. The consumer engagement rates and interaction with these advertisements can be measured before, during, and after each match. Based on the potential use of disparate messaging, digital analytics firms are able to capture and analyze actual consumer behavior, and evaluate and compare the effectiveness of unique sponsorship activities. Through these types of activities, effective messages from sponsors can be identified and improved.

ESPORTS COMMUNICATION AND ANALYTICS

Across nearly every consumer good and service industry, terms such as *data science*, *multivariate analyses*, *data mining*, and other buzz words abound. The catalyst for the increased importance of these areas is in part due to the amount of digital and directly collected consumer data made available to businesses. Current-generation video game consoles are powerful enough to connect to and function on the Internet. For the first time, improved technology underpinning video game consoles allows manufacturers to collect information and player data. For example, video game consoles are capable of collecting tremendous amounts of player data, and they can serve as tremendous repositories for insights into consumers (Palomba 2019). The same is true for streaming services, which can also capture and house tremendous amounts of consumer information. The data is used to enhance the quality of service, but they can also be sold to advertisers. For instance, streaming service Roku has capitalized on its massive audience data matrices by selling it to advertisers who can then target potential customers with more precision (Shields 2018).

These innovations have served as the forerunner to modern esports video game analytics, in which video game play habits can be measured in real time. Because esports are often streamed live, opportunities are plentiful for advertisers, merchants, public relations professionals, television broadcasters, and others to gain precise data about streamers, video game play habits, audience attention spans, consumer sentiments, and other aspects of the consumption experience. This situation differs greatly from live sporting events; with live events, it may be difficult to track how many consumers are directly watching the live event in the arena, on television, at home, or in a third-party location (e.g., restaurant, bar). Another important distinction is the tracking of live broadcasts and on-demand (prerecorded) content. In prior years, it was generally assumed few people watched previously recorded sporting events because the result is already known, eliminating the need to watch a game (Klosterman 2011). Because the consumer desire for on-demand esports content is high, Nielsen has implemented a new live+ metric that measures viewers watching both the live event and on-demand recording (Hitt 2020). As a result, esports analytics are helping to usher in a new era of not only *what* can be measured but also *how* it can be measured.

Several firms are dedicated to looking at analytics. One company, Shadow, has emerged as a pioneer in esports analytics. It currently supports *League of Legends*, *Dota 2*, and numerous other clients (Shadow 2020). These insights are collated around measuring game play performance, task times, player preferences, and other *key performance indicators (KPIs)* that are similar to sports analytics. Stream Hatchet is a platform that allows players to measure numerous important business and performance metrics. These metrics include information on audience reach, streaming sessions, geolocation, consumer demographics, and more (Wooden n.d.). The use of analytics, especially in the context of streaming and broadcasting, empowers organizations to glean salient details about the audience as well as learn how they are perceived by consumers, in addition to deciding how they may want to position themselves according to the needs of potential advertisers. Because many organizations desire to market their goods and services to specific consumer groups or demographics, understanding one's own consumer base, and identifying communication mediums reaching those same consumers, is now an essential process undertaken by many groups.

Digital analytics for advertisers, streamers, and esports organizations is also useful for tracking all types of consumer behavior. A successful esports competition is made up of numerous components, perhaps none more important than the mediums through which the event organizers broadcast the event and how the cognition, emotions, and behaviors of fans are impacted by the messages and information they receive. Through effectively communicating the story behind and throughout the esports competition, fans may express emotions that run the gamut of positive and negative sentiments. Broadcasters and streamers may drive much of the emotion, and the collected analytics can provide feedback on their effectiveness and eventual engagement in consumption behaviors.

ESPORTS COMMUNICATION, FAN EMOTIONS, AND MOTIVATIONS

Esports has blossomed into a massive ecosystem that employs numerous types of organizations and firms. However, the sport has grown due in part to its grassroots user-focused beginnings. The immediacy, ubiquity, and real-time aspects of social media and online video game play streaming have kept microscopic lenses on the sport throughout its growth. Fans are used to being able to learn as much as they wish about a player, and they are also inclined to seek out opportunities for engagement with esports players they like or find interesting.

The connection between fans and players in esports coincides with much literature surrounding how fans experience any type of entertainment. In any hedonic (pleasure-filled) event, emotions are summoned and manipulated to heighten the experience itself. For example, entertainment experiences have been found to influence consumers' moods on a subconscious level (Zillmann 1988; Zillmann and Bryant 1985) and are subject to individual preferences (Zillmann and Knobloch 2001). As a result, consumers emotions are impacted by the messages they receive and information they learn. For example, Diwanji and colleagues (2020) investigated how information and messages consumers received on Twitch affected the experience of streaming content. The results indicated that many consumers who watched Twitch streams were engaged in a process of information seeking, reacting to that information, and subsequent information production. In other words, Twitch consumers both received and produced content through the chat functions that operate in coordination with the stream.

Esports fans' emotions and motivations to view a match are expressed in a variety of manners. While traditional sport fans may scream and shout during a live sporting event, **emojis** and textual esports jargon (e.g., the use of game-specific terminology) may take center stage in the chat function during livestreamed esports competitions. Another area where esports fans may express their emotions is on social media. Because social media is a type of digital media, the tracking of consumer behavior, communications, and messages is also commonplace through these mediums.

ESPORTS COMMUNICATION AND SOCIAL MEDIA

One of the key determinants of consumer engagement with an organization and its brands is relationship marketing. Traditional mass consumption markets created products designed for all types of people to use. However, better understanding of consumer segments and cultivation of interest in specific goods and services (e.g., branding) over a lifetime have pushed marketers to consider different mechanisms through which to engage consumers. Increasingly, marketing activities have been targeted toward individual consumers, requiring precise **customer relationship management (CRM)** strategies, such as tailored communications derived from detailed understanding of psychological processes (e.g., consumers' feelings and motivations about particular goods and services; Kumar and Reinartz 2012). For example, if a group of esports consumers are motivated to watch streamed content in order to learn new techniques and tactics to implement when they themselves play, then organizations may want to produce and market educational esports content in which players' and teams' strategies are succinctly described, explained, and evaluated. When organizations are able to create strong relationships with their customers, oftentimes those individuals may become more invested in the brand, communicate more about the organization and its brand, and evangelize to others about the brand's strengths and opportunities (Taylor 2012).

Esports organizations also rely on social media to enhance fan and streaming engagement during all phases of game play. Social media is an interactive platform that creates additional opportunities for engagement and measurement. Likes, shares or retweets, number of times the content is viewed, and what actions (e.g., clicks) are taken are just some of the metrics available through social media platforms. Twitter analytics allows for educating stakeholders surrounding the number of impressions received for each tweet, as well as the amount of interactions a tweet has received. Metrics such as **engagement rate**, which is determined by engagement divided by impressions (Twitter Business 2017), has also become a popular KPI. Streamers can segment consumer audiences through Google Analytics, Hootsuite, or other proprietary firm software to transform data into information and actionable insights through the previously listed types of data or metrics.

Esports personalities and organizations have benefited tremendously from engaging social media activities. A wide variety of studies have examined how social media has affected professional sports organizations. One study found that professional sport teams have both sport-focused and non–sport-focused groups of fans (Naraine, Wear, and Whitburn 2019). For instance, an esports league may have discernable groups of fans that could be identified by demographics (e.g., gender, ethnicity, cultural background), interests (e.g., sports, music, food, entertainment), and other consumer characteristics (e.g., behaviors). The implications for these types of results suggest that esports organizations may be able to create targeted communication strategies through different media platforms that can focus on influencing consumer behaviors. In fact, esports organizations have invested tremendous numbers of resources in developing and nurturing their fan communities with the goal of creating a communication pipeline between users, organizations, and game developers. Through the development of this communication pipeline, esports game developers and organizations can learn about what their consumers like and engage in activities focused on meeting or exceeding customer expectations. Players and users can influence the direction of games and competitions through providing feedback to the game developer and esports organization. Consequently, through effective communication, stakeholders can gain the benefits and outcomes they want.

ESPORTS COMMUNICATION, PUBLIC RELATIONS, AND CRISIS ACTIVITIES

Unfortunately, sometimes stakeholders do not gain the benefits and outcomes they want. In fact, in some cases, organizations may be forced to confront situations and communicate with stakeholders and the public about unfortunate or unexpected issues. In these situations, organizations often undertake extensive public relations activities. While often perceived as only being done during a crisis, in fact, public relations is a much more holistic field; it is done during any situation in which an organization is communicating with the public.

According to the Public Relations Society of America (PRSA), public relations is defined as "influencing, engaging and building a relationship with key stakeholders across numerous platforms in order to shape and frame the public perception of an organization" (2020, para. 4). In other words, when organizations choose to communicate with the public, they often do so with not just the goal of providing information but also with the hope of influencing opinions, attitudes, and behavior. When communications and public relations are successful, the public is not solely more knowledgeable and informed, their thinking and future actions are also affected.

Over the years, while the esports and video gaming industry has been growing in size and scope, it has not been without issue. As discussed in previous chapters, numerous issues facing esports stakeholders have been put forward, including being cited as a contributing factor to negative physical, mental, and social issues such as increases in aggression and violence, social isolation, obesity, and health and wellness concerns, just to name a few (Chung et al. 2019). When concerns arise, one strategy stakeholders have to counter negative impacts of unflattering portrayals or stories in the media is the opportunity to engage in public relations activities. While public relations activities are not limited to situations when an organization is faced with problems, because of the high level of attention they receive, crisis communications are often the most visible activity.

While entire chapters and even books can and have been written on the topic, the following paragraphs contain some of the basic ideas esports organizations can consider when facing a crisis and engaging in public relations activities. The Institute for Public Relations (2007) defines and explains a crisis as "a significant threat to operations that can have negative consequences if not handled properly . . . a crisis can create three related threats: (1) public safety, (2) financial loss, and (3) reputation loss" (para. 2). When engaging in public relations and crisis communications, organizations and their **spokesperson** may handle a litany of potential activities and responses. These activities include denying the issue exists or is a problem; attacking, blaming, or scapegoating others; excusing or minimizing the problem and the organization's responsibility; justifying the problem or solutions; focusing on other topics; praising others' activities; and apologizing and taking responsibility. Because every situation is different, no single way exists in which an organization may respond to and undertake public relations when faced with a problem or crisis. However, considering the true purpose of public relations (to create relationships with the public), this same goal is also likely to be true when facing problems or crises.

In esports organizations, just as in any organization, problems arise from time to time. Many of the suggestions groups such as the Institute for Public Relations (2007) make about best practices are the same for esports organizations. When engaging in crisis communications, ensuring that communication is timely, accurate, consistent, public focused, safety focused (in the case of harm or injury), widespread through multiple platforms, expresses concern and empathy, and appears sincere and apologetic are all important points for esports organizations and their spokespersons to consider.

ESPORTS COMMUNICATION AND EMPLOYMENT

Social media in esports is one of the fastest-growing areas of employment in the industry. In fact, the esports industry itself has witnessed a groundswell of new positions being opened. For example, Takahashi (2020) notes that esports job website Hitmarker found a rise in the number of esports jobs available around the world; demand increased 87 percent from 2018 to 2019. Much of the growth in esports has likely occurred because of increases in the production of esports events and activities, a dedication to providing exceptional fan experiences, and a multiplatform communication strategy that requires increasing numbers of people with diverse skill sets to help run and manage many of the new activities and events.

Esports is driven by the action, bustle, and dedicated professionals that are behind every matchup and experience. Numerous positions are available in areas such as business development, hospitality, logistics, marketing and sales, operations, production management, public relations and communications, and software engineering, just to name a few (Hitmarker 2020). More paid positions are available, which likely will lead to more stability in the industry (Huggan 2018).

Some positions are more specialized than others, requiring specific skill sets that can still be gained through a university education. Broadcasters, shoutcasters, colorcasters, and play-by-play analysts explain the in-game action and provide excitement with some additional dramatic and theatrical elements. The skills needed to be successful in these positions may be learned in academic programs focused on journalism, communication, media, and public relations. In addition, the same type of skill set required of a shoutcaster could also be applied to becoming an esports journalist where knowledge, skills, and experience in both oral and written mediums are important.

CONCLUSION

Communication lies as the fulcrum of many esports activities. Similar to most physical activities, communication harnesses the power and magnitude of self-expression. Whether a streamer has beaten another streamer or a shoutcaster has passionately described an unprecedented play, these actions reverberate within the human consciousness. Multiple messages are constantly conveyed during competitions and events, and audiences receive them and respond to them. For every completed match is a completed symphony of expression, storytelling, and displayed human emotion. Effective communication can fuel expressions of emotion, while ineffective communication may only be seen later when examining analytics related to engagement and consumer behaviors. Communication activities before, during, and after esports events are used to imbue the activities with value while simultaneously providing opportunities for additional engagement on the part of consumers. As the esports industry continues to develop, so too will the ability of those working in esports and those consuming esports goods and services, not to mention the technology and ways in which emotions and experiences will be recounted.

DISCUSSION QUESTIONS

1. What are the similarities and differences between the broadcasting of traditional sports and the shoutcasting of esports?
2. What are the similarities and differences between streaming platforms?
3. In what ways does esports communication impact sponsorship in the industry?
4. Why is analytics rising in importance within esports communication?
5. How do esports professionals use communications strategies to undertake customer relationship management?
6. What types of esports communications jobs exist? What types of knowledge and skills are beneficial for those interested in jobs in esports communications?

11

Esports Finance and Economics

Gil Fried

INTRODUCTION

In 2019, the global video game market was expected to be around USD $152 billion (Wijman 2019). It is an exciting number, but it is just a snapshot of the financial landscape of the esports industry. Although many people are eager to make money in this field, it's not as easy as it looks. The esports road is not paved with gold; actually, the road is paved with failed companies. These companies often overspent, did not understand their finances, did not track their cash, and made other mistakes. This chapter examines basic financial concepts and explores how they apply to the esports industry.

OBJECTIVES

- Develop an esports event budget.
- Compare and contrast the financial outlooks for two publicly traded esports companies.
- Summarize the financial concepts affecting esports teams.
- Demonstrate the ability to interpret material in a company's annual report.
- Explain how understanding revenue and expenses is critical for those in the esports space.

THE BUSINESS OF ESPORTS

The rapid expansion of and fast-flowing money into esports have reminded some people of the dot-com bubble of 1997-2000 where the value of many Internet companies shot up . . . and then the market burst, bankrupting many smaller companies and losing almost $5 trillion in market capitalization. The concern is that everyone is trying to jump into the space without really understanding what is going on. The industry is in a position where a new game could come out next week and crush the competition, turning today's top game into a has-been virtually overnight. One sport example of this type of volatility is mud runs and obstacle course racing. They were all the rage around 2014. In January 2020, Tough Mudder (an endurance race series involving obstacle courses) owed three creditors over $850,000 and its largest lender, event registration company Active Networks, around $18 million. As part of Tough Mudder's bankruptcy proceedings, rival company Spartan Race offered to pay off the debt and buy the company for a seven-figure amount (Cronin 2020). This story is an example of how a misstep in a market can cause a company to face a harsh economic reality from lenders.

The key to avoiding financial ruin is to understand how economic success is defined. It is not necessarily having the highest total sales. If a company has more expenses than sales, it will lose money, and even a large sales volume cannot keep that company's doors open for long when it is consistently losing money. The following example of two esports-related companies helps highlight that numbers can tell a variety of stories.

Two publicly traded companies dominate China's esports market: Huya (NYSE:HUYA) and DouYu International (NASDAQ:DOYU). Huya and DouYu are often compared to Amazon-owned Twitch. Both also are partially owned by Tencent, the largest gaming company in the world. Both companies' stocks have taken different paths; Huya's has doubled since its initial public offering (IPO), and DouYu's shrunk almost 40 percent since its IPO. How could two companies in the same market with the same supposed upside take such different paths?

Huya focuses on hosting live video game streams and other esports content. Its monthly active users (MAUs) grew to 146.1 million in the fourth quarter of 2019 (a 48% annual increase), and total paying users rose to 5.3 million users (an increase of 29%). Approximately 95 percent of Huya's new revenue comes from selling virtual gifts and items on its livestreaming platform; viewers purchase them for their favorite broadcasters, and Huya takes a cut of the revenue. The remaining 5 percent comes from digital ads.

In the same quarter, DouYu's total MAUs grew 15 percent annually to 163.6 million. DouYu has a larger overall audience, partly because the company offers more video content beyond esports. DouYu's audience is not growing as fast as Huya's and has fewer paid and mobile users. DouYu generates more revenue from ads; its ads generated 11 percent of its revenue, and the remaining 89 percent derived from its livestreaming unit.

If you had $10,000 to invest in either of these companies, which would you choose? In 2019 analysts expected Huya's revenue to grow 71 percent, with DouYu's revenue increasing 98 percent. This projection would seem to indicate that DouYu is a better investment. However, a one-year projection usually is not sufficient to determine the wisdom of a long-term investment. In fact, Huya's revenue was expected to decelerate to 37 percent growth in 2020. These same analysts thought DouYu's revenue would slow to 38 percent growth in 2020. However, revenue is only one number; profits are a different story. While the bottom lines of both companies were improving as of the start of 2019, DouYu was losing money while Huya was making a profit. Huya's net income increased 132 million yuan ($17 million) in the third quarter of 2019, which was a 117 percent increase. At the start of 2019, analysts expected Huya's adjusted earnings to grow 47 percent in 2019 and 80 percent in 2020. In contrast, DouYu's loss narrowed from 220.5 million yuan to 165 million yuan ($23 million) in the last quarter of 2018 (Sun 2019).

In addition to reviewing trends and growth potential, it is also important to monitor how investors and market analysts view an esports business stock, which can rise significantly when a new title is released or drop significantly when a controversy occurs. In terms of Huya and DouYu, the analysts and stock market provide some interesting perspective. Examining the market on January 15, 2020, Huya was selling for $20.63; the stock had sold for as little as $16.40 and as high as $30.00 per share over the span of a year. With such a valuation, the market value for the company was $4.5 billion. In addition, 48 analysts reviewed the stock; 15 rated the stock as a strong buy, and 25 rated it as a buy. These ratings resulted in a ranking between buy and strong buy. Even though the earnings per share reflected a loss of $2.82 per share, analysts expected that the stock price should increase to $27.45.

On the same day, DouYu was selling for $9.02 per share. The price range was not as wide as Huya; over the previous 52 weeks, DouYu's shares had ranged from $7.01 to $11.88. Based on the price, DouYu had a market valuation of $2.93 billion, and the anticipated target price was $9.52. Sixteen analysts over several months rated the stock closer to a buy rather than a strong buy. Four had listed the stock as a strong buy, 10 as a buy, and 2 as a hold over the same period. Based in part on the lower share value, DouYu's board voted in December 2019 to repurchase up to $100 million of their common shares (PR Newswire 2019).

This example helps highlight the importance of examining several different numbers when undertaking a financial analysis. Understanding the critical skill of budgeting is equally important when exploring whether to hold an esports event.

BASIC FINANCIAL CONCEPTS

Economics is the study of what is happening in an economy, such as whether a lot of inflation is occurring or if customers are making buying decisions and why. Esports **finance** describes processes through which to identify where money is being made and spent in an esports business, interpreting these numbers, and making intelligent decisions to guide the business toward profitability. While economics focuses on the big picture of the economy (such as are we in a recession, where is an industry sector going, etc.), finance is more focused on specific companies and how they are making money, paying their bills, and positioned for the future. This section covers a variety of financial topics, but they are all critical for exploring how well an esports organization is doing. It begins with an exploration of assets and liabilities, which represent what is owned and what is owed. Then it considers revenue and expenses; revenue is money coming in, and expenses reflect what is being paid.

Assets

Assets represent something of value. The key to an asset is its ability to generate revenue. Consider what assets you might have. For example, you have this book. Is it an asset? Hopefully, the book will help you land a job and create an opportunity for financial return, so it can qualify as an asset. In contrast, an old magazine you have lying around the house might be interesting reading, but it is not considered an asset.

An important distinction exists between stuff and assets that can generate value. Cash is an asset because it can be invested to help create value. However, if the cash is spent on worthless items, it becomes a missed opportunity to leverage the cash as an asset.

Various asset categories exist. Some assets are considered liquid assets while other assets are long-term assets. A **liquid asset** is an asset that can be converted to cash in a short time frame (usually less than a year), such as gold, stocks, and investments. Some people might consider inventory as a liquid asset. However, some inventory cannot be sold in one year or might not ever be sold. A nonfunctional part of a game might have thousands of hours of programming work already sunk into it, but if the publisher tried to sell this asset, they might not be able to find a buyer. Who would want only part of a game? **Long-term assets** usually refer to assets such as equipment and real estate. An esports publisher always has a variety of assets. They have some cash in the bank that can be used to pay bills, including salaries and taxes. They also have other assets, such as office furniture, computers, and possibly an office building. Depending on whether they own or rent, the asset can also be classified as a liability, such as if they owe rent or have a mortgage on the property. If the company rents, the office building might have some asset-based value; if the company owns the building, it could be one of their biggest assets.

Assets can take many forms; one of the biggest for any esports publisher is their intellectual property. Imagine owning a popular video game. That game can be sold to players. Thus, it is an asset. However, it is more than selling a game; the name itself can be of value. Think of Coca-Cola, Disney, and the National Football League (NFL). These are all household names that have significant value. In the esports space, games such as *League of Legends*, *Fortnite*, *Dota 2*, *Super Smash Bros.*, and *Pokémon* have significant value. They appear on a company's **balance sheet** as an intangible asset (it cannot be touched or held). However, a brand name or a character's name and image can have significant value. Having a well-known history and a strong favorable perception with consumers is a valuable asset that needs to be stewarded. Nintendo and Sony currently have very strong names in the industry. When they launch a new product, they generate a significant buzz just because of who they are and their track record. A new company would not generate the same perception in the minds of the consuming public. Consequently, a great game might not generate any traction, and a small company might struggle generating publicity.

Apex Legends is a free-to-play battle royale game. It was developed by Respawn Entertainment and published by Electronic Arts (EA). The game was released on February 4, 2019 to be played on Windows, PlayStation 4, and Xbox One. The game was released without any prior announcement or marketing. EA has a strong name, but they needed something more when they decided to launch the game. One of the biggest assets an esports publisher can have is the support of a recognizable team or player. In this case, EA purportedly hired Tyler "Ninja" Blevins to promote *Apex Legends*. The 27-year-old esports streamer tweeted about *Apex Legends* on February 5, 2019, and he streamed playing the game to his more than 13 million followers on Twitch. Ninja was apparently paid around $1 million for his support and playing. EA also paid popular streamer Michael "Shroud" Grzesiek, who had 6 million followers, to play the game. This strategy worked; 10 million people downloaded the game in its first three days. EA's stock price and market value rose 16 percent ($4 billion) in those first three days after the game was released, and within one month, they had 50 million users (Panchadar 2019). This example helps highlight a number of assets. A major name backing the game (EA) is an

Zoning

"NINJA" AND OTHER STREAMERS ARE ASSETS

Gil Fried

The esports industry is changing so quickly. The streaming giant Twitch evolved from Justin TV. It all started when one person filmed himself doing everyday things, and it evolved into a platform where people were paid to watch or play games and comment on the games. Twitch grew by leaps and bounds. This growth attracted attention of others wishing to cash in. Success brings competition, and that is why financial strategies always need to be tweaked to anticipate cuts in market share. In esports, that change occurred when YouTube Gaming, Facebook Gaming, Apple TV, and others started trying to get involved in the space. Interestingly, well-known companies have rapidly come and gone. For example, in July of 2020, Mixer (owned by Microsoft), was closed, despite having spent tens of millions of dollars to sign well-known streamers Tyler "Ninja" Blevins and Michael "Shroud" Grzesiek to exclusive contracts just one year earlier. In today's esports industry, these types of changes (i.e., companies appearing and disappearing) will continue to happen on a frequent basis for the foreseeable future.

To maintain their status, in recent years, Twitch signed three new exclusive contracts with top streamers Ben "DrLupo" Lupo, Timothy "TimTheTatman" Betar, and Saqib "Lirik" Zahid. The three gamers have a combined 10.36 million followers and were some of Twitch's biggest stars. The deals are reportedly worth millions of dollars per year. Locking down these three streamers to long-term contracts was essential to maintain the company's status. Similarly, Google-owned YouTube signed players such as Felix "PewDiePie" Kjellberg as it tried to enter the field of livestreaming. Then Rachell "Valkyrae" Hofstetter, Elliott "Muselk" Watkins, and Lannan "LazarBeam" Eacott were signed to exclusively screen their games on YouTube (Thomas 2020). The rush to contractually secure popular streams coincides with the growth of new platforms trying to enter the esports streaming space.

At the end of 2019, Twitch maintained a 75.6 percent hold on the streaming market as of October. YouTube drew 17.6 percent, while Facebook Gaming claimed 3.7 percent of the streaming market. These numbers will keep changing; the landscape of esports is very competitive.

New companies are constantly entering the esports space, which can have a profound impact on revenue and expenses. For example, the talent agency Loaded was launched as an effort to bundle top streamers and shoutcasters into a one-stop shop for talent and sponsors. According to the Loaded website, "We've connected heroic brands and publishers with the right gaming talent for wildly creative, record-breaking promotions and endorsements across the video game industry. Gaming is about more than games and we're here to prove it" (Loaded 2020, para. 1).

Besides new companies, new revenue streams are constantly being developed and explored. Twitch streamer Guy "DrDisrespect" Beahm IV (with 3.8 million followers and with more than 100 million views) has transcended from just being an announcer to becoming a television character. The streamer will aim to take his gaming alter ego from Twitch to a scripted television series. The DrDisrespect character was to be developed into a scripted television series by Skybound Entertainment, the production company helmed by *The Walking Dead* creator Robert Kirkman. Other connected opportunities, such as comics and games, were also being explored (Shanley 2019). All this was in the works before the COVID-19 global pandemic . . . and then for reasons that have yet to be fully explained, Twitch supposedly permanently suspended DrDisrespect on June 25, 2020 (Heck 2020).

asset, the marketing strategy is an asset, paying an influencer is an asset, the influencer's endorsement is an asset, and the people signing up for the game also represent assets.

Liabilities

In contrast to assets, **liabilities**—what is owed to lenders, suppliers, employees, or others—represent an opportunity to wisely invest. Buying an expensive car can make you look good, but if the car does not add significant value to your bottom line then the liability (monthly payments, high insurance premiums, less gas mileage, etc.) might be bad. Most businesses need to borrow money in order to grow. If a company purchases a large facility that can never be used effectively, then the building is a bad liability and can saddle a company with debt for many years. In contrast, if an esports publisher buys a small game developer, it could be a very good liability. The publisher might need to borrow some money to buy the game developer, and it might take years to repay the loan. However, if the game developer has the prospect of creating a valuable game, it could be considered a great investment. That is why it is important to distinguish between good liabilities and bad liabilities. Regardless of their category (liquid liabilities [owed in the short term] and long-term liabilities), liabilities represent an obligation to repay a certain amount, so the company needs to generate enough revenue to keep repaying the obligation. When a publicly traded company borrows money, it can be a sign that they are investing in their future, which can be a positive sign. Many companies do not need to borrow money (or issue) stocks to grow, because they can use **owner's equity** (the value an owner has in money they have invested in the company) to reinvest in the company to keep it growing.

Revenue and Expenses

Revenue is money generated from sales or services. Having revenue on paper (in a budget) and actually selling a product are significantly different concepts. Consider a budget for an esports event that is expected to attract 5,000 people. The budget might have been based on this number, and ticket prices were set accordingly. One week before the tournament, they might only have 500 tickets sold. Should the tournament be cancelled to help reduce losses, or should the event plow forward hoping for the best? Assume that at the end of the day, the event attracted 2,000 people. The actual revenue is significantly less than the projected revenue. Of course, the opposite could happen; 7,000 people could have showed up at the tournament. This example shows that the actual revenue is a fluid amount and can be hard to predict. Past historical data can be useful, but at any time an unexpected issue might arise that could significantly affect possible revenue. For example, a weather concern or other major event could interrupt the tournament.

The first step in the revenue-generating process is understanding all the revenue sources. The same budgeting exercises will need to be applied to **expenses**, money that represents the cost of operations that a company incurs in order to generate revenue. For example, the revenue for a publisher will be considerably different from the revenue of a tournament or an esports team. A college esports team might generate very little money. Yes, they might have some tournament winnings, but that income usually would not cover the cost for facilities, coaching, transportation, and related costs the team might incur. The college team would probably obtain most of their funds from the college itself. These funds could come from admissions scholarships for students, student clubs, recreation departments, or athletic departments. Such a revenue stream would be significantly different from a tournament, where the primary revenue streams would be ticket sales, registration fees, concession fees, sponsorships, broadcasting, and related revenues. Of course, a small tournament would have significantly less revenue, but it would also have significantly fewer expenses. The key point of analysis will always be whether revenue can exceed expenses. When revenues exceed expenses, a company generates a **profit**. For a typical esports team, the typical revenue streams are sponsorship and advertising, merchandising, tournament revenues, broadcasting and media rights fees, and other miscellaneous fees they collect. In the following sections, multiple types of revenue streams are discussed.

Sponsorship and Advertising

Sponsorship (see chapter 7) represents around 58 percent of total esports revenues (Rietkerk 2020).

Sponsorship can include endemic sponsors or non-endemic sponsors. An endemic sponsor is a company in the esports space. Alienware gaming PCs by Dell represents a typical endemic sponsor. Dell might sponsor a tournament and require the tournament to use Alienware equipment and pay a certain amount for signage and other rights such as signage or patches on uniforms. Other endemic sponsors can be keyboard manufacturers, display companies, publishers, esports equipment manufacturers, and similar companies.

Non-endemic sponsors are the big market and more significant potential revenue source. While endemic sponsors are a natural tie-in, a limited number of such companies exist, and everyone in this business is going after the same companies. Every tournament will reach out to staple companies such as Dell, Microsoft, Activision Blizzard, Nintendo, Sony, and GameStop to ask for sponsorship. While many tournaments might get sponsorship with some of these companies, the sponsorship will often be for just trade-outs. Trade-outs will be free products or other small items rather than cash. Non-endemic sponsors, such as soda, snack, fast-food, telecommunications, and numerous other companies, are attracted to esports for their coveted demographics. Consequently, every day stories appear about companies that want to sponsor or get involved in esports. One large international sponsor for esports is AirAsia from Malaysia. AirAsia has sponsored several esports teams throughout Asia. The company does not just sponsor teams; in 2018, AirAsia also became the title sponsor for the ASEAN World Electronic Sports Games (WESG). AirAsia's former head of engagement and internal branding, Allan Phang, was quoted in an interview with *The Esports Observer* saying, "You have sports tourism and health tourism. Esports tourism is the next wave. If you don't start now, you will miss out" (Moncav 2018, para. 6). An airline such as AirAsia realized that many people would be traveling to esports-related events, so naturally they could have them associate AirAsia with esports travel.

As of 2019, *Overwatch* League boasted the strongest and most well-known list of sponsors, including Coca-Cola, HP, Intel, Toyota, and T-Mobile. Such a revenue stream is very attractive as a source of contractually obligated revenue. When sponsors can be locked in to long-term contracts, the future contractually obligated amounts can serve as collateral for loans from banks. All major sport teams use contractually obligated revenue from suite sales, season ticket sales, broadcast contracts, stadium and arena naming contracts, and even sponsorship agreements.

Similar to sponsorship is advertising. Advertising and sponsorship are sometimes grouped together. Advertising can be a component of a sponsorship agreement, but not all advertisers are sponsors. The majority of advertising's revenue stream is generated from ads placed on streamed

Zoning

POKÉMON'S MONEY-MAKING MACHINE

Gil Fried

Revenue can come from a variety of places. Some game developers are leveraging data they get from players to generate additional revenue. Companies such as Facebook and Google leverage that model. Esports companies are no different, and they have a trove of data (e.g., assets) about all their players, how often they play, what they spend, and more. However, data can also be deceiving, as in the following example. So-called Pokémania associated with the game *Pokémon Go* built up a treasure trove for marketers. The game collected geolocation data on what people were buying, where they were going, and how they were getting there. Multiple companies (Yelp, Facebook, Foursquare, Apple, and Google) were getting information from people's phones at all times. About 70 percent of consumers are willing to share their location information if they believe they are getting something of value in return, such as coupons or loyalty points (Zhu 2016). Players with significant computing skills were able to find ways to cheat the game after just the first couple of days it had been out. By tricking a phone's built-in GPS into providing a false set of coordinates, some players were able to trick *Pokémon Go* into letting them "visit" anywhere without leaving their homes (Zhu 2016). This story is yet another example of the Wild West of esports.

content. This advertising revenue could be classified as content-based revenue or revenue generated through streaming platforms. Some of these deals include the right to advertise on a player's individual stream.

Merchandise

Merchandise can take multiple forms, both tangible and intangible. Intangible merchandise can entail electronic tokens or customized skins that fans can play with. Intangible merchandise can be seen as similar to making money from nothing, because once one skin is developed, no real additional costs are required (i.e., no variable costs).

In contrast, a team can sell numerous merchandise elements. One example would be to compare an esports team to a professional sport team. Jerseys, shirts, hats, scarves, blankets, plush toys, bobbleheads, phone covers, and many more items can show that a fan has a connection with a team. While many teams, such as Team Liquid, have stores that carry large numbers of products, some teams go further and have attempted to become a lifestyle brand. That is what 100 Thieves has tried to accomplish. The team's web page provides this description:

> 100 Thieves ("Hundred Thieves") is a premium lifestyle brand and gaming organization. Built at the intersection of competitive gaming, entertainment, and apparel, 100 Thieves was founded in 2017 by Matthew "Nadeshot" Haag, the former OpTic Gaming *Call of Duty* captain, X Games gold medalist, and 2014 Esports Athlete of the Year. After retiring from competitive play, Matt founded 100 Thieves as a creative outlet for his entrepreneurial passions. In its first two years, 100 Thieves has won multiple esports major championships in *Call of Duty*, made the *League of Legends* and *Fortnite* World Championships, launched the top gaming podcasts on iTunes, sold out over a dozen apparel products, and is supported by major partners such as Cash App, General Mills, Rocket Mortgage, and Red Bull. The company has raised $60 million from investors including Drake, Scooter Braun, Artist Capital, and Sequoia Capital. 100 Thieves' mission is to give every gamer something to be proud of. (100 Thieves 2020, para. 1)

Tournaments

Winning tournaments can be a source of income for a team. Some tournaments have large pots, but many smaller tournaments have smaller prizes. Similar to tennis or golf tournaments, first place in esports tournaments gets the highest prize, then the prize money goes down to subsequent finishers. Because one cannot guarantee a specific team will win, budgeting for this revenue stream is difficult.

Other Revenue Sources

Teams have a number of other revenue sources. They can include league-based revenue sources. League- or franchise-based sources can range from broadcasting contract revenue to revenue-sharing agreements between the teams in a league. One such fee that could be split among team members includes integrity fees paid by various gambling-related companies to leagues to ensure accuracy of data. Revenue is the upside, and as stated earlier, it is not guaranteed (except for contractually obligated revenue). Thus, the risks are that merchandise might not sell or a team might not win or place in any tournaments.

Expenses

In contrast, expenses will incur regardless of what revenue may or may not come in. For an average team (remember, some teams compete in six-person games while others might have three-person teams, so average does not truly exist), expenses could range from several thousand dollars to over $100,000 a month to manage a team.

A team needs to pay for their house or other training venue. Then, player salaries can be significant expenses. Other expenses include the following:

- Living expenses for players
- Administrative staff
- Coaching staff
- Nutritionists
- Athletic trainers
- Statistician
- Marketers
- Travel (airfare, hotels, rental cars, food per diem)
- Merchandise
- Electricity and other utilities

- Equipment
- Insurance
- Tournament fees
- Media and content production

The largest expense for any team, besides possibly the $10 to $20 million to buy a franchise, will be the player costs. Personnel costs are usually the largest cost for any business. While 5 to 10 players might live and practice in an esports house, possibly just as many executives, coaches, trainers, and others will be either salaried employees or independent contractors.

In 2017, the professional gamer salary for *League of Legends* team members (for team Ember players) ranged from $65,000 to $75,000 with the potential for performance bonuses. Those salaries started increasing across the board, and by 2018 the salaries had reached the six-figure range. The average starting North America *League of Legends* Championship Series (NA LCS) player salary rose to over $320,000 by mid-2018 (Heitner 2018). This cost is only the salary; it does not include benefits (health insurance, retirement accounts), workers' compensation, and taxes.

BUDGETING FOR AN ESPORTS TEAM

A **budget** represents a potential road map where an esports organization can leverage its assets and liabilities and then explore its future revenue

Zoning

EXAMINING ELECTRONIC ARTS' (EA'S) FINANCES

Gil Fried

While the previous breakdowns of revenue and expenses show how expensive a team might be and the speculative nature of future revenue streams, other companies in the esports space may have different revenue and expense streams. Electronic Arts (EA) is one of the largest and most well-known game publishers. In 2016, EA had a revenue of $1.987 billion from packaged sales and $2.409 billion in digital sales. By 2020, the gap had significantly widened to a projected $1.180 billion in packaged products and $4.230 billion in digital products. Here, the digital revolution could clearly be seen; more people were buying games through digital downloads compared to disks or other hard copies (Electronic Arts 2019).

Not all so-called new delivery methods are doing as well as EA. Personal computers (PCs) and other units are generating $886 million in revenue—an increase of 28 percent from 2019. Console revenue also increased 10 percent, up to $2.476 billion. In contrast, mobile gaming revenue decreased to $521 million, which was a decline of 21 percent. These numbers show that full game downloads differ from live games, and they differ from mobile games. Each is a unique revenue stream and market.

In 2019, EA's 12-month estimate was that its 2020 total net revenue would be $4.230 billion for digital and $1.180 billion for packaged goods and other revenues. It would produce a total of $5.42 billion in revenue. The cost of revenue was expected to be $1.332 billion, while the operating expenses for the company were expected to be $2.746 billion. (Cost of revenue is defined as the total cost incurred to obtain a sale and the cost of the goods or services sold. It does not include all expenses, but it does include marketing, manufacturing, development, and other expenses directly related to making and selling a product.) Operating expenses include research and development, marketing and sales, general administration, and acquisition costs (Electronic Arts 2019a). A fuller list of information about EA's **annual reports** and financial statements can be found on the company's web page under Resources and then Investor (Electronic Arts 2019b).

Every organization will have unique revenue and expense numbers. Teams and leagues will have their revenue and expenses. They would be significantly different compared with a streaming service where advertising revenue or obtaining a percentage of contribution to streamers is a larger revenue stream. The key to success is identifying and maximizing revenue streams while identifying all the expenses and trying to keep those expenses in check. A common refrain is that revenue will normally not be as high as projected, and most organizations underestimate expenses. Being more realistic helps make budgeting for future revenues and expenses easier.

and expenses to be as successful as possible. Any esports organization has multiple budgets. A game publisher might have a budget for each new game being proposed. The budget might start with an expectation of how much of the game can be completed in a given time frame and then how many units can be sold or downloaded. Other budgets could be developed by the publishers for franchises and league play. A team might have a player's budget, a travel budget, a marketing budget, and a housing budget. A high school esports team might have an equipment budget and a travel or tournament budget.

Starting a budget from scratch often occurs when developing a new product or service. The first time an organization runs an event or team might be the most difficult, because so many variables are unknown. In subsequent years, the process often becomes easier because a prior year's budget could serve as a guide. Some organizations might estimate future revenue to increase 10 percent and thus could increase all elements in the budget 10 percent in anticipation of that increase. An organization could also anticipate potential problems, and a college team might obtain a directive from the university administration that the budget needs to be slashed 20 percent. Thus, the college team would have to decide if they are going to reduce all expenses across the board, remove a coach, or not attend future tournaments to reduce future expenses.

Once a budget is developed, it is imperative to track revenue and expenses to determine whether the budget is accurate. If a team anticipates spending $20,000 a year on travel, then all travel expenses should be tracked; at the mid-year mark, the budget might be reexamined. Maybe only $2,000 was spent, so the team knows they may have a lot of money left over to travel to more tournaments. If the team determines that they have already spent over $22,000 on travel, they will realize they have no funds left for travel and that they might have to cut expenses in other areas to balance the budget. Alternatively, if the team has been bringing in a lot of money, the college might allow them to keep spending money and expand beyond the initial budget to incur even more travel expenses. The process of examining what was proposed in the budget and what really happened is called **variance analysis**.

A budget can be examined from different perspectives. One is the **horizontal analysis**, in which the budget for one year (or a quarter) can be examined against that of another year (quarter). Therefore, the budget for the college team in 2018 could be compared with that of 2019. Will more money be needed for a coach if the team is growing? That answer could be reflected in the budgetary comparison. If the club has doubled the number of student members, participates in more tournaments, wins more money, and incurs more travel expenses, the budget would reflect such changes and it could be used to plan for the future.

The other area of analysis is called **vertical analysis**, and one of the most often-used examples is a balance sheet. This process explores all the revenue and expense categories in a budget and then places a percentage on them so that one could explore how revenue and expenses are growing or shrinking. Thus, if the sport team spent $20,000 on a coach, $10,000 on travel and tournament fees, and $10,000 on equipment and other expenses, the common-size expense report would be as represented in table 11.1.

Besides exploring the revenue and expenses, one of the key components of the budgeting process is developing a **break-even analysis**. A break-even analysis focuses on how much it would cost to not make any money but also to not lose any money. For the previous college team, if they knew they had expenses totaling $40,000 and knew the university would give them $20,000 a year, then they would have to find a way to earn $20,000 to help cover the budget and break even.

Table 11.1 Sample Expenses for a Hypothetical Sport Team

Category	Amount	Percentage
Coaching	$20,000	50%
Travel/tournament fees	$10,000	25%
Equipment/supplies/other	$10,000	25%
Total	$40,000	100%

If the club had 200 members, then they might charge $100 for each club member to help cover costs. The break-even analysis looks at what is the ideal number necessary to break even. If the club had only 100 members, then they would have to charge everyone $200 a year. Then some variation might exist, and if the team were to win any tournaments, such sums could help balance the budget. Similarly, if the team found a sponsor to help cover the equipment costs, then that element of the budget could be changed (reduced) and then the amount of money needed to be raised from team members would be less. This analysis shows that a flow exists, but all budgets should start with a basic understanding of what would be the necessary requirements to break even.

The following example might help clarify the break-even concept in the context of managing an esports tournament. Assume an esports tournament will be held at a local college. The tournament managers have indicated that they want to hold the tournament in a manner that breaks even, and they are charging $50 as an entry fee. They have the sample esports tournament information shown in table 11.2.

The list contains both fixed costs and variable costs. **Fixed costs** will occur regardless of the number of people who might register for the event. Insurance, administrative salary, supplies and equipment, facility costs, and prize money all need to be spent and thus taken into consideration. The **variable costs** include the licensing fee and the food expenses. Using the numbers in table 11.2, basic calculations needed to undertake a break-even analysis are shown in table 11.3.

The **contribution margin** is one of the key elements, because it highlights how much money from each entry fee can go to cover fixed costs. This formula can also be manipulated to help determine what to charge for the entry fee. The same contribution margin can be applied to determine how much to charge. Thus, if the contribution margin were $40 and it was anticipated that 200 people would register for the tournament, then the entry fee would have to be $30 per player. This number is calculated by dividing the $4,000 fixed expense by the 200 registrants, which results in $20 needed from each entrant to cover fixed costs. To this $20 another $5 must be added for the licensing and $5 must be added for the food costs, totaling $30. Thus, if this tournament is expecting more people to register, they can reduce the entry fee or they keep the entry fee the same with the idea that they can generate a profit. If

Table 11.2 Sample Esports Tournament Costs

Variables	Costs
Insurance costs	$500
Administrator salary	$1,000
Supplies/equipment	$500
Facility rental	$1,000
Prize money	$1,000
Licensing fee	$5 per player
Food expenses	$5 per player

Table 11.3 Sample Esports Tournament Calculations

Variables	Amount/calculation
Total fixed costs	$4,000
Average variable costs	$10 per player
Average revenue	$50 entry fee per player
Contribution margin per player	$40 ($50 entry fee minus $10 variable cost)
Number of players needed to break even	100 players ($4,000 fixed expense divided by $40 contribution margin = 100)

200 entrants paid $50 each, then the tournament would make a profit of $4,000 ($10,000 revenue minus [$4,000 fixed and $2,000 variable costs]).

Another example of how a budget can help move an esports organization forward can be seen in the following example. The University of New Haven was exploring launching an esports program. The University had a competitive esports team that was started as a club and had over 150 members. The University was interested in developing an esports training lounge, hiring a faculty member, and launching several academic programs. In order to move the proposal to the next level (presidential approval), the proposing faculty member had to develop a budget to explore how much the initiative would cost. The initial budget is displayed in table 11.4.

The proposed budget shown in table 11.4 has no revenue associated with the effort; it was anticipated student fees and tuition revenue would help cover some costs while donors could cover other costs. The equipment costs were broken down even further in a sub-budget. The scope of the estimated required equipment and associated costs are summarized in table 11.5.

The budget appeared sound and was supported. The problem was that the initial estimate for retrofitting an existing space was changed. Instead of building in an existing room, a proposal was made to insert the lounge in a new building being built. The new building was well underway when the proposal moved forward. While walls were not up yet, a lot of infrastructure was in place. The new building

Table 11.4 Initial Budget for Esports Lounge

Category	Projected expenses
Construction/renovations for a 2,800 ft^2 (260.12 m^2) area	$168,000
Equipment	$70,645
Furniture	$42,000
IT infrastructure (including wiring new building)	$100,000
Initial setup expense subtotal	$380,645
STAFFING ESTIMATION (INCLUDING BENEFITS)	
Full-time professor	$120,000
IT support, graduate student reporting to IT	$20,000
Work study students	$15,000
Annual staffing subtotal	$155,000
ANNUAL OPERATING EXPENSES	
IT bandwidth/storage	$15,000
Equipment replacement plan	$15,000
Travel	$15,000
Recruiting	$3,500
Facilities (including electrical costs)	$7,500
Supplies/other	$10,000
NACE membership fee	$2,500
ECAC membership fee	$1,500
Jerseys for players	$3,500
Annual operating expenditure subtotal	$73,500
One-time fixed expense	$380,645
Ongoing variable expense (staffing estimation plus annual operating expenses)	$228,500
Total:	$609,145

Table 11.5 Computer Costs for Proposed Esports Training Arena

Item	Count	Unit cost	Total
Gaming desktops	15	$2,200	$33,000
Gaming monitors	15	$380	$5,700
Gaming mice	15	$80	$1,200
Gaming keyboards	15	$150	$2,250
Gaming headsets	15	$100	$1,500
APC surge protectors	15	$95	$1,425
PC game licenses	75	$50	$3,750
Xbox One console	1	$400	$400
Xbox games	10	$60	$600
PlayStation console	1	$400	$400
PlayStation games	10	$60	$600
Switch console	1	$300	$300
Switch games	10	$60	$600
Streamer microphone	1	$130	$130
Streamer camera	1	$100	$100
Streamer monitors	2	$380	$760
Streamer headphones	1	$80	$80
Green screen	1	$100	$100
Mic boom arm	1	$50	$50
Misc. wiring and adaptors	N/A	$3,500	$3,500
48-in. (121.9 cm) professional-grade displays	7	$1,600	$11,200
Installation	N/A	$3,000	$3,000
		Total:	$70,645

was meant to be a wireless accessible building, and to add the lounge, significant hardwiring was required. Also, additional expense would have been required moving HVAC ductwork and other elements. When the builder priced out everything, the cost for the space alone would have been well over $500,000. The budget did not allow for the addition of such a high unexpected expenditure, so the lounge was moved to another area. The space decreased by close to 1,000 square feet (92.9 m^2). In addition, it was determined that the university needed more than just a teacher to teach esports business classes. Thus, an esports coach was also hired, adding an additional $50,000 plus to the annual budget. The process was very unusual in that it was fluid based on changes advocated by senior executives. Most esports college budgets are very tight with little room for any flexibility. However, an initial investment is always going to be larger than what is originally anticipated because numerous unexpected expenses will arise.

Every esports organization has multiple budgets and individuals in charge of overseeing the **accounting** (the process of calculating how much money is flowing into and out of an organization). It takes time to create a budget. People will make a number of assumptions, and the most effective budgets include extra room for declining revenue and increasing expenses. If revenue drops or expenses rise, the result could be a disaster. Therefore, if some wiggle room exists, it helps with planning. Furthermore, at times upper management might require units within an organization to prove their contribution to the organization. This process is called **zero-based budgeting (ZBB)**. Using ZBB requires every unit to start their budget at zero, then prove the value of their contribution and why funding is needed. This type of budgeting prevents an ever-increasing budget and forces an organization to prioritize where it is spending money so that it can support its most critical initiatives.

HOW TO READ AN ANNUAL REPORT

An annual report can be daunting at first glance; the Activision Blizzard 2018 annual report is 148 pages long. Many people might look at the size of such a document and shy away from reading it. People might go to finance websites to obtain more easily digestible nuggets of information rather than plow through all the information that might be in the annual report. However, the annual report is a treasure trove that can provide some great insight into an organization.

In this case, begin with some basics about Activision Blizzard. The company's stock was trading at just over $60 per share on January 16, 2020. The 52-week range was $39.85 to $60.89. On January 16, over 6 million shares were traded, which is just a little higher than the daily average. The company's market capitalization was $46.426 billion based on the stock price and the number of outstanding shares. The company had earnings per share (EPS) of $2.11, which means every share had earning equal to $2.11. Some companies have a loss for every share, so this earnings number can be analyzed to determine if it is a high-enough return for the investor. The price-to-earning (P/E) ratio was 28.64. The P/E ratio refers to the stock price divided by earnings per share. This number helps show whether a stock is overly priced compared to its competitors. As a frame of reference, EA had a P/E ratio of 12.5, which means that the shares were selling for a price where earnings were closer to the share value. Multiple analysts had rated the stock as a buy. The question is why.

That is where the annual report and other government-required quarterly filings are so critical. They give everyone the same information upon which they can analyze the company. The annual report does more than simply highlight numbers; they tell the story behind each number. It is often in the footnotes that analysts glean important information on the future of the company. Information about lawsuits, debt, order updates, unpaid amounts, and other factors that are mentioned in these footnotes can give someone a better idea about what is going on with the company.

The most recent full annual report at the time of this writing is for 2018, but the 2019 and any subsequent annual report can be found on the company's website (Activision Blizzard 2018). The annual report reflected the 40th anniversary of the company. They started the report with the following announcement:

> To Our Shareholders,
>
> Since 1991, when we first purchased our stake in the company and were given the privilege of managing it, our book value per share has grown at a rate of 31% compounded annually. If you had invested $1,000 in our company 20 years ago, your investment would have been worth $55,236 at the end of 2018, 18 times more than the S&P 500's $2,985 over the same period. (Activision Blizzard 2018, inside front cover)

The company recorded net bookings of $7.3 billion in 2018 and earned $2.72 per share. The annual report went on to reflect that the company did not meet the goals it set for itself in 2018 and that they needed to provide more engaging content. With that said, the report went on to summarize their reach as follows:

> Over 350 million customers consume Activision Blizzard's content each month. And, when they engage, they spend roughly 50 minutes per day in our interactive franchises, invest through online and physical purchasing, and watch digital advertising. (Activision Blizzard 2018, p. 1)

The company also articulated to annual report readers that they would refocus their effort on their strongest games as their research had indicated that esports players were playing fewer games and for longer periods of time for those that they really enjoyed. Thus, the focus on making sure their key games (such as *Call of Duty*, *Candy Crush*, *Warcraft*, *Hearthstone*, *Overwatch*, and *Diablo*) were successful. The company highlighted how they were trying to reduce costs and explore where the market might take them. For example, the company decided they were in a strong position to take advantage of the free-to-play opportunity as they already operated multiple models at scale, including free-to-play titles, microtransaction-based games, games with an upfront charge or with a subscription, and multiple combinations about these models. The company was also very enthusiastic about the advertising model they had developed and derived over $100 million in revenue from advertising associated with King. King Digital Entertainment was purchased by Activision in 2016 for $5.8 billion—funded with $3.6 billion of existing cash and $2.2 billion of cash from new debt issued by the company. Activision Blizzard started the *Overwatch* League in 2018, after selling 12 franchise slots in 2017 with franchise fees reported to be $20 million. During 2018, the company sold an additional 8 *Overwatch* franchises, bringing the total to 20 teams. In the annual report, the company mentions interest in starting a franchise model for *Call of Duty*. The company mentioned they were looking at a 12-team franchised *Call of Duty* League that was to be city based with franchises going for around $25 million each.

The company also mentioned their efforts related to corporate social responsibility and how they created a *Call of Duty* endowment back in 2009 to help veterans returning from deployment. Over the endowment's 10-year history, they had placed more than 54,000 former service members into various jobs and were expecting to place 100,000 veterans by 2024. All this information was discussed just in the introduction of the annual report. The following table of contents for the annual report shows the various categories covered in the document (Activision Blizzard 2018):

Part I

Cautionary Statement

Item 1: Business

Item 1A: Risk Factors

Item 1B: Unresolved Staff Comments

Item 2: Properties

Item 3: Legal Proceedings

Item 4: Mine Safety Disclosures

Part II

Item 5: Market for Registrant's Common Equity, Related Stockholder Matters, and Issuer Purchases of Equity Securities

Item 6: Selected Financial Data

Item 7: Management's Discussion and Analysis of Financial Condition and Results of Operations

Item 7A: Quantitative and Qualitative Disclosures about Market Risk

Item 8: Financial Statements and Supplementary Data

Item 9: Changes in and Disagreements With Accountants on Accounting and Financial Disclosure

Item 9A: Controls and Procedures

Item 9B: Other Information

Part III

Item 10: Directors, Executive Officers, and Corporate Governance

Item 11: Executive Compensation

Item 12: Security Ownership of Certain Beneficial Owners and Management and Related Stockholder Matters

Item 13: Certain Relationships and Related Transactions, and Director Independence

Item 14: Principal Accounting Fees and Services

Part IV

Item 15: Exhibits, Financial Statement Schedule

Item 16: Form 10-K Summary

Exhibit Index

Signatures

The Business section goes through the history of Activision, including its various mergers, acquisitions, and business units, to give investors a broad overview of the company and its primary assets. Also included in this section is a focus on marketing efforts, which discusses digital marketing (e.g., advertising on Google and Facebook) and more traditional advertising such as billboards. In terms of physical products, the annual report highlights as follows:

> Our physical products are available for sale in outlets around the world. These products are sold primarily on a direct basis to mass-market retailers (e.g., Target, Walmart), consumer electronics stores (e.g., Best Buy), discount warehouses, game specialty stores (e.g., GameStop), and other stores (e.g., Amazon), or through third-party distribution and licensing arrangements. (Activision Blizzard 2018, p. 5)

While the company sells directly to end users, a significant amount of sales actually goes to platforms that host a variety of esports games. For the year that ended December 31, 2018, three customers—Apple, Sony, and Google—accounted for 15 percent, 13 percent, and 11 percent, respectively, of net revenues. During the same time period, the top three franchises were *Call of Duty*, *Candy Crush*, and *World of Warcraft*, which collectively accounted for 58 percent of the company's net revenues.

The annual report highlights competition in the esports industry, members of the company's board of directors, and that in December of 2018 the company had approximately 9,900 full-time and part-time employees.

In the Risk Factors section, the company explains how players can be fickle and switch to other games. This uncertainty could significantly affect any one of their games. Other risks that could affect the company include consumers being upset with a game or the company, higher lead time to release more complex games, competition, and a host of other risks that could affect future revenue, expenses, and stock valuation. In fact, so many risks are listed and discussed to cover the company, that the Risk section is 15 pages long. Some risks are necessary components of running a business. For example, the company has approximately 100 facility leases all over the world from various headquarters to sales offices. These areas represent significant fixed costs and are part of doing business. Another possible risk that the company needed to report is two tax-related disputes involving millions of dollars in possible tax liability in both Sweden and France.

The rest of the annual report focuses primarily on financial issues, including a number of key highlights. For example, net revenues from international sales accounted for approximately 54 percent of revenue in 2018. Revenue was bolstered by higher net bookings from the following:

- *World of Warcraft*, driven by *World of Warcraft: Battle for Azeroth*, released in August 2018;
- *Call of Duty: WWII*, which was released in November 2017; and
- higher net bookings from the *Candy Crush* franchise, due to in-game advertisements, increased monetization, and the launch of *Candy Crush Friends Saga*, the latest title in the *Candy Crush* franchise, in October 2018.

The picture was not all rosy; some titles were not doing as well. For example, these three titles did not do as well in 2018: the *Destiny* franchise, driven by the release of *Destiny 2* in a prior year; *Overwatch*, which was released in May 2016; and *Call of Duty: Infinite Warfare*. The document even covers such unique areas as usage patterns to help show in what direction the company is going. For example, in December 2018, the company had 356 million monthly active users. These numbers are broken down as follows: Activision (53 million), Blizzard (35 million), and King (268 million) (Activision Blizzard 2018). These numbers help show how valuable the King acquisition was for the company.

After tightening its belt, the company anticipated pretax restructuring charges of approximately $150 million in 2019. These write-offs were to primarily occur in the first quarter of 2019 through employee severance packages, reducing facilities costs, asset write-downs (an asset write-down is when an asset is recorded for less than the value on the books; i.e., the fair market value is less than what the company had initially reported), and other costs.

The annual report examines so many areas that it would take a number of pages to just cover the highlights. Therefore, readers are encouraged to actually visit the document. It is critical to share two documents contained in both the annual report and all quarterly filings: the **income statement** and the balance sheet. These financial statements help spotlight the revenue and expenses, and assets and liabilities of the company.

The income statement (called the Condensed Consolidated Statements of Operations) from November 2019 reflecting the last three and nine months ending September 30, 2019, is shown in table 11.6 (Activision Blizzard 2019).

The income statement has several key features. First, the sale of products netted $260 million, while subscription, licensing, and other sales resulted in earning over $1 billion in the three-month period ending September 30, 2019. In the nine-month cycle ending September 30, 2019, the total income reached $4.503 billion, which represented a decline from 2018 when during that same time period the company had earned

Table 11.6 Activision's Income Statement (Condensed Consolidated Statements of Operations) From November of 2019

	Three months ended September 30,		Nine months ended September 30,	
	2019	2018	2019	2018
Net revenues				
Product sales	$260	$263	$1,276	$1,447
Subscription, licensing, and other revenues	1,022	1,249	3,227	3,672
Total net revenues	1,282	1,512	4,503	5,119
Costs and expenses				
Cost of revenues—product sales				
Product costs	137	127	388	416
Software royalties, amortization, and intellectual property licenses	9	20	171	214
Cost of revenues—subscription, licensing, and other				
Game operations and distribution costs	246	257	714	777
Software royalties, amortization, and intellectual property licenses	50	109	164	278
Product development	210	263	702	776
Sales and marketing	182	263	580	741
General and administrative	177	208	527	623
Restructuring and related costs	24	—	104	—
Total costs and expenses	1,035	1,247	3,350	3,825
Operating income	247	265	1,153	1,294
Interest and other expense (income), net	(2)	13	(33)	67
Loss on extinguishment of debt	—	40	—	40
Income before income tax expense (benefit)	249	212	1,186	1,187
Income tax expense (benefit)	45	(48)	208	25
Net income	$204	$260	$978	$1,162
Basic earnings per common share	$0.27	$0.34	$1.28	$1.53
Weighted average common shares outstanding	767	763	766	761
Diluted earnings per common share	$0.26	$0.34	$1.27	$1.51
Weighted average common shares outstanding assuming dilution	771	771	770	771

Note: Numbers are in millions.

Reprinted from Activision Blizzard (2019).

$5.119 billion. The major expenses highlighted in the income statement include product costs, game operations and distribution costs, and product development. Sales and marketing and general administration expenses totaled $359 million in the three-month period, which represents 28 percent of the total net revenue going to those expense categories. The total costs declined $212 million from $1.247 billion in the three-month period in 2018 to $1.035 billion in the same period in 2019. Even with the lower income in 2019, lowered expenses meant operating income for the three-month period in 2019 decreased from $265 million to $247 million (an $18 million decrease). This decrease resulted in the earnings per share declining from 34 cents to 27 cents (2018 to 2019 September ending quarter).

The balance sheet, known officially as the Condensed Consolidated Balance Sheet, derived from the 8-K filing by Activision Blizzard (2019), is shown in table 11.7 on page 167.

As is evident from the balance sheet, Activision Blizzard has significant liquid assets, including significant cash reserves. They have some accounts receivables (what is owed to them), they have software in development, and they also have inventories. The company has both current assets and long-term assets associated with software development. The company has intangible assets and other assets worth over $1 billion. One big asset is goodwill (often referred to as the value of their name, name of their games, characters, or something similar), which is valued at close to $10 billion. On the liabilities side, the company has some bills they have to pay as well as a significant amount of deferred revenue (where they owe products and have to deliver). Current liabilities, other liabilities, and long-term liabilities add up to around $5.6 billion for the three-month period ending in September 2019. The remaining amount on the right side of the balance sheet represents retained earnings and owner's equity. It represents money put back into the business to help it grow.

CONCLUSION

Studying esports finance and economics is an opportunity to explore whether the numbers live up to all the hype. Through examining revenue and expenses, a company or organization can determine whether they are in fact generating positive net cash flow. Are esports organizations leveraging their assets, or are they incurring liabilities that do not benefit the bottom line? Can a tournament break even? How much should a game developer charge to sell a game? Is one esports company worth investing in compared to another? Is it a sound financial investment to buy an esports franchise? These questions can be answered through financial analysis. By understanding where the money is in this industry, esports stakeholders can examine issues such as possible trends, how revenue can be increased, and how expenses can be minimized in efforts to make more sound financial decisions.

DISCUSSION QUESTIONS

1. How would you explain the terms assets, liabilities, revenues, and expenses?
2. Based on your own research and reading of annual reports for companies such as EA, Sony, and Nintendo over the same time period, what similarities and differences do you see between the companies?
3. If you were tasked with building an esports facility for a college, where do you think you can generate revenue (be realistic), and how can you reduce possible construction expenses?
4. If you were going to build an esports facility with the highest-quality equipment, what would you buy? Create a projected budget for all of the equipment you would like to buy.

Table 11.7 Activision's Balance Sheet (Condensed Consolidated Balance Sheet) From November of 2019

	September 30, 2019	December 31, 2018
Assets		
Current assets		
Cash and cash equivalents	$4,939	$4,225
Accounts receivable, net	386	1,035
Inventories, net	102	43
Software development	240	264
Other current assets	345	539
Total current assets	*6,012*	*6,106*
Software development	109	65
Property and equipment, net	249	282
Deferred income taxes, net	357	458
Other assets	731	482
Intangible assets, net	583	735
Goodwill	9,764	9,762
Total assets	**$17,805**	**$17,890**
Liabilities and shareholders' equity		
Current liabilities		
Accounts payable	$274	$253
Deferred revenues	695	1,493
Accrued expenses and other liabilities	782	896
Total current liabilities	*1,751*	*2,642*
Long-term debt, net	2,674	2,671
Deferred income taxes, net	23	18
Other liabilities	1,122	1,167
Total liabilities	**5,570**	**6,498**
Shareholders' equity		
Common stock	—	—
Additional paid-in capital	11,116	10,963
Treasury stock	(5,563)	(5,563)
Retained earnings	7,289	6,593
Accumulated other comprehensive loss	(607)	(601)
Total shareholders' equity	*12,235*	*11,392*
Total liabilities and shareholders' equity	**$17,805**	**$17,890**

Note: Numbers are in millions.

Reprinted from Activision Blizzard (2019).

12

Esports Law

Gil Fried | Graciano Gaillard | Jason Chung

OBJECTIVES

- Demonstrate the ability to identify legal issues when hosting esports tournaments.
- Judge the different elements associated with intellectual property.
- Summarize the contract issues that could exist in esports.
- Describe the employment law concerns associated with esports.

INTRODUCTION

Legal challenges in esports are significant. Consider these legal questions:

- Are players under the age of 18 capable of entering into binding contracts?
- Who owns the rights to broadcasted or streamed games?
- Can players unionize?
- Can collegiate esports players keep prize money they win, or would it go to their school?
- Who owns the data you generate from playing games?
- Should game developers be liable for the criminal acts of a player?
- Because some games are made to be addictive, can an addict sue the game developer for their treatment?

These questions represent just a few of the many issues that surface when examining the intersection of esports and the law. Further, from coaches' contracts to arena lease agreements, and employment law to tort liability, numerous areas exist where important legal principles affect the esports industry. Most legal questions have no easy answers, but understanding basic legal concepts is helpful. This chapter first covers some basic legal concepts and then follows with more detailed analysis of some specific topics. The specific topics include intellectual property, criminal law and gambling, contract law, unionization of players, and rights of esports athletes. In addition, the potential unionization of esports athletes is examined.

OVERVIEW OF IMPORTANT LEGAL CONCEPTS

A number of laws can be applied to the esports industry. The list includes international laws, federal laws in the United States, state laws in the United States, and even local laws. Often these laws can conflict. For example, a state law can be more restrictive than federal law. Thus, a state law might punish violators in certain circumstances more significantly than a federal law would punish the same violation. For example, federal antidiscrimination laws under Title VII of the Civil Rights Act apply to employers with more than 15 employees, but the state of Connecticut only requires 3 employees for the equivalent state laws to apply. In contrast, many countries in the world do not have any antidiscrimination laws.

This distinction is important because esports is a truly global enterprise, which means that various laws can be applied. Similarly, a dispute can be heard in multiple venues, and deciding where to bring a claim becomes a chess match. Because different laws might exist across the United States, those with a legal claim might try **forum shopping**, the practice of trying to sue someone in a **jurisdiction** that would be most favorable to a possible claim. Alabama is known for being friendly to people suing for injuries, so someone might try to bring a claim in Alabama to hopefully obtain an easier verdict or a better award. In order for a company or person to be subject to the court (jurisdiction), one has to purposefully avail themselves of the laws of the state. In other words, they have to conduct business in the state. In some states, signing a contract or delivering goods is enough to trigger legal coverage. With esports, games are delivered electronically all over the world. Thus, a question can be where can a publisher be sued if someone was injured by their product? The courts are struggling with this issue. The publisher is not actually doing business in a given area, but the product is being delivered to that area, and someone from that area might be paying money for downloads, skins, or other monetary transactions. This example shows how complex legal issues might be in the esports area.

Various laws can come to play in esports. Swatting (calling the police on someone due to results associated with a game) entails an example of state criminal law; if a phone is used, it can involve federal wire-related crimes. Some people might claim they have a free speech right to say what they want during an online discussion. The federal constitution (and each state in the United States also has a state constitution) provides for free speech, but that means government cannot unreasonably restrain speech. The government can have reasonable time, place, and manner restrictions on speech in order to sustain the public good.

Several key terms are present in this discussion. The first is *government*. Free speech only applies to government actions. That means a public university has limits on what speech they can limit and how. On the other hand, a private university would not have such a limitation, so they can control or limit all speech on their campus. Second, the *reasonable time, place, and manner* restriction means that the government can have content-neutral rules as long as they serve a legitimate government purpose. An example could be requiring marchers to obtain a permit and not march after 8:00 p.m. Now, apply this law to esports: The esports publishers and the streaming and social media accounts are all privately owned. Thus, no free speech rights are guaranteed for esports. Each company might have very specific rules and policies in their user agreements that actually limit what can be said or shown, and many accounts have been cancelled because someone has violated the user agreement (which means a **breach of contract**).

Tort law, which is concerned with legal wrongs that harm someone, is another concept that needs to be addressed in esports. Torts can be intentional or unintentional (negligence). The primary intentional tort seen in esports is **defamation**. Defamation can be either oral (**slander**) or written (**libel**). When someone writes something defamatory about someone else in a chat room, or says something defamatory at an event, a defamation claim could result. A defamatory claim is a false statement that causes or can cause an injury. Thus, saying someone is a horrible player is an opinion rather than a factual statement. In contrast, saying someone won because they cheated is making a factual statement. If the statement is false, and the harmed party loses a sponsor or tournament because of the defamatory comment, then the harmed party can sue for injuries sustained (i.e., monetary loss). The best defense for a defamation claim is the truth. If the person actually cheated, then the defamation claim will fail—as long as someone can prove they cheated.

The other tort claim is **negligence**, where unintentional harm has happened. For example, during an esports tournament hosted at an arena, a fan could slip on spilled liquid in the concourse area, and they could possibly sue for their injuries. The venue could be responsible for damages if they knew or reasonably could have known the hazard was present. Thus, if the spill was reported and was not cleaned up or no sign was posted highlighting the hazard, then the facility could be held liable. Another interesting negligence claim could involve players who are distracted by a game (or notification from a game) while operating a motor vehicle. The number of injuries from people using cell phones while driving has increased greatly in recent years. Can distracted drivers blame esports and various games for causing the distraction?

Contract law is relevant in esports because numerous contracts exist in esports. Some sample contracts include buying a game, user agreements, broadcast agreements, employment contracts, lease agreements, and contracts between players and their agents. To be valid, a contract needs four basic elements: agreement, consideration, capacity, and legality. An agreement entails an offer and acceptance. Some, but not all contracts need to be in writing. **Consideration** entails an exchange of value, such as paying money to receive a skin. **Capacity** means that someone can in fact enter into a contract. You must be over age 18, not intoxicated, and cannot be legally classified incapacitated. The last element of **legality** is simply that a contract must be for legal purposes. If a valid contract exists, a party that breaches a contract could be subject to damages. That is why it is so important to know the contractual terms and abide by them once an agreement is reached. One concern that needs to be addressed with contract law is when someone is under age 18, they technically are not considered capable of entering into a contract. When someone under age 18 enters into a contract, that contract is **voidable**. Therefore, to protect themselves, teams signing a minor would also require the minor's parents to sign. It is similar to a waiver that parents sign to allow their kids to participate in sports.

Intellectual property (IP) represents the need to protect people who produce things (e.g., music, art, poetry) when they put their product into the public domain. If someone produced a song, and anyone else could copy the song, that person would have no incentive to share their talent. Everyone would be taking advantage of everyone else's intellectual capital. To minimize the risk of this happening, laws were developed to protect people and give them the opportunity to profit from their work. The ability to profit is not unlimited. The primary IP issues covered in this text are **copyright** law and **trademark** law. **Patent** law is another topic (which refers to protecting inventions), but patents are not covered in this text. Patents might apply to a gaming console that is unique, but most IP issues faced by esports executives deal with copyright and trademark issues. Copyright law usually provides protection and exclusive rights to a work for the author's life plus 70 years and focuses on creative works such as art, music, books, and even sport games. That is why when a baseball game is broadcast it might say at the start and end of the game that "this has been a copyrighted presentation of Major League Baseball . . ." to protect the rights from someone else using it. Trademark focuses on a name, color scheme, or slogan that a company tries to protect from use by others. The name Kleenex is an example of a trademarked name. The name and how it was written (colors, font, size, etc.) belongs to Kimberly-Clark Corporation, which acquired the rights from another paper company that trademarked the name in 1924 and then sold the name to Kimberly-Clark in 1955. The trademark prevents anyone else from using the name without permission. Even though the name Kleenex has been mistaken for other facial tissues, it is still a trademark that can be defended in federal court. In esports, trademark law protects a game name, color scheme, character names, and other details. For example, Pokémon is a copyrighted character, story line, and game, but trademark protection exists also for the company (Nintendo as the publisher and The Pokémon Company), and such protections are clearly highlighted on the company's web page (The Pokémon Company 2020).

Several major legal issues and privacy concerns are associated with personal data. When a person buys an item or registers with a game publisher, they are asked a number of specific personal questions. What is done with this information? Who owns it? This issue came to full force with the advent of personal motion trackers. Some people thought they were uploading information to a central hub to keep track of their exercise. However, this data was owned by the tracking company and they had the right (under contract law) to sell that information to others, such as health insurance companies. Europe and now California (with the recently passed California Consumer Privacy Act [CCPA]) allow customers to demand that companies delete their personal data. Another privacy right is whether an esports player can refuse to provide a urine sample as part of a drug testing program (Baldwin 2019). If a player wants to play at the highest level, they normally waive their rights to contest drug testing. The court's logic is usually that if a player does not want to be tested because they want to protect their rights, then they do not have to compete in esports.

Employment law concerns abound in esports. Is a player an employee or an **independent contractor (IC)**? This issue might seem minor, but an employee needs to be paid, have taxes withheld, have workers' compensation coverage, and have numerous rights. If a player is an independent contractor, they have very limited rights (and usually only rights specified under contractual terms). This limitation has led to efforts for protecting players' rights. In 2017, Riot Games created the *League of Legends* Players Association (NA LCS Players Association). Shortly thereafter, the *Overwatch* Players Association (OWPA) was launched. While the OWPA is designed to represent players, it does not need to become a union to wield the battle axe of possible antitrust lawsuits against the game publisher. That axe would be dulled if the OWPA was a union and had negotiated a collective bargaining agreement (CBA) to serve as the official union for *Overwatch* players. (For more on CBAs, see the section Unionizing Esports Players.) This situation represents a legal strategy.

Other employment issues to consider are the total number of hours worked each week (training counts as work activity), underage workers, workers' compensation coverage for injuries, immigration concerns for international players, sexual harassment, discrimination concerns, tax implications of being paid, and even age discrimination if a company terminates an older employee to replace them with a younger worker. (In the United States, an older worker is classified as someone at least 40 years old).

Tax law might not seem to be a huge concern, but it can be. For example, where revenue is earned determines where taxes need to be paid, regardless of where a company is technically based. Professional athletes are used to being met by tax collectors at city airports (such as Philadelphia and Pittsburgh) demanding tax payments. The same could happen to esports athletes in the future.

The concept of ethical conduct is not exactly about the law, but it is an important issue to raise. Whether or not something is legal might not be as critical as what is right or wrong. Cheating in the game, whether one is caught or not, raises both legal and ethical concerns. As previously mentioned, doping is not just about players' privacy rights but about integrity in the game and having a level playing field. Riot Games does not have an official antidoping policy, but July 2019, the company entered into a relationship with Sportradar, a data collection and analysis company specializing in sports. Sportradar Integrity Services will monitor the global betting activity taking place with both domestic and international *League of Legends* esports competitions and report potential integrity issues.

These legal topics provide a great entry into understanding and appreciating the various legal concerns found in esports. The following sections offer deeper discussions of some of the most important legal topics and their intersections with esports.

INTELLECTUAL PROPERTY (IP)

Intellectual property (IP) is the branch of law that protects a set of intangible rights produced through human intellectual labor. IP serves as a framework for national legislation. It is also one of the most global areas of law (MacQueen, Waelde, and Laurie 2007). It is fundamentally grounded in international treaties and agreements, such as the Berne Convention for the Protection of Literary and Artistic Works, which protects dramatic and artistic works including computer programs and video games. The following two critical agreements are worth highlighting, because both are administered by the World Trade Organization (WTO).

1. The Paris Convention for the Protection of Industrial Property (covers topics such as patents, trademarks, service marks, and trade names)
2. The Agreement on Trade-Related Aspects of Intellectual Property Rights (TRIPS)

These agreements reinforce the World Intellectual Property Organization (WIPO) Convention (Bently and Sherman 2009) by establishing minimum standards for IP protection. The WIPO Copyright Treaty (WCT), on the other hand, could be described as an internationally agreed extension of the rights protected under the Berne Convention while focusing mostly on the copyright protection of digital works such as computer programs. One of the main policy goals of the 1996 WCT was to address potential infringement of works recorded digitally, such as video games (Waelde et al. 2016). The 1996 WCT led to the enactment of The Digital Millennium Copyright Act (DMCA) in 1998, bringing increased clarity to the digital environment.

The main purpose of copyright is to protect original creative works. Copyright protection allows the rights holder to reproduce, distribute, lend, rent, and produce public performances (Waelde et al. 2016). The rationale for copyright protection is to protect the author's moral rights

(MacQueen, Waelde, and Laurie 2007); it would be unjust if others could benefit from the creator's time, labor, and expenditure if it were possible simply to copy new intellectual property products without fear of reprisal.

Game publishing companies rely and shield themselves on international IP instruments, especially copyright, to prevent plagiarism and/or unfair exploitation of creative work because video games fall under the category of literary and artistic works (Robertson and Nicol 2002). In light of general copyright principles, a game developer or publisher is entitled to a certain level of protection from unauthorized users. Based on that provision, game publishers have the exclusive right to restrict others from using their product without the relevant permission (Van Hoorebeek 2009). Also, publishers can grant licenses to others for a fee.

IP is critical for esports, because most of esports is zeros and ones (binary code, or computer language). While controllers and broadcasting equipment are also part of it, the essence of esports is the coding. In general, computer games can be protected as linguistic works. Not all ideas or products are protected. Only the specific manifestation of a computer program is capable of being protected (meaning both the source code and the object code). In addition, audiovisual elements of a game (items such as special music or sound, landscapes, game characters, and story lines) can be protected by copyright law as long as the elements exceed an originality threshold. If a character is similar to a character in another game, whether face, clothing, name, or something else, then the character might not be copyrightable. Under traditional copyright protection, the various components can each be protected as individual components (such as the cinematographic elements of a fight scene or battlefield) or the work can be protected as a whole.

Another concern is the right to broadcast a game whether through streaming or a major broadcaster. The permanent or temporary reproduction of an esports game requires the express authorization by the rights owner, which is usually the publisher. Publishers often use end-user license agreements to exclude the commercial use of esports games. Thus, a streamer, broadcast network, advertiser, or tournament director needs to obtain appropriate licensing rights from the publisher to avoid getting into trouble.

One other IP concern deals with the players. Most artists can copyright their performance. A singer can copyright their recorded performance (written as well as performed). So, are esports athletes and their play protected, especially if they have a unique playing style? The courts have generally held that traditional athletes, such as soccer players, are not considered performers, so they cannot copyright their play. This example helps show how almost every facet of a game could fall under some type of legal or IP-related coverage.

Copyright infringement occurs when an individual takes a whole or substantial part of a protected work without lawful consent. The law also provides exceptions to exclusive rights and remedies in case of infringement. Commonly, IP infringement carries civil remedies, and financial compensation might be issued by a court (Van Hoorebeek 2009). According to the United States Court of Appeals for the Seventh Circuit, the mere fact that a gamer follows a sequence within a game shall not be considered as the creation of a new work per se, "because the sequence of images generated in playing a computer video games has been held to be a computer rather than player generated work" (Waelde et al. 2016).

In fact, different aspects of a game might attract copyright and other IP protection. Literary copyright exists in the game play, story line, characters or avatars, and soundtrack (Robertson and Nicol 2002). In addition, other aspects attract image rights protection. A logo can be registered as a trademark. A publisher can file a patent for a computer program or a hardware. Once a game is streamed or broadcast on a platform (such as Twitch or YouTube), then it attracts further copyright protection for the broadcasted rights. That is why these platforms are very strict. They will not allow one to play copyrighted music while streaming, as such, airing of the music subjects the platform to possible IP violations or to have to pay a royalty for playing the music. Thus, platforms can send a takedown notice in line with the Digital Millennium Copyright Act (DMCA) Guidelines, and the platform's own community policies might apply.

In the United States, the 1998 DMCA governs copyrights. Section 102 confers protection on artistic works that are *original*, meaning that the person who has created (or commissioned someone else to do the work) enjoys the right of authorship. However, the law clearly establishes a

Zoning

HUMVEE MANUFACTURER ROLLS OUT IP SUIT AGAINST ACTIVISION

Kevin Wenzel

AM General, LLC, the company behind the Humvee military truck, has sued video game maker Activision Blizzard, Inc., over the use of Humvees in their "Call of Duty" video game series and associated tie-in products of the game franchise. In their initial complaint filed on November 11, 2017 in the Southern District of New York, AM General accused Activision of trademark infringement, trade dress infringement, false advertising, false designation of origin and dilution stemming from Activision's use of AM General's Humvee vehicles in its popular "Call of Duty" video game franchise.

In their complaint, AM General claims that Activision's success has come at the expense of AM General, and consumers that are deceived into believing that AM General has granted a license to the game maker for the use of their intellectual property, and that they are involved in the creation of the popular video games. AM General also asserts that Activision has gone beyond including their intellectual property in seven of Activision's video games in the franchise, also alleging that Activision has included Humvees in strategy guides to the games and licensed "Call of Duty" toys such as "Mega Bloks" toy Humvees. AM General mentions that other video games have secured a license from them to include their Humvee vehicles in expressive works, and in Activision not doing so but continuing to use Humvees in spite of not having a license it would imply to consumers that AM General has approved the use of their intellectual property within Call of Duty games.

Activision responded by filing a motion for summary judgment on the case, calling AM General's lawsuit an attack on the First Amendment, and that "to allow AMG to pursue its claim would run directly contrary to the First Amendment and give AMG a stranglehold on virtually any expressive depiction of 21st-century U.S. military history." Activision contends that their Call of Duty video games are subject to First Amendment protections afforded to expressive works, and that "the limited depictions of Humvees in the games (less than ten minutes out of more than 35 hours of gameplay) are artistically relevant to these games."

"Call of Duty" is one of the most commercially successful video game franchises in the world, selling more than 300 million copies globally. Activision has just recently released its latest title in the series, "Call of Duty: Modern Warfare" on October 25th, 2019.

The case pits Activision's First Amendment rights of free expression directly against AM General's trademark rights with regards to expressive entertainment works. Previously, in the case of Rogers v. Grimaldi, the Second Circuit held that the "balance between trademark rights and the First Amendment will normally not support application of the [Lanham] Act unless [1] the title has no artistic relevance to the underlying work whatsoever, or, [2] if it has some artistic relevance, unless the title explicitly misleads as to the source or the content of the work." Much of Activision's argument hinges on their assertion that their work falls within the protections afforded by the case, and that AM General cannot satisfy the Rogers v. Grimaldi test to prevail on their claim.

AM General's case draws several parallels to a lawsuit filed by Bell Helicopter against Electronic Arts, Inc. in 2012 regarding the use of Bell's Cobra Helicopter in Electronic Arts' first-person shooter title 'Battlefield 3'. Although the case was settled without a ruling, it is worth noting that Electronic Arts took a similar stance to that of Activision's in that expressive works, in this case video games, are afforded First Amendment protections that allowed the company to feature realistic depictions of Bell's military vehicles in their game.

difference between unprotectable *ideas* and copyrightable *expressions*. The mere fact of having an idea to develop a game does not enable someone to claim any protection under copyright law. In turn, for a game to be protected under copyright, it must be *fixed in some medium*, which means a hard copy must exist, whether an actual program, a published paper, a video, or something else.

Innovation and creativity form the cornerstone for gaming and esports. International IP protects all assets through its different branches as the gaming ecosystem encompasses different dimensions, spanning from copyright and patents to trademarks. Hence, IP protection is essential as one of the first steps for those looking for business opportunities such as licensing and to prevent unlawful exploitation of one's *intellectual labor*.

CONTRACT LAW

As mentioned in the introduction, four elements are required for a valid contract: an agreement, consideration, capacity, and legality. This section expands beyond those topics to cover a variety of other issues. For example, what happens when children sign up without their parent's or guardian's consent? Do esports players have the right to negotiate the terms of their playing, or is it an **adhesion contract** (i.e., one party has limited rights in the negotiation process and they have to take the contract terms or not enter into the contract)? Also, what happens when someone violates the terms of their contract, whether it is the publisher or the player?

One example of how strict contracts can be is FaZe Jarvis, who was given a lifetime ban by *Fortnite* creators, Epic Games, following his public use of cheating hacks. He was caught using **aimbots**, an in-game cheat that allows players to automatically aim at opponents. The hack greatly increased his shooting accuracy. Epic Games has a strict policy against cheating and exploiting game bugs. Such policy is detailed in the contractual agreement, often referred to as *terms of service*.

FaZe Jarvis is not alone, but he received the harshest penalty to date. In May 2019, gamers Damion "XXiF" Cook and Ronald "Ronaldo" Mach were banned by Epic Games for two weeks for colluding with other players in *Fortnite* World Cup qualifying rounds. Similarly, in September 2018, members of the gamer group FaZe Clan were punished for cheating. As a result, Nate Hill and Trevor "FunkBomb" Siegler were banned from the Fall Skirmish event (Wolfe and Ries 2019).

Epic Games is not alone in enforcing the terms and conditions of its agreements. In 2019, Blizzard suspended three college *Hearthstone* players for six months after they displayed a sign reading "Free Hong Kong, Boycott Blizz." The protesters were upset that Blizzard supported the Chinese government against pro-democracy protesters in Hong Kong. The sign was raised during an official competition stream. An entire team received the ban for violating Blizzard's official rules. The players specifically violated a section of the rules pertaining to good sporting behavior, which provides that players must refrain from performing any gesture that insults a group of people or could incite others to act in a way that is "abusive, insulting, mocking, or disruptive" (Alexander 2019, para. 4). Blizzard had felt that any insult to China would be inappropriate and that is why people were protesting Blizzard's actions.

In terms of buyers or those who download a game, little room exists for negotiation; this situation is similar to cell phone, cable, and car rental agreements. It is a take-it-or-leave-it contract. Because esports games are not a necessity (such as food and housing), courts are rarely interested in intervening. If someone actually reads the terms of service and does not want to accept one of the terms, they have a simple option. They do not have to accept the terms, which means they cannot play the game. If one wants to play a specific game, then they have to agree to the terms. Because some players might play multiple games, they might have several different contracts with different publishers and some that might be with the same publisher for multiple versions of a game.

One often-raised question is what if someone just accepts the terms but does not read the contract? Can they then challenge the terms? The answer is no. Another contractual question is can children sign a contract? Yes, children (those under age 18) can sign a contract, but as mentioned earlier in the chapter, they technically are not considered capable of entering into a contract. Therefore, that contract becomes voidable; in other words, an underage player can back out of the contract. However, if a contract is signed at age 17, and if that player continues to play when they turn 18, then by choosing to continue playing they have

Zoning

IS MY LOOT BOX LEGAL?

Anthony J. Dreyer and David Lamb

The year 2019 saw an appreciable increase in scrutiny directed toward the use of "loot boxes"—in-game rewards (often randomized) that players can purchase while playing a video game. Both domestically and internationally, legislatures, regulatory agencies, and private groups took up the issue of what, if any, legal concerns loot boxes present. However, while discussions concerning loot boxes were certainly more prominent in 2019, they are just the latest in a long line of legislative and administrative reactions to this growing trend in video games. Although, to date, most attempts to ban or regulate loot boxes have been unsuccessful, the increasing government (and private) scrutiny of this practice deserves the attention of anyone with a connection to the video game industry.

The Rise of the Loot Box

The term "loot box" generally refers to any mechanism allowing players to obtain a set of unknown, virtual items for use in a game. A loot box could be a booster pack in a collectible card game, a weapons crate in a first-person shooter, or a llama-shaped piñata in a battle royale game. In most, though not all, instances of loot boxes, the available items have varying degrees of rarity, with more desirable items appearing less frequently. Loot boxes and other micro-transaction mechanics have grown increasingly popular in the last several years, paralleling both the growth of the free-to-play segment of the video game market, as well as rising development costs across the industry.

Are Loot Boxes Legal?

Today, with some few exceptions, most forms of loot boxes remain legal and unregulated worldwide. However, proponents of loot box regulation argue that the chance and rarity mechanics make loot boxes akin to gambling, and constitute predatory practices focused toward minors. While this comparison may seem overblown to some (particularly those with small children who are familiar with the rampant use of "surprise mechanics" in toys), a careful examination of the relevant statutes and analogous cases demonstrates the potential risk posed by loot box systems.

For example, the federal statutes governing online gambling, as well as each state's individual gambling laws, generally require three elements for a particular activity to constitute an illegal "wager": (1) risking something of value, (2) on the occurrence of a chance event, (3) for a potential valuable prize. Arguably, each of these elements may be satisfied by certain loot box systems. In fact, courts have already held that in the context of mobile games, virtual currency may constitute something of value, and thus may satisfy the first element. Further, because many loot box systems involve some aspect of chance, the second element is likely satisfied as well.

With respect to the final element, the Ninth Circuit recently held that in the context of a casino games mobile app, the chips that a player could win constituted an item of value under California's anti-gambling statute, because the chips allowed the player to continue playing the game. Thus, while most courts that have considered the issue in the context of mobile games have found that "prizes" awarded in video games do not constitute a thing of value, there is at least some support for the claim that a virtual good, even if useable only in the game itself, may satisfy the "valuable prize" prong of the gambling analysis.

Given this potential, video game developers and distributors should be aware of the various avenues by which the legality of particular loot box systems may be challenged. For example, state Attorneys General may bring criminal or civil actions, or aggrieved consumers may bring challenges directly under most states' anti-gambling laws.

Additionally, even if loot boxes are presumptively legal and do not constitute gambling, consumers may bring lawsuits based on consumer protection or false advertising laws if they believe that the loot boxes are marketed in an arguably misleading way. In this connection, consumer groups have recently begun questioning whether the odds of receiving certain desirable prizes are manipulated to incentivize continued play. These sensitives are particularly heightened where the loot boxes at issue may be targeted toward minors.

(continued)

IS MY LOOT BOX LEGAL? *(CONTINUED)*

Recent Attempts at Regulation

In light of these concerns, many government officials, both in the U.S. and abroad, have taken steps directed at regulating loot boxes. For example, state legislatures in at least four states have introduced bills aimed at regulating loot box sales, and the Protecting Children from Abusive Games Act, which seeks to prohibit loot boxes in any game played by minors, was introduced in the U.S. Senate this year.

Additionally, in 2019, the U.S. Federal Trade Commission held a public workshop to examine consumer protection issues related to loot boxes. The primary focus was on the information asymmetry present in loot box mechanics, and whether such mechanics are unfair practices requiring FTC regulation.

Internationally, at least a dozen countries have considered the legality of loot boxes, and three—Belgium, the Netherlands, and China—have outlawed loot boxes to some extent. In fact, the gambling commissions of Belgium and the Netherlands found that most forms of loot boxes constituted gambling under the same wager, chance, and valuable prize structure discussed above.

Most recently, both the United Kingdom and Sweden have taken steps suggesting that loot boxes soon may be regulated or banned in those countries as well. For example, the Digital, Culture, Media and Sport Committee of the U.K. House of Commons released a statement that loot boxes purchased with real-world money that do not reveal their contents in advance constitute games of chance, and should accordingly be regulated under the United Kingdom's Gambling Act. The Committee also recommended that loot boxes containing an element of chance should not be sold to children. Similarly, the Swedish Consumer Agency submitted a report to Sweden's Gaming Market Commission highlighting the similarities between loot boxes and real-money gambling, and suggesting loot box regulation.

Best Practices

Given the uncertainties present in the current landscape, video game companies should examine their loot box practices closely, and keep in mind the following strategies to minimize legal risk:

1. Take steps to avoid creating a wager, chance, or win/loss structure required for a finding of gambling. For example:
    - Make the currency used to purchase loot boxes also acquirable from in-game actions, not simply available for direct purchase;
    - Remove chance by showing players in advance what they will get in a loot box (a strategy Fortnite has recently employed);
    - Allow players to use duplicate items to progress in the game in some other way, so loot boxes always provide players with some value; and
    - Prevent players from exchanging items received in loot boxes, and enforce pre-existing prohibitions on sales of items and/or accounts, to minimize perception that in-game items can be converted to real-world currency.
2. Consider substantial parental controls on loot box purchases made by minors;
3. Ensure that loot boxes are promoted transparently, with minimal "fine print" terms or fees that consumers plausibly could contend are "hidden" or obscured; and
4. Continue working with law makers and regulators through self-regulatory bodies like the ESRB to foster an environment of self-regulation. For example, in the first panel of the FTC loot box workshop, it was announced that Nintendo, Sony, and Microsoft will mandate loot box odds disclosures for new games available on their respective platforms, and update existing games with loot box functionality by the end of 2020.

This article is reprinted with permission of Hackney Publications and, specifically, Esports and the Law (https://esportsandthelaw.com/).

ratified the contractual terms and are bound to them. In order for a player to compete at the highest level, many contracts are usually necessary. They include sponsorship, employment, streaming, team contracts, and others. If the player is a minor, then to make sure the contract is valid, the parties might require the player to have an attorney explain the terms to them and have their parents or guardians also sign the contract. To avoid any possibility of impropriety, attorneys are usually involved on both sides of these contracts.

Although attorneys may be involved, they should not be the only ones who can read the contract, so those writing the contract should use plain language that is direct and concise. Courts are willing to construe a contract against the entity who wrote it if any part of that contract is ambiguous. The clearer the language, the easier it is for all parties and the courts to understand the terms. This is not just a legal concern, but a contract is a relationship and it is important for everyone to know what they are supposed to do to avoid violating the contract. It is especially critical when parts of a contract can be cancelled by the courts or a government. For example, a contract might provide for a player to train a certain number of hours every day. However, the Fair Labor Standards Act (FLSA) in the United States limits the number of hours a student can work during the school year. If the contract violates this provision, then a court can either throw out that specific provision or the entire contract depending on the situation.

LIABILITY

Liability can cover a variety of issues from defamation claims to liability for injuries someone might incur from attending an esports event. Imagine if at an esports tournament, a platform or stage on which competitors were playing collapsed. If a player is injured, they might have one remedy. An employee injured on the job has the exclusive remedy of **workers' compensation** insurance, a no-fault insurance program that covers employees injured at work regardless of why or how they were injured. If a player were an independent contractor, they would not have workers' compensation coverage and would have to try to sue someone for negligence if someone were responsible for their injuries. If a fan were injured, they might have a case against the facility, event promoter, and anyone else they could possibly go after who might be responsible. Considering the wide range of ways that people could be injured at an event (e.g., from a small accident to a possible terrorist attack), it is critical to undertake a comprehensive risk management audit before an event. This task starts with examining all contracts, getting all the right people onto the same page, purchasing insurance, monitoring event setup, monitoring during the event, correcting issues during the event, and even monitoring after the event. For example, how safe is the parking lot? How safe is public transportation if cosplay attendees are taking public transportation? Does the facility or event have an alcohol policy, and how is it enforced? Does the facility have any trip and fall hazards? Who is responsible for providing security? These are just a handful of questions that need to be examined. The attention to detail is critical, so it is never too much information. The life safety manual produced for a regular season National Football League (NFL) game fits into a 3-inch-thick (7.62 cm) binder.

For a traditional negligence claim, an injured party needs to prove the event or esports company had a **duty**, breached that duty, the breached duty was the **proximate cause** of a person's injury, and that a person was in fact injured. All four elements are needed for a negligence claim. The event or company can then try to claim a defense. Some of the most common defenses include missing one of the four elements, **assumption of risk (AR)**, contributing to their own injury, or an intervening cause was the real reason for the injury. Through a case, each side is trying to prove they should recover or that someone should not recover. Just because someone was injured does not mean they are entitled to recover. This fact can be seen when some people have sued publishers for the violent acts of someone who played video games.

In August of 2019, Walmart ordered its employees in stores across the United States to remove video game displays that depicted any form of violence. According to the circulated memo, employees were ordered to strip any violent marketing material, unplug Xbox and PlayStation consoles showing violent video games, and turn off any violence depicted on screens throughout the electronics departments. This request came after two mass shootings happened in El Paso, Texas, and then in Dayton, Ohio (Zacarias 2019).

The launch of the *Mortal Kombat* video game series in the early 1990s generated widespread outrage over its graphic content and resulted in the creation of the Entertainment Software Rating Board (ESRB) game rating system (Zacarias 2019). While some games might have warnings indicating potential violence, the Media Psychology and Technology division of the American Psychological Association in 2017 released a statement suggesting that given the lack of evidence of any correlation, reporters and policymakers should cease linking mass shootings to violent media (Zacarias 2019). In fact, only four of the perpetrators of the 33 mass murders at schools in the United States from 1980 to 2018 were known video gamers (Week Staff 2019). With 70 percent of high school students playing video games, it is a stretch to say that the games generate violence when only a small number of people actually commit mass murders. In 2018 a German study showed that there was no more aggression in groups analyzed that played violent games daily for two months compared with those that played nonviolent *Sims 3* or those that did not play any video games. In contrast, a recent analysis at Dartmouth University of 24 studies involving 17,000 adolescents showed that some video gaming correlated with increased physical aggression, especially among kids already prone to antisocial behavior (Week Staff 2019). If games really resulted in violence, why isn't there a great presence of violence in countries with significant gaming populations (and low crime rates) such as in Japan and South Korea?

So, should game manufacturers be held liable for violence caused by gamers? Under negligence law, a party is usually not held responsible for the criminal acts of a third party unless they reasonably knew that the party would engage in a known action and steps could easily have been taken to minimize that risk. The reason for such a legal conclusion is that sometimes it is impossible to know what a person might do. Sport stadiums have been held liable for criminal assaults by third parties when the injured parties have been able to show that the team or facility knew about a risk but failed to undertake reasonable steps to protect patrons (such as more security, alcohol management teams, limiting alcohol sales, undercover officers, etc.).

One early video game liability suit was *James v. Meow Media, Inc.* in 2002 (Nesbitt 2003). On December 1, 1997, Michael Carneal walked into the lobby of Heath High School in Paducah, Kentucky, and shot several of his fellow students, killing three and wounding others. According to the complaint (filed by the injured and the families of those who were killed), Carneal played video games, watched movies, and viewed websites produced by the defendants. These activities allegedly desensitized Carneal to violence and caused him to commit the shooting. The complaint went on to claim that the distribution of this material to impressionable youth constitutes actionable negligence under Kentucky law. The complaint also contended that the defendants purveyed defective products, namely, the content of video games, movies, and websites, triggering strict product liability under Kentucky law.

The defendants contended that Carneal's actions were not sufficiently foreseeable to trigger their liability. The defendants further argued that Carneal's independent decision to kill others constituted a superseding cause of the claimed damages and defeated the proximate cause element of a negligence case. The defendants also argued that tort liability for the nondefamatory ideas and images communicated in their respective media would raise significant First Amendment questions that ought to be avoided. Lastly, the defendants attacked the product liability argument because under Kentucky law, they had not distributed products. The trial court and the appellate court held for the defendants (Nesbitt 2003).

While many want to point their finger at esports and violent games and movies as a cause of violence, there is no clear consensus that an average person is pushed to commit violent acts based on content. Courts have also taken the opportunity to strike attempts to hold game publishers liable, because it is impossible to prove that the playing of games is the proximate cause of any injury by a third party.

UNIONIZING ESPORTS PLAYERS

At the present time, no true player **unions** exist in esports. In contrast, most professional team sports in the United States are unionized. Some leagues may have multiple unions, such as one for players and one for referees. These unions provide protection for players, but they can also provide some protection for companies because they encourage a more stable workforce. To form a union in the United States (all countries approach it differently), employees need to petition to have a vote with the **National Labor Relations Board (NLRB)**. Numerous rules come into play as to how a vote is conducted, what each party can do, and how a union is finalized. If employees vote for a union, then the employer and the union need to negotiate a **collective bargaining agreement (CBA)**, which will set forth all the rules and responsibilities for each party. When a CBA expires, the union can go on strike or possibly sue the employer for various issues such as contractual interference or antitrust violation.

The topic of unions raises a critical issue for esports. Would each esports title require a different union? What would happen if a title cycled out? Would the union need to disband? Who will be involved with the union? If the union were between the players and the teams, are publishers not necessarily bound by the CBA? Thus, would the union agreement have to be between the players, the teams, and the publishers? Would such a three-party system be legal? These and other questions are raising a lot of debate, which might be why at present the only so-called union in the esports space is the *Counter-Strike* Professional Players' Association (CSPPA). It is a democratically run entity made up of more than 180 *Counter-Strike* players from around the world. The focus is on providing better working conditions for team players on some of the top ESL Pro League (EPL) teams. Note that the CSPPA does not have the same legal protections of an official union. It is just a group trying to protect players; it has no CBA and no union vote.

Nonetheless, the CSPPA has had some recent success in inserting the issue of player rights and benefits as part of broader discussions between esports stakeholders. For instance, in early 2020, the Louvre Agreement between the EPL and a select group of elite professional teams (including Evil Geniuses, ENCE, FaZe Clan, Fnatic, G2 Esports, Ninjas in Pyjamas, Team Liquid, and 100 Thieves) provides for what it calls player benefits. The ESL and partner teams have committed to working with the CSPPA on contract standards and minimum standards for events transfer regulations, enshrined a 15 percent revenue share for Pro League and Circuit Events for players, and established a minimum prize pool of $4,500,000 for EPL events. Furthermore, as a consultative body, the CSPPA has also ensured that other operational considerations such as adequate travel and accommodation arrangements, training spaces, and distances between the venue and hotel have included player input (Park 2020).

LEGAL RIGHTS OF ESPORTS ATHLETES

As it applies to sport, unionization means that organized athletes should have a stronger base from which to advocate for player rights. As mentioned in the previous section, collective bargaining refers to the negotiation process that takes place between employers and organized employees, primarily through unions.

The traditional sports industry has long been familiar with the strong correlation between unionization and player rights. In professional leagues such as the National Football League (NFL), National Basketball Association (NBA), and the National Hockey League (NHL), player unions have used the collective bargaining process to secure greater rights for their athletes in virtually all respects. Minimum salaries and other "working conditions" or minimal conditions of employment, such as sick days, travel accommodations, per diems, media appearances, and even injury insurance, are all negotiated with the intention of finding a fair, mutually beneficial agreement (Lowell 1973).

Securing athlete rights is particularly critical in traditional sports given the myriad of health and safety concerns associated with participating in elite sport. Each professional league's collective bargaining agreement and standard player contract regulates, to some extent, players' access to medical treatment for employment-related conditions at the team's expense (McChrystal 2014). Additionally, alternate provisions ensuring player health (e.g., provision of up-to-date safety equipment, mandatory removal from play following suspected injury and major collisions, contract guarantees for injured players) have been part of labor negotiations for several generations.

Esports, with its different modality of physicality emphasizing fine motor skills (clicking and fast-twitch reactions) rather than gross motor skills (running or jumping), may not represent an obvious forum for health and safety concerns, but indicators still show that greater attention is required in this area (Jenny et al. 2017). The well-being and welfare of esports athletes is no longer a trivial matter. It is evident with some professional esports organizations exerting control over players' schedules, accommodations, training, and nutrition.

In fact, overtraining and overexertion are key contributors to long-term injury among esports athletes. Medical issues such as carpal tunnel syndrome, eye fatigue, and tendinitis have been found to occur as a direct result of overuse in esports, and any such injury may significantly inhibit a player's performance for weeks or even months (DiFrancisco-Donoghue et al. 2019). Such downturns in play are not only upsetting for the player but can also have a direct impact on their immediate and future earnings and their role on a team.

In addition, from a mental standpoint, such strenuous competition and training schedules also lead to mental fatigue and burnout. Pressure from living in shared housing with constant training regimens and lack of balancing social releases, such as romantic relationships, have led to significant rates of burnout among esports athletes at relatively young ages (Lajka 2018).

Without a collective representative body, each esports athlete is dependent on publisher mandates, the magnanimity of their employer, and their own ability to negotiate in safeguarding acceptable standards of care. In reality, without collective action, individual players are at the mercy of their employers in this regard due to the potential unequal bargaining power between the two sides. Some esports stars have such significant followings that they might have a better chance to negotiate favorable terms. For others, if esports athletes were able to consolidate around a single or a few strong unions, they would form a representative body or bodies capable of standing toe-to-toe with employers in negotiating and ensuring greater rights for players.

However, athletes' rights do not exist in a vacuum. For such rights to be manifested effectively, the teams or leagues to which athletes belong must be economically sound and capable of absorbing the costs associated with them. Currently, most esports organizations are reputed to be unprofitable. While top organizations have attracted major investors and enjoy impressive market valuations, in fact the revenue streams of esports organizations are still murky and valuations are based on multiples of purported revenues that far outstrip those of the traditional sports industry. For instance, Toronto-based OverActive Media was assigned a Forbes value of $120 million on a mere $5 million of estimated revenue (Settimi 2019). Such valuations do not make sense if esports organizations are analogized as a sports franchise. However, valuations of esports organizations are currently based on their nexus with technology. As such, the valuations of esports organizations mimic those of tech companies at an average of 13 times revenue among the top organizations (Chapman 2019). Therefore, while esports organizations are valuable assets, many currently operate at a loss. Indeed, many organizations are reputed to spend more than 100 percent of revenue on player salaries and operations. Given this fact, their tolerance for poor player performance and desire to bargain regarding athlete rights may be low.

Therefore, for any future negotiation between organized athletes and esports organizations to reach a mutually satisfactory conclusion, both parties must focus on and emphasize the joint value to be gained through negotiated outcomes. For athletes, collectively bargained rights can help lengthen careers by safeguarding player mental and physical well-being. For esports organizations, they can use negotiations as a mechanism to discuss better methods for sharing both risk and opportunity with athletes. Unlike traditional sport unions in which the sport is collectively owned by no one, esports is different. Esports are organized by publishers that might have multiple games in multiple franchises or leagues. Thus, publishers have significant power that they can wield and impact any contractual negotiations between third parties. That is one reason why some publishers may support revenue sharing with teams and players while others might not allow such a model. That relationship could significantly impact bargaining positions and options. For example, Cloud9 was fined by Riot Games for being in violation of a rule regarding employee stock plans for the company's *League of Legends* competitive league after the team issued equity to seven players. The move was a violation of a rule set forth by the league in November 2017 that prohibits LCS team owners from acting as players and players from owning a portion of the team for which they played.

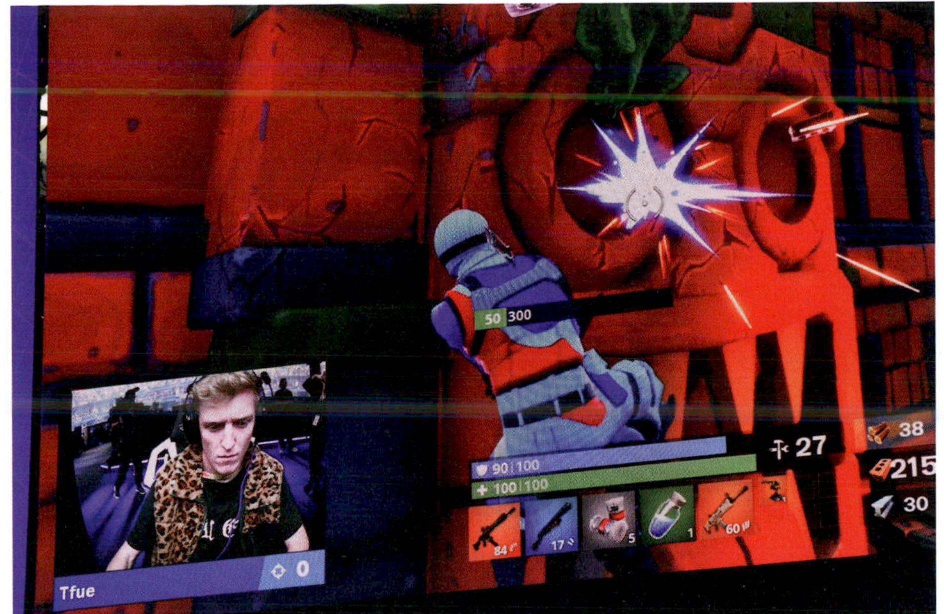

JOHANNES EISELE/AFP via Getty Images

Turner "Tfue" Tenney sued FaZe Clan in a case that highlights issues around player rights.

In 2019, professional gamer Turner "Tfue" Tenney was embroiled in a turbulent separation from the professional gaming organization FaZe Clan. Tfue is best known for his *Fortnite* play and content, which has garnered him over 25 million followers and subscribers across major social media and streaming platforms (Tfue 2020). The 21-year-old sued FaZe Clan in the California Superior Court for what he deemed to be oppressive contracting practices relating to revenue from Twitch streaming and YouTube. The suit alleges that FaZe Clan significantly limited Tfue's ability to pursue his profession and unlawfully claimed 80 percent of earnings on branded content, violating the contractual agreement. Tfue's legal representation argued that the contract should be voided, freeing Tfue from any further obligation to FaZe Clan. The attorneys also argued that these types of predatory practices are common within the industry. FaZe Clan denied the allegations of unfair business practices and maintained that they actively tried to address Tfue's contracting concerns as they arose (Becht 2019).

Tfue's case may center on a contractual dispute, but its complexity exposes a legal void related to player rights and player status. The critical legal question was whether athletes were employees of an organization or simply independent contractors. For Tfue, this undetermined status became central to his argument before the court. It allowed him to identify as an independent contractor and thus prove retroactively that FaZe Clan had infringed on his California Labor Code rights. Contrary to sections 1700 to 1704, FaZe Clan did not submit the contract for review by the California Labor Commissioner and they did not have the required license to enlist the services of an independent contractor such as Tfue (Zaller 2019). Another issue is whether the contract was valid, what would happen if someone willingly agreed to terms, and whether they can then ask to throw out the contractually agreed-upon terms.

Tfue is a cautionary tale of the risks of contracting within the esports industry. As with any sport, uncertainties are always surrounding a player's first contract. Teams must estimate the value of a young, unproven talent while the athlete does their best to demonstrate that their potential is worth a high valuation. Complicating things further, the esports industry also factors in a player's online presence because athletes tend to focus strongly on streaming and social media, both of which are actively encouraged by teams. Teams will devote time and resources to cultivating a player's brand and persona on all platforms. In most cases, the investment proves mutually beneficial because the player is able to tap into an already established fan base while simultaneously bringing in further support for the team. Another wrinkle can be the age of the player; if they are a minor, how can they be legally bound to any contract they sign?

Initially, this was the case for Tfue. Tfue saw a substantial growth across all social media and streaming platforms, leading to new sponsorship and endorsement opportunities. This growth continued, and soon Tfue surpassed FaZe Clan in followers. Clauses that at one point seemed mutually beneficial, later seemed to tilt heavily in favor of FaZe Clan. FaZe sought 80 percent of Tfue's earnings on branded content, which dwarfed the monthly allowance Tfue was receiving from his contract.

Therefore, the argument is made that these types of contracts swindle players by offering upfront salaries and lavish perks while duplicitously ensuring their subjugation. Whether they remain relatively unknown or increase their followers by the millions, these contracts ensure that a player will remain financially tethered to the team for the duration of their contract. The argument is these contracts permit only marginal increases in financial compensation for athletes, while redirecting an overwhelming majority of profits to the team.

As a counterargument, esports organizations bear the risk of promoting unknown esports talent, yet they are alleged to be exploitative if one of their athletes gains a viral following. It is well known that most esports organizations are not profitable and to take a chance on the wrong players could spell the collapse of the team. Furthermore, these front-end-heavy contracts are the norm and give many athletes the chance to enjoy a very comfortable life. This scenario is very similar to player contracts for minor league sports such as hockey and baseball. Teams can invest a significant amount of money on players with only a few of the hundreds of players ever making it to the big leagues. Players like Tfue, who enjoy rapid growth, are not the norm but the exception. If an athlete garners an exceptional number of followers and sponsorships, due in part to the resources they were afforded while with the team, should the team not benefit exceptionally from their gamble on this athlete? Such a question will be answered by the court's ruling and will serve as significant legal precedent for the industry moving forward.

CONCLUSION

Laws are complex. The legal concerns associated with esports are so dynamic because they cross over several legal areas ranging from contract and tort law to workplace laws and intellectual property. The industry is changing rapidly, and the law is trying to catch up. It is similar to how negligence law had to rush and address the risks posed by automobiles and drivers when cars first hit the road. The law will once again be shaped when driverless vehicles hit the road. The same can be said for esports. By the time this book is printed, some of the legal issues raised might be resolved, and new ones will arise.

DISCUSSION QUESTIONS

1. What do you think is the biggest legal risk facing esports?
2. If you were to negotiate a contract between yourself and a professional esports team, what terms would you want? Do you think they are reasonable?
3. Should esports and streaming have free speech?
4. What are some of the workplace rules/laws that can apply to an esports house?
5. What are the risks associated with esports training and playing areas? Conduct a risk audit of the esports training and playing area on campus. If no such space exists, conduct a risk assessment of a recreational facility on campus.

13

Esports Team and Player Management

David P. Hedlund | Matthew Williamson | Aaron Colaiacomo
Joanne Donoghue | Courtney James | Taylor Johnson
Ronald Kim | Raffaele Lauretta | John McDermott
Sheng Qiang | Hallie Zwibel

INTRODUCTION

This chapter provides information about esports team and player management. Similar to traditional sport organizations, numerous personnel beyond coaches are involved in team and player management. While video gaming may have once been stereotypically perceived as individuals playing alone in their basements or bedrooms, nowadays, professional esports organizations (and even a growing number of amateur and collegiate esports teams) have specialized personnel who focus on specific roles and responsibilities. These roles include managers, coaches, scouts, recruiters, athletic trainers, fitness coaches, nutritionists, and psychologists. Today, professional esports organizations have a multitude of tools at their disposal, such as software that analyzes and quantifies players' in-game performance and hardware that can monitor players' health and wellness, just to name a few. Therefore, professionals who can effectively use these tools and aid player and team performance are now important personnel within esports organizations.

Esports players have not always had these tools and resources at their disposal. For example, the highest-level video game and esports players in the 1970s through the early 2000s mostly practiced on their own and looked after themselves. After gamers began to organize activities and competitions and connect with other players both inside and outside the game, gamers—many highly skilled players who could practice, play, and compete with and against each other informally—banded together and helped one another. Over time, organizations arose that formally

OBJECTIVES

- Identify roles and responsibilities for esports coaches and staff.
- Understand the principles and practices used in esports coaching and player management.
- Identify similarities and differences between esports personnel in different roles and organizations.
- Understand unique aspects of esports management from diverse perspectives.
- Draw conclusions from advice, research, and industry examples about the current situation and future opportunities in esports.

signed esports players to contracts to compete for their teams.

In recent years, at least two branding models have been used to create professional esports organizations that encompass multiple teams and players. The first model consists of organizations using the same branded name (e.g., Team SoloMid, Team Liquid, FaZe Clan). In these organizations, the name of every team is the same; even if the organization purchases or acquires a new team that competes with a new game, the branding and name of the team is changed to be consistent with the original brand. For example, in the *Call of Duty* League, FaZe Clan's team is the "Atlanta FaZe," and their logo is consistent with that of FaZe Clan. In addition, their highly acclaimed *CS:GO* team is named FaZe Clan. The second model includes an overarching name for the whole esports organization (e.g., Cloud9), but teams competing in different games may have unique names (e.g., the team name in the *League of Legends* Championship Series (LCS) is Cloud9, but in the *Overwatch* League, the team name is the London Spitfire). An opportunity to undertake a cost–benefit analysis (CBA) about which marketing and branding strategy is superior is provided in HK*Propel*.

Regardless of which marketing and branding strategy is used, both have achieved success based on recent esports organization valuations. Based on research by Settimi (2019), the esports organizations that own or operate esports teams with the highest valuations are shown in table 13.1. The listed organizations own and operate multiple teams in different games. Some of the teams play in organized and franchised leagues in games such as *League of Legends*, *Overwatch*, and *Call of Duty*, while other teams from the organizations may compete in international or game-specific tournaments (e.g., ESL One).

The following sections examine issues related to the esports management and activities performed by coaches, players, operations, and support staff.

THE RISE OF ESPORTS COACHING

Esports has grown rapidly over the years. According to *The Esports Observer* database, in 2019, there were approximately 70 professional international esports tournaments and leagues around the world and over 250 professional esports teams and organizations (The Esports Observer 2019a, 2019b). The number of high school and collegiate esports organizations has also increased. As of 2019, over 2,100 high schools registered with the High School Esports League (HSEL 2019), over 170 colleges and universities have registered with the National Association of Collegiate Esports (NACE n.d.), and more than 55,000 students from 1,800 institutions of higher education in North America competed in Collegiate StarLeague (CSL) esports competitions (CSL n.d.). With increasing numbers of esports players, teams, and competitions have come high expectations from stakeholders and investors for positive outcomes. One of the most important areas for successful esports team and player operations is coaching.

Coaching was not initially an important consideration in the esports industry. When esports gained popularity in the 1990s and early 2000s, teams consisted of individual players or groups of friends who coached themselves. However, the problem many teams experienced was that players could only see the game from their own perspective; no one player could see everything that was occurring during a match. Furthermore, whenever conflicts arose among the players, no one could serve as an independent arbiter to resolve any issues. As a result, teams started to bring in individuals to serve as coaches and analysts.

As more esports organizations hired coaches, tournament and league organizers started to accept the important role coaches served. For example, the Major League Gaming (MLG) Pro Circuit was likely the first esports league to recognize coaches as official members of the team. In 2006, MLG announced that *Halo 2* teams could include a coach on their roster. However, these coaches could not also be a player on the team (MLG 2006). This announcement was one of the first known occurrences involving separate coaches on official esports rosters. Moreover, to ensure teams did not share coaches, MLG required coaches to work with only one team at a particular competition.

The recognition of esports coaches as a member of the team led to similar inclusion in ensuing games and competitions. For example, in 2012, some players involved in *Street Fighter* tournaments coached each other, while other players would have multiple coaches (Chiu 2016). The coaching disparities resulted in some tournament organizers later enforcing a limit of one coach per player (Chiu 2016). In Valve's first *Counter-Strike:*

Table 13.1 Esports Organizations With the Highest Valuations That Oversee Franchises and Teams

Rank	Valuation	Organization	Franchises and teams (league/game)
1. (Tie)	$400 million	Cloud9	Cloud9 (LCS); London Spitfire (*Overwatch* League); and teams competing in *CS:GO*, *Fortnite*, *Hearthstone*, *PlayerUnknown's Battlegrounds* (*PUBG*), *Rainbow Six*: *Siege*, *Rocket League*, *Super Smash Bros.*, *Teamfight Tactics*, and *World of Warcraft*
1. (Tie)	$400 million	Team SoloMid	Team SoloMid (LCS), and teams competing in *League of Legends* Academy, *PUBG*, *Fortnite*, *Hearthstone*, *Super Smash Bros.*, *Overwatch*, *Rocket League*, *Apex Legends*, *Magic: The Gathering*, *Rainbow Six: Siege*, and *Teamfight Tactics*
3.	$320 million	Team Liquid	Team Liquid (LCS), and teams competing in *CS:GO*, *Dota 2*, *StarCraft II*, *Fortnite*, *Rainbow Six: Siege*, *Clash Royale*, *PUBG*, *Apex*, *Hearthstone*, *Smash Melee*, *Smash Ultimate*, *Street Fighter V*, *Tekken*, *Quake*, and *Teamfight Tactics*
4.	$240 million	FaZe Clan	Teams competing in *CS:GO*, *PUBG*, *Call of Duty*, *Fortnite*, *Rainbow Six: Siege*, and *FIFA*
5.	$210 million	Immortals Gaming Club	Immortals (LCS), Los Angeles Valiant (*Overwatch* League), OpTic Gaming Los Angeles (*Call of Duty* League), Immortals (*Clash Royale*), MIBR (*CS:GO*), and MIBR (*Rainbow Six: Siege*)
6.	$185 million	Gen.G	Gen.G (*League of Legends* Champions Korea); Seoul Dynasty (*Overwatch* League); Shanghai (*NBA 2K* League); Team Bumble (*Fortnite*); and teams competing in *Overwatch* Contenders, *PUBG*, *Apex Legends*, and *Clash Royale*
7.	$175 million	Fnatic	Fnatic (*League of Legends* European Championship) and teams competing in *CS:GO*, *Dota 2*, *Fortnite*, *Rainbow Six: Siege*, *Apex*, *Clash Royale*, *Rules of Survival*, and *Street Fighter V*
8.	$170 million	Envy Gaming	Dallas Fuel (*Overwatch* League); Dallas Empire Huntsmen (*Call of Duty* League); and teams competing in *Overwatch* Contenders, *CS:GO*, *Fortnite*, *PUBG*, *Paladins*, and *Super Smash Bros.*
9.	$165 million	G2 Esports	G2 (*League of Legends* European Championship) and teams competing in *CS:GO*, *Rainbow Six: Siege*, *Rocket League*, *PUBG*, *Apex*, *Fortnite*, *Hearthstone*, and *Sim Racing*
10.	$160 million	100 Thieves	100 Thieves (LCS) and teams competing in *CS:GO* and *Fortnite*
11.	$150 million	NRG Esports	San Francisco Shock (*Overwatch* League), Chicago Huntsmen (*Call of Duty* League), and teams competing in *Fortnite*, *Rocket League*, *Clash Royale*, *Super Smash Bros.*, *Apex*, *Gears of War* and *Dragon Ball FighterZ*
12. (Tie)	$120 million	Misfits Gaming	Misfits Gaming (*League of Legends* European Championship); Florida Mayhem (*Overwatch* League); Florida Mutineers (*Call of Duty* League); and teams competing in *Fortnite*, *Marvel vs. Capcom*, and *Clash Royale*
12. (Tie)	$120 million	OverActive Media	Splyce (*League of Legends* European Championship); Toronto Defiant (*Overwatch* League); Toronto Ultra (*Call of Duty* League); and teams competing in *Fortnite*, *Smite*, and *StarCraft II*

Data from Settimi (2019).

Global Offensive (*CS:GO*) Major at DreamHack Winter 2013, the Fnatic and Recursive eSports teams each had an official coach for their respective teams. Fnatic ended up winning the competition (Valve 2013). However, some fans noted the important role their coach and former player Patrik "cArn" Sättermon may have had on the team and its results (u/entfy 2013). In the game *League of Legends*, coaches such as Kim "kkOma" Jeong-gyun were integral for their South Korean teams as early as 2012 (Erzberger 2017). In 2014, Riot Games and the LCS announced official support for team coaches for the 2015 season (LoL Esports Staff 2015). When Blizzard Entertainment began the *Overwatch* League in 2017, teams were also permitted to include coaches on their roster (Blizzard Entertainment n.d.; Szymborski 2016).

ESPORTS COACHING AS A PROFESSION

When esports coaching first became a profession, the only qualification was knowledge of the game(s). For example, if a *League of Legends* team wanted to hire a coach, then the coach was expected to know how to play *League of Legends* at a high level, including knowing the game's rules, strategies, and tactics. As a result, the earliest official esports coaches were generally either current or retired professional players. Their primary responsibilities included analyzing in-game player performance and developing strategies for players and teams. Their focus was on helping teams to become more coordinated and players to improve their game play and mechanics.

As the esports industry grew and competitions became more prominent, the qualifications and expectations for coaches became higher. Having been an experienced professional player was no longer the sole criterion for getting hired as an esports coach. This change occurred because additional issues needed to be managed. For instance, official rosters needed to be created and managed based on factors such as scouting and players' strengths and weaknesses. With more people striving to become professional esports players, organizations also needed to focus on recruiting and retaining the best players by providing long-term contracts (Smith 2019). To help provide structure and alignment within the organization, coaches were included and involved in more and more activities. Esports organizations also started to provide housing accommodations for players so that they could practice together more often. The resulting **gaming houses** meant that players would not only be practicing together, they would be living together, sometimes with their coach (Jacobs 2015). Organizations also learned that taking care of players' mental health, often due to the growing pressure and criticism from the esports community, was critical to the overall wellness of players (Erzberger 2018). As a result, many esports organizations now require coaches to have extensive experience in the esports industry and in-depth knowledge and experience with assisting players with issues such as exercise routines, nutrition, and mental health considerations.

THE ROLE OF COACHES AT ESPORTS COMPETITIONS

The role of coaches in esports competitions varies among tournament organizers. For example, consider the role of *CS:GO* coaches in ESL competitions and tournaments. In the beginning, coaches in the ESL were allowed to watch matches by either viewing the match on a separate computer in spectator mode or standing behind the players. The coaches were also allowed to communicate with the players during the match and call out where the players should go and what the players should do during the game. Having this so-called sixth player resulted in *CS:GO* teams restructuring their rosters by replacing in-game leaders with more mechanically and strategically skilled players, because coaches needed to be able to effectively communicate with their players about which strategies and tactics to use during the game.

Later, Valve, the developer and publisher of *CS:GO*, wanted matches to consist of only the five players on each roster and not having outside assistance during actual games (Chalk 2016). As a result, Valve announced in 2016 that coaches were no longer allowed to communicate with players during official *CS:GO* games. Instead, they were allowed to communicate during warm-up, halftime, and time-outs (Donnelly 2016; Valve 2016). Initially, players, coaches, and teams were upset with this change, but they were obligated to comply if they wanted to compete.

The role of coaches for teams competing in the game *League of Legends* showed similarities and differences compared to the evolution of the role of *CS:GO* coaches. When the LCS began in 2013,

Zoning

WHAT DO YOU NEED TO BECOME A PROFESSIONAL ESPORTS PLAYER?

Ronald "Rambo" Kim

Many young people growing up today dream of reaching the highest levels of esports and video game competition in the professional ranks, but only a small percentage actually live out this dream. As in traditional sports, competition is fierce and there are no guarantees of success, even if one invests countless hours practicing and attempting to be the best. As a former professional *Counter-Strike* player and coach, I lived out this dream. Here, I share my recommendations for anyone wishing to become a professional player:

1. Hardware (computer, monitor, table, chair, Internet speed): The largest monetary investment will be spent purchasing hardware. I suggest investing as much as you can afford, because you do not want in-game performance to be limited by your hardware's performance.
   - Computer components (does not apply to console gamers): How much and what computer components you purchase should be determined by which major components are needed to attain steady high frames per second (FPS) in your chosen game. The major computer components are the graphics processing unit (GPU), central processing unit (CPU), and random-access memory (RAM). The higher the demand and performance of these major components, the more you will need to invest in the motherboard, computer cooling mechanism, and power supply.
   - Monitor: Professional PC gamers use a gaming monitor with a minimum of 144 hertz refresh rate and 1 millisecond response time. If you are a console player, refresh rate does not matter as long as it is a minimum of 60 hertz, but you will still want a monitor with a 1 millisecond response time. These settings matter because they determine how fast your monitor displays the colors and images on your screen, which makes the game visually smoother and gives you an advantage over those with slower monitors.
   - Table and chair: Ideally, you should have a table and chair with as many adjustability features as possible to give you all the options to conform to your comfort level. Too often, I have seen amateur players being forced to align their bodies in awkward positions due to a low-quality table and chair. One of the biggest issues, besides the potential for injury, is that awkward body position can inhibit the proper training of muscle memory needed to be successful in game.
   - Internet speed: Practice and competition mostly occur online, so research and invest in an Internet service provider that provides high download and upload speeds with good routing. Nothing is more debilitating than trying to practice with high ping (latency and lag, in other words the amount of time it takes data to travel between devices or components) and packet loss (the loss of data during transmission, often caused by congestion within the Internet network).
2. Equipment (mouse, keyboard, controller): An ever-increasing number of mice, controllers, and keyboards are available on the market. Because everyone is different, you should try as many combinations as possible to determine which controller, keyboard, and mouse feel best in your hands. I recommend testing every equipment option available in order to find the right shape, weight, and

(continued)

WHAT DO YOU NEED TO BECOME A PROFESSIONAL ESPORTS PLAYER? *(CONTINUED)*

outer surface material for you. Go to your local electronics store, gaming conventions, or gaming center to test equipment. You may not be able to play or compete in an actual game with them, but you can at least feel each one with your own hands. Trying out equipment is more efficient than blindly ordering online. After you find your ideal equipment, you need to commit long term to building your muscle memory with your chosen equipment.

3. Game of choice: The more time you can commit to a single game, the faster you will improve. Constantly switching between the games you play slows down your game-playing progression and also hinders progress toward building experience and muscle memory. You can choose an older, more established game to play, but selecting a newly released game has advantages. A game that has been on the market for many years may have established players, therefore more recently published games allow new players to be not too far behind their competition in terms of developing their knowledge and skill with the game. Try choosing a game with a promising future that is supported by the game developer with a guaranteed tournament and league circuit and with large prize winnings. Keep in mind that a newer game is a riskier investment of your training time compared with an established title, because if the new game does not become popular, the game publisher may stop supporting it.
4. Practice: How efficiently you spend your practice time will determine how quickly you improve. The three fastest ways to improve your game are (1) learning from a mentor or experienced player who is willing and able to teach you, (2) watching demonstrations and replays of the best professionals playing the game, and (3) playing the game with the mindset of learning from every mistake and focusing on improving your weaknesses. Simply playing the game is one method of improving, but practicing with objectives and intentional focus will be the superior path to the fastest rate of improvement.
5. Entering competitive play:
    - After you feel you have reached a level where you are easily beating your current opposition (e.g., competitions at local gaming centers, online, and with friends), then it is time to play in organized competitive league matches. Virtually every popular competitive game has leagues and tournaments where you can test your skills against other competitive gamers and aspiring professionals. The leagues will likely have several divisions divided into the equivalents of beginner, intermediate, advanced, and an area where professionals compete. For the most part, every professional player once started in the beginner division and over time advanced up to the highest level.
    - After you have reached the intermediate or semiprofessional level, gain as much experience as you can through playing in as many matches and tournaments as possible. First-hand experience is the best way to learn at this level. Continue the mindset of learning from every mistake and focusing your practice on improving your weak areas until you are strong in every game facet.

One of the most popular careers for esports players after completion of their playing career is becoming an esports coach. Using the knowledge and experience gained during their playing careers, former esports players can leverage and potentially monetize their knowledge and experience to help other up-and-coming players achieve success.

coaches were allowed to participate in competitions. However, unlike the early days of *CS:GO* competitions, coaches could not participate during the actual games. Coaches could speak with the players before and between games in a best-of-three or best-of-five series. Allowing coaches led to several issues in the LCS. First, not all teams had a coach. Thus, the teams with a coach might have had a competitive advantage over other teams. Second, players (instead of the coach) were responsible for drafting and composing the roster of in-game champions during the "draft pick" phase at the beginning of each game. This responsibility occasionally resulted in players selecting champions that went against the coaches' initial strategies.

The LCS decided to address these issues by providing more support for coaches. They recognized the benefits of having a coach, especially after teams in South Korea that were already using coaches won the 2013 World Championship. As a result, in late 2014, Riot Games (the developer and publisher of *League of Legends* and the organizer of the LCS) announced that they would officially recognize coaches as part of LCS teams (LoL Esports Staff 2015). Not only would Riot Games financially support hiring coaches by each LCS team, but the coaches would also be permitted onstage during the draft pick phase. This permission allowed the coaches (instead of the players) to have an important role in the in-game champions each player would draft and which in-game champions would be banned from each game. Coaches were not allowed to communicate during the actual games, so they would leave the stage at the end of the draft pick phase. These decisions made by Valve and Riot Games in their respective games strongly influenced the roles and responsibilities of what modern-day esports coaches are permitted to do during competitions. The next section examines various roles of esports owners, managers, coaches, and staff.

THE ROLE OF OWNERS, MANAGERS, AND COACHES IN ESPORTS ORGANIZATIONS AND TEAMS

Just as the education, training, and professionalism required of coaches has evolved and increased throughout the years in traditional sports, similar trends are currently happening in competitive esports. In the early years of coaching esports players and teams, coaches were responsible for nearly every aspect of the team, including but not limited to coaching, management, administration, recruiting, scouting, organizing competitions, acting in oversight, referee-like roles, and much more. As more resources have been invested in player development, more opportunities for specialized personnel within esports organizations and teams have arisen.

At the top of an esports organization is an ownership group typically composed of multiple investors. For example, NRG Esports, founded in 2015, is led by cofounders Andy Miller and Mark Mastrov (both co-owners of the Sacramento Kings), co-CEO Hector "H3CZ" Rodriguez, and eight additional investors and advisors, including Alex Rodriguez, Shaquille O'Neal, Jimmy Rollins, Ryan Howard, Jennifer Lopez, Michael Strahan, Marshawn Lynch, and Tiësto (NRG Esports n.d.). Andbox, which oversees the operations of the New York Excelsior (*Overwatch* League) and New York Subliners (*Call of Duty*), is managed by Sterling.VC. Sterling.VC is a venture capital division of Sterling Equities, which is a family-run group of companies, including the New York Mets and Sportsnet New York (Sterling Equities 2017). The ownership group typically hires a managing director who oversees the management and operations of all of the teams and players within the organization. In other organizations, such as institutions of higher education (e.g., colleges and universities), an esports director is typically given the same type of oversight over all the teams.

Below the individual in charge of directing all team and player operations are typically coaches and support staff. Based on a common division of roles and responsibilities, esports coaches can be divided into two general types, **game coaches** and **life coaches** (Hyun 2018). Game coaches, also frequently called head coach, or assistant or **position coaches** for the team are those involved directly with game issues and how the game is played (figure 13.1). Life coaches are involved with a player's or the team's physical, mental, emotional, social, and spiritual well-being (figure 13.2).

Figure 13.1 Types of game coaches.

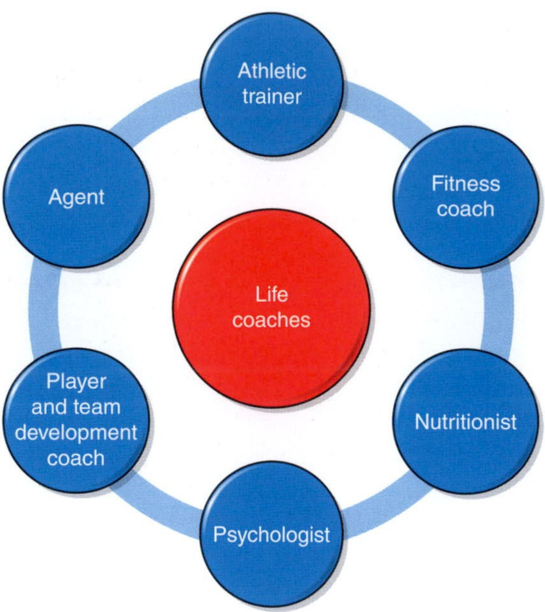

Figure 13.2 Types of life coaches.

Game Coaches

A game coach has a direct effect on the team's or players' actions in preparation for or while playing the game. These coaches analyze game play, tactics, and strategies; identify the team's, players', and opponents' strengths, weaknesses, and playing styles; and develop game plans and strategies for victory based on the team's or players' abilities, the score of the game, and the version of the game being used. In some games and competitions, different maps (versions of the game) may be used. For example, in the 2019 *Call of Duty* release *Modern Warfare*, 23 different maps and 10 different playing modes can be played, including Team Deathmatch (two teams attack each other), Domination (two teams compete to capture positions on the map), Cyber Attack (two teams compete to achieve a goal first), and Gunfight (two teams attack each other in multiple rounds of competitions) (James and Hurley 2019). During a game or competition, game coaches may talk to, coordinate, and aid players while they are playing or during breaks in the competition. In order to provide the most effective aid and instructions, extensive knowledge and experience playing the game is a likely prerequisite.

Position Coaches and Analysts

Due to increasing expansion and complexity of esports games, specialized strategy coaches are being hired by many esports organizations. For example, in a recent version of *League of Legends* (patch 9.24b), 147 heroes are available for players to choose from during a traditional 5v5 match (Riot Games n.d.). In other words, despite the unique features of how heroes are chosen for use at the beginning of *League of Legends* competitions (e.g., opposing team banning heroes during the hero selection or draft process), approximately 64 billion unique combinations of heroes could still be chosen in a particular match. Moreover, because each hero has different qualities, skills, and abilities, and because essentially five different roles exist in *League of Legends* (Top Laner, Mid Laner, Jungler, ADC [Attack Damage Carry], and Support), in recent years, position coaches and **analyst coaches** (for teams and players) have emerged as new coaching opportunities. Position coaches mainly target the most popular multiplayer esports game genres such as multiplayer online battle arena (MOBA), first-person shooter (FPS), battle royale, and survival games, and their role is to coach specific types of in-game characters or roles. Analyst coaches use experiential, professional, statistical, and mathematical knowledge to compile and condense training and competition content into informational pieces and conclusions that are understandable and easily implemented by players and coaches (Yip 2014).

Scouts

In addition to coaching positions responsible for training and competition, opportunities also exist for coaches who focus on analyzing other teams and players (e.g., **performance scouts**). In professional esports, scouting opponents and others who play the game is a common activity for both players and coaches. Whether consciously known or not, players of traditional sports and esports may have tendencies or preferences that affect how they play and compete. Performance scouts are used to identify tendencies and opponent (and one's own) preferences in an effort to potentially predict the in-game decisions players may make. Successful predictions of strategies, tactics, and related decisions can result in competitive advantage for players and teams. Moreover, the opportunity to maximize one's strengths and minimize one's weaknesses is an overarching strategic goal in all sports and esports. Esports organizations will grow in their efforts to identify and train performance scouts and analyst coaches.

Recruiters

Currently, the esports market is mainly concentrated in North America, Europe, Asia, and Australia. In order to increase and expand popularity of esports to every corner of the globe, recruiters and scouts are tasked with finding talent around the world, especially in less-developed esports regions. By implementing talent identification programs in currently underserved or underrepresented areas, esports recruiters and scouts can help raise the status and profile of high-performing players from areas such as the Middle East, Southeast Asia, Africa, and South America. Investing in these rising stars can stimulate a local esports market and help fuel growth in all

Zoning

TEAM AND PLAYER ANALYTICS

David P. Hedlund

One of the areas where little work has been done to date (compared to traditional sports) is analyses and evaluations of esports player and team performance. In traditional sports, such as Major League Baseball (MLB), since at least the 1970s, members of the Society for American Baseball Research (SABR) and individuals such as Bill James have produced evidence indicating the importance of specific types of in-game results (e.g., getting on base in MLB) and their relationship with winning. Undoubtedly because of multiple factors such as the secrecy under which video games are developed, issues related to downloading or exporting data from inside the game to external sources, and the complexity of tools needed to properly analyze the data, only a limited number of organizations are currently undertaking this analytical and evaluative work. However, when limited competition exists, increasing numbers of groups are likely to attempt to carve out entrepreneurial opportunities in the area.

In an undated article published on Intel.co.uk, Wooden (n.d.) describes tools, such as Elgato and AVerMedia, that are used to record game play. These tools, along with traditional streaming and recording tools such as Twitch, YouTube Gaming, and Facebook Gaming (see chapter 10), can provide basic opportunities to watch and review one's own and others' game play. Additional gaming companies such as Shadow, Mobalytics, OP, GYO, Senpai, and Omnicoach have developed various tools such as artificial intelligence (AI) systems, application programming interfaces (API), neural networks, and data visualizations for players, teams, and other stakeholders. These tools help people understand more about areas such as player and team tendencies, effectiveness, efficiency, and performance. Moreover, nonprofit organizations, such as OpenAI, have created automated bots capable of playing esports games such as *Dota 2* at a high level. Yilmazcoban (2018) notes, "If the development of OpenAI's software is anything like that of chess computers like Deep Blue, it won't be long before it's capable of toppling world champions" (para. 4). Moving forward, more tools and services will be available for players, teams, and coaches to use when attempting to garner insights about their own and others' game play. Opportunities will be available for capable entrepreneurs to continue to develop new tools and services that can be used to enhance and improve players' and teams' skills and abilities.

geographic areas. In addition, recruiting esports players is being undertaken with younger players, similar to traditional sports. It is not uncommon for college esports coaches and recruiters for professional teams to scout high school-aged and younger-level players online and at tournaments.

Life Coaches

Game coaches have traditionally received the bulk of attention in both traditional sports and esports. Recently, life coaches and those involved indirectly with the preparation, training, and strengthening of players and teams have taken more prominent places in traditional sports and esports. The preparation can focus on the physical, mental, emotional, social, and spiritual well-being of athletes, and related personnel might include athletic trainers, fitness coaches, nutritionists, psychologists, and player and team development coaches. Due to the professionalization of the esports industry, esports agents are also becoming increasingly commonplace.

Life coaches and personnel focused on the overall health and well-being of the players and team(s) are generally not directly involved in the game, except in cases of injury (Hyun 2018). Some life coaches may not have extensive game knowledge, but their professional knowledge is indispensable for ensuring players' physical and mental health, maintaining a good team atmosphere, and helping to plan players' future development.

Athletic Trainers, Fitness Coaches, and Nutritionists

The first two most common types of life coaches, **athletic trainers** and **fitness coaches**, focus primarily on the physical aspects of players. Athletic trainers tend to focus more on dealing with players' injuries and rehabilitation from injuries while also assisting with strategies to prevent future injuries. Fitness coaches are frequently charged with helping players to enhance and improve their physical fitness, skills, and abilities through exercise and body-training activities. A related and increasingly essential staff member is a **nutritionist**. Beyond the stereotypes of the poor eating and beverage-drinking habits of video game players, traditional sports and esports organizations have recognized the importance of providing healthy food and beverage options for their players. In addition, similar to growth in traditional sports, educating players on proper types of food and drinks to consume in order to achieve maximum performance often requires expertise many players and coaches do not have. As professional esports leagues have been created and have modeled their operations after professional sports leagues, similar issues have arisen. As a result, the need for specialized training and care for esports players' health, well-being, and nutrition due to factors such as frequent travel and high-intensity competitions has increased the demand for athletic trainers and fitness coaches to be employed within esports organizations (Yip 2014).

Psychologists and Development Coaches

Another type of life coach important to overall wellness of players and the team is a **sport psychologist**. Personnel in the role of a sport psychologist use their knowledge and skills to optimize the performance and well-being of athletes; development of the social and competitive aspects of sports participation; and systemic issues associated with sports settings, organizations, and competitions (American Psychological Association n.d.). The high-intensity training and competition environment, critical media evaluations, and harsh public opinion faced by many esports athletes make the hiring of one or more sport psychologists necessary. A related occupation increasingly hired by esports organizations are player and team development coaches. Not only do esports players face criticism and challenges from the public and media, but problems can also arise within the organization and amongst members of the team. In these cases, professionals trained in the development and enhancement of team culture and positive working environments are also important areas for staffing considerations.

Agents

Finally, as noted in chapter 12, an increasing number of legal issues have arisen in esports for which agents and lawyers' expertise may be beneficial to players and teams. Some of these issues include contracts, the signing and trading of players, terminating player or coach contracts, media and public relations activities, retirement, and future career planning. Having professional

Zoning

ESPORTS COACHING IN CHINA

Sheng Qiang

In the past, China's so-called gold medal strategy, which focused on maximizing the number of medals won by heavily investing in men's and particularly women's sports programs, has been seen as an effective way to enhance the national image and pride. However, with the development of China's national power, and after celebrating China's success at the Beijing Summer Olympic Games in 2008, this strategy completed its historic mission. The vestiges of China's gold medal strategy, however, can still be seen in various aspects of its esports industry.

For example, in Chinese esports, players communicate the well-known statement that translates as "There is no runner-up in esports," especially in popular games native to China. After a game or competition is completed, the runner-up (if the champion is not a Chinese team) will not be encouraged and comforted; instead, they will be endlessly criticized, scolded, and mocked. The ultimate pursuit of winning—and only winning—has led to winning becoming almost the only criterion for evaluating an esports team and its coach in China. As noted by Ju-Chih "WarHorse" Chen, head coach of FunPlus Phoenix, *League of Legends* 2019 Season World Champions, the qualities and abilities that a successful coach needs are determined by his or her final result (Chen 2019).

Compared to traditional sports, where international players are frequently popular (e.g., Stephon Marbury), Chinese esports teams are composed of almost entirely domestic players. Even if a Chinese esports team composed of mostly foreign players has achieved high levels of success, it will not be celebrated by most domestic fans in the same way. Within Chinese esports, the labels of patriotism and nationalism as beliefs and motivations possessed by an all-Chinese team have irreplaceable value for Chinese fans. Even if the head coach prefers to use an international player over a domestic Chinese player, as long as the fans believe that the Chinese player has potential, the coach is likely to receive pressure from domestic fans to include the Chinese player on the game-time roster.

Another interesting phenomenon in Chinese esports is what happens after a Chinese player or team becomes a (world) champion. Based on the substantial economic benefits that may accompany becoming a champion and the continuing fan support inherent in this role, a negative outcome that sometimes occurs on the part of players is a lack of obedience and less willingness to take advice from one's coach. For example, highly successful players may only follow or listen to coaches who have extensive game knowledge, excellent experience as players, and similar levels of achievement (e.g., championships). As a result, during competitions, other players on the team may listen more to the highly successful players for advice instead of listening to the coach. Even if the skills and talents of the successful player are on the decline, due to their status, popularity, and prior achievements, other players on the team still may follow them and their instructions rather than those coming from their actual coach. Moreover, because fans often strongly idolize successful players, these fans are frequently willing to defend those successful players and reinforce any messages they may be conveying. As a result, managing the famous personalities that may compose a particular Chinese team can often be a daunting challenge. Tsung-Yu "Xiaogui" Huang, community leader of the Chinese Committee for the 2018 and 2019 *Overwatch* World Cup team, in reference to the challenges of coaching esports, noted that it may be one of the worst jobs (Huang 2019).

One positive aspect of coaching esports in China is the close relationship often developed between players and coaches. Because coaches tend to be older and more experienced than their players, and because players and coaches often live together in some type of team accommodations (e.g., gaming house), Chinese esports coaches often take a very active role in the development and mentorship of younger players. Frequently acting as a big brother or big sister figure, coaches teach younger players about many important things in their daily life (e.g., cooking, laundry), and these relationships can then be leveraged toward successful results while playing and competing in esports.

agents properly trained and educated about how to help prepare esports athletes for careers and life after the conclusion of their playing career is also an important area for staffing consideration, not to mention in the industry as a whole.

In summary, one of the most important characteristics for those working in esports coaching and player operations is knowledge of and experience with the games and competitions in which one would be asked to work. Due to the current and rapid expansion of the esports industry, more specialized and professional positions within esports organizations, especially those that manage multiple teams in different games and competitions, will become available.

COLLEGIATE ESPORTS ORGANIZATION, MANAGEMENT, AND OPERATIONS

In 2014, the first collegiate esports program was launched at Robert Morris University in Chicago, Illinois. As discussed earlier in this chapter, combining participation numbers from multiple collegiate esports organizing groups, it is safe to say more than 2,000 institutions of higher education currently have official or unofficial (e.g., student club) teams. Based on statistics published by *U.S. News and World Report*, during the 2017-18 school year, there were 4,298 degree-granting postsecondary institutions in the United States. (Moody 2019). As a result, it would be reasonable to conclude that at least half of all institutions of higher education currently have student-, faculty-, or staff-organized esports teams or programs.

When further examinations of a cross section of these institutions are conducted, the list includes both public and private colleges and universities, with athletic programs in National Collegiate Athletic Association (NCAA) Divisions I, II, and III, the National Association of Intercollegiate Athletics (NAIA), the National Junior College Athletic Association (NJCAA), and unaffiliated institutions. Given the variety of institutional profiles, it is not surprising to find that no standard operating procedure exists for staffing, coaching, and player operations. Rather, it seems collegiate esports programs exist on a continuum. On one end of the continuum are programs that are completely student managed, with little to no institutional support. On the other end are programs receiving full institutional backing, complete with staffing for program management and established positions for game-specific coaches and other support staff. Some institutions organize and manage esports programs within the student life division, while others have decided to house their activities in athletics departments in order to leverage existing support and experience. Based on the potential for academic study and future careers, other institutions have alternatively decided to organize and administer esports programs from within academic programs (e.g., computer science, sport management, video game studies) where experienced and passionate faculty can manage the operations and make connections with course work and related activities. Several organizations and conferences, including the National Association of Collegiate Esports (NACE), Collegiate StarLeague (CSL), Electronic Gaming Federation (EGF), and Tespa (formerly the Texas eSports Association) organize competitions for collegiate esports teams. As colleges and universities continue to grow and develop their esports programs, academic programs in esports and video gaming (e.g., Shenandoah University, Becker College, University of New Haven) can continue to enhance their curricular offerings and connect industry jobs and careers with opportunities in gaming within each respective institution.

Because every institution is unique, it is essential for schools and colleges to evaluate their own resources and facilities, staffing and coaching opportunities, and institutional goals as they continue to grow and develop their esports programs. While no one-size-fits-all model exists for an esports program at any educational institution, organizations may find themselves in at least five common situations. The following paragraphs identify and discuss five potential paradigms for collegiate esports staffing, coaching, and player operations. In addition, recommendations for practitioners that may be looking to support a program that may find itself in a similar situation, and recommended data collection to maintain your current level of support or perhaps advance to another level, are also provided. While the following information is focused on colleges and universities, similar situations at elementary, middle, and high schools may also exist. As a result, select information can be applied beyond the higher education setting.

1. *Paradigm 1*: The esports program is completely student managed, with little to no institutional support.
    - For many institutions, this is where they are when they first begin exploring and developing a formalized esports program. At this point, teams may be registered as student organizations or club sports, and students are most likely managing all components of their program on their own. These student-led activities include tryouts for the team, tournament participation, and finding coaches, most of whom are likely other students and volunteers.
    - *Recommendations for support at this level*: Given that student-managed organizations often are founded and exist organically, organizing support that allows for coaching and player operations can be as simple as ensuring student organizations have a clear understanding of how to receive resources from the institution. If the university's student activities or involvement office has an opportunity for groups to receive funding, a simple step would be to establish an esports and gaming liaison to answer questions and guide students as they develop their organization and create requests for funding.
    - *Recommended data collection*: In this paradigm, it is important to know the total number of students involved in esports and any related gaming organizations. Gathering this baseline data will provide valuable information about how many students are engaging in esports as a part of their institution's cocurricular experience.
2. *Paradigm 2*: The institution is actively exploring the creation of an esports program or is in early stages of development. In this example, the esports program may receive basic levels of institutional support, but it still relies heavily on students and staff who are doing esports-affiliated work in addition to their day-to-day responsibilities.
    - In this scenario, institutions often have already created a physical space in which esports and gaming occur, but they may not have added staffing resources yet to support these initiatives. Faculty and staff who may be contributing to esports initiatives at this stage are often not doing it as part of their usual job responsibilities. In addition, these faculty and staff instead may be involved because of the establishment of some type of working group within the university, an academic affiliation (e.g., computer science or sport management), a technical affiliation (e.g., information technology), or because of personal interest (i.e., they are gamers themselves). Student engagement at this level is often budding with excitement because they believe more institutional support will be coming in the near future.
    - This paradigm is often a tipping point for college esports programs. From a student engagement standpoint, students are anxious to see what the university will do next and how much support will be provided to the program. Realistically, students have likely seen, heard, or read about programs being established at other institutions, and they potentially believe the same may be coming to their university.
    - *Recommendations for support at this level*: If plans for additional resources such as staffing are not realistic in the immediate future, consider establishing formalized volunteer roles within the program. These positions can be for highly engaged students, eager young alumni, faculty, or staff. If it is possible to add volunteer roles for coaches for teams within the organization, consider connecting with the alumni relations (or similarly titled) office to connect with alumni who may have an interest in volunteering with the program.
    - *Recommended data collection*: While it is always essential to compile data on your program and gage student engagement, this juncture is especially critical in terms of identifying the amount and different types of resources (e.g., personal computers [PCs], consoles [e.g., Xbox, PlayStation, Switch], virtual reality [VR]

devices) that may be needed to facilitate student interest and engagement. If not already collected, create a plan to collect verifiable data about the total number of PC gamers and console gamers, number of teams that exist in which games, and number of competitive and recreational players.

3. *Paradigm 3*: The institution has some part-time staffing resources allocated to the esports program, and the student-managed components have a pipeline to communicate with university administration.
    - When official staffing first comes to an esports program, it often comes in one of two forms. The first type of staff member focuses on management of esports activities, including oversight of space management, student organization support, organizing teams, hosting events, and other related responsibilities. The second focuses on coaching, with a particular focus on overseeing students or a team competing in a particular game, recruitment for the team, and activities focused on helping the players improve and participate in competitions.
    - *Recommendations for support at this level*: When an institution first establishes staffing support for its esports program, it is critical to create expectations and responsibilities for those tasked with team and player operations. It is undoubtedly quite rare to get a single person who can do all of the previously listed tasks exceptionally well, especially when today more than 30 different types of esports games exist in numerous genres and are played on multiple platforms. As a result, it may be a better use of staff resources to focus on areas that may be priorities for the university. For example, if the institution and its students wish to first join and compete in competitions for a game such as *League of Legends*, then it may be more important to prioritize staffing for this team. When it comes to team and player operations, an opportunity exists to create program or organizational standards. For example, the creation of an Esports Code of Conduct for players and coaches can help to communicate rules and expectations and provide a basis for troubleshooting if problems arise in the future. The existence of these types of documents and information can also assist when student transitions occur (i.e., when students and leaders graduate and need to be replaced) and ensure that these processes and new leadership and activities are seamless and without issue. It is also important to seek information, feedback, and updates from various involved stakeholders on a regular basis, especially in the context of exit interviews when students graduate.
    - *Recommended data collection*: Nationwide, colleges and universities are focusing on recruitment and retention initiatives. For many institutions, they are creating esports programs in order to enhance these efforts. In this type of situation, key performance indicators and metrics can be collected (and centralized with an internal group such as institutional research), including retention rates of students involved with the esports program compared to those not involved, GPA of esports students compared with those not involved, and recruitment and admissions data on student interest in esports programs compared to those not involved.
4. *Paradigm 4*: The institution and its esports program have at least one full-time employee, and student-managed components are organized in concert with university-sanctioned activities and staff members.
    - After an esports program has been established and may even achieved some success and recognition, full-time staffing resources may be allocated to support the program. When more staff resources are allocated, students may begin to establish new teams for different games and seek out newly available resources to support expansion. In this situation, staff members may find themselves challenged

to equally support everyone, as students and new teams see resources being invested in one team and attempt to procure similar levels of institutional support. Growth is important in order to maintain student engagement. However, it is highly unlikely that a university esports program can support the establishment of an unlimited number of esports teams. Limits and requirements for the establishment of new teams may need to be put in place by the institution, but many opportunities exist for students to self-organize and compete in more recreational collegiate esports leagues (e.g., CSL, Tespa).

- *Recommendations for support at this level*: As students begin to self-organize new teams, colleges and universities have an opportunity to lead those conversations in order to properly align with a university's mission, goals, and objectives. Often when students self-organize new teams, they attempt to build those teams in line with their perception of what an ideal team looks like. When university administrators participate in these types of conversations with students, they can infuse the university's mission, goals, and objectives from the beginning and help shape expectations and conversations with the students involved, particularly when it relates to their expectations of management of the esports program.
- *Recommended data collection*: In this paradigm, it is important to have and understand comparative data about how many students and teams are served based on current staffing resources. This conversation is often difficult for students because questions are asked about what resources are needed to properly support a team that plays a particular game. Students often request every possible resource, and everyone wants all the teams to receive equitable distributions of resources. Despite these challenges, it is essential to ask these types of questions in order to continually evaluate resource and staffing needs.

5. *Paradigm 5*: In this situation, the esports program receives full institutional backing, complete with staffing for program management and established positions for game-specific coaches. Student-managed teams and activities appropriately integrate staffing support where necessary, and the staff and students undertake activities in tandem with the university's mission, goals, and objectives.

- For both program staff and students, this paradigm is the most desirable scenario. Students have the opportunity to connect directly with staff through a variety of outlets and contact points. Program staff, managers, and game-specific coaches allow for student engagement to thrive, which leads to stronger retention and recruitment efforts directly connected to the esports program.
- *Recommendations for support at this level*: The goal should be to enhance and expand student engagement. In lieu of focusing on creating additional staffing resources, it is an opportunity to instead focus on creating a model for alumni engagement, which may potentially lead to advancement support for years to come. In addition, while staff support may exist for the highest-level (e.g., varsity, intercollegiate) esports teams, an opportunity exists to engage active student leaders and young alumni in other parts of the program, such as team dynamics presentations and communication workshops.
- *Recommended data collection*: At this stage in the development of the esports program, it would be beneficial to create a strategic plan for the esports program and identify data and metrics that can be used to measure and support any initiatives. For example, it is incumbent on universities to prepare students for jobs and careers. While a select few high-level student gamers may be able to use collegiate esports as a platform for reaching the professional ranks of esports players, a multitude of jobs are also available in the industry as a whole. In all likelihood,

the most successful collegiate esports programs should have some students hired for jobs or careers in the esports industry. As a result, data on how students and alumni are utilizing the knowledge and experience gained in the program in their future jobs and careers will be essential as esports programs continue to gain popularity and seek out added resources and opportunities.

As esports in higher education continues to develop, it is essential to continuously evaluate program opportunities and resources such as staffing and team and player operations, not to mention how they may change in the future. While many institutions across the country are experiencing an enrollment and budget crisis, esports and gaming are an emerging trend that may be able to mitigate some of these challenges. However, the programs created to serve students and create additional opportunities for engagement need attention in order to thrive on campus. While additional staffing resources may not always be possible, the five paradigms described in this section can be used to support emerging and established programs at various levels of development.

HEALTH AND WELLNESS CONSIDERATIONS IN GAMING AND ESPORTS

Health and wellness is now a commonly discussed topic in the gaming and esports industry; its impact on both player and team performance is seen as a key ingredient to success. As professional gaming organizations are receiving hundreds of millions of dollars in investments, and the salaries and prize earnings for the players are increasing, the stakes have never been higher. This situation has brought about a shift in how organizations and the players themselves are addressing health and wellness.

When thinking about health and wellness and how it affects performance, a good starting point is understanding the specific demands placed on esports players. A study done by Smith, Birch, and Bright (2019) examined the psychological challenges encountered by elite esports professionals when competing in major contests. They found esports players faced 51 different stress factors, including communication problems and concerns with competing in front of live audiences. Perhaps

Zoning

NEW TECHNOLOGY AND TOOLS IN THE ESPORTS INDUSTRY

Raffaele Lauretta

Due to the rapid growth and constant evolution of esports, virtually limitless potential exists in new tools and technology that can be used to gain unique insights. For instance, consider how traditional and esports athletes currently eat, train, and recover. The methodologies used today are clearly different from how things were done even 10 years ago. Every day, technology is improving, and athletes, teams, and organizations are taking notice. No longer are the days where every athlete, no matter what age, sport, or level they play at, train and eat the same way. Customization in athlete nutrition is propelling the world of sports into the next generation, and esports is no different. As an entrepreneur, I have seen the growth in both sports and esports. Athletes and gamers alike are using every advantage they can get their hands on in order to get even the smallest edge over their competition, and it starts with doing something different than the rest of the pack.

Athletic Genetix, a sports and health genetics company, uses a simple cheek swab and subsequent DNA analysis to create customized blueprints for athletes, with specific guidance for nutrition, training, and recovery. Esports gamers need to be focused, attentive, fast thinkers, have quick hand-eye coordination; above all, they must be in good health. By knowing exactly what foods they should be eating due to possible vitamin deficiencies (e.g., B12), and what foods they should be avoiding due to sensitivities (e.g., gluten and lactose), every gamer can gain an extra advantage. The new age of traditional and esports athlete health, with customized dietary, supplement, and exercise recommendations, has already begun—with guidance based on one's own DNA.

not surprisingly, these stress factors mirrored the mental conditions experienced by professional athletes in traditional sports such as soccer and rugby. The authors also found that gamers are exposed to substantial stress when they compete in top-flight contests. Isolating these stressors can help players develop effective coping strategies for these stressors and optimize performance while playing at the highest level.

The drive to achieve one's personal best along with the inherently competitive nature of the industry comes with costs to players' health and wellness. This result is evident not only in the professional ranks but also at the semiprofessional and collegiate levels. A study by DiFrancisco-Donoghue and colleagues (2019) examined 65 college esports players, showing that the average esports player practices between 5.5 and 10 hours a day prior to competitions. In addition, 15 percent reported three hours or more of sitting and playing without standing to take a break, and 40 percent of the players reported that they do not participate in any kind of physical activity. The largest complaint reported was eye fatigue, followed by back and neck pain, and later followed by wrist and hand pain. The injuries seen in esports athletes are similar to injuries seen in sedentary office personnel. Of the athletes surveyed who suffered from an ailment, only 2 percent sought medical attention (DiFrancisco-Donoghue et al. 2019).

These research studies begin to highlight some key areas to explore that will lend themselves to the broader scope of how to address health and wellness of players. Another area gaining more attention is the mental health and burnout of esports players (Radcliffe 2019). To date, scant research has examined these issues. A further area of need for exploration and research is the potential for esports and gaming to be addictive (Hattenstone 2017).

The current situation presents an opportunity to have an impact on an emerging sport and industry by taking what people know about traditional sports and adapting that knowledge to esports. New areas of research will need to be conducted to continue to explore what is actually happening for esports athletes. It is blending science and esports and creating a new field of esports science and research. Researchers must keep in mind that first and foremost, models of performance should be player centric, meaning that strategies and tactics should be developed based on an individual's needs. In addition, a responsibility exists to promote positive values and offer the tools and resources to allow each individual to become their best version of themselves. A holistic approach to training is needed—one that encompasses key areas such as a balanced lifestyle, psychology, nutrition, movement, and recovery. This balance not only can have an immediate impact but will also be crucial to long-term development and success.

The future of health and wellness and its impact on performance in gaming and esports has never been more exciting and open for discovery. Those who choose to pursue a career along the lines of esports performance and esports science will have the opportunity to have a positive impact on the foundational wellness of an emerging sport and generation. Challenging questions face the esports and video game industry, but further investments in research will help shed light on some of the most important health and wellness issues for players, teams, and organizations.

CONCLUSION

This chapter examined information about the management and coaching of esports teams and players. It described specific information about esports coaching and various roles and responsibilities. In addition, the chapter examined important related topics such as the organization and multiple potential paradigms underpinning how esports organizations may operate. Finally, the chapter provided specialized information about important topics such as esports analytics, the health and wellness of esports athletes, new technology such as the use of DNA testing, and advice from a former professional gamer.

Today, many different types of people play esports. As a result of the investments in sport-focused esports (e.g., *FIFA*, *Pro Evolution Soccer*, *NBA 2K*, *Madden*) and the large number of professional athletes that play or invest in esports, strong connections will continue to exist between traditional sports and esports. Therefore, people who work in traditional sports will undoubtedly continue to accept similar positions within esports organizations. The result will likely be that the jobs and roles of employees within traditional sports and esports will, in many cases, become the

Zoning

RESEARCH INSIGHTS ON THE HEALTH, WELLNESS, AND HABITS OF INTERNATIONAL GAMERS

David P. Hedlund, Hallie Zwibel, Joanne Donoghue, and Raffaele Lauretta

In recent years, whether due to stereotypes, politics, media, or purposeful interest, the issue of the health and wellness of esports athletes and video game players has been thrust into the spotlight. With the proliferation of personal computers, consoles, mobile phones, tablets, and handheld devices all providing platforms on which users can play esports and video games, negatively perceived consumption habits with these devices have raised concerns on the part of numerous stakeholders. Console systems such as the Nintendo Wii, Microsoft Xbox Kinect, and Sony PlayStation Move all involve active movement, termed *exergaming* (*exercise* + *gaming*). These systems are generally considered a separate category of video games, and they have not received the same level of attention or concern as PCs, consoles, and mobile gaming.

As of December 2019, an Internet search revealed more than 22 million results on the topic. A review of the top results indicates two general metatopics. The first metatopic includes concerns expressed about if and how playing sedentary (not exergaming) video games and esports can be good for the health and well-being of players. The second metatopic includes information about strategies and tactics that wellness programs, coaches, players, and other professionals can use to counterbalance some of the negative effects and concerns raised by gaming for long periods of time.

All of these discussions and activities related to potential health and wellness issues and solutions are extremely valuable. However, one challenge facing all of these undertakings is the fact surprisingly little information exists and little organized research has been completed on video games and esports. Moreover, specific challenges also include the many different types of players. Casual players might play a few minutes a day on a mobile device, more competitive players frequently play in local or online competitions, and professional players play for long periods of time nearly every day. Without at least a basic understanding of the health and wellness habits of different types of players, it would be challenging to understand how to go about undertaking specialized research.

As a result of this lack of basic information and research on esports and video game players, academics and practitioners undertook a research collaboration. Collaborators from St. John's University, New York Institute of Technology, and corporate partner Athletic Genetix researched the health, wellness, and habits of a cross section of domestic and international gamers. Here are some of the key findings uncovered during an analysis of the data.

In terms of the demographics of the sample, a total of 1,326 esports and video game players completed an online survey that took on average 20 minutes to complete. The gender composition was 39.2 percent female and 60.5 percent male, and 0.3 percent preferred not to respond. The average age of respondents was 31.68 years old (standard deviation = 8.8 years), and the self-reported age range included those from 18 to 87 years old. In total, 88.3 percent of respondents were between the ages of 18 and 40 years old. The sample included U.S.-based (84.4%) and international (15.6%) respondents. U.S.-based respondents hailed from 48 of 50 states, plus Washington, DC, Puerto Rico, and Guam.

Respondents were asked a number of questions about topics such as how much they play and watch esports; how much sleep they get, when they wake up, and when they go to bed; what types of foods they eat and drink before, during, and after they play; what types of vitamins and other supplements they regularly take; and more. Following are some of the most interesting findings from this research.

- On average, more than 43 percent play esports at least three or more hours per day, 56 percent play esports 1 or 2 times per day, and 29 percent play 3 or 4 times per day.
- On average, more than 48 percent watch esports content on Twitch, YouTube, and other locations 1 to 3 hours per day.

In terms of supplements, drinks, and sleep habits,

- 48 percent take vitamins at least a few times per week.
- 45 percent drink energy drinks at least once per week, and 48 percent drink caffeinated drinks every day.
- Sleep: 38 percent are sleeping less than the recommended 7 hours per night.

Before starting to play esports on an average day,

- 30 percent consume processed and snack foods (e.g., popcorn, chips, pretzels), and 20 percent eat fast food.
- 36 percent drink coffee, 32 percent drink soda, and 24 percent drink energy drinks.

While playing esports on an average day,

- 18 percent consume sugar, candy, chocolate, and the like; and 34 percent eat processed or snack foods (e.g., popcorn, chips, pretzels).
- 30 percent drink coffee, 31 percent drink soda, and 23 percent drink energy drinks.

After playing esports on an average day,

- 25 percent have carbohydrate-loaded foods (e.g., bread, pasta), 20 percent eat processed or snack foods (e.g., popcorn, chips, pretzels), and 16 percent eat fast food.
- 24 percent drink coffee, 26 percent drink soda, and 18 percent have energy drinks.

In terms of some aspects of their overall health and wellness,

- 89 percent of gamers surveyed do not feel they have the best eating habits.
- 86 percent of gamers surveyed do not feel they have the best drinking habits.
- 20 percent smoke cigarettes.
- 40 percent of gamers exercise 0 to 2 times per week.
- 67 percent of gamers do yoga 0 to 1 time per week.
- 65 percent of gamers meditate 0 to 1 time per week.
- 34 percent of gamers believe that something in their DNA helps them play esports better than others.

Overall, these results provide some valuable information about the health and wellness attitudes and habits of U.S.-based and international gamers. For example, areas such as exercise, nutrition (e.g., what players are eating and drinking before, during, and after they play), caffeine consumption, and how much sleep they are getting all suggest that these areas have significant margins for improvement. However, without comparative data for nongamers, it is not known if these results are specific to gamers or more widely systemic in the larger population. By sharing these results, industry professionals, researchers, and academics may become motivated to undertake more collaborative and interdisciplinary research. When results are found, it would be beneficial to try to publish them in the public domain where everyone can read and review them.

same. Preparing for careers in the esports industry has never been more important. Because of the strong connection between organized traditional sports and esports, numerous opportunities exist for careers on the business side of esports. The next chapter explores more careers and opportunities in the industry.

DISCUSSION QUESTIONS

1. What are the roles and responsibilities of different types of esports coaches and staff?
2. What are some of the top esports teams and franchises? What are some of the reasons for their success?
3. What are the unique aspects of coaching and managing esports?
4. What are the five paradigms of collegiate esports?
5. What can you conclude about the current status and future opportunities in esports?

14

Esports Careers

Roger M. Caramanica | Lisa Cosmas Hanson | Taylor Johnson
Moira McArdle | Michael Newhouse-Bailey

INTRODUCTION

Throughout the preceding chapters, various aspects of esports, its ecosystem, and the industry as a whole have been examined. This chapter focuses on providing information about esports jobs and careers. This growing field offers a number of career paths for people with varying skills, in both traditional roles such as marketing and totally new roles generated by the unique needs of this sector.

OBJECTIVES

- Identify careers in the esports and gaming industry.
- Define specific esports job descriptions.
- Summarize examples of career opportunities in the esports and gaming industry.

ESPORTS JOB DESCRIPTIONS AND RÉSUMÉS

A good place to start any discussion of careers and employment is job descriptions and résumés. A **job description** is a written description of the tasks, activities, and outcomes expected for a given role (Brierley 2018a). A job description offers clarity for both the employee and the employer. For an employee, a job description offers a clear view of what they are expected to do while working for the organization. For the employer, the job description offers assurance that expectations have been clearly communicated to the employee and that everyone is on the same page regarding work to be performed. A job description acts as a foundation on which many other aspects within the talent management systems are based. For example, goal setting and performance reviews hinge upon all stakeholders understanding the job description from the beginning.

In practice, creating an esports job description is not materially different than the process that a human resources (HR) professional would follow for any other role within an organization. However, the rapid change of the industry, newness of many roles, and uncertainty in the marketplace require a thorough job analysis. A **job analysis** is the act of studying a role to fully understand the responsibilities, activities, and behaviors required to perform the work expected. This process should help those responsible for hiring to understand and describe the qualifications that will make a candidate well suited for the role. When crafting a job description, it is also important to consider how the organizational structure and competitive landscape of esports influence the required roles, responsibilities, and goals to be executed in the job (Morgeson and Dierdorff 2011). For example, if a college or university is hiring an esports coach, should the coach also be designated as the recruiter? Should they travel to recruit? Do they have the ability to award scholarships? As the competitive landscape of esports changes, so too could the responsibilities and goals of an esports coach change.

Job descriptions should be reviewed often and revised as an organization grows and evolves. Leaving job descriptions unchanged as an organization changes opens the door for communication breakdowns and potential legal risk. According to Cam Brierley of Hitmarker (one of the global leaders in helping organizations hire esports professionals), job functions in a job description should be tied to the purpose of the organization. Hiring professionals should explain to applicants what the organization is about in as much detail as possible, describe the corporate culture and perception of employee roles, and identify potential for career advancement. Vague descriptions such as "We are a new esports organization" does not tell a candidate much about what your organization stands for (Brierley 2019).

A **résumé** is a document that summarizes an individual's knowledge, skills, and qualifications. It can be especially challenging to build a résumé for a job in the esports industry, because many candidates don't have direct experience in this new field. Therefore, candidates have to not only highlight their specific qualifications but also show how knowledge and experience they might have acquired in other fields can translate into the esports industry. For example, if a candidate has experience marketing a sports team, those skills translate very well into marketing for an esports team. Also, if a candidate has experience with accounting, those skills can translate very well to help an esports business with their financials.

Additionally, time spent volunteering in esports can add value to a résumé. Moderating a Twitch channel, volunteering at an esports event, or working in the industry in any voluntary capacity shows passion and interest in the industry and time spent gaining relevant knowledge.

Finally, for a traditional job, outlining one's time spent playing video games would not likely be information to include on a résumé. However, in the esports industry, detailing one's gaming background can be extremely beneficial, especially if it is for a coaching position, product development position, or broadcasting position, since those positions require acute knowledge of the game, tactics, and strategies. Showcasing time spent in game play can show passion for the sport, an understanding of game dynamics, and an interest in the industry as a whole (Brierley 2018b). However, most businesses are not looking for fans of a game to fill a position, they are instead looking to increase revenue or decrease expenses (or both) from a position. As a result, the candidate's résumé should explain how their skills would be an asset to the company.

CAREERS IN ESPORTS

The esports ecosystem has influenced other industries and has been influenced by them as well. The result is an ecosystem with a complex web of interrelated organizations, activities, and stakeholders with a myriad of goals and objectives. With such diversity, it is challenging to effectively describe employment and career opportunities. Within the industry, both esports-specific (unique) and more traditional types of jobs are available. Even some of the traditional jobs are industry specific and existed before the growth and development in the esports industry, but now they require a new knowledge and understanding. Both unique and traditional roles pose opportunities and challenges that personnel interested in the field must understand. The following sections review some careers in the esports and general gaming industry. Sample areas with employment opportunities include the following (Hitmarker 2020):

- Administration
- Art
- Business development
- Coaching
- Community management
- Customer service
- Data science
- Engineering (hardware/software)
- Event management
- Finance
- Hospitality
- Human resources
- Information technology (IT)
- Legal
- Logistics
- Marketing
- Operations
- Photography
- Product management
- Production
- Project management
- Public relations
- Recruiting
- Research
- Sales
- Sponsorship
- Talent management
- Translation
- Videography

In early 2020, Hitmarker published their 2019 Esports Jobs Report, which detailed and compared jobs listed on their website in the 2018 and 2019 calendar years. For example, available esports jobs on the website grew over 87 percent, from 5,896 in 2018 to 11,027 in 2019 (Hitmarker 2020). As shown in figure 14.1, software engineering (1,940 jobs), marketing (1,507 jobs), design (812 jobs), operations (808 jobs), and sales (758 jobs) were the top five largest employment sectors in 2019. In terms of percentage increase in the total number of jobs available from 2018 to 2019, the five largest sectors were data (605.62% growth), project management (531.07% growth), education (436.36% growth), art (375.27% growth), and engineering (358.97% growth).

Traditional Jobs in Esports

With the esports industry gaining momentum during the past two decades, existing talent from other industries have pivoted toward this growing field to fill employment needs. This shift offers an opportunity for career paths that are not often seen in the employment environment. For example, in the 1990s and early 2000s, the creation of the Internet fueled new industries to emerge and new areas of employment were created. Currently, similar types of changes are occurring due to growth in the esports and video gaming industry. Therefore, the need for people who can fill traditional roles (e.g., marketing, finance, sales, product management, service) in the esports industry is increasing. Outside of esports, these jobs are somewhat similar across various employment sectors, in that core responsibilities and skills are required. However, the jobs can vary a great deal according to the organization's product, clients, rules and regulations, and competitive marketplace. For example, most marketing jobs require strong communication skills no matter what type of company one is working for, but a copywriter for a book publisher would need some different strengths and experience as compared to a social media manager for a tech startup.

Unique Jobs in Esports

In the esports and gaming industry, roles have emerged that are unique and not found in other industries. As outlined in chapter 1, the esports industry can trace its history at least back to the 1970s. However, the current rapid growth of competitive play, and interrelated roles and responsibilities of talent required to serve the

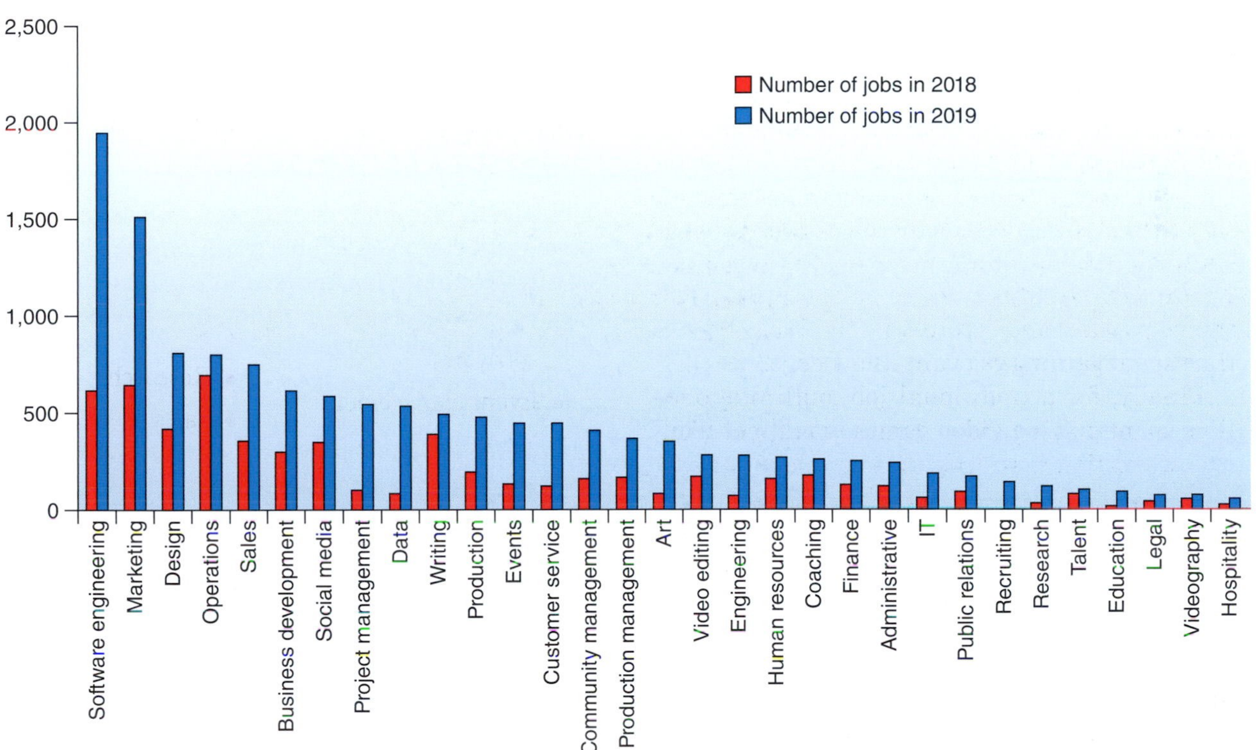

Figure 14.1 Job growth in esports in 2018 and 2019.
Data from Hitmarker (2020).

market, have resulted in a need for a shared understanding of key roles. These roles are often central to competitive play or game design. For example, professional players can vary widely in required knowledge, skills, and abilities regarding the specific game on which they are focused. Knowledge will be game specific, and skills will be honed to master the game dynamics, design of play, and intrinsic ability for hand–eye coordination and elite fast-twitch motor movement. Players' abilities will often be a deep understanding of the logic and interplay of maps, characters, special abilities, and other game play characteristics that give them a competitive edge. Much like pitchers in baseball and softball, or goalkeepers in soccer (football), esports has similar types of "positions" that professional esports athletes with specialized skills and abilities will continue to fill. For example, the game *League of Legends* is usually played with a two-team, 5v5 player competition setup. In this setup, there are five types of positions (Attack Damage Carry [ADC], Top Laner, Mid Laner, Jungler, Support), depending on one's role and location in the game. With over 140 champions available in *League of Legends*, each one with different skills and abilities, players choosing to use different champions and playing different positions requires specialized knowledge, skills, and training in order to be successful. As a result, many esports players specialize in certain types of positions and roles within the game. The same holds true for a coach. Although specific universal talent requirements exist for successful coaches, successful esports coaches will need unique attributes based on the context of the game played.

CAREERS IN COMPETITION

As discussed throughout this book, people seeking a career in competitive video gaming can pursue a wide variety of avenues. Each avenue has its own rules and regulations that should be researched by anyone hoping to begin a career as a competitor. Most professional players are part of either a gaming organization or a local team. The influx of private investment dollars and the growth of gaming arenas has greatly increased the number of career options associated with esports competitions.

Esports Gaming Organizations

Some people find careers in esports organizations or gaming clans. A **gaming clan** is a group of people who play one or more multiplayer games. Team Liquid is one of the larger gaming organizations, and it commanded over $7 million in prize winnings in 2018 with success in *Dota 2*, *Fortnite*, and *League of Legends* (Hayward 2019). With large gaming organizations, players do not need to occupy the same physical space in order to compete together. Moreover, while it is easy to form a small game-specific clan, joining a well-established esports organization is difficult and typically reserved for elite players. One path to an elite organization is to form a small clan and have success in various tournaments. Similar to traditional sports, after players are able to showcase their specific abilities in specific games, they may earn the opportunity to sign with a larger organization.

Beyond competing, other career options are associated with competition, including project management, content creation, broadcasting, sales, and digital marketing. As will be discussed later in this chapter, the esports organization 100 Thieves grew revenue streams by expanding beyond competition and focusing on gaming culture through a highly successful line of apparel (Webster 2019).

Esports Franchises

Significant growth has occurred in local esports teams that closely resemble traditional sport franchises. **Esports franchises** are teams that are located within a city or region and have earned the right (often through the paying of a fee) to compete in a specific esports game. The National Basketball Association's (NBA) NBA 2K League, Major League Soccer's (MLS) eMLS league, and the *Overwatch* League are all examples of esports franchise leagues.

The NBA 2K League launched in 2018. During that season, 17 of the league's 30 teams competed. Players were signed to six-month contracts with a base salary of $32,000 to $35,000 (NBA 2K League 2018a). An additional prize pool of $1 million was available through various contests throughout the season. Players also received housing costs, medical benefits, and were part of the NBA retirement plan (NBA 2K League 2018b). The NBA 2K League holds an open combine to gather data on people who meet the requirements for the *NBA 2K* draft. Following the combine, players' data is provided to the teams and a professional-style draft is held. Players in the NBA 2K League compete in 5v5 matches with members of the team individually controlling all players.

The inaugural season of eMLS debuted in 2018 with 19 of 23 MLS teams competing (Soper 2018). Each eMLS team had one player who represented the team in all eMLS competitions. Teams were able to select their representatives through tryout methods of their own choosing, but typically, teams hosted qualifying tournaments in order to identify the best players. Doolsta won the 2019 eMLS Cup including the $25,000 prize (Rosano 2019).

The *Overwatch* League made its debut in 2018 and peaked with over 360,000 viewers on Twitch for its inaugural matches (Lumb 2018). The league debuted with 12 teams located throughout the world. Players are provided housing and other benefits, including a $50,000 minimum salary for the first year. The *Overwatch* League features a tournament series called *Overwatch* Contenders for professional players to elevate their status in the hopes of being signed by an *Overwatch* League team.

The growth of esports franchise leagues has led to the creation of dedicated gaming arenas and other facilities to host watch parties and other events. Careers associated with gaming facilities include event manager, community outreach specialist, technology specialist, livestream coordinator, marketer, and sales associate.

Competitive Events

With the rise of esports franchises, cities have started investing in dedicated esports facilities to host competitions, leading in turn to an increased need for people who can manage complicated events in a specialized field. People who work in this field need to be able to demonstrate the ability to create a memorable customer experience from conception through planning, design, and execution. The skills that will benefit those who work in esports event management include project management, attention to detail, communication skills, and the ability to manage event staff. Careers in this area include customer service specialist, IT specialist, event coordinator, event manager, and sales.

CAREERS IN STREAMING AND CONTENT CREATION

Various platforms are available to stream either competitive or casual game play. Hundreds of millions of people globally log in to one of the various platform offerings to watch their favorite streamer play games, chat with the viewers, and generally connect. With game play livestreaming viewership rivaling view and revenue volumes of industry names such as HBO, Netflix, and Hulu, the landscape for game streaming platforms is hypercompetitive both among streaming platforms and between livestreaming and traditional prerecorded content providers (Wylde 2017). Streaming would appear to be a natural career path for competitive esports athletes. Competitive players are already in the spotlight and have created a following and fan base. Their elite game play talents also create an enticement for viewership. However, the path to becoming a streamer does not require a person to have played esports competitively. Rather, just about anyone with a microphone, a camera, Internet service, and a way to stream their video games can start streaming. The barrier to entry is low, but it is difficult to translate this activity into a viable career. To be a successful streamer, skills such as the ability to effectively communicate while also being entertaining are important, not to mention also having expertise in game strategies and tactics. Related production, broadcasting, and journalism skills would also be advantageous for streamers.

Self-Employed Streaming

With recent growth and revenue opportunities in esports has also come an opportunity for self-employment. **Self-employment** is the act of working for oneself as a freelancer or owner of one's own business and using an entrepreneurial mindset to drive one's career opportunities. Much like other creative fields such as acting or singing, finding immediate success within the field is challenging. Full-time game play streaming is at its core a complex mixture of talent at playing video games and being able to entertain the audience.

According to industry professionals, some challenges to establishing a full-time career in streaming are market saturation while the industry is in a viewership growth period, long work hours (streamers spending far more time on air than a traditional eight-hour workday), and financial uncertainty as streamers rely on subscriptions, donations, and brand partnerships or advertising for revenue, which can fluctuate wildly.

However, the field can be very rewarding for those with an entrepreneurial mindset, the flexibility and patience to adapt to the ever-changing environment, emotional intelligence, understanding of how to entertain others, and most importantly open-mindedness to interact with the varied audience of viewers. The career offers people the freedom to set their own schedule, make up the rules of their performance, and interact and connect with their audience in a way that resonates with their specific talents and style. Financially speaking, the so-called "streamer wars" that are currently in progress are driving competing platforms to support their streamer population. This competition is resulting in unprecedented dedicated contracts for some of the top streamers, better features and functions to generate revenue, and a push to offer stability to the industry.

Streaming for Esports Teams and Gaming Lifestyle Companies

Esports teams and gaming lifestyle companies can offer a different model of employment for people who are looking to compete and stream or make the switch from esports competitive play to full-time streaming. The transition from esports athlete to streamer is a natural fit for many. However, the landscape for streaming as a member of an esports team or a gaming lifestyle company is more complicated than the pure entrepreneur model discussed previously.

Competitive esports organizations can take various forms depending on the game being played and the organization itself. When considering the game *Overwatch* and the culture developed by its users, it is an example of a game with a very firm competitive code of conduct and a prescriptive design for their streaming (Holt 2019). The *Overwatch* League now has local franchise teams located in 20 cities around the world. These 20 franchises each offer support structures to play at a premier level. The franchises also offer career opportunities in the esports field and a unique cross-pollination for other opportunities. The Boston Uprising Careers page offers links to The Kraft Group's 14 other holdings, creating opportunities for career movement and development beyond esports competitive game play and the support structures within the entire organization (The Kraft Group 2019).

For example, the esports franchise 100 Thieves uses a mixed business model to generate revenue. They are part esports competitors, part marketing agency, and part content creators and streamers, but at their core they are entrenched in the gaming culture and lifestyle. With esports teams competing in *League of Legends*, *Counter-Strike: Global Offensive* (*CS:GO*), and *Fortnite*, and dedicated creators such as founder Matt "Nadeshot" Haag and Twitch turned YouTube sensation Jack "CouRageJD" Dunlop, contracted members of 100 Thieves spend their time working on their individual goals and working toward the collaborative efforts of the 100 Thieves brand and contractual obligations. This model brings some level of structure and security to an individual's career within the esports and gaming space, and the 100 Thieves franchise offers collaborations, brand deals, and support structures. For example, in 2019, 100 Thieves raised $35 million to build a 15,000-square-foot (1,393.55 m^2) training facility in Los Angeles (Perez 2019). As interest in gaming continues to grow and the competitive landscape thrives, potential exists for more organizations of this design to enter the market or pivot to the mixed model with possible continued career openings.

Content Creation

Content creation is often executed hand-in-hand with streaming. In fact, the terms *content creator* and *streamer* are often used interchangeably, but they do differ. Creators can memorialize their streams through editing and postproduction activities to create consumable content for additional platforms. Content hosting services such as YouTube and TikTok are ways for esports athletes to further monetize their knowledge, skills, and abilities. Much like with entrepreneurial streaming, content creation can be a challenging field to make a full-time career out of; it is a creative field, and as such, success can be fickle. New entrants into this space should first learn the skills it takes to become a strong editor, writer, and producer. These technical skills are a must for producing high-quality content. It is best to choose interesting content. If they are enjoying themselves or are passionate about the topic or content, it will show through the resulting production. Finally, understanding how to market and advertise yourself is key to becoming a successful content creator (The eSports Writer 2016).

CAREERS IN EVENT PRODUCTION

Although millions of people love to watch streaming, a large appetite also exists for the experience of attending live esports events. Live events for esports competitions have a high level of technical complexity to produce both at the physical location, often posing technical capability hurdles for traditional event venues, and for the demand to concurrently stream the event for viewers on the Internet. These events also pose unique broadcasting challenges. Unlike a traditional sport event such as a gridiron football game, where everyone can see the field, esports game play must be viewed by broadcasters through customized technology in order to see each player's perspective on the game (Foster 2019). For example, in a 5v5 game, it would mean 10 separate viewpoints could be seen at the same time. In addition, duration for esports events can be quite lengthy, often spanning several days. This uncertainty can pose challenges for organizers in every aspect of the field to keep viewers engaged. Esports are using a wide array of viewing options to broadcast competitions. As the industry converges and consolidates, organizations seek to streamline the viewing experience, such as with a top–down view from above (often called a God's-eye view), or switching between different players' perspectives depending on which one might be engaged in the most important action at a particular moment in time. One thing remains clear: The human capital required to execute a live event has created career opportunities in this space that are only expected to grow in the next decade. Some skills that would be advantageous for those working in event management and production include being organized, detail-oriented, and hardworking. Having a background in organizing activities and events while also bringing an ability to conceptualize and create lists of everything needed to accomplish tasks would also be beneficial. Jobs in this area span the gamut from managing and overseeing events or the run of show, to building and operating different areas or activities at events, to being the one to produce the event.

Zoning

INDUSTRY PROFILE: ROB GONZALES

Roger M. Caramanica

Rob Gonzales is an on-air personality, a content producer for Team Liquid, Twitch, and YouTube, and a host of the HyperX Esports Truck. A veteran in the industry, Rob has spent time in all aspects of the field, but his passion remains within the broadcasting arena. Broadcasters are core in keeping viewers engaged and carrying the product that they are presenting. Broadcasters also bring intrinsic value, leveraging their own span of influence (social media followers) to the event viewership. It starts with a passion for the content. When that passion is combined with education in the space as well as industry experience, a career in the field of esports broadcasting can be lasting and rewarding. Those with an interest in the field must above all else exhibit flexibility. Today, esports broadcasting is somewhat bifurcated from traditional sports broadcasting, but they have begun to converge and it is becoming far more mainstream. Therefore, broadcasters can find themselves in a spectrum of operational situations, including in front of a one-person camera production with limited support staff all the way to a full-scale studio operation with staff in every aspect of the production (Gonzales 2019).

CAREERS IN PLANNING AND CONTROL

Planning and controlling is the act of ensuring that all aspects of an event execute seamlessly. Planning and controlling an event can be the responsibility of a range of stakeholder personas depending on the goals, design, and overall business situation of the event. Some events consist of competitive league play as is the case with *Overwatch* League or *Call of Duty* League, while others are offshoots of a convention offering a competitive space for play such as events at TwitchCon. Still others are driven by brand as a way to create cross-promotional advertisement in the form of a competition tied to a brand sponsor. Planning and controlling an event for hundreds or thousands of people live and thousands to millions of online viewers over the course of a day or multiple days is a complex and daunting challenge (Hayward 2018). The human capital it takes to plan, control, and produce live events spans a vast spectrum of career avenues. Opportunities are available behind the camera in the technical production field; in project management, where staff work to ensure the goals for the event are achieved; for event planners who work out all the details and logistics for the event; for partnership managers who are responsible for working with all sponsors and partners to ensure all plans are properly executed; and for community and social media managers who work before, during, and after the event to advertise, promote, and evaluate important aspects of the event.

CAREERS IN ESPORTS MARKETING

The fundamental activities that link consumers to the content they want—and when, where, and how they want to engage with it—are critical components of esports marketing. Today's successful brands and influencers need to create a welcoming sense of belonging for their fans and prospects, and nowhere is that truer than in the gaming community (Bramble 2019).

Trends across any audience or channel acknowledge that the power of marketing is now in the hands of the consumer, and smart businesses are continually revising their strategies to capture the hearts and minds of their audience. As an emerging segment, esports presents significant opportunity for sales and marketing careers. With hundreds of positions posted monthly on sites such as Hitmarker, marketing jobs were a close second to software engineers as the top roles companies were looking to fill at the end of 2019 (Porter 2019). As esports events and competitors expand, affiliated brands, agencies, and experiential marketing groups will also grow as more businesses, brands, and individuals look to get in on the action.

The Future of Marketing in Esports

With opportunities and interest snowballing, marketing roles are rolling right along with the sport itself. At its core the work is digital, requiring technically savvy, adaptable, risk-taking, consumer-focused thinkers and executors, and success frequently builds on the marketers' own interest in gaming. A leading esports media company, United Esports, is led by experienced digital marketers; brand, PR, and entertainment industry creatives; and committed gamers who have applied their experiences to this targeted niche. Marketers who are hungry to grow in an emerging market can have as much opportunity as traditional sports marketers and committed fans and players to make an impact in esports. OverActive Media Group, owner of teams across three of the largest franchised leagues, combines talent from traditional professional on-field sports and the Olympic Games with early founders of esports teams (OverActive Media 2019). Esports marketing reflects the digital, mobile, influencer, event, social, and user-driven trends that dominate consumer marketing today. Roles today and the future for marketers include positions with franchise owners, agencies, influencers, event producers, and traditional brands that want to play in the esports field. As the industry grows, so too will additional opportunities for jobs and careers.

Roles and Opportunities for Esports Marketers

As discussed in chapter 6, many functions in esports marketing complement the brand, digital, and event marketing responsibilities of more traditional consumer markets, while others are more unique to the niche. Following is a review of current functions that are common in the industry.

Influencer and Celebrity Marketing

According to Business Insider Intelligence/Mediakix data, the advance of social media has spawned an influencer market with brands set to spend up to $15 billion by 2022 (Schomer 2019). Influencer fans get the opportunity to directly engage with online and multimedia celebrities via chats and livestreaming on Twitch and YouTube among other platforms. Frequently initiated by players who want to support their passion for the sport, as their span of influence grows, opportunities for marketers emerge with ambassador programs for major brands, as well as managing and promoting ambassador networks such as PrepReps and Reppr (Barker 2019). PR and marketing managers' roles support and promote influencer programs at agencies, game companies, and directly for celebrities, and they require good project management, writing, speaking, and digital skills.

Content Development and Community Management

High-quality live and recorded content is a critical component of esports, and supporting events, athletes, teams, and game developers creates a broad range of roles for marketing professionals to create written, visual, and interactive content. Creativity, quick thinking, content optimization, strong writing, analytics, and levelheadedness are some of the skills that help digital content and community managers to be successful in a fast-paced industry (Bullas n.d.). In addition, individuals working in this area create strategies and tactics focused on bringing people together face-to-face or online. More and more, having an understanding of research, statistics, and analytics and being able to use that understanding and translate it into actions that will motivate fans and consumers to attend events and engage with content are becoming more and more important.

Event Execution and Sponsorships

Live gaming events offer a range of marketing opportunities, from promotions and ticket sales to media rights and event sponsors. Many of the roles parallel those of traditional sporting events, and the NFL and NBA are already forging partnerships to sponsor and air esports matches. Esports keep their fans engaged in the off-seasons and help them broaden their brand and appeal to a wider audience. Marketing roles to promote events, sell and support partnership opportunities, perform public relations, and create a social media presence are all opportunities in this growing space (Goldman Sachs n.d.). Because individuals working in these areas often collaborate directly with external groups, being outgoing, friendly, and persuasive all are beneficial. Moreover, having an understanding of the goals and outcomes (which are often quantitative) of partners and sponsors and being able to devise and implement action plans to help those groups achieve success are also extremely useful for those in these positions.

CAREERS IN ESPORTS HEALTH AND WELLNESS

The topic of health and wellness is frequently discussed in the gaming and esports industry. As with other sports, esports players' health and wellness have an impact on both individual and team performance. As esports organizations receive large amounts of attention and resource investments, it is critical to ensure players are healthy and ready to compete under pressure. Professional players—as in any other sport—have to practice and develop their skills while keeping their minds and bodies well equipped to perform consistently at a high level. Developing a routine that incorporates general physical fitness activities along with proper nutrition and recovery strategies is crucial for long-term player and skill development.

This discussion opens up an important opportunity for new ways of viewing performance both in research and application. For example, a study conducted by faculty from the New York Institute of Technology examined college-level esports athletes. Based on the results, the authors developed an integrated health management model for gaming and esports athletes. This model provides an overview of the entire health and wellness of an esports athlete and notes areas in which experts will be needed (DiFrancisco-Donoghue et al. 2019). The following sections describe a few of the opportunities available for those interested in pursuing a career in a health-related field in esports.

Physical therapists, athletic trainers, and strength and conditioning coaches help people improve their movement and recovery from injury. They are often an important part of the physical training, rehabilitation, and injury prevention for traditional sport programs; in gaming, it is equally important. Along with providing ergonomic and postural assessments, treatment of acute and chronic pain management, and physical fitness testing, they can design physical training programs that develop specific systems leading to overall health, well-being, performance, and longevity.

Nutritionists and nutrition coaches address behaviors, habits, and lifestyle choices around nutrition and hydration that lead to long-term player development and optimal performance. Just as in any performance endeavor, physical and mental performance are paramount, and understanding how to develop healthy nutrition habits to optimize training, performance, and recovery are a vital part of creating a healthy lifestyle that spans beyond a gamer's career.

Sport psychologists have been core team members in traditional sports for a while now, but esports organizations have recently begun exploring the advantages of employing professionals for their players. Many esports psychologists work closely with teams, sometimes even embedding themselves in team houses. Team members are required to embrace the psychologist's plan in order for the desired results to come to fruition, so being an accessible member of the team is a common tactic for psychologists who are working with a team (Davidson 2019).

CAREERS IN GAME DESIGN AND DEVELOPMENT

The esports industry would not exist if it were not for the games themselves. Game design and development is not a new industry. *Tennis for Two*, often credited as the world's first video game, was created in 1958 by a physicist named William Higinbotham (Tretkoff 2008). Technology has advanced in leaps and bounds in the six-plus decades since, with the required roles, responsibilities, and prescriptive process of game design and development taking form. In addition, opportunities for graphic designers, artists, and animators will also be important to the industry. As mentioned throughout this textbook, the video game industry grew into a $152 billion industry in 2019 with an expected growth nearing the USD $200 billion mark by 2022 (Anderton 2019). This growth has created and will continue to create a

Zoning

SEEKING EMPLOYMENT IN ESPORTS HEALTH AND WELLNESS

Taylor Johnson

Offering health and wellness guidance and care requires the practitioner to understand not only the science of the field but also how to implement the strategies and tactics relative to needs of the teams and individuals. Here is advice for young professionals getting started in the health and wellness aspect of the gaming and esports industry:

1. Do internships, and put yourself out there to learn from those who are already in the position you want to be in. Some of the best knowledge, experience, and relationships I have gained in my career came from doing internships and learning from the top people in the field of human and sport performance.
2. Understand yourself and identify your strengths and weaknesses. Spend time to acquire new skills and knowledge to enhance your strengths. Also, welcome the exposure of your weaknesses because it is valuable feedback.
3. Seek mentors. Whether you are just starting out in your career or you are well established, when you've identified someone you want to connect with, remember that it never hurts to reach out to simply ask questions and advice.
4. There is no failure, only feedback. As you progress in your career, you will make mistakes. The goal is to never make the same mistake twice.
5. Never stop learning. Follow your curiosity; see where it takes you and with whom it connects you.

market need for a wide array of talent focused on the science and art of game creation (U.S. Bureau of Labor Statistics 2019). Those working in these areas often have a background in computer science or programming, graphic design or visual arts, or business (e.g., management, marketing, analytics).

Game Development

The **software development lifecycle (SDLC)** is a holistic development process that accounts for identifying need, planning, designing, building, testing, deploying, and maintaining software (Liming and Vilorio 2011). A myriad of careers are in the game design and development space to support the overall SDLC process in game making, including developers, software engineers, testers, and troubleshooting specialists. According to the U.S. Bureau of Labor Statistics (2019), software development as a general industry was expected to grow 21 percent from 2018-2028.

Careers in related areas, such as software development and computer engineering, often require applicants to show a deep understanding of computer science principles and practice (U.S. Bureau of Labor Statistics 2019). Practical knowledge of various coding languages (e.g., Python, Ruby, JavaScript, C#, Java, and C++) is generally required (Calvello 2019). The creation of video games is both an art and a science. If the technical development process is to be considered the science of the process, the artistic side of the equation should also be considered when it comes to career paths.

Writers

Not all games are driven by a captivating story, but many at least have some form of written content to drive the interest of the player. On one end of the spectrum, a game may include a multifaceted story line that unfolds for the player as they progress through the game. The story may be as much a part of the game play as the game mechanics, the audio, or the on-screen visuals. On the other end of the spectrum, a game may have no story line and could simply be based on accomplishing the same task again and again. In order to captivate users, game developers can seek to bring added depth and interest to the title by creating story lines. As a result, the writing of gaming story is another type of career path. As would be expected, abilities to write and communicate well while offering creative and captivating story lines are beneficial for those seeking employment in this area.

Music Scoring

Another important aspect of gaming is the music to which it is set. The musical score of a game serves to set the tone and create a sense of urgency, and it offers an interesting stimulus to enrich the game play experience (ANR 2019). Throughout recent history, the music for games has gone from an interesting background to a high-quality musical experience that can often stand on its own. The caliber of music desired in games and the sheer volume of new titles released each year offers an interesting career opportunity for musicians. As would be expected, a strong background in music and musical composition are need for those seeking employment in this area.

Voice Artists

Video games often include characters who talk on screen and within the narrative of the story line. Behind the voice of a character is someone who was hired to create those sound bites. Although voice artists put a high level of artistic effort into bringing their characters to life, they tend to be underappreciated; not as visible as a traditional actress or actor, their talents can be taken for granted. Combined with hyperrealistic visuals delivered through modern graphics cards, a quality voice artist can transform a video game into an immersive experience that rivals and even surpasses other mediums (Frankel 2017). While there are many reasons why and ways one might be able to secure work in this area, much is likely just based on the strength and caliber of one's own voice.

INTERNATIONAL CAREERS

The international market for esports is robust and growing (see chapter 3). Audience awareness is increasing globally; 1.8 billion people are aware of esports across the globe. As IT infrastructure and urbanization advance, this number will continue to increase (Newzoo 2019). Moreover, additional growth will result in increases in career opportunities. These opportunities span the entirety of the industry but are also layered with the complexity of opportunities and challenges that are part of any career in a global market.

Zoning

INDUSTRY PROFILE: LAURA BAILEY

Roger M. Caramanica

Laura Bailey is a multitalented voice and screen actor who is the voice behind some of the biggest video game and cartoon characters on screen today. She is also a founding member of the wildly popular *Dungeons & Dragons* (*D&D*) stream, *Critical Role,* which has a peak view count of at least 65,000 viewers (Twitch Tracker 2019). Laura is a prime example of a person with an entrepreneurial spirit; she has at least 460 credits to her name, and her success has been multifaceted. According to IMDB (n.d.), she also has been credited for soundtracks and visual effects as well as producing. Specifically, she has been the voice behind some flagship game titles such as *Gears of War 5*, where she voiced Kait Diaz, *World of Warcraft*, where she voices Jaina Proudmoore, and most recently as Abby in the second installment of the *Last of Us*. Laura has shown success in her career as a key content contributor in the games' overall production lifecycles. Careers in this space are part creative, part understanding of the game play audience, and part understanding of the technical aspects of game design.

Diversity

Understanding the diverse culture and unique characteristics that make up the esports industry is an important aspect of an international career in esports. **Deep-level diversity** relates to the differing psychological attributes in a culture such as differences in beliefs, values, and personalities (Gardenswartz and Rowe 1993). These differing attributes, in part, drive the buying and playing habits of different types of consumers. Interests and expectations for gaming vary from culture to culture. Anyone seeking an international career in esports should develop a deep understanding of the nuances of the markets and cultures in which they seek to work.

Market Dynamics

From a business standpoint, market dynamics are the various factors that affect a business and its overall model. Some unique market dynamics vary in the esports ecosystem. They can take the form of legal and governmental system differences, licensing complexities, Internet access, and access to social media variations. These complexities have resulted in the creation of firms that specialize in markets in the esports space. They offer consulting, data, and analysis of the given market to various stakeholders in order to ensure that they are best positioned to succeed in this market. For example, Niko Partners is the leader in Asia games market intelligence. They have on-the-ground experience and native speaking analysts in the countries they cover who understand the marketplace, understand regulations, and meet with important local stakeholders in order to gather consumer research (Niko Partners 2019). Market research and intelligence like that provided by Niko Partners is an example of a career opportunity in working with dedicated market dynamic experts in the esports space.

CONCLUSION

This chapter discussed careers in esports, including those involved with playing and coaching; managing organizations and franchises; producing, managing, and running events; broadcasting and creating content; marketing; health and wellness; game development and design; and international careers. It provided information about the knowledge and skills needed to successfully undertake careers and highlighted profiles of numerous individuals and companies currently working in the esports industry. It covered creating job descriptions and résumés for jobs in esports. The future of esports appears bright, but the industry as a whole is just starting to gain momentum. The hiring and employment of knowledgeable and passionate people will benefit the industry. Over time, the experience people develop in other professions will also contribute to esports as it continues to grow and prosper.

Zoning

BUILDING A CAREER IN INTERNATIONAL MARKET RESEARCH

Lisa Cosmas Hanson

My journey in the field of international market research started when I was in high school and I found my calling for policy and international relations in a course called American Government and World Affairs. The course enthralled me, and I went on to get a bachelor's degree in international relations from the University of California, Los Angeles (UCLA) and a master's (MA) degree in international affairs (specializing in international economic policy) at American University in the School of International Service. I got my MA in 1992, a year in which global policymakers were still marveling at the success of Japan's economic miracle. My focus in graduate school was U.S.-Japan economic competitiveness. I loved it. I knew that if I were truly going to be an expert on the topic, I needed to learn about it from the Japanese perspective as well as the American.

One needs to understand various perspectives to truthfully analyze a topic. In fact, my personal motto is *Peace through intercultural understanding.* I believe with my whole heart that if we take time to learn and understand each other in a global world, we can economically and politically stand a better chance at peace and fairness. Life is imperfect and not fair, but we can do our best.

So I flew to Japan and landed in Tokyo, and through connections I had, I wound up taking a job at a Japanese stock brokerage house. Then I moved from Tokyo to London and worked in another financial institution, but my true interest remained in Asia. I eventually moved from London to Silicon Valley and got a job as a senior analyst of Asia markets in a multinational market research firm. The job posting that I had answered was actually looking for a Latin America analyst. I answered the (newspaper) ad and said, "I don't know anything about Latin America, but I do know a lot about Asia, and I'd like to work for you." They hired me, and I spent three years talking to U.S. clients and traveling to our Asia offices to do research and learn as much as I could.

From there I went to a tech consulting firm in Silicon Valley in the dot-com bubble. I was a lead strategist, and I had lots of cool international work, such as heading for Asia to help open a Hong Kong office. But then the bubble burst, and that was the end of that.

So, I partnered with one friend from the market research firm and one from the consultancy, and we formed Niko Partners as a consultancy to help multimedia software companies expand internationally. It wasn't even a market research company (yet)! I was tasked with looking at Asia, one friend looked at Latin America, and the other at Europe. When the dot-com bubble burst, the only software companies with money for consulting were video game companies, and the only region they really wanted to figure out was Asia, and within Asia the big black box was China. My partners left for more reliable and better jobs, and I pivoted Niko Partners to become a market research firm covering China's video game industry. It worked.

In my job as president of Niko Partners, I work with people from all over the world as clients and sources of information. In addition, my team is made up of people from parts of Asia to parts of Europe and in between, and its cultural and gender diversity serve as assets. Our small Niko family is truly building peace through intercultural understanding as a company, through the work that we do and provide for our clients, and for readers of our interviews and articles in the media.

My advice to someone seeking employment is do what you are passionate about; if you are lucky enough to make that passion fall into an industry that everyone is clamoring to be part of, you will do even better. The games industry brings humans together. Esports is truly the most international, borderless type of entertainment that exists. People who identify as any gender, people from all countries, people of all ages, and people of all religions play games, and many of them love esports. The fact that my career has brought me to a place where the topic I study embodies my personal motto, well, that is pretty cool stuff.

DISCUSSION QUESTIONS

1. What documents and information should job seekers in the esports area prepare?
2. What are the career areas that employers are seeking to hire in the esports industry?
3. For those wishing to work in the esports industry, what are some of the skills needed?
4. Do specialized areas exist where employment opportunities abound?

An Expert Perspective on the Future of Esports

Tobias M. Scholz

Tobias M. Scholz is an assistant professor of human resource management and organizational behavior at the University of Siegen in Germany. Beyond his involvement in esports since 2001, he published the book *Esports Is Business: Management in the World of Competitive Gaming* in 2019 and founded groups such as the Esports Research Network and the University of Siegen's Esports Lab. Among other contributions to the field, he is a frequent writer and contributor to esports publications such as *The Esports Observer* and is also a frequent speaker on the topic of esports. On October 22, 2019, Dr. Scholz published the article "Esports Is More Than Just Sports—A Proposition to Move Beyond the Existing Discourse" on the Esports Research Network website, in which he details some of his ideas about the future of esports. He has graciously provided the article and image included here.

Recently the German Olympic Sports Confederation presented a legal opinion on esports, claiming that it is not a sport based on the currently applicable law and consequently it cannot be categorized as a nonprofit. In many European countries, activities classified as sport can be nonprofit and receive subsidies. Therefore, because esports were not classified as a sport, they are not eligible for governmental support. However, laws can be changed, and they should be changed to be consistent with an evolving society. Especially in current times of digitalization, we are observing a massive transformation, and we need to deal with this change. We are experiencing the fourth industrial revolution. Moreover, this struggle of dealing with esports is emblematic of the struggle of the world transforming into a digitalized society. Existing rules, regulations, and laws do not necessarily fit the current times.

Consequently, we have to rethink the categories we are using; putting esports into traditional sports categories may no longer be fitting. It may be reasonable to understand esports as an evolution of sports into digitalized society. For me, with a human resource background, this concept is nothing new. It could be compared to the continuous transformation from blue-collar worker to white-collar worker, the move from body labor to mental labor. Especially at the beginning of computerization in the 1980s, many managers struggled to understand and adapt to the changes in their work environment.

Nobody today would say that administrative work is not work just because it is not primarily physical labor. Blue-collar work and white-collar work are utterly different work and should be treated that way. That difference can be seen as analogous to the difference between sports and esports. Esports no longer fits into the existing category of traditional sport, and maybe it is time to learn from human resource management. A white-collar worker needs to be treated differently from a blue-collar worker. Esports is something different from sports; it is *electronic* sports, and therefore it should be categorized differently.

What is esports, then? Above all, it is an allegory for the struggle of society to deal with digitalization. Digitalization changed the rules, and so did esports. It is a sociotechnological phenomenon that we observe in real time (Scholz 2017). Technology enforces change in society; at the same time, society enforces change in technology. If an imbalance occurs, society cannot advance and may stagnate. Nevertheless, the role of esports does not have such a great impact on society, but it provides a good sense of how society is dealing with digitalization.

Labeling esports as sport may seem insufficient and may not give credit to this digital phenomenon. The fourth industrial revolution changes the way sport can be understood. For the first time in sport history, the fundamental understanding of it is challenged. However, esports will never replace sport, just as blue-collar work still exists but its relevance may shift. Still, understanding the inner structure of esports could be helpful in dealing with the struggle of transforming into a digitalized society. Esports is about the person and the role everybody is playing.

Before deconstructing esports in contrast to sports, consider these two assumptions: First, esports is simply an umbrella term for over 400 titles that can be played competitively (Besombes 2019). That means the complexity of esports and the variety of esports titles may rival traditional sports. Playing *Counter-Strike* and playing *Hearthstone* are fundamentally different, just as playing football and archery are fundamentally different. Furthermore, the sheer number of potential games also puts the claim that game developers abuse their power of owning an esports title into perspective. Players can choose to play the *FIFA* game or *Pro Evolution Soccer*; soccer players have to submit to the regulations of FIFA.

Second, esports is competitive gaming not only on a professional level but also on an amateur level. This assumption is essential for discussing the status of for-profit and nonprofit esports. Naturally, the professional level is for profit, as this is the case in the majority of traditional sports. However, the amateur level is similar to many amateur teams in traditional sports. They meet up, play in a tournament or league, and have a good time. Both assumptions may be debatable, but they are necessary to compare esports with traditional sports accurately.

Looking back on the history of esports, it becomes evident that the connection to sports was not always the dominant driver for defining esports, because esports were a sociocultural phenomenon. Michael Wagner stated that "eSports is a phenomenon that has become a fundamental element in today's digital youth culture" (2006, p. 437), and in 2015, a report from Superdata even summarized "that a new phenomenon like eSports can be described in terms of the old is to misunderstand it entirely" (Superdata 2015, p. 3). Esports may not fit entirely into the sports category; nevertheless "it has its taste" (Arnaud 2010, p. 11). That the sports aspect is only one facet of esports, can also be seen in the seminal work of T.L. Taylor (2012), who focused on the interwovenness of esports in terms of play, work, and sport, as well as spectatorship. Therefore, an ongoing discourse exists that esports may not fit in the category of sports.

As stated before, esports is linked with a cultural phenomenon and especially with a digital cultural phenomenon. Back in 2006, Wagner said that esports were youth culture; one can assume now that esports is no longer solely a youth phenomenon. Therefore, the esports culture had time to find its place in society and create structures, rituals, and tools to foster communities. The way communities are built varies vastly from the way traditional sports create communities. The physical aspect is not necessarily needed, and that makes esports a prime example for the way communities are built in the digitalized world. Where is the benefit of playing at one location in a traditional sports club when people can play with people all around the world? In the digitalized and globalized world, people tend to relocate more often. In esports, it is possible to play with an old school friend even though this person may now live in a different country.

Furthermore, some people may prefer these digital communities over the physical club environment. They are not less social, but they have a different understanding of what social means. As these new communities, teams, clans, or guilds are in the digital or virtual world, they are not captured by traditional ways of measuring it. They are virtually invisible with the existing tools. Many people in esports do volunteer work in a variety of grassroots projects and even the management of a team, but media coverage often neglects that fact. Esports is a digital phenomenon and, consequently, most of the community interaction happens online. The way digital communities are built is different from how physical communities are built. Therefore, understanding esports may contribute to understanding digital communities.

Many esports players are entertainers, and esports tournaments are designed to be entertaining. This development exploded recently due to the popularity of battle royale games such as *Fortnite.* These games, and most importantly the players, are focusing on the entertainment aspect of their work (Friedman 2019). Examples like Tyler "Ninja" Blevins show the potential of an entertainer. Despite not being the best *Fortnite* player, his exclusive partnership with the streaming platform Mixer immediately brought massive attention to this platform in 2019 (Miceli 2019). In addition, many players and esports organizations test new ways of entertaining their audience, be it through memes, drops, or using augmented reality (AR) in an opening ceremony as in the *League of Legends* 2018 World Finals having elements of AR in it (Takahashi 2018). Esports is continuously pushing the limits of entertainment, thereby creating a novel category: the esports entertainer.

Finally, esports also had a substantial impact on the modern media landscape. Mainly due to the rise of livestreaming, esports (and video games in general) contributed to a massive transformation in the media landscape. However, this evolution is rooted in the negligence of traditional media toward esports in the mid-2000s. As no traditional media such as television wanted to broadcast esports besides South Korea, it was necessary to

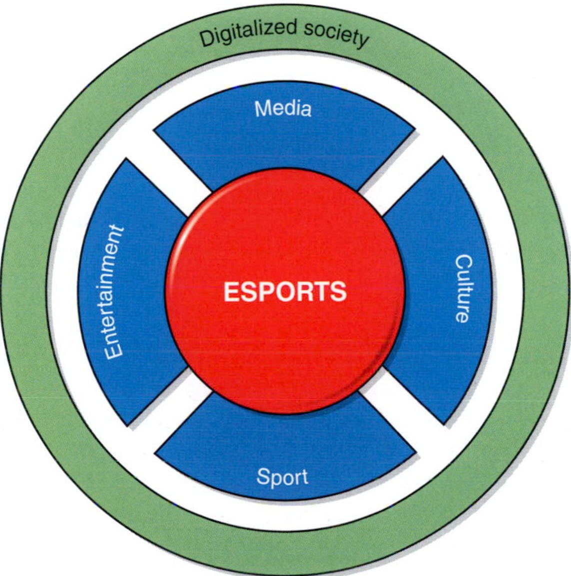

Figure A.1 Esports is an evolution of sport, media, entertainment, and culture in the digitalized society.
Reprinted by permission from Tobias Scholz.

find alternatives. Internet Protocol Television (IPTV) was the only way to stream tournaments, and with the emergence of Twitch.tv, this technology was broadly usable (Scholz 2019). Twitch filled a void and extended the watching experience with a dimension of social interaction. Consequently, people were motivated to watch the games online rather than go offline (Neus et al. 2018). People could watch from everywhere and still be able to interact. Furthermore, through video on demand, it was possible to rewatch matches soon after they were completed. Many traditional sport organizations try to experiment with ways to attract a young audience by enabling the use of a second screen mimicking the idea of social interaction through chat (Cunningham and Eastin 2017). It may be debatable how strong the impact of esports were on the transformation of the media landscape through livestreaming, but esports were the driving force of livestreaming in early times and had a significant role in the way the modern media landscape looks. Esports pushed the limits of the media ecosystem, most importantly, because traditional media ignored esports for too long. The actors in esports created their own media landscape, thereby creating a way to successfully propagate content in digitalized society.

In summary, it is evident that putting a traditional label on esports is difficult, because it is something unique and requires different labels. Similar to the example of blue-collar and white-collar workers, it becomes evident that esports is an evolution of sports exposed to digitalization. As digitalization is a new transformative sociotechnical change for everyone, it also has an impact on media, entertainment, and culture. Deduced from this transformative change, the following denotation of esports may be more fitting: Esports is a cultural phenomenon with a resemblance to its roots in sport, media, entertainment, and culture, but it emerged in a digitalized environment. It evolved beyond the constraints of traditional sport, media, entertainment, and culture.

In the sense of philosopher Ludwig Wittgenstein (1953), this description should not be seen as a definition but rather an analysis of the usage of a word in society. It may not be useful as a legal definition but should describe the usage of the word *esports* in today's world. As the current discussion shows, esports is part of sport but not entirely part of traditional sport. However, it gave meaning to the word *electronic sports*. This logic can be applied to media, entertainment, and culture. Moreover, it seems that putting esports into traditional categories may not be productive at all; subsequently, using traditional regulation may also be harmful to the evolution of esports as the meaning of esports is forced into the sports category or any other category. In short, esports is esports.

In the end, this proposed understanding is also revealing that an essential agenda for any person involved in esports should be to fill esports with meaning. Esports is a case for a microcosm of people based on digitalization. Therefore, esports could act as a test laboratory for digitalized society.

What should this society look like? Discussions about esports being sport may be a waste of time; instead, people should focus on these essential questions: How can we create a sustainable ecosystem for all stakeholders? How can we achieve the triple bottom line (a balance in social, environmental, and financial factors)? What is an adequate form of regulation for a complex environment like esports? How can this complexity be managed without losing the flexibility and dynamic of esports? Solutions for those questions will help to grow esports organically and sustainably. Furthermore, these solutions could initiate a discussion about the digitalized society in which we want to live.

Reprinted by permission from Tobias Scholz.

Glossary

accounting—The process of calculating how much money is flowing into and outside the organization.

activations—Activities used to create awareness among potential consumers of sponsorship-related marketing opportunities.

addiction—A compulsive, chronic, physiological or psychological need for a habit-forming substance, behavior, or activity that has harmful physical, psychological, or social effects.

adhesion contract—Where one party has limited rights in the contract negotiation process and they have to take the contract terms or not enter into the contract.

aimbot—An in-game cheating mechanism that allows someone to automatically aim.

analyst coach—A type of coach involved with examining how players and teams play, and then using that information to improve results.

annual report—A document required for publicly traded companies to inform investors of how the company did and what issues they might face in the future.

assets—Representations of something of value, such as gold, stocks, inventory, and equipment. In terms of sponsorship, goods or services that can be offered by a sponsored property and accessed, used, or sold to a sponsor, often with exclusive opportunities for the sponsor to leverage what they receive.

association—A group of individuals or entities that agree to work together for a common purpose or goal.

assumption of risk (AR)—When someone engages in conduct voluntarily with the risks known, then they should not recover if they were injured from those known risks.

athletic trainer—A professional who is focused on helping players deal with injuries, rehabilitation, and preventive strategies.

average minute audience (AMA)—"The average number of individuals (or homes or target group) viewing a TV channel, which is calculated per minute during a specified period of time over the program duration" (Ashton 2019, para. 4).

balance sheet—A calculation of an organization's worth at a given point in time that explores assets, liabilities, and owner's equity.

brainstorming—The process of throwing out ideas in a group to develop further and on which to base future action.

brand activation—A marketing strategy to encourage purchasing products such as in-store samples of products to encourage buying.

brand equity—The value consumers place on the name and the image they have of a brand.

breach of contract—Occurs when one party does not follow the terms or conditions of a contract.

break-even analysis—Explores how many units need to be sold to cover all costs (fixed and variable).

budget—A road map highlighting where the organization wants to go in the future based on sound financial analysis that can be examined at a later date for accuracy.

cannibalization—The process of one eating another. Applied to esports, it means if there are too many games it can harm an industry; when one game grows, it reduces the players of another game.

capacity—The ability to enter into a contract, which means being over age 18, not being intoxicated, and not being legally considered incapacitated.

cash-flow statement—Statement that indicates where money is coming and going in an organization.

collective bargaining agreement (CBA)—A contract between a union and an employer that gives specific rights and responsibilities to each party.

colorcaster—A broadcaster or commentator who provides explanations of strategies, tactics, story lines, and strengths and weaknesses of players and teams.

color commentary—The action of providing explanations of strategies, tactics, story lines, and strengths and weaknesses of players and teams.

computer maintenance management systems (CMMS)—Computer systems that track various activities in a facility to help it operate more effectively.

consideration—An exchange of value required to complete a contract. It need not be a specific monetary value; the parties simply need to feel there is value.

contract—An agreement between multiple parties with specific terms and conditions and meeting specific requirements in order to be valid.

contribution margin—The amount of sales that help contribute to covering the fixed costs.

copyright—A protection afforded to works produced by someone, such as books, programs, compositions, artwork, and broadcasts.

cosplayers—People who dress up as their favorite characters from games, movies, or literature.

culture—The customary beliefs, social forms, and material traits of a racial, religious, or social group. The set of shared attitudes, values, goals, and practices that characterizes a group.

customer relationship management (CRM)—Using quantitative and qualitative data in an attempt to identify and determine ideal ways in which an organization can retain customers and increase their future consumption.

deep-level diversity—Related to the differing psychological attributes within a culture, such as differences in beliefs, values, and personalities.

defamation—A written or oral statement about a person or an organization that causes harm to another's reputation. The defense against a defamation claim is the truth.

duty—A responsibility one owes to another to protect them from known or reasonably identifiable harms they should protect someone from.

economics—The study of what is happening in an economy, such as whether a lot of inflation is occurring or if customers are making buying decisions and why.

emoji—Electronic symbols created to represent the expression of thoughts or emotions.

endemic—Typically used in reference to brands, sponsorship, marketing, and advertising activities of goods and services that are native and have a direct connection to a particular category or population segment.

endemic sponsors—Organizations that produce goods and services used in the actual playing or production of esports competitions and events.

engagement rate—A quantitative measure of how much those individuals who see particular content engage with it through actions such as reading or learning more about it.

esports—Any video game that allows for organized multiplayer non–geographically bound real-time competitions with or against other players or teams, where the primary aspects of the game are facilitated by electronic systems, and the input of players and teams as well as the output of the electronic systems are mediated by human–computer interfaces.

esports franchises—Teams that are located within a city or region and have earned the right (often through the paying of a fee) to compete in a specific esports game.

esports tourism—Travel to a particular destination that occurs in order to attend or participate in an esports event or activity.

event bidding—The process of competing with other entities to win the rights to host an event.

expenses—The cost of operations a company incurs that are needed to generate revenue.

federation—A group of organizations that agree to be bound by certain rules and regulations to achieve a common purpose or goal.

finance—The art and science of financial planning for a person, business, or organization.

first-mover advantage—Idea that the first one to market with a product or idea has the ability to be the first to sell and can make a profit before others.

fitness coach—A type of coach involved with helping players to enhance and improve their physical fitness, skills, and abilities through exercise and body training activities.

fixed costs—Costs incurred to make a product regardless of how many units are made. A mortgage on a building needs to be paid regardless of how many units are sold.

flat rate—A charge that is set in advance so that the organization knows the cost from the very beginning.

forum shopping—The process of searching for the best location to sue someone to take advantage of laws or favorable legal environment.

frontline employees—Staff who directly interact with customers.

furniture, fixtures, and equipment (FFE)—Represent any items added to a facility beyond the structure and key systems, including furniture, paintings, carpeting, scoreboards, speakers, and more.

futuristic fantasy—A type of game which is completely unrealistic and associated with what might happen in the future.

game coach—A type of coach involved with issues related to how the game or competition is being played or how players are identified and prepared to compete.

gaming clan—A group of people who play one or more multiplayer games.

gaming house—Shared housing used by esports players in which team members live, practice, and play together.

gender diversity—The inclusion of different genders in a group or organization.

goals—Specific requirements an organization must meet to help achieve its mission; they should be measurable and time bound.

governance—The culture and institutional environment where people interact.

high fantasy—Type of game that happens outside the realm of possibility.

horizontal analysis—A process of comparing a company's financial information from one year to another year or other period to see growth or decline.

incident management system (IMS)—Computer-based system that tracks incidents in a building so that management can track and analyze what is going on in the building.

income statement—A statement that examines revenue and expenses over a given time period to see if the organization made or lost money.

independent contractor (IC)—Someone who performs work under the terms of a contract and is not considered an employee.

influencer marketing—Creating marketing activities for individuals who have the power to influence large numbers of potential consumers to communicate and use.

information technology (IT)—The system (hardware and software) in place to help solve information- or computer-related needs, from making sure computers work to identifying viruses and other threats.

in-stream promotional content—The ability to sell or market a product or service during the streaming of an event or personal stream.

intellectual property (IP)—The legal means to protect someone's ideas, name, expressions, and products; IP laws are written so that the originator can protect their creation.

job analysis—The act of studying a role to fully understand the responsibilities, activities, and behaviors required to perform the work expected.

job description—A written document that memorializes the tasks, activities, and outcomes expected for a given role.

jurisdiction—A legal venue where a case is filed and where the court can rule on the merits of a given case.

key performance indicator (KPI)—Important data or metrics used to measure and evaluate success.

legality—Something that is legal such as a speed limit on a road. Also, an element stating that a contract needs to be undertaken for a legal purpose (i.e., an illegal drug deal is a void contract).

level up—To move from a lower level of a game to a higher or more advanced version of a game, often coinciding with players earning access to new in-game opportunities and resources.

leverage—In terms of sponsorship, using resources to make consumers aware of a sponsor's existence and marketing activities.

liabilities—What an organization owes, whether to a lender, suppliers, employees, or others.

libel—A written defamatory statement about someone that harms their reputation.

life coach—A type of coach involved with a player's or team's physical, mental, emotional, social, and spiritual well-being.

line item—In a budget, these are single entries of money coming in or going out.

liquid assets—Assets that can quickly be turned to cash to cover expenses (e.g., cash, stocks, and certificates of deposit).

loge seat—Similar to a luxury box, it is often much smaller and can sit four to six people in a more intimate area where food might be shared with other loge box owners.

long-term assets—Assets that will be held for longer than five years, such as large equipment, patents, or a building.

loot boxes—Virtual items, developed by game publishers, purchased with real money by players for items that may enhance and improve their game play or in-game experience.

magnetometer—A metal detector; it can be a handheld detector or one that people walk through.

marketing—Activities designed to create, communicate, and deliver value to potential consumers.

mission—The primary directive motivating how an organization can achieve its vision.

National Labor Relations Board (NLRB)—The U.S. governmental organization designed to help facilitate the formation of unions in a lawful manner and to make sure unions and employers act appropriately.

negligence—The act of causing harm to another through breaching a duty, and that breach caused an injury.

non-endemic—Typically used in reference to brands, sponsorship, marketing, and advertising activities of goods and services that are not native and have no direct connection to a particular category or population segment.

non-endemic sponsors—Organizations that produce goods and services not directly used in the playing of the game or production of esports competitions and events.

nutritionist—A professional who is focused on educating players about healthy nutrition habits and often overseeing the preparation of balanced meals meant to enhance performance.

objectives—Strategies that help an organization achieve its goals. They are more specific than goals but not as specific as tactics.

owner's equity—The value an owner has in money they have invested into the company.

patent—A legal protection provided to one who creates a product. The item needs to be tangible rather than just a concept or idea.

paywall—A way in which access is restricted to digital content, and only those who pay the required fee can access it.

PC bang—Literally "PC room," a small dedicated gaming facility in South Korea.

per capita—For each person. In esports it is related to what each fan is paying for various elements of an event such as expenditure on concessions at an event.

percentage of sales—Payment to a vendor based on a percentage of total sales rather than a contracted flat rate price.

performance scout—A type of coach involved in identifying players' and teams' tactics and strategies in advance of competitions, and communicating that information to the coaches and players in an effort to predict what might happen before it happens.

personal seat license (PSL)—A dedicated seat at a facility where someone has bought the rights to buy tickets associated with the seat.

play-by-play analyst—A broadcaster or commentator who provides information about what players and teams are doing during the game moment by moment.

player versus environment (PvE)—Video games in which one participant competes alone, typically against competitors or situations managed by the computer.

player versus player (PvP)—Video games in which two or more participants compete in real time.

position coach—A specific type of coach involved in coaching specialized types of players who are often using particular types of in-game roles.

pouring rights—An agreement made between an organization and a beverage distributor for the exclusive rights to sell specific beverages at the location or venue.

profit—If an organization's expenses are less than its revenue it has made a profit.

proximate cause—The actual cause that resulted in an injury. An intervening cause breaks the chain of causation and eliminates potentially negligent liability.

ratified (contract)—Agreeing to the terms of a contract, again. If someone enters into a contract when they are younger than 18 and then keep playing after they are 18, they will be stopped from saying the contract is void because their behavior has ratified the contractual terms.

realistic fantasy—A type of game that is part fantasy, but elements are plausible and technically could be accomplished.

relationship marketing—Designing marketing activities in order to create relationships with the organization and between its consumers.

résumé—A document that summarizes your knowledge, skills, and qualifications.

return on investment (ROI)—A measurement of the benefit of an action divided by the costs associated with that same action.

revenue—The amount of money generated from sales and services.

rights holder—The person or group owning the intellectual property or license for a particular good or service.

run of show—Often called an event script, a timeline that highlights how the event will run minute by minute.

secondary ticket market—The marketplace composed of tickets frequently being resold by the original purchaser.

segment—A way to divide a group such as fans or customers. Marketers often segment their customers for ease in marketing to the correct group.

self-employment—The act of working for oneself as a freelancer or owner of one's own business and using an entrepreneurial mindset to drive one's career opportunities.

sense of community—A feeling of kinship and connection felt amongst a group of people.

shoutcaster—An esports broadcaster or commentator that provides play-by-play or color commentary during the often online broadcasting of esports games or competitions.

shoutcasting—The action of providing play-by-play or color commentary during the broadcasting of esports games or competitions.

sizzle reel—A short promotional video highlighting the highest-quality content.

slander—An oral defamatory statement about another person or group that harms their reputation.

smurf account—When a highly experienced or ranked player establishes an additional in-game player account, often at a much lower level or rank. While the purposes of these accounts vary, players often use them to hide their identity and play casual games without pressure.

software development lifecycle (SDLC)—A holistic development process that accounts for identifying need, planning, designing, building, testing, deploying, and maintaining software.

spatial resolution—A measure of the accuracy or detail of a graphics display, often expressed as dots per inch and related to how accurate an image is.

spokesperson—An individual who communicates on behalf of an organization with the public and media.

sponsor—The person or group buying the intellectual property or license for a particular good or service from the rights holder.

sponsor reads—The announcement made over the loudspeaker or scoreboards conveying a message from a sponsor (an advertisement).

sponsorship—"A cash and/or in-kind fee paid to a property (typically in sports, arts, entertainment or causes) in return for access to the exploitable commercial potential associated with that property" (IEG 2017a, p. V).

sport psychologist—A professional who is focused on helping players and teams optimize their performance and well-being, developing the social and competitive aspects of sports participation, and addressing systemic issues associated with sports settings, organizations, and competitions.

stakeholders—Parties who are affected by and affect a given industry or organization.

staying power—The ability to continue to exist or operate through trials and tribulations.

stereotype—A standardized mental picture members of a group hold in common; it represents an oversimplified opinion, prejudiced attitude, or uncritical judgment.

stigma—A mark of shame or discredit.

streaming services—Specialized software, paired with video and audio recording technology, that facilitates the recording of content from one user and broadcasting of that content to other users, often over the Internet.

swatting—The act of calling police and sending them to a fake emergency as a way to harass esports opponents.

tactics—The smallest details or action items that, when done, will help lead to attaining goals and objectives.

target market—The ideal market most likely to attend an event or purchase something. The market can be based on criteria such as demographics (age, gender, race, location) or psychographics (buying patterns, interest).

tort—A legal wrong that harms someone. There are intentional torts such as defamation and the unintentional tort of negligence.

toxic gamers—People who engage in frequent negative behaviors while playing or watching esports, and who create (through words and actions) an environment in which others do not want to play.

trademark—A protection of a company's or product's name, color, design, or other elements from those wishing to copy it and cause consumer confusion.

trolling—Antagonizing others online by deliberately posting inflammatory, irrelevant, or offensive comments or other disruptive content.

union—A group of employees who have formally joined together to negotiate with an employer to secure rights and opportunities for workers.

upsell—To increase purchasing behavior such as selling an initial game and then trying to sell other elements to the same buyer as they have already made one purchase and shown interest.

variable costs—Costs that vary based on the total number of units produced. Usually more units produced reduces the variable costs per unit.

variance analysis—The ability to compare an initial budget with the actual results to help identify where inaccuracies may have occurred. This process helps with better future planning.

vertical analysis—Often called common-size analysis, it compares one element with another on the income statement to see what percentage sales (and other elements) were from one period to another. For example, sales of one game might represent 20 percent of revenue one year and 10 percent for the next year.

vision—The overarching reason for an organization to exist.

visual processing—The ability to make sense of information taken in through the eyes.

Voice over Internet Protocol (VoIP)—Using digital technology (the Internet) instead of traditional analog telephone lines to make phone calls and perform voice chatting.

voidable—Refers to a contract where a party does not need to follow the contractual terms.

workers' compensation—A no-fault insurance program that covers employees injured at work regardless of why or how they are injured.

zero-based budgets (ZBB)—A budget that starts at zero and all expenses need to be justified to be approved.

PREFACE

CNN. 2018. "Drake and Ninja's 'Fortnite' battle sets a new Twitch record." Last modified March 15, 2018. www.cnn.com/2018/03/15/entertainment/drake-ninja-fortnite-twitch-battle/index.html.

IMDB. 2020. "Make Love, Not Warcraft." Last modified 2020. www.imdb.com/title/tt0850173.

Jabr, Ferris. 2019. "Addicted to Video Games." Last modified December 13, 2019. https://theweek.com/articles/883863/addicted-video-games.

Lapin, Tamar. 2019. "Teen Wins Fortnite World Cup Solo Championship and $3 Million." Last modified July 29, 2019. https://nypost.com/2019/07/29/teen-wins-fortnite-world-cup-solo-championship-and-3-million.

McHugh, Alex. 2019. "Echo Fox Esports Organisation Officially 'Gone'." Last modified November 13, 2019. www.greenmangaming.com/newsroom/2019/11/13/echo-fox-esports-organisation-officially-gone.

Newzoo. 2020. "Key Numbers." Last modified 2020. https://newzoo.com/key-numbers.

Price, Lilly, and Mike Snider. 2018. "Video Game Addiction Is a Mental Health Disorder, WHO Says, but Some Health Experts Don't Agree." Last modified June 19, 2018. www.usatoday.com/story/tech/nation-now/2018/06/18/gaming-disorder-who-classifies-video-game-addiction-health-disorder/709574002.

Upton, Nicholas. 2019. "Why Esports Franchises Are Big Business Beyond Gamers." Last modified May 30, 2019. www.franchisetimes.com/June-July-2019/Why-esports-franchises-are-big-business-beyond-gamers.

Werner, Ben. 2019. "Navy Drops TV Ads: Trades Super Bowl Spots for Esports, YouTube." Last modified December 18, 2019. https://news.usni.org/2019/12/18/navy-drops-tv-ads-trades-super-bowl-spots-for-esports-youtube.

CHAPTER 1

Agarwal, Shubham. 2018. "7 Reasons Why Console Gaming Is Better Than PC Gaming." Last modified December 17, 2018. www.makeuseof.com/tag/reasons-console-gaming-better-pc-gaming.

Alexander, Julia. 2019. "The Golden Age of YouTube Is Over." Last modified April 5, 2019. www.theverge.com/2019/4/5/18287318/youtube-logan-paul-pewdiepie-demonetization-adpocalypse-premium-influencers-creators.

Austin, Sarah. 2018. "Where Have All the Viners Gone?" Last modified May 24, 2018. www.entrepreneur.com/article/313038.

Baker, Chris. 2016. "Stewart Brand Recalls First 'Spacewar' Video Game Tournament." Last modified May 25, 2016. www.rollingstone.com/culture/culture-news/stewart-brand-recalls-first-spacewar-video-game-tournament-187669.

Blizzard Entertainment. n.d. "Teams." Accessed December 30, 2019. https://overwatchleague.com/en-us/teams.

Bogorad, Nataly. 2020. "Top 5 Video Game Streaming Platforms in 2020." Last modified January 8, 2020. www.movavi.com/learning-portal/gaming-streaming-sites.html.

Boyd, Jordan. 2019. "What Gears 5 Looks Like As A First-Person Shooter." Last modified September 10, 2019. https://screenrant.com/gears-5-first-person-shooter-glitch.

BBC (British Broadcasting Corporation). 2018. "Paris 2024 Olympics: Esports 'in Talks' to Be Included as a Demonstration Sport." Last modified April 25, 2018. www.bbc.com/sport/olympics/43893891.

Bryksin, Gleb. 2018. "VR vs. AR vs. MR: Differences and Real-Life Applications." Last modified February 13, 2018. www.upwork.com/hiring/for-clients/vr-vs-ar-vs-mr-differences-real-life-applications.

Casey, Dan. 2017. "Why Atari's PONG Matters 45 Years Later." Last modified November 28, 2017. https://nerdist.com/article/atari-pong-45th-anniversary-history-video-game.

Celera, Lex. 2019. "For the First Time Ever, eSports Will Be a Medal Event in the Southeast Asian Games." Last modified April 2, 2019. www.vice.com/en_asia/article/zmaa5y/for-the-first-time-ever-esports-will-be-a-medal-event-in-the-southeast-asian-games.

Chalk, Andy. 2008. "Cyberathlete Professional League Shuts Down." Last modified March 14, 2008. www.escapistmagazine.com/news/view/82350-Cyberathlete-Professional-League-Shuts-Down.

Chalk, Andy. 2014. "League of Legends 2014 World Championship Draws 27 Million Viewers." Last modified December 2, 2014. www.pcgamer.com/league-of-legends-2014-world-championship-draws-27-million-viewers.

Chau, Jeff "SuiJeneris." 2019a. "My WCG 2019 Presentation: East vs West, Parallels of PC and Mobile Esports and Why Mobile Is the Future of Esports." Last modified July 21, 2019. https://medium.com/@SJeneris/my-wcg-2019-presentation-east-vs-west-parallels-of-pc-and-mobile-esports-and-why-mobile-is-the-59500c29dbe4.

Chau, Jeff "SuiJeneris." 2019b. "Why Mobile Esports Will Displace PC/Console Esports: The Rise of Multiplayer Action Mobile Gaming." Last modified November 14, 2019. https://medium.com/@SJeneris/mobile-esports-is-starting-to-displace-other-esports-4c53bb68ae1e.

Cifaldi, Frank. 2015. "The Story of the First Nintendo World Championships." Last modified July 14, 2016. www.ign.com/articles/2015/05/13/the-story-of-the-first-nintendo-world-championships.

Comen, Evan. 2018. "Check Out How Much a Computer Cost the Year You Were Born." Last modified October 3, 2018. www.usatoday.com/story/tech/2018/06/22/cost-of-a-computer-the-year-you-were-born/36156373.

Dave, Paresh. 2013. "Online Game League of Legends Star Gets U.S. Visa as Pro Athlete." Last modified August 7, 2013. www.latimes.com/business/la-xpm-2013-aug-07-la-fi-online-gamers-20130808-story.html.

Deloitte. 2019. "The Rise of Esports Investments." Accessed January 12, 2020. www2.deloitte.com/content/dam/Deloitte/us/Documents/finance/drfa-rise-of-esports-investments.pdf.

Esports Arena. n.d. "About Esports Arena." Accessed December 30, 2019. www.esportsarena.com/OrangeCounty/about.html.

Esports Earnings. n.d. "Top Games Awarding Prize Money." Accessed December 28, 2019. www.esportsearnings.com/games.

Evans-Thirlwell, Edwin. 2017. "The History of the First Person Shooter." Last modified October 20, 2017. www.pcgamer.com/the-history-of-the-first-person-shooter.

Fitch, Adam. 2019. "Real Estate Giant Simon to Invest in Allied Esports." Last modified July 1, 2019. https://esportsinsider.com/2019/07/simon-allied-esports-investment.

Fogel, Stefanie. 2018. "Esports Arena Opens Venues Inside Walmart Stores." Last modified November 9, 2018. https://variety.com/2018/gaming/news/esports-arena-opens-walmart-venues-1203024499.

Fortnite Team. 2019. "The Fortnite World Cup: A Record-Setting Tournament." Last modified July 31, 2019. www.epicgames.com/fortnite/en-US/news/the-fortnite-world-cup-a-record-setting-tournament.

Funk, Daniel C., Anthony D. Pizzo, and Bradley J. Baker. 2018. "Esport Management: Embracing Esport Education and Research Opportunities." *Sport Management Review, 21* (1): 7-13.

Hamari, Juho, and Max Sjöblom. 2017. "What Is eSports and Why Do People Watch It?" *Internet Research, 27* (2): 211-232.

Harris, Todd. 2020. "Average Age of Esports Fans vs. Traditional Sports Fans." Last modified January 6, 2020. www.linkedin.com/in/toddalanharris/detail/recent-activity/.

Heitner, Darren. 2015. "New Counter-Strike: Global Offensive (CS:GO) League announces $1.2 Million Prize Pool." Last modified December 4, 2015. www.forbes.com/sites/darrenheitner/2015/12/04/new-counter-strike-global-offensive-csgo-league-announces-1-2-million-prize-pool/#6b2645fe613f.

Hillier, Brenna. 2012. "Battle.net World Championship Detailed, 28 Countries Involved." Last modified April 5, 2012. www.vg247.com/2012/04/05/battle-net-world-championship-detailed-28-countries-involved.

Horowitz, Ken. 2018. *The Sega Arcade Revolution: A History in 62 Games.* Jefferson, NC: McFarland & Company.

Intel. 2019. "Intel Technology Propels Olympic Games Tokyo 2020 Into the Future." Last modified September 11, 2019. https://newsroom.intel.com/news-releases/intel-2020-tokyo-olympics/#gs.sagmev.

Iqbal, Mansoor. 2019. "Fortnite Usage and Revenue Statistics (2019)." Last modified December 13, 2019. www.businessofapps.com/data/fortnite-statistics.

Janas, Mark. 2019. "Motorsports Simulation: The Closest Esports Get to the Real Thing?" Last modified September 12, 2019. http://thesportdigest.com/2019/09/motorsports-simulation-the-closest-esports-get-to-the-real-thing.

Jenny, Seth E., R. Douglas Manning, Margaret C. Keiper, and Tracy W. Olrich. 2017. "Virtual (ly) Athletes: Where Esports Fit Within the Definition of 'Sport'." *Quest, 69* (1): 1-18.

Kahn, Jeremy. 2020. *The Quest for Human-Level A.I.* New York: Fortune Media.

Kent, Steven. 2001. *The Ultimate History of Video Games: From Pong to Pokemon—The Story Behind the Craze That Touched Our Lives and Changed the World.* New York: Three Rivers Press.

Larch, Florian. 2019. "The Emergence of Gaming Culture in South Korea: Seoul—The Home of Esports." Last modified January 10, 2019. www.ispo.com/en/markets/seoul-how-city-addicted-esports.

Leong, Lewis. 2019. "The Future of Mobile Gaming: The Push for Fully Immersive Gaming Will Be Led by AR and VR (Part 3)." Last modified February 6, 2019. https://blog.applovin.com/future-of-mobile-gaming-part-3-vr-ar-mr-gaming.

Li, Roland. 2016. *Good Luck Have Fun: The Rise of Esports.* New York: Skyhorse.

Liquipedia. 2019a. "2012 Battle.net World Championship." Last modified October 24, 2019. https://liquipedia.net/starcraft2/2012_Battle.net_World_Championship.

Liquipedia. 2019b. "Eleague." Last modified January 10, 2019. https://liquipedia.net/counterstrike/ELEAGUE.

Liquipedia. 2019c. "CPL." Last modified November 14, 2019. https://liquipedia.net/counterstrike/CPL.

Marr, Bernard. 2019. "The Important Difference Between Virtual Reality, Augmented Reality and Mixed Reality." Last modified July 19, 2019. www.forbes.com/sites/bernardmarr/2019/07/19/the-important-difference-between-virtual-reality-augmented-reality-and-mixed-reality/#3183263a35d3.

Martin, Douglas. 2014. "Ralph H. Baer, Inventor of First System for Home Video Games, Is Dead at 92." Last modified December 7, 2014. www.nytimes.com/2014/12/08/business/ralph-h-baer-dies-inventor-of-odyssey-first-system-for-home-video-games.html.

McAloon, Alissa. 2019. "Apex Legends Already Beat Fortnite's Single-Day Viewership Record on Twitch." Last modified February 14, 2019. www.gamasutra.com/view/news/336715/Apex_Legends_already_beat_Fortnites_singleday_viewership_record_on_Twitch.php.

McVerry, Eryn, and Janelle E. Wells. 2019. "Embarking on Pop Culture: The Entertainment of Gaming." In *The Business of Esports: The Wild Wild West*, edited by Janelle E. Wells and Michelle G. Harrolle, 104-134. Tampa, FL: MGH Research.

Minor League Baseball. n.d. "Teams by Name." Accessed December 30, 2019. www.milb.com/about/teams.

Mlot, Stephanie. 2014. "VIDEO: Teens React to the Original NES." Last modified September 9, 2014. www.pcmag.com/news/327169/video-teens-react-to-the-original-nes.

MLS Soccer Staff. 2018. "eMLS 2019 Details Revealed: Expanded Competition, New Teams for 2nd Season." Last modified November 19, 2018. www.mlssoccer.com/post/2018/11/19/emls-2019.

Murray, Trent. 2018. "An Introduction to Watching Fighting Games as Esports." Last modified February 26, 2018. https://esportsobserver.com/introduction-fighting-games-esports.

NBA 2K League. 2018. "$1 Million Prize Pool for Inaugural NBA 2K League Season." Last modified February 9, 2018. https://2kleague.nba.com/news/1-million-prize-pool-for-inaugural-nba-2k-league-season.

Newzoo. 2019. "Key Numbers." Last modified 2019. https://newzoo.com/key-numbers.

Newzoo. n.d. "Custom Consumer Research." Accessed January 14, 2020. https://newzoo.com/solutions/custom-consumer-research.

Niko Partners. n.d. "Homepage." Accessed January 14, 2020. https://nikopartners.com.

Parker, Max. 2018. "Interview: Lakers' Josh Hart Talks Esports and His Love for the Games at CWL." Last modified June 17, 2018. http://communityvoices.post-gazette.com/arts-entertainment-living/the-game-guy/item/41401-interview-lakers-josh-hart-talks-esports-and-his-love-for-games-at-cwl.

PocketGamer.biz. n.d. "Count of Active Applications in the App Store." Accessed January 14, 2020. www.pocketgamer.biz/metrics/app-store/app-count/.

Potkin, Fanny. 2018. "Esports: Move to Less Violent Games for 2022 Asiad—Alisport CEO." Last modified September 2, 2018. www.reuters.com/article/us-games-asia-alisports/esports-move-to-less-violent-games-for-2022-asiad-alisport-ceo-idUSKCN1LI0RI.

Prizetrac.kr. 2019. "The International 2019." Last modified 2019. dota2.prizetrac.kr/international2019.

Purcaru, Ion B. 2014. *Games vs. Hardware. The History of PC Video Games: The 80's*. Seattle, WA: Amazon Digital Services.

Rinaldi, Casey. 2018. "Learn the Story of the Evolution Championship Series, as told by theScore Esports." Last modified August 20, 2018. http://shoryuken.com/2018/08/10/learn-the-story-of-the-evolution-championship-series-as-told-by-thescore-esports/.

Robehmed, Natalie, and Madeline Berg. 2018. "Highest-Paid YouTube Stars 2018: Markiplier, Jake Paul, PewDiePie and More." Last modified December 3, 2018. www.forbes.com/sites/natalierobehmed/2018/12/03/highest-paid-youtube-stars-2018-markiplier-jake-paul-pewdiepie-and-more/#56996607909a.

Rouse, Isaac. 2019. "Undefeated Produces Custom Kits for Esports Team New York Excelsior." Last modified July 26, 2018. https://hypebeast.com/2018/7/undefeated-new-york-excelsior-jerseys-overwatch-league-finals-barclays.

Simon. n.d. "About." Accessed January 12, 2020. https://business.simon.com/about.

Spangler, Todd. 2019. "Fortnite World Cup Finals 2019 Draws Over 2 Million Live Viewers." *Variety*. Last modified July 29, 2019. https://variety.com/2019/digital/news/fortnite-world-cup-finals-2019-live-viewers-championship-1203282771.

Starcade. n.d. "The Games of Starcade!" Accessed December 30, 2019. www.starcade.tv/starcade/games/games.html.

Statista. 2019a. "Esports Market Revenue Worldwide From 2012 to 2022." Last modified March 14, 2019. www.statista.com/statistics/490522/global-esports-market-revenue.

Statista. 2019b. "Esports Market Revenue Worldwide in 2019, by Segment." Last modified February 21, 2019. www.statista.com/statistics/490358/esports-revenue-worldwide-by-segment.

Statista. 2019c. "Share of Worldwide Esports Market Revenue in 2019, by Region." Last modified March 14, 2019. www.statista.com/statistics/443147/estimate-of-global-market-revenue-of-esports-by-region.

Statista. 2019d. "Esports Audience Size Worldwide From 2012 to 2022, by Type of Viewers." Last modified August 9, 2019. www.statista.com/statistics/490480/global-esports-audience-size-viewer-type.

Statista. n.d. "About us." Accessed January 14, 2020. www.statista.com/aboutus/.

Steam. n.d. "Steam: About." Accessed January 12, 2020. https://store.steampowered.com/about/.

Stephen, Bijan. 2019. "Mixer Adds Another Top Streamer to Its Roster, Which Means Its Plan Is Working." Last modified October 28, 2019. https://www.theverge.com/2019/10/28/20936859/mixer-twitch-king-gothalion-shroud-ninja.

SuperData Research. n.d. "Homepage." Accessed January 14, 2020. www.superdataresearch.com.

Switzer, Eric. 2020. "If You Aren't Playing Pokémon Trading Card Game Online, You Should Be." Last modified January 2, 2020. www.thegamer.com/why-you-should-be-playing-pokemon-trading-card-game-online.

Tangermann, Victor. 2019. "A Guy Trained on Video Games Just Beat a Formula 1 Driver on a Real Track." Last modified January 21, 2019. https://futurism.com/sim-racing-virtual-motorsport-beat-formula1.

Tassi, Paul. 2013. "League of Legends Finals Sells Out LA's Staples Center in an Hour." Last modified August 24, 2013. www.forbes.com/sites/insertcoin/2013/08/24/league-of-legends-finals-sells-out-las-staples-center-in-an-hour/#3d6c2e1132b8.

Taylor, Tina L. 2012. *Raising the Stakes: E-sports and the Professionalization of Computer Gaming*. Boston: MIT Press.

Twitch Tracker. 2020. “Twitch Statistics & Charts.” Accessed January 12, 2020. https://twitchtracker.com/statistics.

U.S. Citizenship and Immigration Services. n.d. “P-1A Athlete.” Accessed December 28, 2019. www.uscis.gov/working-united-states/temporary-workers/p-1a-internationally-recognized-athlete.

Volk, Peter. 2016. “League of Legends Now Boasts Over 100 Million Monthly Active Players Worldwide.” Last modified September 13, 2016. www.riftherald.com/2016/9/13/12865314/monthly-lol-players-2016-active-worldwide.

Waddell, Cooper. 2019. “Gamer Segmentation Report.” Last modified October 16, 2019. https://s3-us-east-2.amazonaws.com/igda-website/wp-content/uploads/2019/10/16161926/NPD-2018-2019-Gamer-Segmentation-Report-White-Paper.pdf.

Wagner, Michael G. 2006. “On the Scientific Relevance of Esports.” In *Proceedings of the 2006 International Conference on Internet Computing and Conference on Computer Game Development*, 437-440. Las Vegas: CSREA Press.

Webster, Andrew. 2019. “Offset Joined Faze Clan Because Its Players Are ‘Rock Stars.’” Last modified August 28, 2019. www.theverge.com/2019/8/28/20835760/offset-migos-faze-clan-esports-gaming-interview.

Webster, Andrew. 2020. “NFL Star Jay Ajayi Is Now a Pro Gamer.” Last modified January 7, 2020. www.theverge.com/platform/amp/2020/1/7/21054962/jay-ajayi-nfl-mls-esports-fifa-philadelphia-union.

Williams, Katie. 2020. “Clash of Clans Grossed $727 Million in 2019, a 27% Increase Over 2018.” Last modified January 8, 2020. https://sensortower.com/blog/clash-of-clans-revenue-2019.

Wijman, Tom. 2018. “Mobile Revenues Account for More Than 50% of the Global Games Market as It Reaches $137.9 Billion in 2018.” Last modified April 30, 2018. https://newzoo.com/insights/articles/global-games-market-reaches-137-9-billion-in-2018-mobile-games-take-half.

Witkowski, Emma. 2012. “On the Digital Playing Field: How We ‘Do Sport’ With Networked Computer Games.” *Games and Culture* 7 (5): 349-374.

World Cyber Games (WCG). 2019. “Latest Event: WCG 2019 Xi’an.” Last modified July 21, 2019. www.wcg.com.

Wright, Steven. 2018. “Twin Galaxies Aims to Be Arbiter of Not Just High Scores but Competitive Gaming.” *Variety*. Last modified July 24, 2018. https://variety.com/2018/gaming/features/twin-galaxies-billy-mitchell-jace-hall-high-scores-1202883050.

Zampella, Vince. n.d. “A Message From Vince Zampella on Apex Legends.” Accessed January 13, 2020. www.ea.com/games/apex-legends/news/apex-legends-10-million-players.

CHAPTER 2

Anderson, Monica, and Jingjing Jiang. 2018. “Teens, Social Media & Technology 2018.” Last modified May 31, 2018. www.pewresearch.org/internet/2018/05/31/teens-social-media-technology-2018.

Baker, Suzanne. 2017. “‘Minecraft’ and Other eSports Compete for Legitimacy as Kids’ Activities.” Last modified April 14, 2017. www.chicagotribune.com/suburbs/naperville-sun/ct-nvs-minecraft-league-for-kids-st-0409-20170414-story.html.

Buzby, Jon, and Josh Shannon. 2020. “UD creates varsity gaming team, opens state-of-the-art arena.” Last modified February 22, 2020. www.newarkpostonline.com/news/ud-creates-varsity-gaming-team-opens-state-of-the-art/article_c547842f-9f70-506f-b843-3e4dbd06077b.html.

College AD. 2018. “eSports and the Mountain West: A Winning Combination.” Last modified November 26, 2018. https://collegead.com/mountain-west-esports.

Collins, Y. 2019. “Kyle ‘Bugha’ Giersdorf ‘surprised’ to win Esports Player of the Year at the 2019 Esports Awards.” Last modified November 17, 2019. https://www.skysports.com/more-sports/esports/news/34214/11863136/kyle-bugha-giersdorf-surprised-to-win-esports-player-of-the-year-at-the-2019-esports-awards.

Conditt, Jessica. 2017. “Overwatch League Pro Players Will Earn at Least $50,000 a Year.” Last modified July 26, 2017. www.engadget.com/2017/07/26/overwatch-league-salary-esports-players-health-insurance-blizzard.

Doran, Leo. 2017. “How ‘eSports’ Is Changing the College Sports Scene.” Last modified February 27, 2017. www.insidesources.com/gamers-receive-college-scholarships-esports-culture-scrutiny.

Esports Ohio. 2020. “Getting Started Esports Presentation.” Last modified 2020. www.esportsohio.org/resources.

Game Arena. 2019. “Game Arena: Esports Facility.” Last modified 2019. www.game-arena.co.

Hayward, Andrew. 2019. “NCAA Votes to Not Govern Collegiate Esports.” Last modified May 17, 2019. https://esportsobserver.com/ncaa-nogo-collegiate-esports.

Heilweil, Rachel. 2019. “Infoporn: College Esports Players Are Cashing In Big.” Last modified January 21, 2019. www.wired.com/story/infoporn-college-esports-players-cashing-in-big.

Hendrickson, Brian. 2018. “Game On.” *Champion*, Spring: 50-55. https://issuu.com/championmag/docs/champion_magazine_spring_2018.

Hendrickson, Brian. 2019. “SCAC Joins Expanding List of Conferences, Schools to Plug Into Esports Trend.” Last modified April 17, 2019. www.ncaa.org/champion/scac-joins-expanding-list-conferences-schools-plug-esports-trend.

HSEL. 2020. “Want Esports Taught at Your School?” Last modified 2020. www.highschoolesportsleague.com/high-school-partnership/#curriculum.

Kalinowski, Bob. 2019. “More NEPA Colleges Forming Esports Programs.” Last modified April 21, 2019. https://apnews.com/25cd9fcece514a2bad875ccc0d0f33a8.

Lenhart, Amanda. 2015. “Chapter 3: Video Games Are Key Elements in Friendships for Many Boys.” Last modified August 6, 2015. https://www.pewresearch.org/internet/2015/08/06/chapter-3-video-games-are-key-elements-in-friendships-for-many-boys/.

MAAC. 2019. "MAAC Partners with Riot Games, Introduces New Opportunity for Postseason Play." Last modified November 7, 2019. https://maacsports.com/news/2019/11/7/esports-maac-partners-with-riot-games-introduces-new-opportunity-for-postseason-play.aspx.

NACE. 2020a. "Home: Collegiate Esports Governing Body." Last modified 2020. https://nacesports.org.

NACE. 2020b. "NACE Announce CSGO Competition." Last modified January 16, 2020. https://nacesports.org/nace-csgo-competition-spring-2020.

NASEF. 2020. "Esports + Middle School." Last modified 2020. www.esportsfed.org/learning/curriculum/ms.

Phillips, Caron. 2018. "Phillips: Collegiate Esports Are on the Rise but Will Have to Figure Out How to Be More Appealing and Welcoming to Female Gamers." Last modified July 20, 2018. www.nydailynews.com/sports/ny-sports-eports-college-schorlarships-20180719-story.html.

Ryan, Kevin J. 2019. "In Just One Year, This Startup Got Two-Thirds of U.S. High Schools to Adopt E-Sports." Last modified March 10, 2020. Retrieved from www.inc.com/kevin-j-ryan/playvs-esports-high-schools-series-c-delane-parnell.html.

Schaffhauser, Dian. 2019. "Eastern Conference Esports Grows to 57 Schools." Last modified October 7, 2019. https://campustechnology.com/articles/2019/10/07/eastern-conference-esports-grows-to-57-schools.aspx.

Schaffhauser, Dian. 2020. "Athletic Conferences Partner With ESL Collegiate for Greater Esports Reach." Last modified February 19, 2020. https://campustechnology.com/articles/2020/02/19/athletic-conferences-partner-with-esl-collegiate-for-greater-esports-reach.aspx.

Smith, Michael. 2019. "NJCAA to Create Collegiate Esports National Championship." Last modified September 10, 2019. https://esportsobserver.com/njcaa-national-college-esports.

Smith, Michael, and Ben Fischer. 2018. "Final Four-Nite? NCAA Explores Move to Sponsor Esports." Last modified November 19, 2018. www.sportsbusinessdaily.com/Journal/Issues/2018/11/19/Esports/Esports.aspx.

Stoller, Eric. 2019. "An Epic Update on Collegiate Esports." Last modified May 16, 2019. www.insidehighered.com/blogs/student-affairs-and-technology/epic-update-collegiate-esports.

Tespa. 2020. "What Is Tespa?" Last modified 2020. https://tespa.org/about.

Yee, Nick. 2017. "Beyond 50/50: Breaking Down the Percentage of Female Gamers by Genre." Last modified January 19, 2017. https://quanticfoundry.com/2017/01/19/female-gamers-by-genre.

CHAPTER 3

Abrams, Olivia, and Christina Settimi. 2019. "Gen.G And Bumble Team Up For An All-Female Esports Partnership." Last modified August 6, 2019. https://www.forbes.com/sites/oliviaabrams/2019/08/06/geng-and-bumble-hook-up-and-create-an-all-female-gaming-partnership/#341c6a249127.

Almasy, Steve, and Melissa Alonso. 2019. "His 'Swatting' Call Led to the Death of a Man. Now He is Going to Prison for 20 Years." Last modified March 30, 2019. www.cnn.com/2019/03/29/us/swatting-suspect-20-year-sentence/index.html.

American Psychiatric Association. 2018. "Internet Gaming." Last modified June 2018. www.psychiatry.org/patients-families/internet-gaming.

Anselimo, Tim. 2014. "[CS:GO] coL.n0thing swatted (STREAM HIGHLIGHTS)." Last modified July 11, 2014. www.youtube.com/watch?v=AQ8T0CZ0sbA.

AnyKey. 2020a. "About AnyKey." Last modified 2020. https://www.anykey.org/en/about.

AnyKey. 2020b. "GLHF Pledge." Last modified 2020. www.anykey.org/en/pledge.

Bartle, Richard A. 2004. *Designing Virtual Worlds*. San Francisco: New Riders.

Bian, Mingyu, Carina Carbetta, Olivia Green, Dan Hoyt, and Joan Rodriguez. 2019. "Exploring an Equity and Inclusivity Problem: Gender and Ethnic Diversity in Video Games." Last modified October 24, 2019. https://amt-lab.org/blog/2019/10/gender-amp-ethnic-diversity-in-video-games-exploring-core-games-inclusivity-problem.

Blumenthal, Ralph. 1976. "Death Race." Last modified December 28, 1976. www.nytimes.com/1976/12/28/archives/death-race-game-gains-favor-but-not-with-the-safety-council.html.

Bruckman, Amy. 1994. "Programming for Fun: MUDs as a Context for Collaborative Learning." In *Proceedings of the National Educational Computing Conference*. Eugene, OR: International Society for Technology in Education.

Buckels, Erin E., Paul D. Trapnell, and Delroy L. Paulhus. 2014. "Trolls Just Want to Have Fun." *Personality and Individual Differences 67*: 97-102. https://doi.org/10.1016/j.paid.2014.01.016.

Chadborn, Daniel, Patrick Edwards, and Stephen Reysen. 2018. "Reexamining Differences Between Fandom and Local Sense of Community." *Psychology of Popular Media Culture 7* (3): 241.

Cole, Helena, and Mark D. Griffiths. 2007. "Social Interactions in Massively Multiplayer Online Role-Playing Gamers." *Cyberpsychology & Behavior 10* (4): 575-583.

Cowherd, Colin. 2015. "Cowherd: eSports is for booger-eaters | THE HERD." Last modified September 29, 2015. www.youtube.com/watch?v=_Rwt9NNNJIk.

Dunkey. 2015. "I'm Done with League of Legends." Last modified September 12, 2015. www.youtube.com/watch?v=VjzgbZL12VI.

Flatow, Ira. 1993. *They All Laughed . . . From Light Bulbs to Lasers: The Fascinating Stories Behind the Great Inventions That Have Changed Our Lives*. New York: HarperCollins.

Glanville, Jennifer L., and Elisa Jayne Bienenstock. 2009. "A Typology for Understanding the Connections Among Different Forms of Social Capital." *American Behavioral Scientist 52* (11): 1507-1530.

Hamilton, William A., Oliver Garretson, and Andruid Kerne. 2014. "Streaming on Twitch: Fostering Participatory Communities of Play Within Live Mixed Media." In *Proceedings of the SIGCHI Conference on Human Factors in Computing Systems*, April: 1315-1324. https://doi.org/10.1145/2556288.2557048.

Harris, Eric. 1999. "Eric Harris' Journal." Last modified 2019. www.columbine-guide.com/columbine-eric-harris-journal.

Hernández, Javier C., and Albee Zhang. 2019. "90 Minutes a Day, Until 10 P.M.: China Sets Rules for Young Gamers." Last modified November 8, 2019. www.nytimes.com/2019/11/06/business/china-video-game-ban-young.html.

Huang, Zheping. 2018. "Gaming addiction under spotlight in China as regulators tighten control on industry." Last modified September 4, 2018. https://www.scmp.com/tech/apps-social/article/2162773/gaming-addiction-under-spotlight-china-regulators-tighten-control.

Kuss, Daria J., Halley M. Pontes, and Mark D. Griffiths. 2018. "Neurobiological Correlates in Internet Gaming Disorder: A Systematic Literature Review." *Frontiers in Psychiatry 9*: 1-12. https://doi.org/10.3389/fpsyt.2018.00166.

Lenhart, Amanda. 2015. "Chapter 3: Video Games Are Key Elements in Friendships for Many Boys." Last modified August 6, 2015. www.pewresearch.org/internet/2015/08/06/chapter-3-video-games-are-key-elements-in-friendships-for-many-boys.

Link, Bruce G., and Jo C. Phelan. 2001. "Conceptualizing Stigma." *Annual Review of Sociology 27* (1): 363-385.

Ministry of Human Resources and Social Security (MOHRSS) of The People's Republic of China. 2019. "Notice from the General Office of the Ministry of Human Resources and Social Security, the General Office of Market Supervision Administration, and the Statistics Office on the release of professional information regarding artificial intelligence engineering and technical personnel." Last modified April 1, 2019. www.mohrss.gov.cn/gkml/zcfg/gfxwj/201904/t20190402_313702.html.

Naskar, Subrata, Robin Victor, Kamal Nath, and Chiradeep Sengupta. 2016. "'One Level More:' A Narrative Review on Internet Gaming Disorder." *Industrial Psychiatry Journal 25* (2): 145-154. https://doi.org/10.4103/ipj.ipj_67_16.

Ning, Jizhe. 2019. "2019 Sports Industry Statistics Classification, Order No. 26 from the National Bureau of Statistics." Last modified April 9, 2019. www.stats.gov.cn/tjgz/tzgb/201904/t20190409_1658556.html.

North American Scholastic Esports Federation. 2018. "Why Should Educators Embrace Esports?" Last modified on October 30, 2018. https://www.nasef.org/news/blog/why-should-educators-embrace-esports/.

Reysen, Stephen, and Nyla R. Branscombe. 2010. "Fanship and Fandom: Comparisons Between Sport and Non-Sport Fans." *Journal of Sport Behavior 33* (2): 176-193.

Rogers, Ryan. 2016. *How Video Games Impact Players: The Pitfalls and Benefits of a Gaming Society*. Lanham, MD: Lexington Books.

theScore esports. 2019. "What is Trolling? The Complex Art of Being an @$$hole Gamer | OverExplained." Last modified December 22, 2019. www.youtube.com/watch?v=OCPjqlNZJ_w.

Vella, Kellie, Daniel Johnson, Vanessa Wan Sze Cheng, Tracey Davenport, Jo Mitchell, Madison Klarkowski, and Cody Phillips. 2019. "A Sense of Belonging: Pokémon GO and Social Connectedness." *Games and Culture 14* (6): 583-603. https://doi.org/10.1177/1555412017719973.

World Health Organization. 2018. "Gaming Disorder." Last modified September 2018. www.who.int/features/qa/gaming-disorder/en.

Xia, Fei. 2000. "Computer games aimed at children, electronic heroin." Last modified May 9, 2000. www.people.com.cn/GB/channel1/13/20000509/58873.html.

CHAPTER 4

Baym, Nancy K. 2007. "The New Shape of Online Community: The Example of Swedish Independent Music Fandom." Last modified August 6, 2007. https://kuscholarworks.ku.edu/bitstream/handle/1808/7545/Baym_ShapeofOnlineCommunity.pdf?sequence=1.

Betwayesports. 2020. "Betting help." Last modified May 30, 2020. https://esports.betway.com/policies/betting-help/.

Bhatt, Neelay. 2019. "Esports: The Next Big Thing for Parks and Rec." Last modified September 1, 2019. www.nrpa.org/parks-recreation-magazine/2019/september/esports-the-next-big-thing-for-parks-and-rec.

Bowles, Nellie, and Michael Keller. 2019. "Video Games and Online Chats Are 'Hunting Grounds' for Sexual Predators." Last modified December 7, 2019. www.nytimes.com/interactive/2019/12/07/us/video-games-child-sex-abuse.html.

British Esports Association. 2019. "Esports Job Spotlight: Coach / Analyst." Accessed December 2, 2019. https://britishesports.org/careers/coach-analyst.

Cohen, Andrew. 2019. "The NFL Invests in Mobile Esports Platform Skillz." Last modified November 21, 2019. https://sporttechie.com/nfl-invests-mobile-esports-skillz.

Crecente, Brian. 2018. "Nearly 70% of Americans Play Video Games, Mostly on Smartphones (Study)." Last modified September 11, 2018. https://variety.com/2018/gaming/news/how-many-people-play-games-in-the-u-s-1202936332.

Esguerra, Tyler. 2019. "Dignitas Merges With Clutch Gaming's LCS franchise." Last modified June 6, 2019. https://dotesports.com/league-of-legends/news/dignitas-merges-with-clutch-gamings-lcs-franchise.

Everett, Angeline. 2019. "eSports online betting projected to hit $13 Billion in 2020: Analysts USA Casino Online.com." Last modified March 15, 2019. https://www.usaonlinecasino.com/casino-news/esports-online-betting-projected-to-hit-13-billion-in-2020-analysts/.

Ewoldsen, David R., Cassie A. Eno, Bradley M. Okdie, John A. Velez, Rosanna E. Guadagno, and Jamie DeCoster. 2012. "Effect of Playing Violent Video Games Cooperatively or Competitively on Subsequent Cooperative Behavior." *Cyberpsychology, Behavior, and Social Networking 15* (5): 277-280.

Granic, Isabela, Adam Lobel, and Rutger C.M.E. Engels. 2014. "The Benefits of Playing Video Games." *American Psychologist 69* (1): 66-78. https://doi.org/10.1037/a0034857.

Henry, Jasmine. 2019. "Professional Overwatch Team Possibly Has Ties to Organized Crime." Last modified September 24, 2019. https://gamerant.com/overwatch-league-australia-esports-organized-crime.

Influencer Marketing. 2019. "Top 10 eSports Teams, Earnings, and Salaries." Last modified March 15, 2019. https://influencermarketinghub.com/top-10-esports-teams-earnings-and-salaries.

iResearch Center. 2019. "2019 China Esports Industry Research Report." Last modified March 2019. www.iresearch.com.cn/Detail/report?id=3352andisfree=0.

Jackson, Linda A., Edward A. Witt, Alexander Ivan Games, Hiram E. Fitzgerald, Alexander Von Eye, and Yong Zhao. 2012. "Information Technology Use and Creativity: Findings From the Children and Technology Project." *Computers in Human Behavior 28* (2): 370-376.

Kim, Hongje "Koer," and Junseok "Tonny" Bae. 2018. "How to Become a Pro Gamer - Seung Heun Lee at Game Coach, Esports Academy." Last modified November 18, 2018. www.invenglobal.com/articles/6767/how-to-become-a-pro-gamer-seung-heun-lee-at-game-coach-esports-academy.

Kim, Max. 2018. "Want to Be a Pro Gamer? Look No Further than Game Coach Academy." Last modified September 21, 2018. www.espn.com/esports/story/_/id/24754523/game-coach-academy-seoul-south-korea-max-kim.

MTG. 2020. "Esports." Last modified 2020. www.mtg.com/esports.

Pannekeet, Jurre. 2019. "Zooming in on the Biggest Franchises in Esports: 71% of Fans Watch Only One Game." Last modified August 21, 2019. https://newzoo.com/insights/articles/zooming-in-on-the-biggest-franchises-in-esports-71-of-fans-watch-only-one-game.

Perrin, Andrew. 2018. "5 facts about Americans and Video Games." Last modified September 17, 2018. www.pewresearch.org/fact-tank/2018/09/17/5-facts-about-americans-and-video-games.

Pike, Nicole, and Stephen Master. 2017. "The Esports Playbook." Last modified 2017. https://nielsensports.com/reports/esports-playbook-2017.

Pike, Nicole, and Guy Port. 2018. "The Esports Playbook Asia: Maximizing Investment Through Understanding the Fans." Last modified 2018. https://nielsensports.com/reports/esports-playbook-asia-maximizing-investment-understanding-fans.

Raghuram, Vignesh. 2018. "5 National Governments in Asia that Support Esports in Their Country." Last modified December 13, 2018. https://afkgaming.com/archive/articles/5-national-governments-in-asia-that-support-esports-in-their-country.

Skillz. "The Skillz Team." Last modified 2020. www.skillz.com/about-us/.

Thier, Dave. 2019. "Report: EA Paid Ninja $1 Million To Play 'Apex Legends', Which Is Way Too Little." Last modified March 14, 2019. https://www.forbes.com/sites/davidthier/2019/03/14/report-ea-paid-ninja-1-million-to-play-apex-legends-which-is-way-too-little/#71b27d6f27f3.

World Health Organization. 2018. "Gaming disorder." Last modified September 14, 2018. www.who.int/features/qa/gaming-disorder/en.

Wragg, Mike. 2017. "Fan Revolution, Global Fans in the Information Age." Last modified 2017. https://nielsensports.com/fanrevolution.

Xinhua. 2019. "Esports New Growth Point of China's Gaming Industry: Report." Last modified December 19, 2019. www.xinhuanet.com/english/2019-12/19/c_138643724.htm.

CHAPTER 5

Beck, Kellen. 2016. "Owner-Operated PEA Wants to Improve Player Pay in Esports." Last modified September 8, 2016. https://mashable.com/2016/09/08/pea-esports-organization/#PrYdsxN0Msq4.

ECAC. 2020. "Home page – ECAC Esports." Last modified 2020. http://www.ecacesports.com/.

Gardner, David. 2018. "Forget Friday Night Lights, Esports Is Becoming the Next Varsity Obsession." Last modified June 14, 2018. https://bleacherreport.com/articles/2780847-forget-friday-night-lights-esports-is-becoming-the-next-varsity-obsession.

Geracie, Nick. 2019. "NASEF and JHSEF Announce International Collaboration for Esports Youth." Last modified November 9, 2019. www.invenglobal.com/articles/9574/nasef-and-jhsef-announce-international-collaboration-for-esports-youth.

International Esports Federation. 2019. "IESF'S Players' Commission Invites All Players to Participate." Last modified April 22, 2019. https://ie-sf.org/news/3488.

Kennedy, Clint. 2019. "Dr. Kennedy's Guide to Building the Ideal Esports Program." Last modified November 25, 2019. www.playvs.com/news/dr.-kennedy-gets-into-the-details-of-what-a-healthy.

Partin, Will. 2019. "The Esports Pipeline Problem." Last modified July 11, 2019. www.polygon.com/features/2019/7/11/18632716/esports-amateur-pro-players-teams-talent-process.

Scholz, Tobias M. 2019a. *eSports is Business. Management in the World of Competitive Gaming*. Cham, Switzerland: Palgrave.

Scholz, Tobias M. 2019b. "How Over-Regulation Endangers the Long-Term Success of the Overwatch League." Last modified August 1, 2019. https://esportsobserver.com/opinion-owl-regulations.

Takahashi, Dean. 2019. "PlayVS Raises $50 Million More for High School Esports Platform." Last modified September 18, 2019. https://venturebeat.com/2019/09/18/playvs-raises-50-million-more-for-high-school-esports-platform.

WESA. 2019a. "WESA Mandates ESIC Commissioner, Ian Smith, to Conduct Independent Third-Party Review of Allegations Against Ninjas in Pyjamas (NIP)." Last modified August 21, 2019. www.wesa.gg/2019/08/21/nipallegations.

WESA. 2019b. "Ian Smith (ESIC Commissioner) Presents Report Regarding Allegations Against Ninjas in Pyjamas (NiP) to WESA." Last modified September 4, 2019. www.wesa.gg/2019/09/04/mediastatement_re_nip.

CHAPTER 6

American Marketing Association (AMA). 2017. "Definitions of Marketing." Retrieved January 22, 2020. www.ama.org/the-definition-of-marketing-what-is-marketing.

Arkenberg, Chris, Doug Van Dyke, J.D. Tengberg, and Nathan Baltuskonis. 2018. "eSports graduates to the big leagues." Last modified July 23, 2018. www2.deloitte.com/us/en/insights/industry/telecommunications/capitalizing-on-growth-of-esports-industry.html.

Association of National Advertisers (ANA). 2020. "Brand Activation Disciplines." Retrieved January 30, 2020. www.ana.net/content/show/id/brand-activation-disciplines.

Bailey, Jason M. 2019. "Adaptive Video Game Controllers Open Worlds for Gamers With Disabilities." Last modified February 20, 2020. www.nytimes.com/2019/02/20/business/video-game-controllers-disabilities.html.

Barcraft. n.d. "The International Dota 2 Championships Pubstomp Listing." Retrieved January 31, 2020. www.barcraft.com.

CBS News. 2017. "That Dragon, Cancer: A Game for Joel." Last modified March 12, 2017. www.cbsnews.com/news/that-dragon-cancer-a-game-for-joel.

Chen, Yuyu. 2017. "Inside Activision's 'Call of Duty' Marketing Playbook." Last modified April 26, 2017. https://digiday.com/marketing/call-of-duty-marketing.

Cunningham, George B., Sheranne Fairley, Lesley Ferkins, Shannon Kerwin, Daniel Lock, Sally Shaw, and Pamela Wicker. 2018. "Esport: Construct Specifications and Implications for Sport Management." *Sport Management Review 21* (1): 1-6.

Duran, Heidi. 2017a. "Do Microinfluencers Really Work? Brands (And Results) Say Yes." Retrieved January 26, 2020. www.ion.co/microinfluencers-really-work-brands-results-say-yes.

Duran, Heidi. 2017b. "Brands Are Recruiting Video Game Characters As Spokespeople." Last modified September 27, 2017. www.alistdaily.com/strategy/brands-recruiting-video-game-characters-spokesmen.

Duran, Heidi. 2019. "Ninja's Successful Mixer Move Shows Influencers Can (and Should) Diversify Platforms." Last modified August 7, 2019. www.alistdaily.com/lifestyle/ninjas-successful-mixer-move-shows-influencers-can-diversify-platforms.

Engine Group. 2019. "Esports: The Future of Digital Marketing." Last modified October 2, 2019. https://enginegroup.com/us/news/stay-curious/esports-the-future-of-digital-marketing.

Entertainment Software Association. 2019. "2019 Essential Facts About the Computer and Video Game Industry." Last modified May 2019. www.theesa.com/wp-content/uploads/2019/05/ESA_Essential_facts_2019_final.pdf.

Favis, Elise. 2020. "Activision Raises $1.6 Million Via Call of Duty: Modern Warfare for Australia Fire Relief." Last modified February 3, 2020. www.washingtonpost.com/video-games/2020/02/03/activision-raises-16-million-via-call-duty-modern-warfare-australia-fire-relief.

Funk, Daniel C., Anthony D. Pizzo, and Bradley J. Baker. 2018. "Esport Management: Embracing ESport Education and Research Opportunities." *Sport Management Review 21* (1): 7-13.

Futian, Shi. 2019. "Phoenix Rises to Conquer the World." Last modified November 20, 2019. www.chinadaily.com.cn/a/201911/20/WS5dd48e9ea310cf3e355788ca.html.

Gamepedia. 2019. "The International 2019 Battle Pass." Last modified October 31, 2019. https://dota2.gamepedia.com/The_International_2019_Battle_Pass.

Gilbert, Ben. 2019. "8 Reasons Why 'Apex Legends' is the Best Battle Royale Game Available." Last modified April 15, 2019. www.businessinsider.com/apex-legends-best-battle-royale-game-2019-4.

Griffin, Andrew. 2018. "FIFA 19: Real Madrid Fans Furious After Club Signs Virtual Player Alex Hunter." Last modified August 9, 2019. www.independent.co.uk/life-style/gadgets-and-tech/gaming/fifa-19-real-madrid-alex-hunter-transfer-deadline-day-player-real-virtual-a8485006.html.

Grubb, Jeff. 2020. "Activision Blizzard Brings Overwatch, Call of Duty Esports Exclusively to YouTube." Last modified January 24, 2020. https://venturebeat.com/2020/01/24/activision-blizzard-google-youtube-esports-deal/.

Hamari, Juho, and Max Sjöblom. 2017. "What Is Esports and Why Do People Watch It?" *Internet Research 27* (2): 211-232.

Hamilton, Daniel. 2018. "Shoutcasting and Sportscasting Have Similar Elements; Both Can Be Throaty." Last modified November 13, 2018. www.sportsbroadcastjournal.com/shoutcasting-and-sportscasting-have-similar-elements-both-can-be-throaty.

Hayward, Andrew. 2018. "Inside ESL's Inventive DHL Dota 2 Activation for ESL One Hamburg." Last modified October 31, 2018. https://esportsobserver.com/inside-esls-inventive-dhl-dota-2-activation-for-esl-one-hamburg.

Hedlund, David P. 2019. "The Motivations of Esports Players." In *Understanding Esports: An Introduction to the Global Phenomenon*, edited by Ryan Rogers, 95-114. Lanham, MD: Lexington Books.

Joseph, Stephen. 2016. "7 Qualities of Truly Authentic People." Last modified August 29, 2016. www.psychologytoday.com/us/blog/what-doesnt-kill-us/201608/7-qualities-truly-authentic-people.

Liffreing, Ilyse. 2017. "'A Whole New World': Coke Has a Sponsorship Deal with a Virtual Soccer Star in 'FIFA 18'." Last modified September 21, 2017. https://digiday.com/marketing/whole-new-world-coke-sponsorship-deal-virtual-soccer-star-fifa18.

Liquipedia. 2019. "The International." Last modified December 6, 2019. https://liquipedia.net/dota2/The_International.

Marketing Accountability Standards Board (MASB). n.d. "Experiential Marketing." Retrieved January 30, 2020. https://marketing-dictionary.org/e/experiential-marketing.

Millennial Esports. 2019. "Millennial Esports' Esports Data Division Highlights 41% Streaming Growth at Vegas Esports Business Summit." Last modified September 9, 2019. www.newswire.ca/news-releases/millennial-esports-esports-data-division-highlights-41-streaming-growth-at-vegas-esports-business-summit-893550423.html.

Mullin, Bernard J., Stephen Hardy, and William A. Sutton. 2014. *Sport Marketing*. 4th ed. Champaign, IL: Human Kinetics.

Naraine, Michael L., and Henry Wear. 2019. "The Esports Consumer Experience." In *Understanding Esports: An Introduction to the Global Phenomenon*, edited by Ryan Rogers, 85-93. Lanham, MD: Lexington Books.

Nelson, Randy. 2019. "Clash of Clans Earns $27 Million in One Week as Revenue Grows 145% Following Season Pass Debut." Last modified April 9, 2019. https://sensortower.com/blog/clash-of-clans-gold-pass.

Newzoo. 2019. "Global esports market report." Retrieved January 15, 2020. https://newzoo.com/insights/trend-reports/newzoo-global-esports-market-report-2019-light-version.

Nielsen. 2019. "Esports Playbook for Brands 2019." Retrieved January 28, 2020. www.nielsen.com/wp-content/uploads/sites/3/2019/05/esports-playbook-for-brands-2019.pdf.

Niko Partners. 2019. "Special Report: Evolution of Mobile Esports for the Mass Market." Last modified August 25, 2019. https://nikopartners.com/wp-content/uploads/2019/08/Evolution-of-Mobile-Esports-for-the-Mass-Market.pdf.

Pannekeet, Jurre. 2019. "Zooming in on the Biggest Franchises in Esports: 71% of Fans Watch Only One Game." Last modified August 21, 2019. https://newzoo.com/insights/articles/zooming-in-on-the-biggest-franchises-in-esports-71-of-fans-watch-only-one-game.

Pe, Gabriel. 2019. "China, Europe Set to Conquer League of Legends World Championship." Last modified November 4, 2019. www.spin.ph/esports/china-europe-league-of-legends-world-championship-a2186-20191104.

Pizzo, Anthony D., Sangwon Na, Bradley J. Baker, Mi Ae Lee, Doohan Kim, and Daniel C. Funk. 2018. "Esport Vs. Sport: A Comparison of Spectator Motives." *Sport Marketing Quarterly 27* (2): 108-123.

Qian, Tyreal Yizhou, Jerred Junqi Wang, James Jianhui Zhang, and Laura Zhenqiu Lu. 2019. "It Is In the Game: Dimensions of Esports Online Spectator Motivation and Development of a Scale." *European Sport Management Quarterly*. https://doi.org/10.1080/16184742.2019.1630464.

Qian, Tyreal Yizhou, James Jianhui Zhang, Jerred Junqi Wang, and John Hulland. 2019. "Beyond the Game: Dimensions of Esports Online Spectator Demand." *Communication & Sport*. https://doi.org/10.1177/2167479519839436.

Reuters. 2019. "Call of Duty League to Kickoff Jan. 24 in Minneapolis." Last modified October 29, 2019. www.espn.com/esports/story/_/id/27958880/call-duty-league-kickoff-jan-24-minneapolis.

Riot Games. 2019. "Riot Games Forms the Riot Scholastic Association of America." Last modified May 22, 2019. www.prnewswire.com/news-releases/riot-games-forms-the-riot-scholastic-association-of-america-300855269.html.

Rogers, Charlotte. 2018. "Understanding the Esports Community: What Brands Need to Know." Last modified May 18, 2018. www.marketingweek.com/understanding-esports-community.

Rovell, Darren. 2017. "U.S. Venues that Should Have Esports Events in 2017." Last modified January 11, 2017. www.espn.com/esports/story/_/id/18452114/2017-venues-esports-events.

Schau, Hope Jensen, Albert M. Muñiz Jr, and Eric J. Arnould. 2009. "How Brand Community Practices Create Value." *Journal of Marketing 73* (5): 30-51.

Scholz, Tobias. 2019. *Esports Is Business: Management in the World of Competitive Gaming*. Cham, Switzerland: Palgrave Macmillan.

Seo, Yuri. 2013. "Electronic Sports: A New Marketing Landscape of the Experience Economy." *Journal of Marketing Management 29* (13-14): 1542-1560.

Seo, Yuri, and Sang-Uk Jung. 2016. "Beyond Solidarity Play in Computer Games: The Social Practices of Esports." *Journal of Consumer Culture 16*: 635-655.

Takahashi, Dean. 2019. "Call of Duty League: How Activision Reimagined its City-Based Esports Structure." Last modified October 18, 2019. https://venturebeat.com/2019/10/18/call-of-duty-league-how-activision-reimagined-its-city-based-esports-structure.

The Story Mob. 2020. "Seven Commandments of Esports Communications." About The Story Mob. Retrieved January 22, 2020. www.thestorymob.com/s/The_Story_Mob_White_Paper_Seven_Commandments_Of_Esports_Communications_2018.pdf.

Tobin, Ben. 2019. "Mobile Video Game Players' Mindset: They Don't Consider Themselves 'Gamers,' Survey Finds." Last modified February 13, 2019. www.usatoday.com/story/tech/2019/02/13/smartphone-owners-play-video-games-but-deny-gamer-label/2847788002.

Turner, Ash. 2020. "How Many Smartphones Are In The World?" Last modified January 2020. www.bankmycell.com/blog/how-many-phones-are-in-the-world.

U.S. Chamber of Commerce Foundation. 2019. "Corporate Social Responsibility in the Gaming Industry." Last modified February 27, 2019. www.uschamberfoundation.org/reports/corporate-social-responsibility-gaming-industry.

Valve. n.d. "The International Battle Pass." Retrieved January 31, 2020. www.dota2.com/international/battlepass.

Van Boom, Daniel. 2020. "Call of Duty Outback Relief Pack raises $1.6M to combat Australian bushfires." Last modified February 3, 2020. https://www.cnet.com/news/call-of-duty-outback-relief-pack-raises-1-6m-to-combat-australian-bushfires/.

Westcott, Kevin, Jeff Loucks, David Ciampa, and Shashank Srivastava. 2019. "Digital Media Trends: Video Gaming Goes Mainstream." Last modified June 10, 2019. www2.deloitte.com/us/en/insights/industry/technology/digital-media-trends-consumption-habits-survey/trends-in-gaming-esports.html.

Wijman, Tom. 2019. "The Global Games Market Will Generate $152.1 Billion in 2019 as the U.S. Overtakes China as the Biggest Market." Last modified June 18, 2019. https://newzoo.com/insights/articles/the-global-games-market-will-generate-152-1-billion-in-2019-as-the-u-s-overtakes-china-as-the-biggest-market.

Wong, Steven. 2017. "Experts Explain How Brands Should Approach Esports." Last modified Spetember 29, 2017. www.alistdaily.com/media/experts-explain-brands-approach-esports.

YouTube. 2014. "Warriors (ft. Imagine Dragons) | Worlds 2014 - League of Legends." Retrieved January 22, 2020. www.youtube.com/watch?v=fmI_Ndrxy14.

YouTube. 2020. "Call Of Duty League 2020 Season | Launch Weekend." Retrieved January 24-26, 2020. www.youtube.com/codleague/live.

CHAPTER 7

Ali, Amna. 2020. "Red Bull Limited 'Ninja' Edition." Last modified February 12, 2020. https://ninjamerchstore.com/ninja-red-bull.

Ashton, Graham. 2019. "Esports' Quest for the Average Minute Audience." Last modified September 11, 2019. https://esportsobserver.com/nielsen-owl-ama-viewership-intro.

Berzen, Jake. 2019. "Navigating Esports." Last modified February 20, 2019. https://lumency.co/2019/02/20/navigating-esports.

CORSAIR. n.d. "Team CORSAIR Esports: Sponsored Teams." Retrieved on February 15, 2020. www.corsair.com/us/en/esports.

D'Anastasio, Cecilia. 2019. "Shady Numbers And Bad Business: Inside The Esports Bubble." Last modified May 23, 2019. https://kotaku.com/as-esports-grows-experts-fear-its-a-bubble-ready-to-po-1834982843.

Dell. n.d. "ALIENWARE x RIOT GAMES." Retrieved February 14, 2020. www.dell.com/en-us/member/gaming/esports-partners.

Fanelli, Jason. 2019. "Tyler 'Ninja' Blevins Inks Adidas Sponsorship." Last modified August 28, 2019. www.hollywoodreporter.com/news/tyler-ninja-blevins-inks-adidas-sponsorship-1235039.

Fischer, Ben. 2018. "Esports' Next Big Mission: Win Over Sponsors." Last modified May 28, 2018. www.sportsbusinessdaily.com/Journal/Issues/2018/05/28/In-Depth/Esports.aspx.

Hayward, Andrew. 2019. "MTN DEW AMP GAME FUEL's Gaming Focus Driving Sales, Says PepsiCo CEO." Last modified July 11, 2019. https://esportsobserver.com/pepsico-mtn-dew-soda-share.

Hitt, Kevin. 2020a. "LCS Adds Mastercard 'Player of the Week' Activation, Partners With GreenPark Sports." Last modified January 16, 2020. https://esportsobserver.com/lcs-2020-mastercard-greenpark.

Hitt, Kevin. 2020b. "Nielsen and LCS Implement Live+ Metric to Measure VOD Viewing." Last modified February 27, 2020. https://esportsobserver.com/lcs-nielsen-viewership-tools.

Holland, Frank, and Fahiemah Al-Ali. 2019. "Puma Teams Up with Cloud9, Becoming the Latest Sports Apparel Brand to Join the Esports Trend." Last modified October 10, 2019. www.cnbc.com/2019/10/10/puma-teams-up-with-cloud9-esports-in-an-apparel-deal.html.

IEG. 2017a. "IEG's Guide to Sponsorship." Chicago, IL: IEG, LLC. www.sponsorship.com/ieg/files/59/59ada496-cd2c-4ac2-9382-060d86fcbdc4.pdf.

IEG. 2017b. "Sponsor Survey Reveals Dissatisfaction With Property Partners." Last modified December 18, 2017. www.sponsorship.com/Report/2017/12/18/Sponsor-Survey-Reveals-Dissatisfaction-With-Proper.aspx.

IEG. 2018. "What Sponsors Want & Where Dollars Will Go in 2018." Last modified 2018. www.sponsorship.com/IEG/files/f3/f3cfac41-2983-49be-8df6-3546345e27de.pdf.

IEG. 2019. "IEG Esport Sector Update." Last modified 2019. www.sponsorship.com/getattachment/cbe957cb-7c51-453d-8969-b2813acdce75/IEG_Esports_Infographic_2019--3-.pdf.aspx.

iSpot.tv. 2016. "Arby's TV Commercial, 'ELEAGUE: Rush B.'" Last modified 2016. www.ispot.tv/ad/AK8S/arbys-eleague-too-real.

Lindner, Rob. 2020. "EMLS League Series One Social Analysis." Last modified January 23, 2020. https://zoomph.com/blog/emls-league-series-one-social-analysis.

Logitech G. n.d. "Esports Teams and Pro Gamers Win with Logitech G." Retrieved February 15, 2020. www.logitechg.com/en-us/esports.html.

LoL Esports Staff. 2019. "Dell Alienware Joins LoL Esports as Official PC & Display Partner." Last modified January 2019. https://nexus.leagueoflegends.com/en-us/2019/01/dell-alienware-joins-lol-esports-as-offi.

Major League Soccer. 2019. "Playstation Giveaway!" Last modified March 18, 2019. https://twitter.com/emls/status/1107643116264267776.

Martin, Ken. 2020. "US Air Force Joins 'Call of Duty' Sponsors for 2020 Season." Last modified January 24, 2020. www.foxbusiness.com/technology/us-air-force-call-of-duty-sponsors.

Mastercard. 2018. "Mastercard Debuts Priceless Experiences for Fans at the League of Legends 2018 World Championship." Last modified October 25, 2018. https://newsroom.mastercard.com/press-releases/mastercard-debuts-priceless-experiences-for-fans-at-the-league-of-legends-2018-world-championship.

Miceli, Max. 2018a. "Red Bull Leverages New Sponsorship With Ninja to Promote Unique Fortnite Event." Last modified June 18, 2018. https://esportsobserver.com/red-bull-ninja.

Miceli, Max. 2018b. "MTN DEW Works With Call of Duty World League for Game Fuel Release; Sponsors OpTic Gaming." Last modified December 5, 2018. https://esportsobserver.com/mtn-dew-cwl-optic.

MLB. 2019. "2019 MLB Season Generates Increases in Consumption and Youth Participation." Last modified September 30, 2019. www.mlb.com/press-release/press-release-2019-mlb-season-generates-increases-in-consumption-and-youth-parti.

MLS Communications. 2018. "MLS Announces PlayStation® as Presenting Sponsor of Inaugural eMLS Cup." Last modified April 3, 2018. www.mlssoccer.com/post/2018/04/03/mls-announces-playstation-presenting-sponsor-inaugural-emls-cup.

MLS Communications. 2019. "MLS Announces eMLS 24 Hours of FIFA 20 Live Stream as Part of 6th Annual MLS WORKS Kick Childhood Cancer Campaign." Last modified September 17, 2019. www.mlssoccer.com/post/2019/09/17/mls-announces-emls-24-hours-fifa-20-live-stream-part-6th-annual-mls-works-kick.

Muncy, Julie. 2019. "Ninja Is Being Immortalized on a Red Bull Can." Last modified March 29, 2019. www.wired.com/story/ninja-red-bull-can.

Nichols, Matt. 2017. "Endemics Vs. Non-Endemics: Esports Expanding Its Sponsorship Horizons." Last modified August 2017. http://sponsorship.org/wp-content/uploads/2017/08/Sportcals-Endemics-vs-Non-Endemics-eSports-expanding-its-sponsorship-horizons.pdf.

Nielsen. 2019a. "Esports Playbook for Brands 2019." Retrieved January 28, 2020. www.nielsen.com/wp-content/uploads/sites/3/2019/05/esports-playbook-for-brands-2019.pdf.

Nielsen. 2019b. "Games 360 U.S. Report." Last modified 2018. www.nielsen.com/wp-content/uploads/sites/3/2019/04/games-360-2018.pdf.

Red Bull. 2019. "How Else Would We Surprise @ninja With the Ninja Red Bull Can? *drone incoming* Available in the U.S. beginning April 1." Last modified March 27, 2019. https://twitter.com/redbull/status/1110873123899895808.

Red Bull Gaming. 2018. "Step Into Ninja's Ultimate Stream Room!" Last modified November 12, 2018. www.youtube.com/watch?v=QgRVDRpLbbc.

Ring, Oliver. 2018. "HyperX Acquires Naming Rights for Allied Esports Arena Las Vegas." Last modified November 16, 2018. https://esportsinsider.com/2018/11/hyperx-acquires-naming-rights-for-allied-esports-arena-las-vegas.

Rolander, Niclas. 2019. "ESports Makes a Deal With Nielsen Deal to Measure Its Audience." Last modified September 27, 2019. www.bloomberg.com/news/articles/2019-09-26/esports-nears-adulthood-with-nielsen-deal-to-measure-audience.

Russ, Hilary. 2019. "Nike to Sponsor China's League of Legends Esports League." Last modified February 28, 2019. www.reuters.com/article/us-nike-tencent-holdings-videogames/nike-to-sponsor-chinas-league-of-legends-esports-league-idUSKCN1QH2IW.

Sinclair, Brendan. 2019. "ESL, Dreamhack Partner With Nielsen for Esports Data." Last modified September 26, 2019. www.gamesindustry.biz/articles/2019-09-26-esl-dreamhack-partner-with-nielsen-for-esports-data.

Singer, Dan, and Jayson Chi. 2019. "The Keys to Esports Marketing: Don't Get 'Ganked.'" Last modified August 2019. www.mckinsey.com/industries/technology-media-and-telecommunications/our-insights/the-keys-to-esports-marketing-dont-get-ganked.

Stern, Adam. 2019a. "Esports Faces New Debate Over Shooter Games." Last modified August 19, 2019. www.sportsbusinessdaily.com/Journal/Issues/2019/08/19/Esports/Esports-violence.aspx.

Stern, Adam. 2019b. "Overwatch League Releasing Nielsen Viewership Figures For First Time." Last modified September 4, 2019. www.sportsbusinessdaily.com/Daily/Issues/2019/09/04/Esports/OWL.aspx.

Swant, Marty. 2019. "Nielsen Is Partnering With Riot Games to Measure Esports Sponsorships." Last modified June 27, 2019. www.adweek.com/digital/nielsen-is-partnering-with-riot-games-to-measure-esports-sponsorships.

Sweeney, Erica. 2019. "Red Bull Partners With Pro Gamer Ninja on Experiential Contest." Last modified March 28, 2019. www.marketingdive.com/news/red-bull-partners-with-pro-gamer-ninja-on-experiential-contest/551486.

Takahashi, Dean. 2018. "Inside Team Liquid's High-End Esports Training Facility." Last modified January 28, 2018. https://venturebeat.com/2018/01/28/inside-team-liquids-high-end-esports-training-facility.

Takahashi, Dean. 2019. "Nielsen: How to Properly Measure the Impact of Esports for Brands and Advertisers." Last modified August 30, 2019. https://venturebeat.com/2019/08/30/nielsen-how-to-properly-measure-the-impact-of-esports-for-brands-and-advertisers.

Wallace, Mitch. 2018. "Mountain Dew's New 'Game Fuel' Drink Has A Seriously Interesting Can." Last modified December 5, 2018. www.forbes.com/sites/mitchwallace/2018/12/05/mountain-dews-new-game-fuel-drink-has-a-seriously-interesting-can/#500c0e582377.

Young, Jabari. 2019. "National Football League television viewership increases 5% for 2019 regular season." Last modified December 31, 2019. www.cnbc.com/2019/12/31/nfl-television-viewership-increases-5percent-for-2019-season.html.

CHAPTER 8

Datanyze. 2020. "Ticketing Systems." Last modified 2020. www.datanyze.com/market-share/ticketing-systems--123.

Duran, Heidi. 2019. "Riot: LEC Spring Split Finals Contributed $2.6M to Rotterdam Economy." Last modified July 11, 2019. https://esportsobserver.com/riot-tourism-lec-spring-rotterdam/.

Lush, Tamara, and Russ Bynum. 2018. "Gaming Tournament Shooting Highlights Security or Lack of It." Last modified August 27, 2018. https://apnews.com/56692f0fa5e444eeb1dc90041845d2bb.

Sweet, Laurel J. 2015. "Bail Doubled for Two Pokemon Plot Suspects." Last modified November 18, 2018. www.bostonherald.com/2015/11/10/bail-doubled-for-two-pokemon-plot-suspects.

CHAPTER 9

AT&T. 2019. "AT&T to Deliver North America's First 5G-Enabled Esports Event Live Stream Coverage." Last modified November 15, 2019. https://about.att.com/newsroom/2019/dreamhack_5g.html.

Dallas Fuel. 2020. "Dallas Fuel - Home." Last modified 2020. https://dallasfuel.com.

Danziger, Pamela. 2018. "The Fall Of The Mall And How To Make Them Rise Again." Last modified October 14, 2018. www.forbes.com/sites/pamdanziger/2018/10/14/the-fall-of-the-mall-and-three-ways-to-make-them-rise-again/#57f590922a26.

GameCraft Arcade and Bar. 2020. "GameCraft Arcade and Bar." Last modified 2020. www.gamecraft-arcade.com.

Malone, David. 2019. "Fortress Melbourne Will Be the Largest Esports Complex in the Southern Hemisphere." Last modified September 30, 2019. www.bdcnetwork.com/fortress-melbourne-will-be-largest-esports-complex-southern-hemisphere.

New York Excelsior. 2020. "Tickets." Last modified 2020. https://excelsior.overwatchleague.com/en-us/tickets.

Populous. 2018. "Populous Designs the Gaming House of the Future." Last modified November 1, 2018. https://populous.com/populous-designs-the-gaming-house-of-the-future.

Populous. 2020. "Fusion Arena." Last modified 2020. https://populous.com/fusion-arena.

UCI Esports. 2020. "Arena - UCI Esports." Last modified 2020. https://esports.uci.edu/arena.

CHAPTER 10

Alexander, Julia. 2020. "YouTube Is Using Massive E-sports Leagues to Take on Twitch in Big Live-Streaming Bet." Last modified January 27, 2020. www.theverge.com/2020/1/27/21082612/youtube-blizzard-activision-esports-leagues-twitch-live-streaming.

Amazon. 2020. "Twitch Prime." Last modified 2020. https://twitch.amazon.com/tp.

Brathwaite, Brandon. 2018. "Breaking Down the Major Streaming Platforms in Esports." Last modified August 31, 2018. https://esportsobserver.com/breakdown-streaming-platforms.

Brewster, Thomas. 2019. "Discord: The $2 Billion Gamer's Paradise Coming to Terms With Data Thieves, Child Groomers and FBI Investigators." Last modified January 29, 2019. www.forbes.com/sites/thomasbrewster/2019/01/29/discord-the-2-billion-gamers-paradise-coming-to-terms-with-data-thieves-child-groomers-and-fbi-investigators/#391de1723741.

Chiu, Stephen. 2019. "The Battle for the Sixth: Bjergsen vs Doublelift." Last modified April 12, 2019. https://upcomer.com/lol/story/1415736/the-battle-for-the-sixth-bjergsen-vs-doublelift.

Chung, Thomas, Simmy Sum, Monique Chan, Ely Lai, and Nanley Cheng. 2019. "Will Esports Result in a Higher Prevalence of Problematic Gaming? A Review of the Global Situation." *Journal of Behavioral Addictions 8* (3): 384-394.

Discord. 2020. "Discord – Company." Last modified 2020. https://discordapp.com/company.

Diwanji, Vaibhav, Abigail Reed, Arienne Ferchaud, Jonmichael Seibert, Victoria Weinbrecht, and Nicholas Sellers. 2020. "Don't Just Watch, Join In: Exploring Information Behavior and Copresence on Twitch." *Computers in Human Behavior 105* (April): 1-11. https://doi.org/10.1016/j.chb.2019.106221.

Esports Charts. 2020a. "Viewership Statistics of 2019 Esports & Streaming." Last modified 2020. https://escharts.com/2019.

Esports Charts. 2020b. "Streaming Platforms." Last modified 2020. https://escharts.com/platforms.

Gamepedia. 2019a. "Fiddlesticks." Last modified November 19, 2019. https://lol.gamepedia.com/Fiddlesticks.

Gamepedia. 2019b. "Ramus." Last modified December 11, 2019. https://lol.gamepedia.com/rammus.

Geracie, Nick. 2019. "Rivington Bisland III: 'My Favorite Game I've Ever Cast Was When Misfits Took SKT to 5 Games at Worlds.'" Last modified April 19, 2019. www.invenglobal.com/articles/8058/rivington-bisland-iii-my-favorite-game-ive-ever-cast-was-when-misfits-took-skt-to-5-games-at-worlds.

Hilvert-Bruce, Zorah, James Neill, Max Sjöblom, and Juho Hamari. 2018. "Social Motivations of Live-Streaming Viewer Engagement on Twitch." *Computers in Human Behavior 84* (July): 58-67.

Hitmarker. 2020. "Esports Jobs - Hitmarker." Last modified February 2020. https://hitmarkerjobs.com.

Hitt, Kevin. 2020. "Nielsen and LCS Implement Live+ Metric to Measure VOD Viewing." Last modified February 27, 2020. https://esportsobserver.com/lcs-nielsen-viewership-tools.

Huggan, Rich. 2018. "Esports Is Hiring - and You Don't Need to Be a Player." Last modified August 30, 2018. https://venturebeat.com/2018/08/30/esports-is-hiring-and-you-dont-need-to-be-a-player.

Imah, John, and Nick Miller. 2018. "Introducing the Facebook Gaming Creator Level Up Program." Last modified June 7, 2018. www.facebook.com/fbgaminghome/blog/introducing-the-facebook-gaming-creator-level-up-program.

Institute for Public Relations. 2007. "Crisis Management and Communications." Last modified October 30, 2007. https://instituteforpr.org/crisis-management-and-communications.

Jargon, Julie. 2019. "The Dark Side of Discord, Your Teen's Favorite Chat App." Last modified June 11, 2019. www.wsj.com/articles/discord-where-teens-rule-and-parents-fear-to-tread-11560245402.

Klosterman, Chuck. 2011. "Space, Time and DVR Mechanics." Last modified June 10, 2011. http://grantland.com/features/space-time-dvr-mechanics.

Koczwara, Michael. 2014. "Mobile Games Hotspot: 'Clash of Clans' hit $722M in 2019; 'Pokemon Home' App Sets Release Window." Last modified September 25, 2014. www.hollywoodreporter.com/news/mobile-games-hotspot-clash-clans-hit-722m-2019-1268314.

Kumar, V., and Werner Reinartz. 2012. *Customer Relationship Management.* 2nd ed. Heidelberg, Germany: Springer.

Lorenz, Taylor. 2019. "How an App for Gamers Went Mainstream." Last modified March 12, 2019. www.theatlantic.com/technology/archive/2019/03/how-discord-went-mainstream-influencers/584671.

Marks, Tom. 2016. "One Year After Its Launch, Discord Is the Best VoIP Service Available." Last modified May 13, 2016. www.pcgamer.com/one-year-after-its-launch-discord-is-the-best-voip-service-available.

McCormick, Rich. 2014. "This Is Why People Want to Watch Other People Play Video Games." Last modified August 26, 2014. www.theverge.com/2014/8/26/6068993/this-is-why-people-want-to-watch-other-people-play-video-games.

Menegus, Bryan. 2017. "How a Video Game Chat Client Became the Web's New Cesspool of Abuse." Last modified February 6, 2017. https://gizmodo.com/how-a-video-game-chat-client-became-the-web-s-new-cessp-1792039566.

Moncav, Melany. 2019. "Counter Logic Gaming beats TSM for first time since 2016." Last modified July 9, 2019. https://win.gg/news/1622/counter-logic-gaming-beats-tsm-for-first-time-since-2016.

Mumble. n.d. "About Mumble." Accessed January 28, 2020. www.mumble.info.

Napoli, Phil M. 2011. *Audience evolution: New technologies and the transformation of media audiences.* New York, NY: Columbia University Press.

Naraine, Michael L., Henry T. Wear, and Damien J. Whitburn. 2019. "User Engagement From Within the Twitter Community of Professional Sport Organizations." *Managing Sport and Leisure 24* (5): 275-293. https://doi.org/10.1080/23750472.2019.1630665.

Nielsen. 2020. "Esports Playbook for Brands 2019." Last modified 2020. www.nielsen.com/wp-content/uploads/sites/3/2019/05/esports-playbook-for-brands-2019.pdf.

Olebe, Leo. 2019. "Bringing More Esports Content from ESL to Facebook Gaming on a Non-Exclusive Basis." Last modified February 12, 2019. www.facebook.com/fbgaminghome/blog/bringing-more-esports-content-from-esl-to-facebook-gaming-on-a-non-exclusive-basis.

Palomba, Anthony. 2019. "Digital Seasons: How Time of the Year May Shift Video Game Play Habits." *Entertainment Computing 30*: 1-7.

Public Relations Society of America. 2020. "About Public Relations." Last modified 2020. www.prsa.org/about/all-about-pr.

Riot Games. n.d. "David 'Phreak' Turley." Accessed January 10, 2020. https://leagueoflegends.fandom.com/wiki/David_%27Phreak%27_Turley.

Shadow. 2020. "Shadow – Game-changing Esports Analytics." Last modified 2020. https://shadow.gg.

Shields, Ronan. 2018. "Roku Is Leveraging Its First-Party Data to Better Help Advertisers Target Cord Cutters." Last modified June 27, 2018. www.thedrum.com/news/2018/06/27/roku-leveraging-its-first-party-data-better-help-advertisers-target-cord-cutters.

Stern, Adam. 2020. "Turner Sports, Twitch Team Up For New Digital/Linear Show." Last modified January 21, 2020. https://esportsobserver.com/turner-sports-twitch-tv-show.

Supercell. 2020. "Supercell – Our Story." Accessed February 3, 2020. https://supercell.com/en/our-story.

Takahashi, Dean. 2020. "Hitmarker: Esports Jobs Grew 87% in 2019." Last modified February 8, 2020. https://venturebeat.com/2020/02/08/hitmarker-esports-jobs-grew-87-in-2019.

Taylor, Nicholas. 2016. "Now You're Playing With Audience Power: The Work of Watching Games." *Critical Studies in Media Communication 33* (4): 293-307.

Taylor, Tina L. 2012. *Raising the Stakes: E-sports and the Professionalization of Computer Gaming.* Boston: MIT Press.

TeamSpeak. 2020. "What makes TeamSpeak the number 1 choice for pro gamers?" Last modified 2020. https://www.teamspeak.com/en/features/overview/.

Tweedie, Steven. 2014. "Why 'Clash of Clans' Is So Incredibly Popular, According to a Guy Who Plays 16 Hours a Day." Last modified September 25, 2014. www.businessinsider.com/why-clash-of-clans-is-so-popular-2014-9.

Twitter Business. 2017. "7 Useful Insights You Can Learn From Twitter Analytics." Last modified November 6, 2017. www.marketingprofs.com/articles/2017/33063/seven-sets-of-useful-insights-you-can-gain-from-twitter-analytics.

Wooden, Andrew. n.d. "How Do You Play a Perfect Game? Modern Esports Is Turning to Big Data to Find the Answers." Accessed January 26, 2020. www.intel.co.uk/content/www/uk/en/it-management/cloud-analytic-hub/big-data-powered-esports.html.

Zaidi, Taha. 2019. "BM at the LCS Finals | Zven can't see Jensen. . . or Xmithie's Skarner." Last modified April 14, 2019. www.dailyesports.gg/bm-lcs-finals-zven-cant-see-jensen-xmithie-skarner.

Zillmann, Dolf. 1988. "Mood Management Through Communication Choices." *American Behavioral Scientist 31* (3): 327-340.

Zillmann, Dolf, and Jennings Bryant. 1985. "Affect, Mood, and Emotion as Determinants of Selective Exposure." In *Selective Exposure to Communication*, edited by Dolf Zillmann and Jennings Bryant, 157-190. Hillsdale, NJ: Lawrence Erlbaum Associates.

Zillmann, Dolf, and Silvia Knobloch. 2001. "Emotional Reactions to Narratives About the Fortunes of Personae in the News Theater." *Poetics 29* (3): 189-206.

CHAPTER 11

Activision Blizzard. 2018. "Annual Reports." Last modified 2018. https://investor.activision.com/annual-reports.

Activision Blizzard. 2019. "Current Reports." Last modified November 7, 2019. https://investor.activision.com/current-reports.

Cronin, Ben. 2020. "Tough Mudder Co-Founder Consents to Spartan Sale Through Bankruptcy Proceedings." Last modified January 16, 2020. www.sportbusiness.com/news/tough-mudder-co-founder-consents-to-spartan-sale-through-bankruptcy-proceedings.

Electronic Arts. 2019a. "Electronic Arts Reports Q2 FY20 Financial Results." Retrieved October 29, 2019. https://s22.q4cdn.com/894350492/files/doc_financials/2020/q2/Q2-FY20-Earnings-Release.pdf.

Electronic Arts. 2019b. "Annual Reports." Last modified 2019. https://ir.ea.com/financial-information/annual-reports-and-proxy-information/default.aspx.

Heck, Jordan. 2020. "Why is Dr Disrespect banned on Twitch? Here's what we know." Last modified July 6, 2020. https://www.sportingnews.com/us/other-sports/news/why-dr-disrespect-banned-twitch/1khyhre2e71om1ujvujfnmy2b8.

Heitner, Darren. 2018. "A Look Inside Riot Games, From $320,000 Player Salaries to Using Esports as a Catalyst for Sales." Last modified May 2, 2018. www.forbes.com/sites/darrenheitner/2018/05/02/a-look-inside-riot-games-from-320000-player-salaries-to-using-esports-as-a-catalyst-for-sales/#6cd2f8ef2c6a.

Loaded. 2020. "Loaded." Last modified 2020. https://loaded.gg.

Moncav, Melany. 2018. "AirAsia Announces Three New Sponsors for Esports Centre." Esports Insiders. Last modified August 28, 2018. https://esportsinsider.com/2018/08/airasia-announces-three-new-sponsors-for-esports-centre.

100 Thieves. 2020. "About Us - 100 Thieves." Last modified 2020. https://100thieves.com/pages/about-us.

Panchadar, Arjun. 2019. "Top Gamer 'Ninja' Made $1 Million to Promote EA's 'Apex Legends' Launch: Source." Reuters. Last modified March 13, 2019. www.reuters.com/article/us-electronic-arts-apexlegends/top-gamer-ninja-made-1-million-to-promote-eas-apex-legends-launch-source-idUSKBN1QU2AC.

PR Newswire. 2019. "DouYu International Holdings Limited Announces Share Repurchase Program." Last modified December 20, 2019. https://finance.yahoo.com/news/douyu-international-holdings-limited-announces-090000196.html.

Rietkerk, Remer. 2020. "Newzoo: The Global Esports Audience Will Be Just Shy of 500 Million This Year." Last modified February 25, 2020. https://newzoo.com/insights/articles/newzoo-esports-sponsorship-alone-will-generate-revenues-of-more-than-600-million-this-year/.

Shanley, Patrick. 2019. "Streamer Dr Disrespect Inks TV Development Deal With 'Walking Dead' Creator's Skybound (Exclusive)." Last modified December 6, 2019. www.hollywoodreporter.com/news/streamer-dr-disrespect-inks-tv-development-deal-walking-dead-creators-skybound-1260034.

Sun, Leo. 2019. "Which Esports Stock to Buy: Huya or DouYu?" Last modified December 6, 2019. www.fool.com/investing/2019/12/08/which-esports-stock-to-buy-huya-or-douyu.aspx.

Thomas, Zoe. 2020. "YouTube signs three top gamers away from rival Twitch." Last modified January 14, 2020. www.bbc.com/news/technology-51101606.

Wijman, Tom. 2019. "The Global Games Market Will Generate $152.1 Billion in 2019 as the U.S. Overtakes China as the Biggest Market." Last modified June 18, 2019. https://newzoo.com/insights/articles/the-global-games-market-will-generate-152-1-billion-in-2019-as-the-u-s-overtakes-china-as-the-biggest-market/.

Zhu, Yehung. 2016. "How Niantic Is Profiting Off Tracking Where You Go While Playing 'Pokémon GO'." Last modified July 29, 2016. www.forbes.com/sites/yehongzhu/2016/07/29/how-niantic-is-profiting-off-tracking-where-you-go-while-playing-pokemon-go/#41cab2136df9.

CHAPTER 12

Alexander, Julia. 2019. "Blizzard Bans Three College Hearthstone Players for Hong Kong Protest Sign." Last modified October 16, 2019. www.theverge.com/2019/10/16/20917574/blizzard-ban-hearthstone-college-students-grandmaster-china-hong-kong-protests.

Baldwin, Alan. 2019. "Targeted Tests Having an Impact in Eesports, says Verroken." Last modified April 17, 2019. www.reuters.com/article/us-sport-doping/targeted-tests-having-an-impact-in-esports-says-verroken-idUSKCN1RT2D4.

Becht, Eli. 2019. "Tfue Suing FaZe Clan Over 'Oppressive' Contract." Last modified May 2, 2019. www.dexerto.com/entertainment/tfue-suing-fa-ze-clan-over-oppressive-contract-642021.

Bently, Lionel, and Brad Sherman. 2009. *Intellectual Property Law*. Oxford, England: Oxford University Press.

Chapman, Josh. 2019. "Esports Teams: Valued as Tech Companies." Last modified February 9, 2019. https://hackernoon.com/esports-teams-valued-as-tech-companies-a2df287e02ee.

DiFrancisco-Donoghue, Joanne, Jerry Balentine, Gordon Schmidt, and Hallie Zwibel. 2019. "Managing the Health of the Esport Athlete: An Integrated Health Management Model." *BMJ Open Sport and Exercise Medicine 5* (1): 1-15. http://doi.org/ 10.1136/bmjsem-2018-000467.

Jenny, Seth E., R. Douglas Manning, Margaret C. Keiper, and Tracy W. Olrich. 2017. "Virtual(ly) Athletes: Where Esports Fit Within the Definition of 'Sport'." *Quest 69* (1): 1-18. doi:10.1080/00336297.2016.1144517.

Lajka, Arijeta. 2018. "Esports Players Burn Out Young as the Grand Takes Mental, Physical Toll." Last modified December 21, 2018. www.cbsnews.com/news/esports-burnout-in-video-gaming-cbsn-originals.

Lowell, Cym H. 1973. "Collective Bargaining and the Professional Team Sport Industry." *Law and Contemporary Problems 38* (1): 3-41.

MacQueen, Hector L., Charlotte Waelde, and G.T. Laurie. 2007. *Contemporary Intellectual Property: Law and Policy*. Oxford, England: Oxford University Press.

McChrystal, Michael. 2014. "No Hiding the Ball: Medical Privacy and Pro Sports." *Marquette Sports Law Review 25* (1): 163-180.

Nesbitt, Stephen G. 2003. "James v. Meow Media, Inc.: When Life Imitating Art Goes Awry, Should We Silence Its Expression." *Northern Kentucky Law Review 30*: 229-247.

Park, Gene. 2020. "Counter-Strike's New Esports Framework Allows for Profit-Sharing, Transforms League." Last modified February 18, 2020. www.washingtonpost.com/video-games/esports/2020/02/18/counter-strikes-new-esports-framework-allows-profit-sharing-transforms-league.

Press, Tim. 2013. *Intellectual Property Law*. Oxford, England: Oxford University Press.

Robertson, Geoffrey, and Andrew G.L. Nicol. 2002. *Media Law*. London: Penguin.

Settimi, Christina. 2019. "'Awful Business' or the New Gold Rush? The Most Valuable Companies in Esports are Surging." Last modified November 5, 2019. www.forbes.com/sites/christinasettimi/2019/11/05/awful-business-or-the-new-gold-rush-the-most-valuable-companies-in-esports-are-surging/#70cc71a9324d.

The Pokémon Company. 2020. "Legal Information." Last modified 2020. https://www.pokemon.com/us/legal/.

Van Hoorebeek, Mark. 2009. *Intellectual Property Law*. London: Sweet and Maxwell.

Waelde, Charlotte, Abbe E.L. Brown, Smita Kheria, and Jane Cornwell. 2016. *Contemporary Intellectual Property: Law and Policy*. 4th ed. Oxford, England: Oxford University Press.

Week Staff. 2019. "Video Games and Violence, Explained." Last modified September 20, 2019. https://theweek.com/articles/864451/video-games-violence-explained.

Wolfe, Elizabeth, and Brian Ries. 2019. "A Fortnite Superstar Has Been Banned for Life for Cheating." Last modified November 6, 2019. www.cnn.com/2019/11/06/entertainment/faze-jarvis-fortnite-ban-trnd/index.html.

Zacarias, Michelle. 2019. "Video Games Become the Latest Target in Mass Shooting Outrage." Last modified August 14, 2019. www.peoplesworld.org/article/video-games-become-the-latest-target-in-mass-shooting-outrage.

Zaller, Anthony. 2019. "Tfue v. Faze Clan – Esports Lawsuit Raises Many California Employment Legal Issues." Last modified May 24, 2019. www.californiaemploymentlawreport.com/2019/05/tfue-v-faze-clan-esports-lawsuit-raises-many-california-employment-legal-issues.

Zavian, Ellen M., and Jim Schmitz. 2019. "Genesis of an Industry: The Emerging Workforce and Regulations of Esports." Last modified April 4, 2019. www.accdocket.com/articles/emerging-workforce-and-regulations-of-esports.cfm.

CHAPTER 13

American Psychological Association. n.d. "Sport Psychology." Accessed December 2, 2019. www.apa.org/ed/graduate/specialize/sports.

Blizzard Entertainment. n.d. "The Overwatch League." Accessed December 28, 2019. https://overwatchleague.com/en-us.

Chalk, Andy. 2016. "Valve Explains Why It's Restricted Coaches at CS:GO Tournaments." Last modified August 19, 2016. www.pcgamer.com/csgo-coach-ban.

Chen, Ju-Chih. 2019. "Interview with FPX: How much influence does BP have on the game?" Last modified December 3, 2019. www.bilibili.com/video/av77937155.

Chiu, Stephen. 2016. "Coaches Across Esports." Last modified August 22, 2016. www.espn.com/esports/story/_/id/17365945/coaches-esports.

Collegiate Starleague (CSL). n.d. "What Is CSL?" Accessed December 31, 2019. https://cstarleague.com/about.

DiFrancisco-Donoghue, Joanne, Jerry Balentine, Godron Schmidt, and Hallie Zwibel. 2019. "Managing the Health of the Esport Athlete: An Integrated Health Management Model." *BMJ Open Sport & Exercise Medicine 5* (1): e000467. http://doi.org/10.1136/bmjsem-2018-000467.

Donnelly, Joe. 2016. "CS:GO Coaches Banned From Helping Teams During Competitive Matches." Last modified August 18, 2016. www.pcgamer.com/csgo-coaches-banned-from-helping-teams-during-competitive-matches.

Erzberger, Tyler. 2017. "kkOma -- a Reflection on SK Telecom's Legendary, Unbeatable Brain." Last modified May 20, 2017. www.espn.com/esports/story/_/id/19424995/kkoma-reflection-sk-telecom-legendary-unbeatable-brain.

Erzberger, Tyler. 2018. "Mental Health Issues Remain Pervasive Problem in Esports Scene." Last modified August 20, 2018. www.espn.com/esports/story/_/id/24427802/mental-health-issues-esports-remain-silent-very-real-threat-players.

Hattenstone, Simon. 2017. "The Rise of Esports: Are Addiction and Corruption the Price of Its Success?" Last modified June 16, 2017. www.theguardian.com/sport/2017/jun/16/top-addiction-young-people-gaming-esports.

High School Esports League (HSEL). 2019. "Homepage." Accessed December 31, 2019. www.highschoolesportsleague.com.

Huang, Tsung-Yu. 2019. In discussion with the author, July 30, 2019.

Hyun, Woo "Ready." 2018. "The Importance of Esports Coaches in League of Legends: Their Role Within a Team." Last modified December 13, 2018. www.invenglobal.com/articles/7010/the-importance-of-esports-coaches-in-league-of-legends-their-role-within-a-team.

Jacobs, Harrison. 2015. "Here's What Life is Like in the Cramped 'Gaming House' Where 5 Guys Live Together and Earn Amazing Money by Playing Video Games." Last modified May 5, 2015. www.businessinsider.com/inside-team-liquids-league-of-legends-gaming-house-2015-4.

James, Ford, and Leon Hurley. 2019. "Modern Warfare Maps: The Complete List of Maps in Call of Duty This Year." Last modified December 12, 2019. www.gamesradar.com/call-of-duty-modern-warfare-maps.

Kain, Erik. 2018. "'Fortnite: Battle Royale' Has Made Over $1 Billion As It Completely Dominates Video Game Streaming." Last modified July 18, 2018. www.forbes.com/sites/erikkain/2018/07/18/fortnite-battle-royale-has-made-over-1-billion-as-it-completely-dominates-video-game-streaming/#7fb26a5015ce.

LoL Esports Staff. 2015. "Team Coaches Officially Part of LCS in 2015." Last modified 2015. https://nexus.leagueoflegends.com/en-us/2015/09/team-coaches-officially-part-of-lcs-in-2015.

Major League Gaming (MLG). 2006. "2006 MLG Season Official Announcement." Last modified February 16, 2006. www.majorleaguegaming.com/news/2006-mlg-season-official-announcement.

Moody, Josh. 2019. "A Guide to the Changing Number of U.S. Universities." Last modified February 15, 2019. www.usnews.com/education/best-colleges/articles/2019-02-15/how-many-universities-are-in-the-us-and-why-that-number-is-changing.

National Association of Collegiate Esports (NACE). n.d. "School Directory." Accessed December 23, 2019. https://nacesports.org/school-directory.

NRG Esports. n.d. "About - NRG Esports." Accessed December 22, 2019. www.nrg.gg/about.

Radcliffe, Noam. 2019. "As Esports Evolves, Burnout Becomes a Potential Problem for Players." Last modified April 17, 2019. www.dbltap.com/posts/as-esports-evolves-burnout-becomes-a-potential-problem-for-players-01d8kake8e4r.

Riot Games. n.d. "Champions." Accessed December 21, 2019. https://na.leagueoflegends.com/en/game-info/champions.

Settimi, Christina. 2019. "'Awful Business' Or The New Gold Rush? The Most Valuable Companies In Esports Are Surging." Last modified November 5, 2019. www.forbes.com/sites/christinasettimi/2019/11/05/awful-business-or-the-new-gold-rush-the-most-valuable-companies-in-esports-are-surging/#78215815324d.

Smith, Matthew J., Phil D.J. Birch, and Dave Bright. 2019. "Identifying Stressors and Coping Strategies of Elite Esports Competitors." *International Journal of Gaming and Computer-Mediated Simulations 11* (2): 22-39. http://doi.org/10.4018/IJGCMS.2019040102.

Smith, Noah. 2019. "Debate: What Does a Fair Esports Contract Look Like? It's complicated." Last modified June 18, 2019. www.washingtonpost.com/sports/2019/06/18/debate-what-does-fair-esports-contract-look-like-its-complicated.

Sterling Equities. 2017. "Sterling.VC Announces Overwatch League Team - New York Excelsior." Last modified October 30, 2017. www.prnewswire.com/news-releases/sterlingvc-announces-overwatch-league-team---new-york-excelsior-300545229.html.

Szymborski, Dan. 2016. "Blizzard to Create Professional Overwatch League." Last modified November 4, 2016. www.espn.com/esports/story/_/id/17968297/blizzard-announces-professional-overwatch-league.

The Esports Observer. 2019a. "2019 Competitions." Accessed December 31, 2019. https://esportsobserver.com/database/leagues?search=2019.

The Esports Observer. 2019b. "Teams." Accessed December 31, 2019. https://esportsobserver.com/database/teams.

u/entfy. 2013. "Massive Change in CSGO Metagame? [Spoilers]." Last modified 2013. www.reddit.com/r/GlobalOffensive/comments/1ruar1/massive_change_in_csgo_metagame_spoilers.

Valve. 2013. "CS:GO Blog: DreamHack 2013 Champions." Last modified December 1, 2013. https://blog.counter-strike.net/index.php/2013/12/8278.

Valve. 2016. "Counter Strike Blog: Coaching." Accessed December 10, 2019. https://blog.counter-strike.net/index.php/coaching.

Wooden, Andrew. n.d. "How Big Data Is Revolutionising The Future of Esports." Retrieved January 1, 2020. www.intel.co.uk/content/www/uk/en/it-management/cloud-analytic-hub/big-data-powered-esports.html.

Yilmazcoban, Olcay. 2018. "AI Is Esports' Newest Weapon." Last modified December 11, 2018. https://venturebeat.com/2018/12/11/ai-is-esports-newest-weapon.

Yip, Robert. 2014. "Coaching in Esports: A Comprehensive Look." Last modified July 16, 2014. www.liquiddota.com/forum/dota-2-general/462152-coaching-in-esports-a-comprehensive-look.

CHAPTER 14

Anderton, Kevin. 2019. "The Business of Video Games: Market Share for Gaming Platforms in 2019." Last modified June 26, 2019. www.forbes.com/sites/kevinanderton/2019/06/26/the-business-of-video-games-market-share-for-gaming-platforms-in-2019-infographic/#1dc2da447b25.

ANR Team. 2019. "The Evolution of Audio in Video Games." Last modified July 21, 2019. https://audionewsroom.net/2019/07/the-evolution-of-audio-in-video-games.html.

Barker, Shane. 2019. How to Make Money on Social Media as an Influencer. Last modified April 25, 2019. https://shanebarker.com/blog/influencer-make-big-money-on-social-media.

Bramble, Julia. 2019. "Could 'Belonging' Be the Next Marketing Revolution?" Last modified December 11, 2019. https://businessesgrow.com/2019/12/11/marketing-revolution.

Brierley, Cam. 2018a. "Defining the Role You're Hiring for." Last modified April 25, 2019. https://hitmarkerjobs.com/recruitment-advice/define-the-role-youre-hiring-for.

Brierley, Cam. 2018b. "Write an Esports Job Description." Last modified April 25, 2019. https://hitmarkerjobs.com/recruitment-advice/write-an-esports-job-description.

Brierley, Cam. 2019. "Zoom Interview With Cam Brierley." Interview conducted by Roger Caramanica on December 10, 2019.

Bullas, Jeff. n.d. 10 Essential Skills a Social Media Manager Needs to Have on Their Resume. www.jeffbullas.com/10-essential-skills-a-social-media-manager-needs-to-have-on-their-resume.

Calvello, Mara. 2019. "How to Become a Software Engineer (+4 Tips From the Pros)." Last modified November 19, 2019. https://learn.g2.com/software-engineer.

Camerato, Jessica. 2017. "Sixers Owners Josh Harris, David Blitzer Form Sports and Entertainment business." Last modified September 25, 2017.

Davidson, Jack. 2019. "The Role of an Esports Psychologist." Last modified November 19, 2019. www.pinnacle.com/en/esports-hub/betting-articles/educational/role-of-an-esports-psychology/7wl2k4fdskszqlch.

DiFrancisco-Donoghue, Joanne, Jerry Balentine, Gordon Schmidt, and Hallie Zwibel. 2019. "Managing the Health of the E-Sport Athlete: an Integrated Health Management Model." *BMJ Open Sport & Exercise Medicine* 5 (1). http://doi.org/10.1136/bmjsem-2018-000467.

Epstein, David. 2019. *Range: How Generalists Triumph in a Specialized World*. London: Macmillan.

Foster, Alana. 2019. "Looking Behind Live Esports Production." Last modified November 14, 2019. www.ibc.org/create-and-produce/looking-behind-live-Esports-production/5213.article.

Frankel, Todd C. 2017. "In $24 Billion Video Game Industry, Voice Actors Struggle to Make a Living." Last modified October 29, 2019. www.chicagotribune.com/business/blue-sky/ct-wp-bsi-video-game-voice-actors-20171029-story.html.

Gardenswartz, Lee, and Anita Rowe. 1993. "Recognizing the power of diversity." *Physician Executive 19* (6): 64-68.

Goldman Sachs. n.d. "Esports Joins the Big Leagues." Retrieved January 15, 2020. www.goldmansachs.com/insights/pages/infographics/e-sports.

Gonzales, Rob. 2019. "Zoom Interview With Rob Gonzales." Interview conducted by Roger Caramanica on December 10, 2019.

Hayward, Andrew. 2018. "What Is Needed to Run an Esports Event? Experts Discuss Challenges and Opportunities." Last modified October 6, 2018. https://esportsobserver.com/hive-esports-event-recap.

Hayward, Andrew. 2019. "The 10 Highest-Earning Esports Organizations of 2018 by Total Winning." Last modified January 2, 2019. https://esportsobserver.com/10-earning-esports-orgs-2018.

Hitmarker. 2020. "Esports Jobs | Hitmarker." Last modified March 1, 2020. https://hitmarkerjobs.com.

Holt, Kris. 2019. "Overwatch League Lets Fans Choose How to Watch the Action for $15." Last modified January 31, 2019. www.engadget.com/2019/01/31/overwatch-league-2019-all-access-pass-twitch.

International Movie Database (IMDB). n.d. Laura Bailey Credits List. www.imdb.com/name/nm1154161.

Liming, Drew, and Dennis Vilorio. 2011. "Work for Play: Careers in Video Game Development." *Occupational Outlook Quarterly 55* (3): 2-11.

Lumb, David. 2018. "Overwatch League's debut stream ruled Twitch last night." Last modified January 12, 2018. www.engadget.com/2018/01/12/overwatch-leagues-debut-stream-ruled-twitch-last-night.

Morgeson, Frederick P., and Erich C. Dierdorff. 2011. "Work analysis: From technique to theory." *APA Handbook of Industrial and Organizational Psychology* 2: 3-41.

NBA 2K League. 2018a. "Introducing the NBA 2K League Combine." Last modified February 9, 2018. https://2kleague.nba.com/news/introducing-the-nba-2k-league-combine.

NBA 2K League. 2018b. "$1 Million Prize Pool for Inaugural NBA 2K League Season." Last modified February 9, 2018. https://2kleague.nba.com/news/1-million-prize-pool-for-inaugural-nba-2k-league-season.

NBA 2K League. n.d. "League Info." Retrieved January 15, 2020. https://2kleague.nba.com/league-info.

Newzoo. 2019. "Global Esports Market Report." Retrieved January 15, 2020. https://newzoo.com/insights/trend-reports/newzoo-global-esports-market-report-2019-light-version.

Niko Partners. 2019. "Niko Partner Services." Retrieved January 15, 2020. https://nikopartners.com/services.

100 Thieves. n.d. "Homepage." Retrieved January 15, 2020. https://100thieves.com.

OverActive Media. 2019. "About Us." Retrieved January 15, 2020. www.overactivemedia.com.

Perez, Matt. 2019. "Esports Company 100 Thieves Raises $35 Million in Series B." Last modified July 16, 2019. www.forbes.com/sites/mattperez/2019/07/16/esports-company-100-thieves-raises-35-million-in-series-b/#3e53f17c4b15.

Porter, Matt. 2019. "Esports Job Website Hitmarker Launch Crowdfunding Campaign." Last modified November 1, 2019. www.dexerto.com/business/esports-job-website-hitmarker-launch-crowdfunding-campaign-1204596.

Rosano, Nick. 2019. "Philadelphia Union's Doolsta Wins eMLS Cup 2019 presented by Playstation." Last modified March 30, 2019. www.mlssoccer.com/post/2019/03/30/philadelphia-unions-doolsta-wins-emls-cup-2019-presented-playstation.

Schomer, Audrey. 2019. "Influencer Marketing 2019: Why Brands Can't Get Enough of an $8 Billion Ecosystem." Last modified December 17, 2019. www.businessinsider.com/the-2019-influencer-marketing-report-2019-7.

Soper, Taylor. 2018. "MLS Launches eMLS, a New FIFA Esports League With One Pro Gamer Representing Each Team." Last modified January 12, 2018. www.geekwire.com/2018/mls-launches-emls-new-fifa-esports-league-one-pro-gamer-representing-team.

The eSports Writer. 2016. "The Secret of Becoming a Successful Esports Content Creator." Last modified April 5, 2016. https://medium.com/@FionnOnFire/the-secret-of-becoming-a-successful-esports-content-creator-3ebed258f3f9.

The Kraft Group. 2019. "Careers at The Kraft Group." Retrieved January 15, 2020. www.thekraftgroup.com/careers.

Tretkoff, Ernie. 2008. "October 1958: Physicist Invents First Video Game." Last modified October 15, 2008. www.aps.org/publications/apsnews/200810/physicshistory.cfm.

Twitch Tracker. 2019. "Critical Role." Retrieved January 15, 2020. https://twitchtracker.com/criticalrole/statistics.

U.S. Bureau of Labor Statistics. n.d. "Occupational Outlook Handbook, Software Developers." Last modified September 4, 2019. www.bls.gov/ooh/computer-and-information-technology/software-developers.htm.

Webster, Andrew. 2019. "How 100 Thieves Became the Supreme of E-sports." Last modified September 5, 2019. www.theverge.com/2019/9/5/20849569/100-thieves-nadeshot-esports-supreme-drake.

Wilde, Tyler. 2017. "More People Watch Gaming Videos and Streams than HBO, Netflix, ESPN, and Hulu Combined." Last modified April 20, 2017. www.pcgamer.com/more-people-watch-gaming-videos-and-streams-than-hbo-netflix-espn-and-hulu-combined.

AFTERWORD

Arnaud, Jean-Christophe. 2010. "ESports – A New Word." In *eSports Yearbook 2009*, edited by Julia Christophers and Tobias M. Scholz, 11-12. Norderstedt, Germany: Books on Demand.

Besombes, Nicolas. 2019. "Esports & Competitive Games by Genre." Last modified July 26, 2019. https://medium.com/@nicolas.besombes/esports-competitive-games-by-genre-61fcaf9c6a8f.

Cunningham, Nicole R., and Matthew S. Eastin. 2017. "Second Screen and Sports: A Structural Investigation into Team Identification and Efficacy." *Communication & Sport* 5 (3): 288-310.

Friedman, Daniel. 2019. "Battle Royale Blurs the Line Between Entertainment and Esports." Last modified March 6, 2019. www.polygon.com/2019/3/6/18244946/fortnite-apex-legends-league-competitive-ninja-esports.

Miceli, Max. 2019. "Mixer Reaps Immediate Benefits from Exclusive Partnership With Ninja." Last modified August 3, 2019. https://esportsobserver.com/ninja-mixer-viewership.

Neus, Florian, Fred Nimmermann, Katja Wagner, and Hanna Schramm-Klein. 2019. "Differences and Similarities in Motivation for Offline and Online Esports Event Consumption." In *Proceedings of the 52nd Hawaii International Conference on System Sciences*, edited by Tung X. Bai, 2458-2467. Honolulu, HI: University of Hawaii at Manoa.

Scholz, Tobias M. 2017. *Data in Organizations and the Role of Human Resource Management. A Complex Systems Theory-Based Conceptualization*. Frankfurt, Germany: Peter Lang.

Scholz, Tobias. 2019. *Esports Is Business: Management in the World of Competitive Gaming*. Cham, Switzerland: Palgrave Macmillan.

Superdata. 2015. *Esports – The Market Brief 2015*. New York: Superdata.

Takahashi, Dean. 2018. "Riot Games Uses AR Imagery to Kick Off League of Legends 2018 World Finals." Last modified November 3, 2018. https://venturebeat.com/2018/11/03/riot-games-uses-ar-imagery-to-kick-off-league-of-legends-2018-world-finals.

Taylor, T.L. 2012. *Raising the Stakes: E-Sports and the Professionalization of Computer Gaming*. Cambridge, MA: MIT Press.

Wagner, Michael G. 2006. "On the Scientific Relevance of eSport." Proceedings of the *2006 International Conference on Internet Computing and Conference on Computer Game Development*, edited by Hamid R. Arabnia, 437-440. Las Vegas, NV: CSREA Press.

Wittgenstein, Ludwig. 1953. *Philosophical Investigations*. Oxford, UK: Basil Blackwell.

Index

Note: The italicized *f* and *t* following page numbers refer to figures and tables, respectively.

About the Editors

David P. Hedlund, PhD, is the chairperson of the division of sport management at St. John's University, where he is also a faculty expert and faculty leader on research and topics related to esports.

Hedlund earned his PhD in sport management and a certificate in measurement and statistics from Florida State University. He has more than 20 years of domestic and international experience in sport, esports, coaching, business, education, and analytics. He has published more than 30 journal articles and book chapters on related topics. He is a research committee member for the International Esports Federation, an educational program assistant for the United States Esports Federation, and a member of the Esports Research Network.

In recent years, Hedlund has also acted as a consultant for dozens of domestic and international high school, college, and professional esports teams as well as business and entrepreneurial ventures, including the World Cyber Games and the Global Esports Executive Summit.

Gil Fried, JD, is a professor at the University of New Haven in Connecticut. He has taught sport law, sport finance, and sport facility management for more than 25 years and has written numerous articles, books, and book chapters on various sport management issues. He taught the first business-school-based esports class several years ago and has worked to expand the professionalism of the esports industry. Fried speaks throughout the United States on issues such as building and financing facilities and dealing with risk management concerns.

Fried was a practicing attorney before becoming an academician. Before that, he was a collegiate coach, helped run major events, and was the vice president of marketing for a women's professional basketball league. 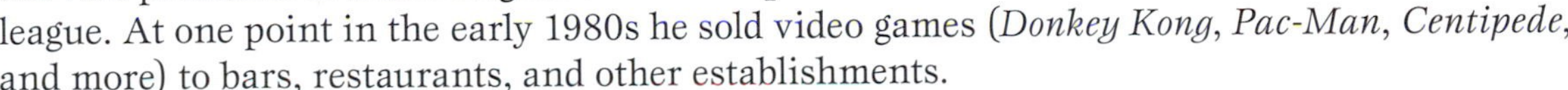 At one point in the early 1980s he sold video games (*Donkey Kong*, *Pac-Man*, *Centipede*, and more) to bars, restaurants, and other establishments.

In addition to researching and writing about sport management, Fried enjoys playing badminton, collecting stamps, farming, being with his wife and kids, and traveling.

Courtesy of Marietta College.

R.C. Smith III, MAA, MSJ, is an assistant professor of sport management in the department of business and economics and the director of esports at Marietta College. Smith has over 12 years of work in higher education in various roles, including alumni relations, teaching, and collegiate athletics. He has earned two master's degrees—one from Seton Hall University School of Law in intellectual property and one from the University of the Incarnate Word in sport management—and he earned his bachelor's degree in multimedia journalism from Florida Atlantic University. Smith's areas of strength are event management, fan engagement, innovation, and revenue generation. Recently, Smith became a software trainer and consultant for sports teams and organizations in the areas of game management and fan engagement.